EARLY MODERN CULTURAL STUDIES

Ivo Kamps, Series Editor

PUBLISHED BY PALGRAVE MACMILLAN

Idols of the Marketplace: Idolatry and Commodity Fetishism in English Literature, 1580–1680
by David Hawkes

Shakespeare among the Animals: Nature and Society in the Drama of Early Modern England
by Bruce Boehrer

Maps and Memory in Early Modern England: A Sense of Place
by Rhonda Lemke Sanford

Debating Gender in Early Modern England, 1500–1700
edited by Cristina Malcolmson and Mihoko Suzuki

Manhood and the Duel: Masculinity in Early Modern Drama and Culture
by Jennifer A. Low

Burning Women: Widows, Witches, and Early Modern European Travelers in India
by Pomp Banerjee

Shakespeare and the Question of Culture: Early Modern Literature and the Cultural Turn
by Douglas Bruster

England's Internal Colonies: Class, Capital, and the Literature of Early Modern English Colonialism
by Mark Netzloff

Prose Fiction and Early Modern Sexualities in England, 1570–1640
edited by Constance C. Relihan and Goran V. Stanivukovic

Turning Turk: English Theater and the Multicultural Mediterranean
by Daniel Vitkus

Money and the Age of Shakespeare: Essays in New Economic Criticism
edited by Linda Woodbridge

Arts of Calculation: Numerical Thought in Early Modern Europe
edited by David Glimp and Michelle Warren

The Culture of the Horse: Status, Discipline, and Identity in the Early Modern World
edited by Karen Raber and Treva J. Tucker

The Figure of the Crowd in Early Modern London: The City and its Double
by Ian Munro

Citizen Shakespeare: Freemen and Aliens in the Language of the Plays
by John Michael Archer

Constructions of Female Homoeroticism in Early Modern Drama
by Denise Walen

Localizing Caroline Drama: Politics and Economics of the Early Modern English Stage, 1625–1642
edited by Adam Zucker and Alan B. Farmer

Re-Mapping the Mediterranean World in Early Modern English Writings
edited by Goran V. Stanivukovic

Islam and Early Modern English Literature: The Politics of Romance from Spenser to Milton
by Benedict S. Robinson

Women Writers and Public Debate in 17th Century Britain
by Catharine Gray

Global Traffic: Discourse and Practices of Trade in English Literature and Culture from 1550 to 1700
edited by Barbara Sebek and Stephen Deng

Remembering the Early Modern Voyage: English Narratives in the Age of European Expansion
by Mary C. Fuller

Memory, Print, and Gender in England, 1653–1759
by Harold Weber

Memory, Print, and Gender in England, 1653–1759

Harold Weber

palgrave
macmillan

MEMORY, PRINT, AND GENDER IN ENGLAND, 1653–1759
Copyright © Harold Weber, 2008.

First published in 2008 by
PALGRAVE MACMILLAN®
in the US—a division of St. Martin's Press LLC,
175 Fifth Avenue, New York, NY 10010.

Where this book is distributed in the UK, Europe and the rest of the world,
this is by Palgrave Macmillan, a division of Macmillan Publishers Limited,
registered in England, company number 785998, of Houndmills,
Basingstoke, Hampshire RG21 6XS.

Palgrave Macmillan is the global academic imprint of the above companies
and has companies and representatives throughout the world.

Palgrave® and Macmillan® are registered trademarks in the United States,
the United Kingdom, Europe and other countries.

ISBN-13: 978–0–230–60791–0
ISBN-10: 0–230–60791–8

Library of Congress Cataloging-in-Publication Data is available from the
Library of Congress.

A catalogue record of the book is available from the British Library.

Design by Newgen Imaging Systems (P) Ltd., Chennai, India.

First edition: August 2008

10 9 8 7 6 5 4 3 2 1

Printed in the United States of America.

Transfered to Digital Printing 2009

CONTENTS

Series Editor's Preface   vii

Acknowledgments   ix

Introduction: The Invention of Modern Memory   1

1   "Building Castles in the Air": Margaret Cavendish
and the Anxieties of Monumentality   27

2   "A Space for Narration": Milton and the
Politics of Collective Memory   65

3   "Oh grant an honest Fame, or grant me none!":
The Ethics of Memorialization in Pope's
Archives of Dulness   103

4   "Graven with an iron pen and lead in the book for ever!":
Paper and Permanence in Richardson's *Clarissa*   137

Conclusion: From the "Garbage Heap" of Memory to
the Cyborg: The Exhaustion and Revitalization of
Memory in the Twentieth and Twenty-First Centuries   175

Notes   203

Bibliography   233

Index   253

SERIES EDITOR'S PREFACE

The Early Modern Cultural Studies series is dedicated to the exploration of literature, history, and culture in the context of cultural exchange and globalization. We begin with the assumption that in the twenty-first century, literary criticism, literary theory, historiography, and cultural studies have become so interwoven that we can now think of them as an eclectic and only loosely unified (but still recognizable) approach to formerly distinct fields of inquiry such as literature, society, history, and culture. This series furthermore presumes that the early modern period was witness to an incipient process of transculturation through exploration, mercantilism, colonization, and migration that set into motion a process of globalization that is still with us today. The purpose of this series is to bring together this eclectic approach, which freely and unapologetically crosses disciplinary, theoretical, and political boundaries, with early modern texts and artifacts that bear the traces of transculturation and globalization.

This process can be studied on a large as well as on a small scale, and the volumes in this series are dedicated to both. The series is just as concerned with the analyses of colonial encounters and native representations of those encounters as it is with representations of the other in Shakespeare, gender politics, the cultural impact of the presence of strangers/foreigners in London, or the consequences of farmers' migration to that same city. This series is as interested in documenting cultural exchanges between British, Portuguese, Spanish, or Dutch colonizers and native peoples as it is in telling the stories of returning English soldiers who served in foreign armies on the continent of Europe in the late sixteenth century.

IVO KAMPS
Series Editor

ACKNOWLEDGMENTS

Although writing a book affords many pleasures—and creates much anxiety as well—few activities are as satisfying as composing the acknowledgments page, for it signals not simply the completion of what is often years of work, but the moment when debts that one has accrued can be gratefully recognized, acknowledged, and, to the extent possible, repaid.

I owe many thanks to Elizabeth Meese, who was reading and responding to the essays that were to become this book even before I realized that it might be a book; over the last two decades she has remained my most constant and demanding reader. I want to thank Brean S. Hammond and Scott R. MacKenzie for reading the entire manuscript in its penultimate form; Brean provided trenchant criticism particularly of the conclusion, which benefited greatly from his critique of an argument that I suspect he still regards skeptically, while Scott pushed me in directions that I refused to contemplate on my own. Kay Gilliland Stevenson deserves special thanks for her reading of the manuscript, not simply because her perceptive criticism has left its mark on every chapter, but because we've never met: a chance exchange of emails about another matter entirely led her to provide the type of careful reading that I hardly expect even from close friends.

Shannon Reed read chapter one in its earliest incarnation and her suggestions helped determine its final form. Cori Perdue's ideas about monumentality in Milton helped shape the writing of chapter two, while Ellen Rosenman secured research materials otherwise unavailable to me at a crucial point in the writing of chapter three. Deanna Kreisel allowed me to read her unpublished essay on *Clarissa* and then provided helpful criticism of chapter four; the direction of this chapter was also effected by conversations with Maaja Stewart, whose knowledge of textiles and sewing helped determine my focus on material culture. Joel ("Dutch") Brouwer was kind enough to read my treatment of W.G. Sebald in the conclusion and his insight and advice helped me to better understand this complex and demanding author.

The second chapter is a revised and expanded version of an essay first published in the *Journal for Early Modern Cultural Studies* [4 (2004): 62–88], while an early version of chapter three appeared in *Eighteenth-Century Studies* [33 (1999): 1–19]. I am obliged to both journals for permission to republish the material here.

The University of Alabama has provided research and sabbatical leaves, spent at the British Library, without which this book could not have been written. Although I lament no longer being able to work at the BL's old location in the British Museum, the new library is a splendid facility, and the staff has remained as friendly, helpful, and knowledgeable as ever. I wish to thank Sharon O'Dair for introducing me to Ivo Kamps, and to thank Ivo for encouraging me to place the manuscript with his series on early modern culture. I also want to thank the still anonymous reader whose two readings of the manuscript had a profound impact on the final form of this book. I have stolen shamelessly from her reports and benefited from her engagement with my work. Emily Conner spent many hours helping me prepare the manuscript for publication; I want to express my gratitude for her hard work. I want to express my gratitude for her hard work, and to thank Bill Ulmer and the Department of English at UA for appointing Emily as my research assistant.

Much of this book was written during my travels abroad, and I want to end by thanking those friends whose homes provided the comfortable spaces that helped make writing this book such a pleasure: Francesca Kazan and Martin Monk in London, the former in fashionable West Hampstead and the latter in lovely Crouch End, where visits to the fishmonger and greengrocer punctuated my hours of writing; Ross Bond and Brenda Brand in bucolic Poplar Point, Manitoba; Rosemary Hooley at Skaigh Stables on the edge of Dartmoor, a paradise for horseback riding; und ein spezielles Dankeschön an meine deutschen Freunde in Bodnegg, Baden-Württemberg, Bruno und Paula Schuler, Roland und Rita Schuler, Petra Schuler, und Mario Schuler.

INTRODUCTION

THE INVENTION OF MODERN MEMORY

I

I first became interested in memory, the subject of this book, during the early 1990s, after I turned forty and, ironically but not surprisingly, began gradually to lose my own. There is nothing dramatic or tragic about this process (so far), which has merely measured the slow but inexorable passage of time and the apparently inevitable diminution of a faculty that I once took for granted. Like most people entering middle age, I suspect, I began to wonder about the significance of a language that had previously seemed unremarkable: what did apparently simple phrases such as "commit to memory" or "keep in my head" really mean when I attempted to describe that which I seemed to be losing?

What I discovered as I began tentatively to research the phenomenon of memory was an extraordinarily rich and dynamic literature formed by contributions from an array of scientific and humanistic disciplines. Certainly the most astonishing came from the burgeoning field of cognitive neuroscience, which, with increasing precision, was beginning to explain the relationship between mental activity and brain chemistry. Advances in medical and scientific research—particularly those involving new techniques in cerebral imaging such as Magnetic Resonance Imaging and Positron Emission Tomography—allowed molecular biologists to refine and even redraw the map of the brain, to isolate the chemical messengers and their receptors utilized in the learning process, and to study the information-gathering capabilities of the neuron. Driven to some extent by a growing concern with the vulnerability of an aging population (of which I was a member) to Alzheimer's disease, medical and scientific practitioners began to reexamine the relationship between behavior, memory, and anatomy. In the words of Daniel L. Alkon, professor of neurology and biophysics, "Memory has behavioral expression, electrical coding, and a molecular basis. Memory is all of these and has to be describable at each different level of biological complexity."[1] During the 1980s the pace of change in the field was so rapid and promising that both the first President Bush and the U.S. Congress designated the 1990s as the Decade of the Brain, inaugurating a formal governmental and bureaucratic commitment to new research.[2]

The last two decades of the twentieth century also saw a renewed attention to memory in the social sciences and humanities, to some extent driven by advances in the natural sciences but responding as well to long-term international concerns about ethical responses to traumatic historical events, particularly the Holocaust, and, especially in the United States, to questions raised by a series of criminal and legal cases in the 1980s and 1990s involving child abuse, "recovered memories," and "false memory syndrome."[3] In a number of related but distinct academic disciplines, including psychology, sociology, anthropology, criminal justice, and history, researchers devoted themselves to exploring the ways in which memory sustains both personal identity and cultural history, both the individual consciousness and the collective bonds that unite particular groups and societies. Although advances in these fields could never be as dramatic as those in the natural sciences, there developed a growing consensus that memory as a social and cultural construct possessed a number of "histories" that could be profitably studied and described from diverse but related perspectives.[4]

This book assumes that technologies of storage and transmission govern both the form and content of what individuals and societies can remember. My history of memory will be shaped by the literary history of seventeenth- and eighteenth-century England, and specifically by the way in which the printing press effected the memorial aspirations of writers concerned with how a commercial print trade might determine their place in cultural memory. This project grew out of my last book, *Paper Bullets: Print and Kingship Under Charles II* (1996), in which I examined the relationship of print culture to political power in England during the latter half of the seventeenth century. My new book deals not with political but with literary authority and the challenges presented to classical models of memory and authorship by the new technologies of print reproduction and distribution.

My inquiry will consider the publication of four works, Margaret Cavendish's *Poems, and Fancies* (1653), John Milton's *Paradise Regain'd. A Poem. In IV Books. To which is added Samson Agonistes* (1671), Alexander Pope's *The Dunciad* (1728–43), and Samuel Richardson's *Clarissa* (1747–59), the complex publication histories of the last two—reflected in their extended dating—an integral part of my narrative of the literary struggle to achieve memorial authority and certainty. All four of the writers I examine were committed to a classical conception of cultural memory and the literary vocation epitomized in Horace's bold assertion that "I have finished a monument more lasting than bronze and loftier than the Pyramids' royal pile."[5] Yet all recognized that a new age of mechanical reproduction had rendered this trope of literary monumentality and immortality problematic, and that their identity as "poor Moderns" (in Pope's phrase) compromised their ability to achieve it.[6] I will argue that the century covered by my study reveals the genesis of a particularly modern conception of memory in which gender becomes crucial to the processes of memorialization, and the professional author central to the struggle for the mastery of cultural memory.

During the last twenty years, scholarship on the evolution of "the modern author" has moved progressively further back in time, suggestive aspects of the history of authorship in the British Isles derived from both Chaucer and Langland.[7] After the establishment of the first printing press in England, significant figures in that history would include, from the late sixteenth and early seventeenth centuries, both Sir Philip Sidney and Ben Jonson. While the former refused to publish during his lifetime, the posthumous publication of his works in three volumes from 1590 to 1595 established an authoritative although perhaps ambiguous precedent for a gentleman to enter the literary marketplace.[8]

Although he was certainly no gentleman, Jonson's 1616 *Workes* has long been recognized as a decisive moment in the affirmation of a new sense of authorial importance and privilege, one tied directly and explicitly to the printed book. Richard C. Newton argues that "Jonson establishes the printed text as the primary object of literature," his efforts to appropriate a classical authority for his texts marking "the birth of the printed book in English literature."[9] Everything about the *Workes*, from its size and shape to the layout of its pages, from Jonson's refusal to include a dedication to his revisions of the play texts, speaks to the monumental aspirations of the volume and its author's willingness to court the disapproval of his literary peers and social superiors by insisting on the cultural authority and authorial power manifest in his book. The elaborate triumphal arch on the volume's title page visually represents the memorial ambitions that drove Jonson to proclaim himself a literary classic while still in mid-career.[10]

Near the end of his professional life Jonson reiterated his insistence on the primacy of the printed book in the octavo printing of *The New Inne*, where the title page flaunts his determination to appropriate the energy and authority of the theater for the book: *The New Inne. Or, The light Heart. A Comoedy. As it was neuer acted, but most negligently play'd, by some, the Kings Seruants. And more squeamishly beheld, and censured by others, the Kings Subjects. 1629. Now, at last, set at liberty to the Readers, his Maties Seruants, and Subiects, to be iudg'd. 1631. By the Author, B. Ionson.*[11] This extraordinary title page—whose conventional recording function is pressed into the service of Jonson's wish to revenge himself on the theatrical world that first brought him success—exhibits his contemptuous rejection of the stage, and his hopes for redemption on the printed page. True judgment here resides with the reader, the theatrical spectacle condemned as neglectful and even reckless, sickly, distant, and ungenerous. The emphasis on the difference between acting and playing suggests that on the stage Jonson's play possessed a mere shadow life from which the printed page has rescued it. Even the clash of rival dates insinuates the insubstantiality of the theater, the primacy of 1631 over 1629 affirmed by the authoritative MDCXXXI at the bottom of the page.

The title page condemns both actors and spectators, but Jonson displays a particular scorn for the latter, who, as "The Dedication, to the Reader" contends, participate in a narcissistic ritual in which "to be seen" is more important than "to see" the play before them. Such auditors, filled with a pride wrought by the expensive "clothes of credit" that they display "between the acts," are without "understanding," having reduced themselves to mere objects, "as the stage-furniture, or arras-clothes." Juxtaposed to their "solemn ignorance" stands the reader, to whose "rustic candour" Jonson will "trust myself and my book." The "Dedication" ends with this idealization of the reader, whose unsophisticated purity and openness of mind—a simplicity and stainlessness of character made even more precious by the "fastidious impertinents" who fill the theater—will presumably underwrite the integrity of the act of reading: "Fare thee well, and fall to. Read."

But Jonson begins the "Dedication" betraying some hesitation, recognizing the perhaps Faustian bargain that he has struck with a reader whose person he cannot observe, whose skills he cannot validate:

The Dedication, to the Reader

If thou be such, I make thee my patron, and dedicate the piece to thee: if not so much, would I had been at the charge of thy better literature. Howsoever, if thou canst but spell, and join my sense, there is more hope of thee than of a hundred fastidious impertinents, who were there present the first day.

The implied question with which the "Dedication" opens—"If thou be such"—reveals the uncertainty that accompanies Jonson's negotiations with a reader who must remain far more insubstantial than a theater audience delighted to parade their clothing and vanity before the dramatist. "Are you a *reader?*" Jonson asks: "how can I identify a *reader?* how can I judge the fitness of my *reader?* who precisely is *reading* my book, and how well are they *reading* it?" "If thou be such" betrays the fundamental indeterminacy that conditioned relations between an early-modern author and the anonymous and private reader who purchased a book. In the following chapters I will examine the ideal reader imagined by Cavendish, Milton, Pope, and Richardson, all of whom fret about the necessarily obscure figure who concludes the long commercial chain of production and consumption set in motion by the author's initial act of composition.

In removing himself from the theater to the book, in making the reader his patron, Jonson inaugurates a relationship between reader and author whose mystery and uncertainty play a significant part in the anxiety with which seventeenth- and eighteenth-century authors greeted the complex print trade that brought their work to the public. The readers Jonson addresses in his dedication were joined by booksellers, stationers, publishers, and printers in a commercial network that created, marketed, and consumed the book upon which the new memorial aspirations of authorship rested. The book, of course, had long represented one of the most powerful metaphors in the

Western tradition, but its significance was transformed and reanimated by its status as the first mass-produced commodity in the West, as Joseph Addison recognized when he dismissed the "mouldering materials" employed by painters, sculptors, and architects:

> The Circumstance which gives Authors an Advantage above all these great Masters, is this, that they can multiply their Originals; or rather can make Copies of their Works, to what Number they please, which shall be as valuable as the Originals themselves. This gives a great Author something like a Prospect of Eternity.[12]

My study concerns itself with the ways in which early-modern authors understood and responded to "something like a Prospect of Eternity," to a world in which, although Addison doesn't quite realize it, the distinction between "Copy" and "Originals" has lost much of its previous meaning. The printing press initiates immense changes in the memorial processes of early-modern culture, for the printed book helped transform the world of learning, the nature of scientific achievement, the storage and transmission of knowledge, and the shape of modern memory. During the seventeenth and eighteenth centuries, as the European print industry expands and evolves, new intellectual categories such as copyright and plagiarism arise, as do the new professional identities of scientist, inventor, and author. In the scientific community, for instance, the act of publication became essential to the marketing and dissemination of new inventions, discoveries, and ideas.[13]

Early in the seventeenth century, Jonson's determination to link his visions of immortality to the book remains uncommon, not shared by many of his contemporaries. While he used the publication of the First Folio in 1623 to famously announce that Shakespeare represents "a monument without a tomb, / And art alive still while thy book doth live," Stephen Greenblatt speculates that this understanding of the book and its relationship to futurity was not shared by the object of Jonson's admiration: "even though as a poet Shakespeare dreamed of eternal fame, he does not seem to have associated fame with the phenomenon of the printed book...He never, it seems, anticipated what turned out to be the case: that he would live as much on the page as on the stage."[14]

By the early eighteenth century, however, the link between the book and posterity has become commonplace, as Addison reveals in a series of metaphors that demonstrate how books are both uniquely embedded in and uniquely abstracted from the world of bodies:

> There is no other Method of fixing those Thoughts
> which arise and disappear in the Mind of Man, and
> transmitting them to the last Periods of Time; no
> other Method of giving a Permanency to our Ideas,
> and preserving the Knowledge of any particular Person,
> when his Body is mixed with the common Mass of Matter,

and his Soul retired into the World of Spirits. Books
are the Legacies that a great Genius leaves to Mankind,
which are delivered down from Generation to Generation,
as Presents to the Posterity of those who are as yet
unborn.[15]

Addison's movement in this passage from "the Mind of Man" to the "common Mass of Matter," from the "Body" to the "Soul" and "World of Spirits,"
from the way in which thoughts "arise and disappear" to "Posterity" and
"the Legacies that a great Genius leaves to Mankind," points to one of the
fundamental paradoxes about the book that puzzled, fascinated, and excited
the authors who contemplated the place of the book in an early-modern
memorial economy. Firmly located in the material world, made of little more
than paper, ink, and leather, and constructed as commercial commodities
in crowded, filthy industrial spaces, books nonetheless seemed to possess an
intellectual and even spiritual essence that could communicate to future generations and conquer time. In the chapters that follow I will examine how
the paradoxical mixture of substance and insubstantiality that characterizes
the book supports a broader paradox in which confidence in the relative
permanence of the page as a repository of cultural memory is haunted by
anxieties concerning uncontrollable replication, rampant individualism, and
cultural devaluation.

   The division between the material and the ethereal in perceptions of
the book is connected to, or even derived from the way print technology
obscures the difference between the functions of formation and transmission. The book becomes both an object in a material realm of industrial
production and the bearer of an intellectual essence expected to survive centuries; as literary monuments books are both the means of transmission and
the object being transmitted. Addison is certainly alive to the complexities of
this paradoxical relationship when he focuses on the way in which books *fix*
the transient "Thoughts" of men, "transmitting them to the last Periods of
Time." So too was Gabrial Naudé, whose *Advis pour dresser une bibliothèque*
(1627)—generally regarded as the first European attempt to rationalize the
selection and classification of books within a library—was translated into
English in 1661 by John Evelyn as *Instructions Concerning Erecting of a
Library*. Naudé opens his first chapter by celebrating those who would create
libraries, an activity

   which breathes nothing but Immortality, to draw out of oblivion, conserve,
   and erect...all these Images, not of the Bodies, but of the Minds of so many
   Gallant men, as have neither spared their time, nor their Industry, to transmit to us the most lively features and representations of whatsoever was most
   excellent and conspicuous in them.[16]

Like Addison, Naudé moves between the poles of "Bodies" and "Minds,"
between "Immortality" and "oblivion" when thinking about how books and
the libraries that will preserve them "transmit" images and representations

from one age to the next. The modern library takes its shape in England during the seventeenth and eighteenth centuries, the archival impulse, as we shall see particularly in the career of Alexander Pope, central to the new intellectual dispensation of the book.

For my purposes, that dispensation begins with the intersection of the political and commercial in the decade after the lapsing of the government's ability to control printing in 1641, when the struggle between Parliament and Crown led the former to abolish the Court of Star Chamber, the most important of the Prerogative Courts and the customary legal authority that successive royal governments had used to control the print trade.[17] While Parliament, and, later, the Commonwealth government, adopted their own measures and procedures for regulating the industry—press freedom possessed very few advocates during the mid-seventeenth century—the political vacuum created by the increasing hostilities between the king and his opponents occasioned a sudden and enormous growth in the publication and distribution of printed matter dealing with the civic crisis that transformed the political landscape, the print trade, and the republic of letters in England. From his relatively privileged position as a successful bookseller in St. Paul's Churchyard, George Thomason succeeded in documenting the exponential growth of printed matter that both accompanied and helped create the English Revolution, the over twenty-two thousand pamphlets and other ephemera he collected and annotated—perhaps 80 percent of everything published in London during the years 1640–1661—providing an unprecedented window into the print trade's involvement in mid-seventeenth-century English politics.[18] George Thomason's extraordinary archive remains a crucial source for scholars constructing the history of revolutionary England, its significance as a part of England's cultural heritage and political memory recognized even at the time of its formation. The careers of both Cavendish and Milton, with whom I begin, were directly effected by the civic, economic, and social changes that attended the transformed commercial print industry of the 1640s.

Accompanying the print explosion of the mid-seventeenth century, and the evolution of the modern archive and library dedicated to its preservation, are both the excitement occasioned by the exhaustive knowledge that the print revolution seemed to promise, and the anxiety that accompanied the as yet inadequately understood world of the commercial print trade. If one specific source of that anxiety is the new relationship between author and reader, a second source concerns the archive itself, where the infinite accumulation of books that the modern library promises leads not necessarily to liberation but entrapment, not to freedom but instead to a specifically modern experience of paralysis and bondage. The possibility of what Roger Chartier has called "libraries without walls" represented for early modern Europe a fantastic vision in which "the closed world of individual libraries could be transformed into an infinite universe of books noted, reviewed, visited, consulted and, eventually, borrowed." Yet such a vision could never be realized: "a universal library...could not be other than fictive,...The irreducible gap between ideally exhaustive inventories and necessarily incomplete collections was experienced with intense frustration."[19] During the seventeenth and eighteenth centuries, the printed book and library come to represent both the dream and nightmare generated by print's ability to standardize, accumulate, catalog, and preserve the diverse productions of the human mind.

In a 1605 letter to Sir Thomas Bodley, whose restored Oxford library had in that year published its first catalog, Sir Francis Bacon suggests the centrality of the book to the transformation from a medieval to modern world when he insists that "books are the shrines where the Saint is, or is believed to be: and you having built an Ark to save learning from deluge, deserve propriety in any new instrument or engine, whereby learning should be improved or advanced."[20] For all of Bacon's cynicism here, his amused recognition that the modern book may be as empty as the medieval shrine, he nonetheless registers the way in which the book has replaced the saint's shrine, and the library the church, as the spiritual center of a new intellectual regime. In the new age of the book, Bodley's library has become central to the preservation and advancement of learning, the ark that alone can save civilization from possible annihilation.[21] In this unpredictable movement from the book as a shrine to the library as an ark, which can alone provide memorial salvation from a second deluge, Bacon captures perfectly the excitement generated by the book as well as the simultaneous fear of cultural extinction that accompanies its rise. In the *Advancement of Learning*, Bacon's puzzlement about how the book achieves its memorial authority perhaps explains this association between excitement and extinction:

> But the images of men's wits and knowledges remain in books, exempted from the wrong of time and capable of perpetual renovation. Neither are they fitly to be called images, because they generate still, and cast their seeds in the minds of others, provoking and causing infinite actions and opinions in succeeding ages…how much more are letters to be magnified, which as ships pass through vast seas of time.[22]

While the sexual imagery in this passage points to memory's organic base, Bacon's concern for a reader from "succeeding ages" also acknowledges the way in which books function as social and historical constructs, as objects whose meanings were ultimately supplied by that distant and unknowable auditor. Bacon's triumphant image of letters and printing as a ship that passes through the "vast seas of time" is certainly not undermined by his uncertainty about the precise status of the book, but his momentary hesitation about the term "image," and its propriety as a way to describe what and how books transmit "their seeds in the minds of others," suggests how difficult it was to understand and rationalize the book's generative power.

II

My study of the printed book and modern memory is situated within three contemporary critical discourses. The first—which I have already begun to survey—was inaugurated by Elizabeth Eisenstein's *The Printing Press as an Agent of Social Change* and Michel Foucault's "What Is an Author?" It has focused on the construction of the professional author, and the ways in which this figure came to enjoy and exploit a privileged status in the literary marketplace.[23] Early in the seventeenth century, for instance, Milton's decision to pursue cultural authority forced him reluctantly to enter the world of print and reject many of the political, economic, and class interests represented by the practice of manuscript circulation. By the early eighteenth century, on the other hand, an ambitious poet like Pope could enter a literary marketplace transformed by the Copyright Act of 1710, and construct himself as a cultural monument not simply through his poetic genius, but by his cunning, innovative, and energetic business practices. Richardson, a highly successful printer as well as author, enjoyed another sort of privilege, dictated by the control he possessed over the printing and obsessive revision of his massive novels. Indeed, I conclude my survey of the seventeenth and eighteenth centuries not with a poet, but with Richardson's *Clarissa* because the novel remains, more than any other modern literary form, marked by its longing to achieve monumentality; the frequency with which the term *history* appears in both the titles and subtitles of "novels" from the mid-seventeenth to mid-eighteenth centuries is only the most obvious sign of the form's desire to appropriate the memorial stability and aspirations of other more prestigious, nonfictional forms.[24]

Yet the challenges presented by new technologies and markets concern all three men, who betray a profound anxiety about how the new conditions of authorship will transform the cultural memories of their society, and their ability to participate in and even control that process. Moreover, in *Samson Agonistes, The Dunciad,* and *Clarissa,* the struggle to achieve a monumentality that will provide a second life in time assumes a specifically gendered form, Dalila in Milton, "The Mighty Mother" in Pope, and Clarissa in Richardson's novel the primary threats to the memorial aspirations of the male protagonists. In Milton's poem, Samson can take his "rightful" place in history only by erasing Dalila's interpretation of their marriage and her "betrayal," while in Pope's *Dunciad* the survival and transmission of classical male culture is itself threatened by the dirty and revolting female body of Dulness. Richardson's novel stages a similar battle in the confrontation between Clarissa and Lovelace, who, by the novel's conclusion, clash over whose version of their intertwined story will achieve the status of "history."

The challenges presented to masculine preeminence by female competition lead me to discourses of gender theory, in particular current attempts by Margaret J.M. Ezell, Jennifer Summit, and Wendy Wall, among many others, to rewrite early modern literary history by charting the struggle by female poets to achieve literary authority.[25] I will begin my inquiry by examining Margaret Cavendish's first published book, *Poems, and Fancies,* in which she articulates like no English woman before her a relationship to authorial fame and cultural memory that allows her to imagine herself within the precincts of a literary present and future previously constructed primarily in terms of male succession. In this volume Cavendish attempts to achieve and retain visibility within a literary history in which the woman writer normally functioned, as Jennifer Summit argues, as a figure of loss or exteriority, and for whom fame as a writer promised not immortality but death.[26] Cavendish, rejecting this customary role, defiantly situates herself within a contemporary intellectual and literary context while attempting to construct herself as a future figure of cultural memory.

At the same time, Cavendish's volume engages issues that concerned all writers, male as well as female, during a period when the protocols of authorship remained fluid and uncertain, and the expanding print industry raised concerns about social hierarchy and rank, cultural consumption and economics. As early as the sixteenth century, according to Wendy Wall, "the press engendered outcries that far exceeded its political force, for the circulation of texts created anxieties and benefits that tapped into vast cultural problems."[27] For writers who possessed literary aspirations, these problems included questions involving authorial survival, memorial authority, and archival permanence. Cavendish, for instance, recognized the importance and consequences of the act of publication much earlier in her career than Milton did in his, and her attention to the ways in which cultural memory privileged some writers and marginalized others represents a notable attempt to understand how poets and authors might achieve their second life in time. *Poems, and Fancies* demonstrates the strategies that allowed one woman to simultaneously disregard and exploit her elevated social position, and to envision and then realize a career as a "professional" woman writer in Interregnum and Restoration England.

These two primarily literary discourses of authorship and gender will be employed within a context formed by current scholarship—taken primarily from the social sciences—concerned with how print helped to shape the formation of a distinctly modern conception of collective memory. The printed book and modern library accelerate the movement toward what James Fentress and Chris Wickham refer to as "the textual model of memory," which revolutionized Western society by transforming the content and mechanisms of collective memory: "In Western society, the history of memory is one of its steady devaluation as a source of knowledge—a devaluation which proceeds in step with the evolution, and increasing dominance, of the textual paradigm of knowledge." England's long and gradual transformation from a primarily oral to a primarily written culture was accompanied by important political changes, for, as Fentress and Wickham have noted, "the reconstitution of memory through texts...sets into relief the issue of who controls commemoration in any given society,"[28] a process punctuated by the unstable, dramatic, and sometimes violent politics of the seventeenth century. While the desire for literary immortality takes different forms for the four writers I will consider, their attempts to claim memorial authority reveal the modern author's centrality to negotiations for the mastery of collective memory, what Frances Dolan describes as the "political conflict in

seventeenth- and eighteenth-century England . . . self-consciously and openly
to shape national memory."[29]

Although terms such as "national" or "social," "cultural" or "collective
memory" remain anachronistic when used to describe the early modern,
there can be little doubt that the tumultuous politics of sixteenth- and
seventeenth-century England intensified an already increasing attention to a
new, secular, and rational history that both depended on and helped to shape
a national identity and consciousness no longer determined or limited primarily by providential history or the two bodies of the divine monarch. The
collective, national identity of a new British nation was beginning to take
recognizable form during these centuries, separating itself from an older
political and cultural regime, for instance, in Henry VIII's dramatic break
with Rome during the 1530s, and, a century later, the traumatic 1649 execution of Charles I. David Cressy has argued that during the sixteenth and
seventeenth centuries, "England's past became an issue in England's present to a degree unknown elsewhere in early modern Christendom": "The
Protestant leaders of early modern England developed a distinctive view of
English history, and buttressed their position by the invocation and manipulation of memory."[30]

A poem such as Dryden's "To My Honored Friend, Dr. Charleton," in
spite of its commitment to a zealous, even mystical celebration of Charles II's
Restoration, represents the ways in which both England's national identity
and cultural heritage came to be separated from the person of the monarch.
In *The Material Word* (1991), Richard W.F. Kroll has described the poem as
"a critical meditation on those motives by which a literate culture can dif-
ferentiate among, revise, and translate older sources of authority."[31] Insofar
as the poem attempts to provide a critique of its own intellectual history, and
to examine the memorial structures that govern the transmission of cultural
forms and ideas, it can help us to understand the parameters of the nascent
modern, collective memory that began to take shape during the seventeenth
century in England.

Dryden almost certainly composed his commendatory poem sometime
during 1662, barely two years after Charles II's Restoration, and the poem's
mixture of political playfulness, intellectual exhilaration, and nationalistic
fervor suggests the not yet diminished excitement of the king's supporters.
From the opening reference to "The longest Tyranny that ever sway'd," to
the final evocation of Charles's "Restor'd . . . *Throne*," the poem insists that
we understand its examination of cultural achievement and intellectual labor
within the context of what Dryden regarded as England's recent political
liberation and triumph.[32] Learning, scholarship, and scientific advancement
are, within the poem, implicitly and inextricably linked to civic stability,
national identity, and the political imaginary.

The cultural tyranny with which the poem begins discovers an intellectual continuum that runs unbroken from classical Greece to Dryden's
own England, a two-thousand-year history that the poem simultaneously celebrates and questions. The poem clearly glories in the long and

rich cultural heritage that it uncovers, even as it insists on the necessity to break with the past and affirm the intellectual superiority of the present. Dryden venerates Aristotle and the classical heritage that he represents, but the poem's admiration for the past, and its evident appreciation of its own valuable cultural inheritance, cannot prevent the poet from seeking to overthrow "the Stagirite," for his tyranny has circumscribed the world within which contemporary society lives. The very first of the moderns who Dryden celebrates is Columbus, whose discovery of a "*Temp'rate* in a *Torrid* Zone" has transformed both the physical geography and the mental landscape of the seventeenth-century world that Dryden inhabits:

> Had we still paid that homage to a *Name*,
> Which onely *God* and *Nature* justly claim;
> The *Western* Seas had been our utmost bound,
> Where *Poets* still might dream the *Sun* was drown'd:
> And all the *Starrs*, that shine in *Southern* Skies,
> Had been admir'd by none but *Salvage* Eyes. (15–20)

In these lines, the cultural and intellectual traditions that societies inherit shape not only the physical world in which they live, but regulate both individual dreams and the materials available to the poetic imagination. Our cultural past determines the present, what "we" as moderns can apprehend and experience in the contemporary moment dependent on the memorial structures provided by our forebears. In the first verse paragraph, which the lines above conclude, that which distinguishes civilized from savage is precisely the existence of a shared cultural history. The noble savages who Columbus discovers, "guiltless *Men*, who danc'd away their time," remain "*Fresh* as their *Groves*, and *Happy* as their *Clime*" (13–14) because they possess no past, no collective memory that inspires both the excitement of intellectual achievement and the burden of guilt. Although Dryden would not have expressed himself in the language of the twenty-first-century neurobiologist, Steven Rose's description of "artificial memory" captures the impoverishment that for Dryden characterizes the mythology of the noble savage: "Where there is no artificial memory, each individual animal lives in its own unique and personal set of memories, memories which begin with its birth and end with its death and can represent only its own experience."[33] I will return to this subject in both chapter one—for the ostensible inability of the bestial mind to participate in a collective memory particularly concerned Margaret Cavendish—and in my conclusion, where I will briefly examine the figure of the cyborg, whose confusion of the animal and mechanical, the human and the technological, questions this comfortable distinction between people and beasts, and represents a new, postmodern conception of memory.

In the second verse paragraph, the poem's emphasis shifts to "Fame," and the question of how individuals can forge a place for themselves and participate in their society's collective memory. Having begun with a foreign explorer, Dryden turns his attention to the English scientists, physicians,

and members of the Royal Society who are remaking the intellectual land-
scape of Restoration England. "Th'*English* are not the least in Worth, or
Fame" (22), asserts the proud Englishman, as he points to Francis Bacon,
William Gilbert, Robert Boyle, William Harvey, George Ent, and, of course,
Walter Charleton himself, as men whose names have been saved "from dark
Oblivion." For all of his English pride, however, Dryden recognizes that
the simple dichotomy between Oblivion and Fame does not quite capture
the complexity and richness of the cultural memory he wants to describe.
Although the poem insists on its celebration of a specifically English worth,
at the same time it doesn't wish to consign its heroes to only a local fame.
The poem looks toward a European, if not a global context within which to
determine genuine cultural value:

> Nor are *You*, Learned Friend, the least renown'd;
> Whose Fame, not circumscrib'd with *English* ground,
> Flies like the nimble Journeys of the Light. (33–35)

In making Charleton a candidate for this larger fame, Dryden must
enlarge his list of worthies, including the scholar and antiquarian as well as
the explorer and scientist, for the book of Charleton's that the poem com-
memorates, *Chorea Gigantum; or, the most famous antiquity of Great-Britain,
vulgarly called Stone-Heng, standing on Salisbury plain, restored to the Danes,*
is not a work of natural science or discovery, but of history and scholarship.
The lines that testify to Charleton's worth are quite different from those that
credit Harvey's discovery of the circulation of blood, or Gilbert's work with
magnetism:

> What ever *Truths* have been, by *Art*, or *Chance*,
> Redeem'd from *Error*, or from *Ignorance*,
> Thin in their *Authors*, (like rich Veins of Ore)
> Your Works unite, and still discover more.
> Such is the healing virtue of Your Pen,
> To perfect Cures on *Books*, as well as *Men*. (37–42)

The awkwardness of Dryden's imagery here, which points not to the individual achievement of a Columbus, Harvey, or Gilbert but instead to Charleton's
scholarly dependence on other writers and their books, may suggest a certain defensiveness in the poem, a recognition that, for all of Charleton's
undoubted fame, the nature and magnitude of his achievements did not
quite place him in the select company Dryden describes in the poem.[34]
But Dryden's movement in these lines to *Authors* and their *Books* suggests
the ways in which, as Richard W.F. Kroll argues, "knowledge now derives its
main metaphors from the atomistic model,...[its] coherence from cultural
atoms (such as texts)"[35]; and Dryden concludes his poem with a demonstration of the book's power to shape contemporary knowledge and collective
memory when he considers how Charleton's scholarship has altered society's

understanding of the monumental antiquity of Stonehenge: "You well may give / To Men new vigour, who make Stones to live" (43–44). In attributing the otherwise inarticulate stones to the Danes, giving them a contemporary voice and demonstrating their function as throne rather than temple, Charleton's book rewrote the cultural and political history of Restoration England, reestablishing the importance of Danish culture—"the DANES (their short Dominion lost) / A longer Conquest than the Saxons boast" (45–46)—thus providing a way for Dryden to legitimize Charles' kingship by turning the military defeat at Worcester into a symbolic victory. Such a public representation, according to the Popular Memory Group, provides one of the most powerful ways to produce a collective sense of the past, to generate "a public 'theatre' of history, a public stage and a public audience for the enacting of dramas concerning 'our' history, or heritage, the story, traditions, and legacy of 'the British People.'"[36] Charleton's scholarship allows Dryden, in the final verse paragraph of the poem, to transform the "Ruines" of Stonehenge into a living public theater in which the past can be reproduced in the image of the triumphant present, the collective memory of Restoration England refashioned in the restoration of Stonehenge's "original" purpose and meaning.

With his characteristic cultural perspicuity, Dryden articulates many of the questions, issues, and assumptions that governed early-modern considerations of what today we most commonly refer to as collective memory, specifically the dialectical relationship between fame and oblivion, the meaning of monumentality and status of the literary monument in the new age of the book, the way in which national identity shapes the memorial imagination, the importance of the archive to the transmission of modern knowledge, and the centrality of the book to collective memory. Indeed, Dryden's attention to the book and cultural memory in a poem about England's most important monument of antiquity is not coincidental. Jennifer Summit has shown the way in which, during the sixteenth century, monuments and books (as well as the Eucharist) had become part of a "memorial vocabulary" that transformed "loss into memory, and memory into posterity."[37] The *monumental* status of the printed book was a significant issue during the sixteenth through eighteenth centuries, its complexity figured, according to the *Oxford English Dictionary*, in the now obsolete definitions of a monument as "a piece of information given in writing," "a written document or record," or, in law, as "a legal instrument."

This juxtaposition between, and affiliation of book and monument in the poem speaks to the complex relationship between the material form memory takes and its political, intellectual, and even spiritual content. Stonehenge's monumental status seemed self-evident to those in mid-seventeenth-century England who sought to understand its grandeur, but its content, its meaning, what precisely its creators had intended to memorialize, remained embarrassingly opaque. In Dryden's poem, after all, for all of Stonehenge's eminence as temple or throne, in the Restoration present it lies in "Ruins," a mystery obscured and to a large extent even destroyed by time. The difficulty of establishing with any certainty the original function and significance of the site was part of a continuing seventeenth-century concern for the material decay of its past, a process, according to John Weever, in which the nation was even devouring its own history. In his *Ancient Funerall Monuments within the United Monarchie of Great Britaine, Ireland, and the Islands Adiacent with the Monasteries Therein Contained* (1631) Weever laments "the shame of our time," in which "the Monuments of the dead" in Great Britain have been "barbarously...broken downe, and utterly almost all ruinated":

> Grieuing at this vnsufferable iniurie offered as well to the liuing, as the dead, out of the respect I bore to venerable Antiquity, and the due regard to continue the remembrance of the defunct to future posteritie; I determined with my selfe to collect such memorials of the deceased, as were remaining as yet vndefaced; as also to reuiue the memories of eminent worthy persons entombed or interred.[38]

Weever's tone here, as he protests the Reformation's destruction of his nation's heritage, differs dramatically from that of Bacon, Addison, and Naudé when they celebrate the book's ability to transcend and defeat time. Weever, on the other hand, contemplates memorial forms shorn of their content, physical remains, "their brazen Inscriptions erased, torne away, and pilfered," which can no longer transmit a "venerable Antiquity...to future posteritie." This contrast between the divergent memorial potentials of monument and book underlines the significance of Weever's "Funerall Elegie vpon the Death of Sir Robert Cotton Knight and Baronet," for he celebrates Cotton as "this worthy repairer of eating-times ruines, this Philadelphus, in preseruing old Monuments, and ancient Records: this Magazin, this Treasurie, this Storehouse of Antiquities." Sir Robert Cotton's private library was one of the most extensive in London during the first half of the seventeenth century; his collection of manuscripts even became politically controversial, according to Ann Baynes Coiro, because "it contained the scraps from which competing versions of a national identity were being constructed...A whole new sense of historiography, of time, of change and continuity, and of legitimacy rested in the physical evidence of these manuscript documents."[39] Cotton's collection fulfilled just such a function for Weever, for it allowed him to repair some of the damage he discovered during his survey when Cotton "lent me out of his inestimable Librarie, such Bookes and Manuscripts as were most fitting for my vse."

For both Dryden and Weever, the book and the monument participate in a symbiotic relationship within which the book might articulate memorial content for otherwise dumb or defaced stone and "brazon Inscriptions." Indeed, in seventeenth- and eighteenth-century England, book and monument both took their place in a larger memorial economy that included diverse material objects, the reciprocal, supplementary relationship between them necessary to achieve a more accurate picture of the past. In a long 1689 letter to Samuel Pepys, John Evelyn talks at length about how Pepys should adorn and present his "Choice Library." At the center of Pepys's "precious Collection" stands, of course, the book, but Evelyn urges his friend to surround his library with a variety of other objects that can act as a "necessary Adjunct" in the recovery of "Antiquitie." Evelyn begins by discussing Pepys' plan to hang "pictures of Men Illustrious for their parts and Erudition," and then moves on to the importance of also exhibiting "Medals and Medalions," "Ancient and Modern Coines," and, from the title pages of books, "Effigies and Icons of those who have made such a noise and bussle in the World." Evelyn provides a careful description, for instance, of how the "Image and Superscription" displayed on "Medalls" might supplement "the Text of Vitruvius, and all his Commentators," providing for "the Recovery of the Antient and magnificent Architecture, whose real Monuments had ben so barbarously defac'd by the Goths etc, that without this light, and some few Ruines yet extant, that so usefull Order and Ornament of Columns and their decent members, were hardly to be knowne."[40] Image, text (in the form of a superscription), book, "real Monuments," and "Ruines," all contribute to save the past for the present, functioning, according to Kroll as a "collection of concretized moments of history" in which "poetry and history here work together"[41] to monumentalize the cultural heritage that both Pepys and Evelyn cherish.

The printed book certainly played a privileged role in the memorial economy described in the seventeenth century by Bacon, Evelyn, and Dryden, for, according to Bacon, "the monuments of wit and learning are more durable than the monuments of power."[42] Yet this very durability, which fueled the burgeoning literary marketplace that, from the early seventeenth to early eighteenth centuries, transformed and enlarged the status and aspirations of the author, was also undermined by that marketplace and the increasing sense, according to Aleida Assmann, that "far from being the guarantor of the perpetuity of texts, by the eighteenth century,... The literary market, with its laws of production and consumption and short-lived whims of fashion, became paradigmatic for different experiences of time."[43] As commercial commodities trying to find their way in a fiercely competitive and uncertain market, books, for all of their potential durability, were now subject to the caprice of buyers and the fickle tastes of those readers whom Jonson had enthroned. Here is yet a third specific site of anxiety raised by the Janus-faced nature of the print trade, whose promises of a second life in literary monuments that might outlive a Stonehenge depended on transient commercial commodities and transactions that might not survive the next change in fashion. In the "Preface" to his *Works* of 1717, Alexander Pope deplores the throwaway economy that surrounded him, where "the utmost we can hope, is but to be read in one Island, and to be thrown aside at the end of one Age": "I am altogether uncertain, whether to look upon my self as a man building a monument, or burying the dead?"[44] A half century after Dryden's poem to Charleton, Pope laments a contemporary literary world that has perhaps doomed him to a fleeting, local fame, his ability to construct a durable literary monument compromised by the language in which he writes and the cultural milieu he inhabits.

This complex, reciprocal, and dynamic relationship between book and monument is visually and architecturally represented in the history of the south transept of Westminster Abbey, which became popularly known as "Poets' Corner." Although Chaucer was buried there upon his death in 1400—because of his status as clerk of the king's works rather than as a poet—the site didn't achieve its preeminent literary status until the seventeenth century, and only in the eighteenth century, when memorials to Milton and Shakespeare were erected, did it attain widespread recognition as a public monument to the nation's literary heritage. The evolution of the Abbey as a symbol and protector of the national literary canon was accompanied, according to Philip Connell, by the same type of relentless commercialization that defined the place of the book in the literary marketplace.[45] By the end of the eighteenth century, both book and monument were subject to an economic marketplace in which immortality seemed both uniquely possible and entirely impossible. If, as Richard Kroll suggests, the "literate culture" of Restoration and early-eighteenth-century England manifested itself in the public world of books and monuments, that culture was perceived to have grounded itself on material foundations that both promised and betrayed longevity.

III

While Dryden's "To My Honored Friend, Dr. Charleton" celebrates the monumental status of the printed book, it also unwittingly reveals that the new sphere of collective memory inscribed in the book was in fact marked specifically as a site of contestation. Although the poem pretends that Charleton's discovery of Stonehenge's origins possessed all the cultural authority and weight of Harvey's or Gilbert's science, few of his contemporaries accepted Charleton's conclusions, which could establish their legitimacy, and Charleton's memorial ascendancy, only by confronting rival claims in the new marketplace of books and ideas. In the four authors I will examine, collective memory takes its modern shape as part of a triadic relationship with fame and history, the former representing the transitory and uncertain, a dubious celebrity that may fade as quickly as mortal breath, the latter embodying a realm of ostensibly unchanging, institutionalized certainties; during the seventeenth and eighteenth centuries, modern memory teeters between archaic models of *fame* and emergent conceptions of *history*. The four early-modern writers I consider apprehend collective memory as the contested middle ground between these two extremes, a modern purgatory in which the author might achieve a cultural authority allowing him or her to pass from the loud and ragged Bartholomew Fair of fame to the hallowed precincts of a history figured as the quiet, sacred library that promises eternal life.

My emphasis on the central position of memory in this triadic relationship does not deny that as intellectual categories both fame and history possess their own rich and complex histories. According to Leo Braudy, in *The Frenzy of Renown: Fame and Its History* (1986), fame had long expressed itself "in two aspects, as something transitory that only fools seek and as something permanent that is the reward of true greatness." Braudy delineates, in fact, a specifically English resistance to "brazen fame" that Chaucer as well as Sidney share. But he also recognizes that the proliferation of images and texts that resulted from the print revolution decisively changed early-modern understandings of fame. Particularly for writers, new print technologies transformed the way in which posterity would be apprehended, represented, and even desired: "Petrarch sought by scholarship to rescue language from corruption and writers from being forgotten. How much easier would the task be when aided with the new technology of moveable-type printing. How much more certain would be the way out of personal death and into posterity."[46]

What Braudy fails to appreciate here is one of the fundamental paradoxes of print, for his rhetorical questions ignore the ways in which the relationship between print and posterity led inevitably to increased doubts about the survival of literary culture and the writer's second life in time. The dream of print immortality was always accompanied by its nightmare twin, in which the seemingly endless proliferation of books and the flimsy paper on which they were printed—the subject of my chapter on Richardson—represented the corruption and destruction of civilized life. In the new age of the book, as we have seen, the meaning of monumentality, and the status of the literary monument in particular, comes under renewed scrutiny, the disparity between paper and stone, the apparent fragility of the former contrasted to the brute materiality of the latter, a fascinating but also disquieting subject for authors concerned with achieving their own place in a timeless cultural memory. Fame alone could not allay or confront these fears, for fame, as Bacon wrote dismissively in "Of Praise," is "like a River, that beareth up Things Light and Swolne, And Drownes Things waighty and Solide."[47] By the mid-eighteenth century, fame, according to Richard Terry, had become reified within the literary marketplace, semantic change having shifted its connotative meaning from posterity to reputation, a transformation that Andrew Sabl has charted in Hume's skeptical and ultimately unsuccessful attempts to define the nature of true fame.[48]

The four authors I examine turn to memory to provide the type of memorial certainty that Donne alludes to when he contemplates the possibility of death and insists that "to be no part of any body is to be nothing." He derides "the greatest persons" as "but great wens, and excrescences;...except they be so incorporated into the body of the world that they contribute something to the sustentation of the whole."[49] Memory in the seventeenth and eighteenth centuries becomes one of the primary human faculties through which this act of incorporation can take place. Achsah Guibbory argues that in Donne's religious writing, "memory becomes not simply something private and individual, but rather a kind of typological memory linking Donne with biblical history and mankind as a whole."[50] Although, according to the *Oxford English Dictionary*, the two meanings of *memory* that specifically define it in terms of "the faculty by which things are remembered"—or that

faculty "residing in the awareness or consciousness of a particular individual
or group"—can be traced to the turn of the fifteenth century, only in the
seventeenth and eighteenth centuries do these meanings begin to assume
the primacy that they maintain today. Other meanings and uses of *memory*
slowly become obsolete: the last *OED* citation for *memory* as "a commemorative account" is found in 1730; as "a memento" in 1624; as a "memorial
tomb, shrine,...or monument" in 1691.

"Goodfriday, 1613. Riding Westward" dramatizes the type of typological
memory that Guibbory describes above, and the individual or group "consciousness" that is part of the *OED* definition, when, at the emotional and
spiritual climax of the poem, the narrator experiences the crucifixion that
might save him:

> Though these things, as I ride, be from mine eye,
> They'are present yet unto my memory,
> For that looks towards them; and thou look'st towards mee
> O Saviour, as thou hang'st upon the tree.

Memory's ability in these lines to embody and realize the truth of Christ's
sacrifice—to allow the distracted narrator to "behold those hands which
span the Poles" and "behold that endlesse height which is/Zenith to us"[51]—
provides an opportunity for salvation. Not mere fame, but this type of
incorporation into the fabric of collective memory becomes the ambition of
Cavendish, Milton, Pope, and Richardson, although each understands and
expresses this act of inclusion in a different fashion, and, except for Milton,
certainly not within the religious context imagined here by Donne.

The complexities of fame, of course, are dwarfed by those of history,
a rich and problematic intellectual field, particularly in the seventeenth
and eighteenth centuries when a new, secular history, utilitarian, progressive, political, and analytical, began to challenge an older conception of
Christian universal history.[52] During these centuries, history transformed
itself from the study of first to second causes, as the analysis of cause
and effect, particularly in the political realm, became central to a renewed
emphasis on accuracy, method, and impartiality. Even biblical history came
under the scrutiny of empirical methods of analysis, while the concept of
anachronism transformed Europe's sense of historical time.[53] Bacon, for
instance, in *New Organon*, derides the Greeks for their "narrow and meager
knowledge either of time or place," directly linking their temporal limitations to their historiographic failures: "they had no history worthy to be
called history that went back a thousand years—but only fables and rumors
of antiquity."[54] And both Jonson and Dryden possessed more than a casual
interest in history: Jonson was appointed historiographer of London in
1628, while Dryden became historiographer royal in 1670, and both register in their poetry this new historical consciousness, in which, according
to the former, history stands as "Time's witness, herald of antiquity, / The
light of truth, and life of memory."[55]

Jonson's tribute to history as "Time's witness" reveals the pretensions to memorial authority and reliability that the new history promised. History's growth and transformation during the early modern was accompanied by an insistence that new methods of research and writing, including a renewed attention to authenticity and anachronism, privileged the discipline, confirming its status as an enduring record. Today we are much more aware that history's certainties remain not simply unfulfilled but illusory. History is not simply an objective record of the past, for it can produce what it pretends only to record, and the archives that underwrite its ostensible objectivity represent a "range of institutions including libraries, museums, local records and special collections [that are] all designed to create a particular vision of society."[56] The evolution of the modern conception of history to some extent depends on such illusions:

> Since ancient times, the archive had been the location of the record. Refined in the early modern period with the establishment of diplomatics, archives were increasingly regarded as the location of "authentic" records. The idea of authority embedded in the notion of an authentic record privileged the archives as an authoritative source in understanding the past.[57]

In modern societies, history is constructed by and through the struggle to establish dominance over archival materials that can never tell their own story, but must instead be interpreted by historians whose powers to a large extent stem from the untenable objectivity of what the archive preserves. Such interpretation and preservation, as Derrida insists, are always political acts: "There is no political power without control of the archive, if not of memory. Effective democratization can always be measured by this essential criterion: the participation in and access to the archive, its constitution, and its interpretation."[58]

The particularly intimate as well as problematic relationship between history and memory that Derrida implies here was figured in antiquity by a Greek mythology that cast Mnemosyne, the goddess of Memory, as the mother of Clio, or History. In the twentieth century that relationship has come under particular scrutiny, its precise formulation still a matter of enormous debate among academicians.[59] The questions raised by this relationship have, in fact, engaged numerous academic disciplines throughout the century, the intellectual figure most responsible for the theorizing of collective memory possessing disciplinary links to the fields of philosophy and law, as well as psychology and sociology. Maurice Halbwachs' *Les Cadres sociaux de la mémoire* (1925) and *La Mémoire collective* (published posthumously in 1950) remain two of the foundational texts of collective memory, which in his work becomes an object of sociological inquiry conceptualized not as a biological but as a cultural phenomenon. Halbwachs recognized that neither groups nor institutions actually remember—for there exists no abstract or mystical collective consciousness—and that only in the individual can the memory of particular groups actually manifest and realize itself. But at the same time he insists that without the temporal, spatial, intellectual, and linguistic forms provided by society there would be no individual memory: "No memory is possible outside frameworks used by people living in society to determine and retrieve their recollections." In complex, modern societies, in which each individual participates in many, often diverse groups, these frameworks effectively envelop the individual, saturating the individual consciousness with collective memorial structures: "It is in this sense that there exists a collective memory and social frameworks for memory; it is to the degree that our individual thought places itself in these frameworks and participates in this memory that it is capable of the act of recollection."[60]

In *La Mémoire collective*, Halbwachs distinguishes between two types of memory, the autobiographical and the historical, the first concerned with the internal, personal life that the individual directly lives and experiences, the second with the social life, lived within different groups, that people normally experience only indirectly. Yet these two sorts of memory rarely exist isolated and apart, but "are often intermingled. In particular, the individual memory, in order to corroborate and make precise and even to cover the gaps in its remembrances, relies upon, relocates itself within, momentarily merges with, the collective memory."[61] Historical memory can cover a vast expanse of time, which it knows in a condensed and schematic fashion; rarely can it claim to "remember" events that it experiences primarily through others. Autobiographical memory, on the other hand, possesses both a deep continuity provided by the individual life, and the dense, rich, particular texture of a life experienced at first hand.

During the last half century Halbwachs' conceptualization of collective memory has certainly come under interrogation, modified and revised by some, questioned and challenged by others. Raphael Samuel, for instance, interested in a popular history based on oral tradition, local lore, and printed ephemera, rejects the opposition that Halbwachs constructs between history and memory; he sees the two as dialectically related, emphasizing the way in which memory dynamically shapes the past rather than passively storing it.[62] James Fentress and Chris Wickham, on the other hand, representing the fields of anthropology and history, critique Halbwachs for what they consider an exaggerated emphasis on the collective nature of social consciousness. They employ the term "social memory," rather than Halbwachs' more famous phrase, in order to posit a greater balance between the collective aspects of consciousness and the individual will.[63] Recently the sociologist Barbara A. Misztal has suggested that since the 1980s Halbwachs' social conception of collective memory has been forced to share the discipline with a number of different perspectives concerned specifically with issues of power and its containment. She describes a field in which some scholars emphasize the ways in which dominant groups in the present manipulate the past, in which others maintain that memory can be constructed from the bottom up, and in which still others envision collective memory as a continual process of negotiation that in fact limits the ability of any group in the present to control the past.[64]

Jan Assmann's critique of Halbwachs focuses not just on issues of power and control but of time, for Assmann identifies Halbwachs' conception of collective memory with what he calls "communicative memory," an everyday, informal, and primarily oral form of memory that possesses a limited temporal existence. Assmann distinguishes this from "objectivized culture," a "cultural memory [that] has its fixed point; its horizon does not change with the passing of time. These fixed points are fateful events of the past, whose memory is maintained through cultural formation (texts, rites, monuments) and institutional communication (recitation, practice, observance)." Participating in the processes of both cultural formation and institutional communication, literary authors are particularly well placed to dominate the content of cultural memory as well as some of the forms it might take:

> The distribution and structure of participation in the communicative memsory are diffuse. No specialists exist in this regard. Cultural memory, by contrast, always depends on a specialized practice, a kind of "cultivation." In special cases of written cultures with canonized texts, such cultivation can expand enormously and become extremely differentiated.[65]

In the creation of cultural memory, all literary authors might be considered "specialists," although this was particularly true during the seventeenth and eighteenth centuries when the English literary canon and its history achieved their modern shape.[66] Those involved in the corporate enterprise of the early-modern print trade, booksellers and printers, critics and poets, "Grubstreet hacks" and government censors, all participated in the institutionalization of a cultural and collective memory that, according to Assmann,

> comprises that body of reusable texts, images, and rituals specific to each society in each epoch, whose "cultivation" serves to stabilize and convey that society's self-image. Upon such collective knowledge, for the most part (but not exclusively) of the past, each group bases its awareness of unity and particularity.[67]

My aim in this book is not to intervene in the disciplinary debates of other fields, but to illuminate the contribution that literary studies can make to the sociology of collective memory. Larry Ray insists that "understanding memory as a contested terrain is central to understanding the particular character of modernity,"[68] and the poets and novelists of seventeenth- and eighteenth-century England were especially sensitive to the contested nature of this modern landscape. The worlds of both politics and letters, as Andrew Marvell recognized, would necessarily be transformed by the printing press, contestation and mortality—linked by the lead that formed bullets as well as type—essential to the changes it would initiate: "Lead, when moulded into Bullets, is not so mortal as when founded into Letters."[69] The commercial print industry, which played an important part in the political upheavals of the seventeenth century, assumed just as significant a role in the formation and evolution of English literary history, the promise of an everlasting textual future accompanied by the uncertainty and anxiety occasioned by a technology whose material and memorial consequences were not yet fully understood.

Indeed, the mingled excitement and fear occasioned by a technological revolution whose profound memorial effects can hardly be imagined characterizes our own age as well: "For each of us as individuals and for all of us as a society, technologies, some as old as the act of writing, some as modern as the electronic personal organizer, transform the way we conceive of and the way we use memory."[70] Steven Rose's linking of writing and the computer at two ends of a long historical spectrum suggests a memorial continuum that runs through the printing press to the computer, and in my conclusion I want to suggest at least some of the ways in which postmodern memory will differ from the modern memory whose seventeenth- and eighteenth-century origins primarily concern me here.

There were, of course, many stages on which that modern history of memory would play itself out. During the seventeenth and eighteenth centuries, an age devoted to civic pageantry and lavish displays of state power, what one scholar has called "spectacular politics,"[71] the English "public theatre of history" described by the Popular Memory Group provides one way to survey changes that overtook conceptions of collective memory. Another way to explore the evolution of modern memory is through the diary, a protean "literary" genre that raises important questions about public versus private memory forms. The seventeenth and eighteenth centuries usher in the golden age of the diary, which has proven to be an extraordinarily valuable vessel of memory, both social and personal. Yet Pepys and Evelyn, both of whom I will employ in chapter one, kept their diaries with no intention of seeing them in print; that is, as first conceived and written, they were essentially outside of print culture, although certainly a part of literate culture. So voracious is the god of print, however, that both have become part of the print culture from whose public scrutiny they would originally have shrunk.

During an age of scientific and philosophical ferment, when René Descartes' "animal spirits" theory of memory had a powerful influence on English philosophers, it is also possible to pursue changing conceptions of memory in the works of Robert Hooke, Thomas Hobbes, Henry More, and John Locke.[72] Hobbes, for instance, thought that "Memory begets Judgement, and Fancy," its prominent place in the creative process the reason "the Ancients therefore fabled not absurdly, in making memory the Mother of the Muses. For memory is the World (though not really, yet so as in a looking glass)."[73] For John Locke, on the other hand, memory provided a personal continuity that linked individuals with their own pasts and histories: "It is of so great moment, that where it is wanting, all the rest of our Faculties are in a great measure useless." Yet at the same time, memory's "defects," its tendency to lose ideas entirely or to move too slowly, compromised its power and undermined our abilities. "The Print wears out," according to Locke and

> Thus the *Ideas*, as well as Children, of our Youth, often die before us: And our Minds represent to us those Tombs, to which we are approaching; where

> though the Brass and Marble remain, yet the Inscriptions are effaced by time, and the Imagery moulders away. *The Pictures drawn in our Minds, are laid in fading Colours.*[74]

In Locke's famous depiction of memory, metaphors of print and monumentality convey the frightening prospect of an intellectual existence threatened by its own vulnerabilities, reduced to the status of a tomb that cannot be deciphered, the human identity it represents lost forever; psychologically Locke confronts the type of memorial destruction that Weever described physically a half century earlier. The history of philosophy contains few more poignant accounts of memory than Locke's, whose model of mind in *An Essay Concerning Human Understanding* is potentially undermined by the defects of memory.

There can be little doubt, however, that early-modern literary authors register with particular acuity both the impact of the act of publication, and its relationship to modern memory.[75] Indeed, the literary imagination, from Augustine to Proust, has always been responsive to the mysteries of human memory and the ways in which technologies of writing, reading, and publication condition our understanding of memorial processes; these represent cultural dynamics often encountered most directly in literary texts. In what follows I will attend to four authors who understood that both their literary careers and future lives depended on a commercial print industry whose precise effects they could only imagine. But all recognized, in the words of Margaret Cavendish, that the individual life, lived on its own terms, possessed almost no meaning: "For since Nature hath made our Bodily Lives so short, that if we should Live the full Period, it were but the Flash of Lightening, that Continues not, and for the most part leaves black Oblivion behind it."

To live beyond that brief flash of lightening, to keep at bay the long night of oblivion, the individual, physical life must be recreated in another, immaterial form: "I am industrious to Gain so much of Nature's Favour, as to enable me to do some Work, wherein I may leave my *Idea*, or Live in an *Idea*, or my *Idea* may Live in Many Brains, for then I shall Live as Nature Lives amongst her Creatures, which onely Lives in her Works."[76] The tension here between work and idea, between the material and the immaterial, points to the investment all four authors I will examine have in the books that represent the human attempt to negotiate the gulf between these polarities. For Cavendish and Milton, Pope and Richardson, books are the "Work," the physical manifestation of the creative act, which can at least approximate the generative powers of nature, her ongoing life in her "Works." The repetition of "Idea" here suggests Cavendish's uncertainty about the precise mechanism that can translate the individual's mundane, material existence into the immaterial, intellectual essence that can live in the collective memory for which she possesses as yet no name. Does one become an idea? Does one live in an idea? Does one become an idea that lives in another's brain? Her uncertainty also suggests an inability to fully explain or even understand exactly what she wanted remembered—was it her good name? Her personal identity? Her work alone? The tentativeness of Cavendish's conclusions here suggests the recognition, as Paul Ricoeur expresses it, "that we have no other resource, concerning our reference to the past, except memory itself... we have nothing better than memory to signify that something has taken place, has occurred, has happened *before* we declare that we remember it."[77] Cavendish's prose here betrays her fear that having "nothing better than memory" to stave off oblivion will not be enough, that memory remains too ill-defined and understood to bear the weight we place upon it. Yet her uncertain prose also reveals the vigor of her intellectual curiosity, the commitment all four authors maintained to apprehend the mysterious relationship between the literary imagination and the processes of human memory.

CHAPTER 1

"BUILDING CASTLES IN THE AIR":
MARGARET CAVENDISH AND
THE ANXIETIES OF MONUMENTALITY

I

Published in 1653, thirty-seven years after Jonson's *Workes*, Margaret Cavendish's *Poems, and Fancies* presents itself with all the self-importance and monumental pomp of its more famous predecessor. Although *Poems, and Fancies* represents a first book by an entirely unknown poet who possessed no place in the literary landscape of Interregnum England, rather than the collected poetry and plays of one of the foremost dramatists of his day, its author claims for herself and her book memorial aspirations that rival those of Jonson:

> But at all other things let *Fancy* flye,
> And, like a Towring *Eagle*, mount the *Skie*,
>   Or lik the *Sun* swiftly the World to round,
>   Or like pure *Gold*, which in the *Earth* is found.[1]

In lines that might even remind us of *Areopagitica* (published only nine years before), with its triumphant vision of "an Eagle muing her mighty youth, and kindling her undazl'd eyes at the full midday beam,"[2] Cavendish calls forth the powers of language and fancy in order to "build me a Pyramid, a Praise to my Memory." While *Poems, and Fancies* certainly acknowledges the inexperience of its newly minted author—the lines above, for instance, are followed by the admission that if her book betrays "a drossie *Wit*, let't buried be, / Under the *Ruines* of all *Memory*" (*Memory*, A7ᵛ)—it nonetheless reveals a ferocious and consuming desire to achieve fame and an enduring place in literary history.

If generations of readers and scholars have failed to acknowledge or take seriously Cavendish's claims to memorial power, to juxtapose her monumental book to Jonson's, this stems, to at least some extent, from the unfamiliar and even outlandish ways in which Cavendish articulates her desires. However turbulent and straitened his youth, Jonson was educated in the classics at Westminster School by the great antiquarian and scholar William Camden; although unable to pursue a university degree, he possessed a classical vision and understanding of learned culture that remained forever closed to Cavendish, who, for all of her wealth and privilege, never received a formal education or learned the Latin and Greek that defined cultural literacy during the seventeenth century. The patterns of gender proscription that determined Cavendish's estrangement from literate culture were not unusual, nor were they restricted only to the arts and literature. In his book on the evolution of experimental science during that century, Steven Shapin depicts "the institutionalized systems of exclusion that effectively prevented the vast majority of women from having a significant voice in formal culture or even from proposing the possibility of speaking in those forums."[3] In all professionalized fields during the seventeenth century, literary, scientific, judicial, political, and economic "formal culture" to a large extent took its shape from the exclusion of women. In her *Reflections upon Marriage* (1700), Mary Astell laments the ways in which the marginalization of women removes them from the public world in which men routinely act:

> Have not all the great Actions that have been Perform'd in the World been done by Men? Have not they founded Empires and overturn'd them? Do not they make Laws and continually repeal and mend them?...What is it they cannot do? They make Worlds and ruine them, form Systems of universal nature and dispute eternally about them; their Pen gives worth to the most trifling Controversie.[4]

Astell's depiction of the "great Actions" performed by men reveals at once her contempt for male self-congratulations, her scorn for a masculine preeminence built on the arbitrary transformation of the trivial into the substantial, and her bitterness at being excluded from this "vast" realm of male privilege. Her final reference to the "Pen [that] gives worth" suggests her conviction that masculine authority remains to a large extent underwritten by male control of language and specifically writing. Male power depends on the textual, representational economy of valuation that literacy, writing, and publication alone provide. "Possession of the Pen," she will reiterate in her discourse, remains crucial to the subordination of women. As long as women are denied its use, they can never write themselves into a society's collective memory.

Yet Astell's own life demonstrates that by the first decade of the eighteenth century women could claim possession of that pen both as private individuals and as public figures. For herself and her friends Astell wrote both letters and poetry, while during the years 1694–1709 she published a series of essays on matters of gender, education, religion, and ethics. During the 1670s and 1680s, Aphra Behn established herself as a successful professional writer, demanding "the Priviledge for my Masculine Part the Poet in me, (if any such you will allow me) to tread in those successful Paths my Predecessors have so long thriv'd in, to take those Measures that both the Ancient and Modern Writers have set me." Like Cavendish, Behn demanded a place for herself in literary history, unashamed to announce that "I am not content to write for a Third day only. I value Fame as much as if I had been born a *Hero*."[5] Although Behn must represent her poetic self as "my Masculine Part," and assert herself as if "born a *Hero*," she nonetheless imagines herself as a woman within a tradition that has long described the model for authorial fame and a second life in time.

Women certainly remained an unusual and even alien presence in the republic of letters: Katie Whitaker reckons that in the first four decades of the seventeenth century women published fewer than eighty books, one-half of 1 percent of all books published, while Elaine Hobby estimates that women wrote less than 1 percent of the texts published during the years 1649–1688.[6] Such figures, and the powerful cultural restraints responsible for them, have led at least two scholars to suggest that before the eighteenth century the term "woman writer" might be considered an oxymoron.[7] Nonetheless, the last twenty years have seen the recovery of a great deal of literature written and circulated by women during the late sixteenth, seventeenth, and early eighteenth centuries. As Lynette McGrath argues, women were in fact active in a variety of literary, political, religious, and medical forms that include "dramatic and lyric poetry...prose romances, women's petitions to Parliament, anti-male broadsheets, public speeches by middling-sort women, letters from serving maids, diaries, medical handbooks, religious testimonies and travel journals."[8]

As McGrath's list suggests, and Margaret J.M. Ezell and Paula McDowell have demonstrated, much of this writing took place outside of the formal, conventional, "authorized" channels of literary production. During the seventeenth and early eighteenth centuries much of the writing produced by women was circulated in manuscript, or participated in what has been described as "peripheral book trade activity"; it was written primarily by working-class women or women from the middling ranks of society; it was most often religious, and presented itself as self-consciously collaborative, collective, or anonymous; and much of it "was inseparable from an older oral culture...but one phase in an ongoing *oral* religio-political dialogue."[9]

From such a literary culture Margaret Cavendish remained throughout her career resolutely aloof. I have chosen to begin with Cavendish's *Poems, and Fancies*, in fact, precisely because it articulates her determination to separate herself from such a culture, which she regarded as inevitably transient, and it exemplifies her investment in the printed book and the memorial promises that it represented. A number of recent commentators have celebrated the work's importance by identifying it as the first volume of English poetry published by a woman, while others have argued that it inaugurates the career of the first English woman to fashion herself as a poet or author.[10] While the first of these claims is patently false, and the second problematic, *Poems, and*

Fancies nonetheless demands our attention, for in it Cavendish claims the right to incorporate herself within a textual and memorial economy that had previously defined itself primarily in terms of male succession.[11]

Cavendish confronts this problem in the first pages of *Poems, and Fancies*, justifying her decision to "Print this *Book*" in the context of "the truth…[that] our *Sex* hath so much waste Time, having but little imployments, which makes our *Thoughts* run wildly about, having nothing to fix them upon, which *wilde thoughts* so not onely produce unprofitable, but indiscreet Actions; winding up the *Thread* of our *lives* in *snarles* in *unsound bottoms*" ("An Epistle to Mistris Toppe," A5). Beginning in the dedicatory epistle that opens the volume, *Poems, and Fancies* juxtaposes a heroic, masculine realm of books and letters to the diminished and restricted world of women, whose conventional, domestic employments circumscribe the nature and possibilities of female ambition, effectively removing women from the pursuit of honor, fame, and truth. Cavendish's first volume of poetry refuses to acquiesce in these exclusions, and instead contemplates how women might themselves understand the nature of fame and memory, and participate in the literary immortality that the book seems to promise.

In this chapter I will examine the ways in which Cavendish addresses these issues in *Poems, and Fancies*, privileging herself as a poet and fashioning herself as a figure worthy of a place in cultural memory. Before turning to Cavendish's poetry, I will begin by attending to the circumstances of the volume's publication, its physical appearance, and its extensive and self-conscious use of paratext, for in such matters *Poems, and Fancies* reflects Cavendish's lifelong effort to understand and exploit the monumentality of the modern book. Cavendish possesses a rich and varied, if sometimes unusual, vocabulary for addressing such questions, utilizing not only the conventional architectural metaphors examined in my introduction—with a particular attention to the library and its archival expectations—but a range of textile images, including clothing itself, how it is worn, as well as the sewing through which garments took shape. And at one particularly telling moment near the beginning of *Poems, and Fancies*, Cavendish uses the image of a child to imagine the relationship of her book to a monumental futurity. Although he writes only about architectural monuments built of stone and metal, Sanford Levinson's insistence that "all monuments are efforts, in their own way, to stop time"[12] remains true even when applied to the paper and leather objects produced by the modern print trade, which assert their ability to cheat time and conquer oblivion in spite of their apparent fragility. This is particularly true in Cavendish's books, where the questions she raises about a woman's relationship to literary history and collective memory reveal her investment in incorporeal and intrasubjective memory forms even as she celebrates the materiality of the book itself.

II

Considering how few volumes of verse women had published in England before 1650, the three volumes that appeared during the years 1650–1653 represent a significant publishing event. While I don't want to insist that this dramatically heralds a new era in female publication, within the next quarter of a century three women, Margaret Cavendish, Aphra Behn, and Katherine Philips, were to enjoy public careers as writers (the last, albeit, with a great show of reluctance). The appearance of three volumes within four years, all published by commercial London presses, suggests at least an apprehension on the part of those in the book trade that there existed a clientele receptive to female poets, that money might be made by marketing what the volume published in 1650 trumpeted as "the tenth muse." Briefly examining the two volumes that accompanied Cavendish into print will provide a context for understanding not only this marketplace, but Cavendish's unusual and even unique place within it.

The Tenth Muse Lately sprung up in America. Or Severall Poems, compiled with great variety of Wit and Learning, full of delight was published by Stephen Bowtell in 1650.[13] The title cleverly draws a prospective buyer's attention to the doubly exotic nature of the volume, which presents not just the *rara avis* of a female poet, but one who has unaccountably "sprung up" like a fair flower amidst the weeds in the untamed wilderness of the New World. A London bookseller since 1643, Bowtell published primarily works of a political and religious cast, and in 1647 he had enjoyed great success with *The Simple Cobler Of Aggawam in America*, a political satire in which Nathanial Ward, a former neighbor of the Bradstreets, adopts the pose of a rustic, frontier shoemaker in order, as part of the long descriptive title puts it, "To help 'mend his Native Country, lamentably tattered."[14] At a time when Parliament was preparing to depose and ultimately execute the king, the book's conservative opposition to religious toleration found a ready audience, and Bowtell sold four editions in that year. The professional relationship that Ward established with Bowtell—who marketed three more works of Ward's in 1647 and a further one in 1649—almost certainly brought Anne's brother-in-law John Woodbridge to Bowtell when the former returned to England from the colonies in 1647 with the manuscript of *The Tenth Muse.* Ward even contributed one of the introductory verses to the 1650 volume, in which Bowtell may have tried to emulate his earlier success by exploiting an interest in Americana, particularly when, as in Bradstreet's "A Dialogue between Old England and New, concerning their present Troubles," which was featured on the title page, an English audience could see themselves from the perspective of their colonies.

While the marketing of *The Tenth Muse* may have had a political agenda, it also played a very knowing and self-conscious gender game with its audience, refusing on the title page to identify its modest author—referred to only as "a Gentlewoman in those parts"—and then engaging in a decorous striptease as it slowly reveals her name and identity. Only after a prose letter and four poems do two verses disclose her name, which, once revealed, even becomes the subject of two anagrams. Finally, the poet herself appears to address her audience, first in a poem directed to her father and then in a verse "Prologue" clearly directed to the reader. The extended prefatory matter, which, as Pattie Cowell has observed,[15] consists primarily of short poems easily consumed as blurbs by bookshop browsers, tries to wring maximum suspense out of the revelation of the unknown female poet's identity. This protracted sport with Bradstreet's identity and name suggests that Robert J. Griffin is right to insist that, like the legal and fictional name, anonymity can function as a type of mask, and that the opening to *The Tenth Muse* flaunts a "play of subject positions" that involves both gender and economics.[16]

Although we cannot know with certainty whether her family published *The Tenth Muse* with Bradstreet's knowledge or not, this studied and knowing opening of the volume, as well as the sheer conventionality of its denials, gives a cynical modern reader pause. Both Bradstreet's poem to her father and the "Prologue" could have been composed and designed for manuscript circulation, but they suit so well a public, printed discourse that one can be forgiven for regarding Bradstreet as complicit in the book's performance of a modesty that carefully measures the tone of her first two poems. Repeated references in the first to "My lowly pen," "humble hand," "harsh rimes," and "ragged lines" emphasize the hesitancy with which Bradstreet puts herself forward and claims the privilege and ability to grasp the male pen. As Jonathan Goldberg insists in *Writing Matter: From the Hands of the English Renaissance*, "it all starts...in the hand...that propriety of hand and text is re-marked within the elementary scene of the teaching of writing."[17] The force of cultural prohibitions governing the act of writing were such that even in 1680, thirty years after the publication of Bradstreet's book, Aphra Behn's narrator in *Oroonoko* feels compelled to apologize for her female identity in precisely the same terms, lamenting the harsh fate that left her hero with "only a Female Pen to celebrate his Fame."[18] Indeed, the scene of writing, and particularly the inauguration of an authorial career, intimidated men as well as women, Milton's "forc'd fingers rude" and "harsh and crude" plucking in the opening lines of *Lycidas* comparable to Bradstreet's hesitancy here.

The "Prologue" begins in a similar register, references to "my mean pen" and "obscure Verse," to "My foolish, broken, blemish'd Muse," reiterating Bradstreet's ostensible uncertainty on such an occasion. Yet in stanza five she begins to clear a space for herself, in the process revealing the highly developed sense of irony that she shares with Aphra Behn concerning how questions of fame and infamy govern the fate of "a Female Pen," for suddenly she explicitly challenges the dictates of a disapproving male culture that both of these poems imagine themselves in a dialogue with: "I am obnoxious to each carping tongue, / Who sayes, my hand a needle better fits, / A Poets Pen, all scorne, I should thus wrong" (4).[19] I will have more to say about needlework when I consider *Poems, and Fancies* and *Clarissa*, but the juxtaposition between the male pen and the female needle marked a foundational cultural trope in early modern Europe, one that Bradstreet must negotiate here in order to empower herself as a poet.[20] She signals her eagerness to do so in the decisive fashion with which her book abandons the pose of anonymity assumed by the title page; and in the two anagrams on her name she might even be said to revel in the assumption of her legal name and the rejection of an anonymity that convention has tried to thrust upon her.

The final stanza of the "Prologue" demonstrates her success in seizing the male pen and appropriating an authorial identity, for the irony and even sarcasm of these last lines is striking, and may remind us of the controlled rage of Astell's references to the "great Actions" and "vast Minds" of the male sex. Here Bradstreet's final address to "ye high flown quills, that soare the skies" suggests the ridiculousness of male ambitions, which such dramatic images present as exaggerated and overblown. The rhetoric of the poem's final four lines emphasizes even more the absurdity of male pretensions, as Bradstreet mimics the poses of female abjection:

> If e're you daigne these lowly lines, your eyes
> Give wholesome Parsley wreath, I aske no Bayes:
> This meane and unrefined stuffe of mine,
> Will make your glittering gold but more to shine. (4)

Here female modesty reveals itself as scorn, and apparent debasement as contempt, the "glittering gold" of male egotism given its value only through the corresponding devaluation of women. The recuperative gesture of the second line, in which a humble household herb triumphs over one of the primary masculine symbols of poetic preeminence, will be repeated frequently by Cavendish, as both women utilize the domestic and familiar to define a new conception of aesthetic merit.

The book as a whole, in fact, gives the lie to the repeated gestures of self-effacement that mark these opening two poems, for Bradstreet breaks the promise with which the "Preface" begins: "To sing of Wars, of Captaines, and of Kings, / Of Cities founded, Common-wealths begun, / For my mean Pen, are too superiour things" (3). Although this small duodecimo that fits comfortably in a reader's or browser's hand appears a modest volume, at two hundred and seven pages it represents an ambitious work that includes poems on the greatest political empires, significant political issues, and elegies on important public figures such as Sir Philip Sidney, Du Bartas, and Queen Elizabeth. Even the decision to publish the book in London suggests the desire for as wide and cosmopolitan an audience as possible.[21]

Ann Rosalind Jones has suggested that we understand the sixteenth- and seventeenth-century system of interdictions and permissions concerning women's writing as a spectrum: at one end is the possibility of dealing only with the "domestic and religious concerns considered appropriate for women and to write without any ambition for publication...Slightly further along the spectrum, women translated religious texts, sheltering under the masculine authority of their originals...Other women wrote religious meditations themselves."[22] While Bradstreet's volume of verse would lie at a far remove from the end of the spectrum described here, An Collins' *Divine Songs and Meditacions*, which appears, like Cavendish's *Poems, and Fancies*, in 1653, falls comfortably within parameters already established by Aemilia Lanyer's *Salve Deus Rex Iudaeorum*, published over forty years earlier in 1611. The tensions apparent in Bradstreet's attempts to negotiate cultural prohibitions are hardly visible in the opening to Collins' small, modest octavo, where the bounds of a caring Christian community unite the faithful: "And now (Courteous Reader) I have delivered unto you, what I intended, Onely it remaines that I tell you, That with my Labours, You have my Prayers to God through Jesus Christ; whose I Am, and in him, *Yours, in all Christain affection*, An Collins."[23] In this address "To the Reader" Collins doesn't even feel the necessity to raise the issue of her gender. Guided by her sympathy for "disconsolate Spirits," Collins imagines a "Courteous Reader," rather than the "carping tongue" of the censorious critics who disturb Bradstreet's imagination.

In the verse "Preface" that follows this opening address, Collins implicitly raises the question of her sex when she laments the "homly dresse...[of] my works" (lines 80–81), but only in the first stanza of her long seven hundred and fifteen line "Discourse" does Collins explicitly reveal her sex, when she asks if her readers will "Dain to survey *her* works that worthlesse seem" (6; my emphasis). In asking for our indulgence in spite of the "defects herein may be espide" (11), Collins admits that "Vnto the publick view of every one / I did not purpose these my lines to send, / Which for my private use were made alone" (15–17). The distinction between public and private was fundamental to the prohibitions that governed women's writing, and in explicitly addressing that issue here Collins acknowledges its profound cultural power. Collins insists that she began to write without any intention of transgressing this boundary, and she provides four reasons that justify her decision to do so.

The first three of these reasons highlight Collins' "proper" female humility and her religious faith. Although Collins' fourth reason ends by reiterating the conventional gestures of female modesty enacted throughout the "Preface" and "Discourse," in which women are imaged as bees, children or sucking babes, and here as low servants, this should not blind us to the quiet but powerful act of authorial self-assertion that nonetheless distinguishes these lines:

> 4 And lastly in regard of any one,
> Who may by accident hereafter find,
> This, though to them the Author bee unknown,
> Yet seeing here, the image of her mind:
> They may conjecture how she was inclin'd:
> And further note, that God doth Grace bestow,
> Vpon his servants, though hee keeps them low. (50–56)

When juxtaposed to Cavendish, whose insistent claims to fame and immortality we shall examine in a moment, Collins' still, low voice can almost not be heard. Collins does not presume to court fame or notoriety: a reader will discover her only by "accident" because this author will remain "unknown." Nonetheless, what a reader will discover "here," in this small book, is a true "image of her mind," a reflection of the individuality of this "Author." Even as she puts herself forward in this fashion, Collins at the same time humbles herself: she makes no grand claims for her unique subjectivity as a powerful authorial presence, for she is but one of God's servants, one of the lowly who serves him faithfully and without complaint. Moreover, she assumes this position without any of Milton's anger, frustration, pain, and fear; she wants only to use her talents wisely, never imagining herself as either a victim of God's punishment or a critic of His justice. But her desire for recognition, her wish to touch even one reader who might come to know her mind through this book and her poetry, resonates through these lines.

Collins' projection of her poetic anonymity would prove accurate. Her modern editor, Sidney Gottlieb, admits that we know little about the author and publication or reception of her book beyond what we can tease out of the volume itself.[24] *Divine Songs and Meditacions*, as far as we can tell from the volume itself, appears to have been marketed as a religious work, with little or no attempt made to exploit the gender of its author. Collins, as we have seen, acknowledges but does not emphasize her identity as a woman, and the volume itself does nothing to call attention to the rarity of its female poet. To casual browsers nothing in the volume's presentation automatically suggests that the object before them contains anything transgressive or remarkable.

III

An Collins' book discreetly took its place in the marketplace, and for its tact disappeared modestly and anonymously into the literary abyss. Cavendish might have predicted its fate, for in the course of her career she expressed impatience if not contempt for a sex "more apt to Read then to Write, and most commonly when any of our Sex doth Write, they Write some Devotions, or Romances, or Receits of Medicines."[25] Such quiet, conventional, unpretentious efforts do not suit Cavendish, whose large, handsome, expensive folio volume announces itself and its author with a shout. Cavendish's aristocratic rank and status as wife to one of the most important and notorious nobles associated with the exiled king would in any event have made anonymity difficult if not impossible, and the title page betrays no hesitation in exploiting her social importance by trumpeting the author of *Poems, and Fancies* as "the Right Honourable, the Lady Newcastle." Her privilege and wealth—which in 1653 rested primarily on her husband's ability to finance his exile by securing large amounts of credit—granted Cavendish a freedom available to neither Bradstreet nor Collins, although at the same time her nobility marked a second prohibition that her desire to publish required her to transgress. Had Cavendish wished to pursue her ambitions "properly" she could have circulated her poems in manuscript, the conventional mode of distribution for the upper classes of both sexes. Cavendish even possessed a contemporary model for a socially acceptable literary career in the "Matchless Orinda," Katherine Philips, who actively circulated her poetry during the early 1650s, had published a poem in 1651, and during that same year received public acknowledgment of her poetic abilities in Henry Vaughan's "To the most Excellently accomplish'd, Mrs. *K. Philips.*"[26]

But Philips' poem, one of fifty-four testimonials that introduces a posthumous edition of the *Comedies* of William Cartwright, did not acknowledge the identity of its author, and *Poems, and Fancies* emphasizes from the very beginning that anonymity was not the state in which Cavendish wished to enter the literary marketplace. As we shall see, the decision to "degrade" oneself by entering the realm of commercial printing was a significant one even for Milton, who had neither Cavendish's gender nor her social position to protect. But for Cavendish, publishing both her works and her name was absolutely essential to how she conceived of and constructed her career as a writer. Cavendish not only rejected anonymous publication, but refused as well to adopt a pseudonym, another socially acceptable mode of female publication. The witty play with diverse subject positions that attracted Philips to "Orinda" and Behn to "Astrea" did not recommend itself to Cavendish, who disdained the authorial mystification and polymorphism provided by literary sobriquets; and insisted throughout her career on the formal use of her legal name and aristocratic title.

As befit a peer of the realm, Cavendish attached tremendous importance to the proper presentation of that name and title. The original title page for *Poems, and Fancies,* which read "Written by the Right Honourable, the Lady Margaret Countesse of Newcastle," was only changed at the last minute to "the Right Honourable, the Lady Newcastle" when Cavendish objected to her demotion from marchioness to a mere countess. Although William was a marquess when he married Margaret, Charles I had granted him that title only in 1643, when it was no longer recognized in England by a commonwealth government. Officially William remained the earl of Newcastle—the title granted him in 1628—until Charles II's Restoration. Like an adolescent deciding on a new signature, Margaret experimented with a variety of authorial formulae until 1656, when she fixed on the following: "Written by the thrice Noble, Illustrious, and Excellent Princess, the Lady Marchioness of Newcastle." In the seventeen volumes of poetry, prose, and drama that she prepared for publication from 1656 to 1671, that title remained unchanged except when *Marchioness* became *Duchess* in 1666—after William became the duke of Newcastle in 1665—and when she styled herself "Margaret, Duchess of Newcastle, his wife" on the title page of her husband's biography, *The Life of the thrice Noble, High and Puissant Prince William Cavendishe.* Margaret J.M. Ezell argues that "a text with a woman's name could be read symbolically as a public declaration of her possession of intellectual and artistic property," and there seems little doubt that Cavendish's insistence on a proper and enduring formula for her name and title was designed to declare "her proprietorship of the ideas expressed, [and] her possession of mastery over the artistic techniques employed," particularly early in her career when many charged that her husband had really authored her books.[27]

The care that Cavendish took with her name reflects the attention she devoted throughout her career to both her self-presentation and the publication of her books. With the printing of *Poems, and Fancies*, for example, she began a long-term relationship with the booksellers John Martin and James Allestrye, who had formed a partnership in 1652 that lasted with great success until the latter's death in 1670. According to H.R. Plomer, in the 1660s Allestrye "was one of the largest capitalists in the trade, and his shop was the resort of the wealthy and the learned."[28] Even in 1653, at a relatively early stage in their joint careers, Martin and Allestrye employed Thomas Roycroft to print *Poems, and Fancies*. Although Roycroft had only begun printing under his own name in 1651, he eventually became one of the most distinguished English printers of the seventeenth century, appointed the King's printer in Oriental languages in 1660, and Master of the Stationers' Company in 1675.

Until 1662, Cavendish, in other words, published her works through some of the most distinguished and successful printers and booksellers in the trade. But after Martin and Allestrye published her first volume of *Playes* in that year—her sixth book—Cavendish changed her manner of publication, financing the printing of her works herself and employing the services first of the printer William Wilson and then, after his death in 1665, of Anne Maxwell, a widow who assumed ownership of her husband David's print shop after his death around that same year.[29] According to Katie Whitaker, Cavendish's latest biographer, the move from Martin and Allestrye to smaller London printers, and her assumption of their costs, "gave [Cavendish] much greater control over publication and resulted in more careful printing."[30] In 1662 Cavendish could afford to take more financial responsibility for her publications, the economic health of the Newcastles having revived with Charles' Restoration. But even during the 1650s, Cavendish had lavished money on her books when it became available. Although *Poems, and Fancies*, for instance, was originally published without a frontispiece, the improvement of the Newcastles' finances in the latter half of 1653—after William's brother Charles had his estates discharged from sequestration, and William's son Charles repossessed his inheritance—allowed Margaret to prepare three engravings from portraits designed by Abraham van Diepenbeke, an Antwerp artist. Although these were appended to her third, fourth, and fifth books at the time of their printing, she prepared presentation copies of *Poems, and Fancies* that used all three at different times and for different occasions.[31]

Both Newcastles, in fact, spent great sums on the publication of their works, and, in a letter written in 1667, Walter Charleton, the subject of the Dryden poem considered in the introduction, praises her specifically for her willingness to subsidize the production of her works: other writers "imploy only their wit, labour, and time, in composing Books. You bestow also great sums of Money in Printing Yours: and not content to enrich our Heads alone, with your rare Notions, you go higher, and adorn our Libraries, with your elegant Volumes."[32] The elegance of *Poems, and Fancies* is particularly striking, since poetic debuts rarely merited folio production. Abraham Cowley, for instance, published his poetry for over twenty years and made himself one of the preeminent poets of the age before Humphrey Moseley published his 1656 *Poems* in folio form.

But the look and place of her books in the library, as we shall see, obsessed Cavendish, who thought deeply about the relationship of the archive to the cultural memory within which she longed for a home. Charleton's transparent flattery should not blind us to his insight that books operate in dual registers, both in "our Heads" and in "our Libraries," both intellectual and material counters in the transmission of cultural immortality; the book both constructs the textual memory of modern society, and transmits it. Indeed, Charleton's letter was later reprinted in the 1676 *Letters and Poems in Honour of the Incomparable Princess, Margaret, Duchess of Newcastle*, prepared by her husband and published after her death as a memorial to her fame. This volume contains numerous letters thanking her for the gift of her many books, which have been lodged "in the richest Cabinet that we have, our publick Liberary; for the perusal of the present, and succeeding generation"; or which "have turned a sorry Study into a rich Library."[33] Throughout her career, Cavendish understood the memorial importance of the library, aware that women maintained only an insecure tenure on its shelves, that, as Andreas Huyssen writes, the institutional archives preserved in museums and libraries "helped define the identity of Western civilization by drawing external and internal boundaries that relied as much on exclusions and marginalizations as it did on positive codifications."[34] All of Cavendish's books confront the marginalizations wrought by gender, part of their distinctive mien stemming from the aggressive way in which they set their faces against this exclusion and attempt to secure an incontestable place for themselves within the archive.

Determined that her books present themselves to their best advantage to "succeeding generations," Cavendish attended not only to her name and to their material elegance, but, once she learned the role she needed to play in reviewing the progress of her books through the press, to how they were printed.[35] The prefatory matter appended to her fourth book, *The Philosophical and Physical Opinions* (1655), complains at some length about the printing of her first three books, a period when she clearly didn't understand the personal care she needed to take in inspecting the work of the printer. In "To the Reader" she laments that her last book, *The Worlds Olio*, was grossly misprinted, "yet I must Confesse that this book is much truer Printed than my book of Poems [*Poems, and Fancies*], for where this book hath one fault, that hath ten; for which I can forgive the Printer and Corrector ten times easier than I did for the other."[36] Whoever Cavendish finally blamed for the poor printing of *Poems, and Fancies*, and wherever the responsibility for its many defects may lie, Cavendish's decision to leave Martin and Allestrye in 1662 and assume the entire cost of publishing her works allowed her to reprint the volume, in a "Second Impression, much altered and corrected" according to the title page of the 1664 edition printed by William Wilson. When Cavendish moved to the house of Alice Maxwell, she even printed a third edition in 1668. During her lifetime, only *The Blazing World* was reprinted as often.

Whatever the state of its printing, *Poems, and Fancies* presents itself as a serious and ambitious volume of poetry. Although today we have become rather cynical about claims for originary status, the second part of the boast in one of the book's prefatory letters that "You are not onely the first English Poet of your Sex, but the first that ever wrote this way" may well be true. *Poems, and Fancies* is an extraordinary volume of poetry, over two hundred, large, folio pages long, containing a multitude of poems on an enormous range of subjects in a bewildering number of genres. It also contains a great deal of paratextual matter, not only nine letters or poems introducing the volume, but prose addresses throughout designed to appeal to specific audiences. If Cavendish's volume looks nothing like that of An Collins, or even Anne Bradstreet's, it also bears no resemblance to Milton's first volume, the *Poems of Mr. John Milton*, published just eight years before. It is not a volume that can be mistaken for anyone else's, supporting the poet Alice Fulton's recent characterization of Cavendish as one of those "feral poets whose work Robert Lowell characterized as raw rather than cooked."[37]

Although Cavendish's first collection of poems is a loose, baggy monster of a book, she nonetheless attempts to provide at least a species of structural unity by linking its many different genres and sections through a recurring device called "The Claspe," which at one point is described as a "Phantasmes Masque" in which "THE Scene is Poetry" and "The Stage is the Braine, whereon it is Acted" (155). "The Claspe," which appears four times in the course of the volume, usually functions as a brief, lyrical moment when Cavendish self-consciously reflects on her poetry, as in its first appearance when she describes how she "tooke great paines" to liberate the "*Thoughts*" and "*Fancies*" that "breake my Braines" (47), or, in the second, where she celebrates "the *Free*, and *Noble Stile*" in which she composes her poetry, "a *Stile* that *Nature* frames, not *Art*" (110). These short poetic reflections on her art are followed within five–ten pages by a prose address to a particular audience suggested by the poems that will follow: "To Morall Philosophers" is linked to dialogues and moral discourses, "To ALL Writing Ladies" introduces poems on fairies and pastorals, while before a section of poems devoted to types of battles she writes "To Souldiers."

Cavendish also attempts to provide a structural logic for the volume by beginning the collection, after the extended prefatory matter, with a creation myth, "Nature calls a Councell, which was Motion, Figure, matter, and Life, to advise about making the World." She follows this poem with a long series of poems—lasting until the first appearance of "The Claspe"—on scientific matters, particularly the atom and the nature of matter. A reader, however, may have difficulty discovering any type of continuing or progressive logic in the presentation of her poetry subsequent to this first section, for after it a bewildering array of verse types and subjects follow each other in no order that I can discern.

While the conclusion of the volume doesn't necessarily provide a sense of narrative closure, it does end, just before its concluding "Finis," with an important promise: "Reader, I have a little Tract of Philosophicall Fancies in Prose which will not be long before it appear in the world." Cavendish had worked frantically to complete the material that eventually became her second book, *Philosophicall Fancies*, so that it could be included in *Poems, and Fancies*, but that finally proved impossible and Martin and Allestrye published the second volume on its own later in 1653. However unwieldy such a combined volume might have been, Cavendish clearly relished the symmetry provided by the juxtaposition of poetical and philosophical fancies. But her concluding promise to the reader, while prompted by a failure to meet a deadline, represents a significant claim nonetheless, for it explicitly announces the expectation of a literary career. To the best of our knowledge, An Collins never published again, and while Anne Bradstreet prepared a revised edition of *The Tenth Muse*, it was not published until 1678, six years after her death. The single volume describes the norm for female poets who sought to publish their works in the sixteenth and seventeenth centuries. As if aware of this, Cavendish publishes her first volume with the announcement that it is *only* the first, that more will follow, that she wishes to establish a relationship with her readers that will go beyond the volume before them. Supported by her wealth and rank, of course, Cavendish could afford to make such a claim. The financial and aesthetic vagaries of the marketplace could not interfere with her ambitions, since she could both subsidize her own publication and rely on the scandal of her impropriety to generate an audience for her writings. Cavendish entered the literary marketplace very much on her own terms, and could afford to present herself with an audacity and ambition that few poets of the century, male or female, could emulate. Cavendish as an author was made possible only by the immense privilege she enjoyed; at the same time, however, that privilege also defined her extreme vulnerability, the very advantages she enjoyed making visible her poetic and cultural transgressions.

IV

Cavendish's awareness of her vulnerability accounts in large measure for the paratextual practices of not only this first volume, but of her use of paratext throughout her career. The prefatory matter appended to *Poems, and Fancies* consists of six prose addresses and three poems, all but one written by Cavendish herself. This wealth of prefatory material is not designed to titillate the reader—there is no slow revelation of the author's identity here—nor "sell" the volume, for few of the sometimes ponderous letters function like blurbs readily consumed by curious browsers. And, although many of the individual letters and poems not only betray the hesitations and nervousness of a fledgling author but directly address these fears, we cannot characterize the volume's prefatory inflation as the defensive, self-protective gesture of a timid authorial virgin, for extended prefaces characterize almost all of the original books Cavendish published during her lifetime. None of Cavendish's first six books, for example, contain fewer than seven prefatory elements, her 1662 *Playes* boasting a whopping sixteen. Although some of her books include assorted epilogues, Cavendish relies on paratextual matter primarily to introduce her work, for here she could anticipate expected criticism and respond to past rebukes.

Bronwen Price has argued that while prefaces, epistles, and apologia are a conventional form in seventeenth- and eighteenth-century texts, "in women's writing they have a particular significance in that they often become the place in which the sexual politics of speaking, writing, and knowing is highlighted. Indeed, one might argue that the prefaces to women's writing form a gendered genre."[38] This is particularly true for Cavendish, who accomplishes an essential part of what she considered the business of her writing, whether poetry, science, biography, drama, or prose fiction, in the numerous prefaces, poems, and letters that begin her books. Moreover, this prefatory matter is almost always composed entirely by Cavendish herself, although after the publication of her third volume—*The Worlds Olio*—her husband William usually contributed one or two letters or poems to each volume. The only exceptions to this Newcastle monopoly on paratextual utterance come in *Poems, and Fancies*, where Cavendish solicited a testimonial from her former servant and lifelong companion Elizabeth Toppe (nee Chaplain), whose letter makes the insistent claim for the volume's originary status that we have already examined; and in her life of William, where her husband's long-serving secretary, John Rolleston, includes a letter attesting to the truth of the accounts of William's conduct during the civil war. Aside from her husband and these two dependents, Cavendish allows no one else to interrupt her textual monologues.

Although the final shape of a seventeenth-century book, including the inclusion of paratextual matter, was not always or even usually determined by the author, Cavendish's social and economic privilege gave her control over the prefatory letters, poems, and addresses that crowd her books. Her refusal to allow others to participate in her text distinguishes her from many seventeenth-century authors, who normally included—or were forced to include—their own paratextual contributions along with those of others (as in Anne Bradstreet's volume, for example). Paratext, in fact, was precisely where the author's friends or other individuals responsible for a text's production—printers, booksellers, editors, translators—could have, as it were, their say. In the sixteenth and seventeenth centuries, books did not yet belong solely to the privileged author, and paratext could give voice to at least some of the others involved in transforming a manuscript into a book, or to the intellectual community that welcomed the volume's appearance. A book's paratextual apparatus could be the site of a collective and social collaboration, where literary and textual authority might be dispersed rather than consolidated.

As an author, however, Cavendish clearly possessed little interest in compromising her individuality by presenting herself as part of a larger, more broadly defined literary or intellectual community. During the years 1651–1653, while she was living in London with her brother-in-law Sir Charles as they saw to their financial affairs, Cavendish visited the house of the musician and composer Henry Lawes, where she would have encountered what remained of royalist court culture. Katherine Philips frequented Lawes' home as well, and it is reasonable to assume that had Cavendish desired to participate in the production and circulation of manuscript collections such opportunities would have presented themselves; this was, after all, the period when she was furiously writing the poems that would become the volume *Poems, and Fancies*. Cavendish's failure to participate in manuscript culture, and her refusal to solicit paratextual material from others, suggests her insistence throughout her life on "owning" her books entirely, on not allowing other perspectives or voices to intrude on the performance of authorial singularity that to some extent all of her books enact.[39]

William provides the one exception to this policy, signaling the unique role he played in Margaret's construction of her vast authorial self. In *Poems, and Fancies*, however, William does not appear until Margaret refers to him at the end of the volume, in a concluding poem that I shall examine later. In this volume Cavendish chooses to open not with her husband but with "The Epistle Dedicatory: To Sir Charles Cavendish, My Noble Brother-in-Law," in which she pays tribute to, after husband William and brother John, her most important intellectual mentor. Charles was a serious scholar and European intellectual through whom Cavendish met some of the most important men of the day.[40] In dedicating her book to Charles she thus establishes not just a genealogical pedigree for herself, but an intellectual one as well, both defined by their exclusivity. While doing so, Cavendish wastes no time in addressing the fundamental cultural problem raised by her sexual identity: "True it is, Spinning with the Fingers is more proper to our Sexe, then studying or writing Poetry, which is the Spinning with the braine…[I] endeavour to Spin a Garment of Memory, to lapp up my Name, that it might grow to after Ages" (A2–A2ᵛ). The symbolic and imagistic equivalence that Cavendish draws here, at the very start of her literary career, between spinning, poetry, and memorial aspirations, was to have a profound effect on her aesthetic self-fashioning.

In the first place, it draws together the female spinning and male writing that conventional gender ideology attempted to segregate from one other. In this early-modern version of cultural apartheid, spinning, sewing, needlework, and embroidery described the matrix of cultural activities that both signified and inculcated femininity.[41] Cavendish acknowledges the crucial ideological separation between these traditional markers of femininity and the intellectual activity that defined masculinity in her second prefatory letter, "To All Noble, and Worthy Ladies":

> But I imagine I shall be censur'd by my owne Sex; and Men will cast a smile of scorne upon my Book, because they think thereby, Women incroach too much upon their Prerogatives; for they hold Books as their Crowne, and the Sword as their Scepter, by which they rule, and governe. And very like they will say

to me, as to the Lady that wrote the Romancy, "Work Lady, Work, let writing Books alone, For surely wiser Women nere wrote one." (A3–A3ᵛ)

The lady here is Lady Mary Wroth, the "romancy" *The Countess of Montgomery's Urania*—in 1621 the first English romance published by a woman—and the original author of the verse quoted by Cavendish, Sir Edward Denny. He concluded his poem attacking Wroth for disclosing family secrets—in which he damned her as an "Hermophradite in show, in deed a monster"—with the following couplet: "Work o th'Workes leave idle bookes alone / For wise and worthier women have writte none."

In the two letters of complaint that Lord Denny wrote to Wroth, the stress falls on "so vaine a booke," for he contrasts the romance she had written—"lascivious tales and amorous toyes"—to a volume of "heavenly layes and holy love": "followe the rare, and pious example of your vertuous and learned Aunt, who translated so many godly books." Denny's poem was never printed during the seventeenth century, so Cavendish almost certainly knew of it through its circulation in manuscript collections and commonplace books, where it might have taken the form she quotes. But in Cavendish's articulation the juxtaposition between secular and religious texts is lost, and Wroth's hermaphroditic monstrosity arises solely from her attempt to abandon the "work" that makes her a woman, needlework, for the work, writing books, that defines manhood. Although Denny might permit women to write or translate "holly psalmes" and "devine meditations," in Cavendish's "revision" of Denny's original complaint, to transgress the strict boundaries that divide the one activity from the other disrupts the gendered cultural economies that guarantee sexual integrity and difference.[42] Cavendish acknowledges the power of such regulatory prohibitions by quoting as anonymous, proverbial wisdom a dictate that had circulated for thirty years. Like Astell half a century later, Cavendish clearly understands the way in which men fashion their superiority through the control of books, which no woman should presume to write. Cavendish also recognizes that the internalization of female inferiority—a basic element in the gender ideology of early-modern England—will make her a victim of female censure, which, along with the male scorn she anticipates, will generate a problematic relationship between her "Book" and the "Fame" she so desires. But Cavendish's equation of spinning and writing in her dedication represents a way to subvert what she presents as a fundamental sexual and cultural divide; strategically, the figurative link between "Spinning with the Fingers" and "Spinning with the braine" generates equivalence where before only difference existed.

Second, this equivalence guided Cavendish in her self-presentation not simply as a poet and author, but as an exemplar of fashion. In her own day, Cavendish was as well known for her distinctive dress as for her writing. Although she did not make her own clothing—for she would rather "write with the pen then work with a needle"[43]—she possessed a mode of dress that she regarded as essential to her creative self-expression. As she explains in *A True Relation of My Birth, Breeding and Life*, her attention to clothing originally arose as a compensatory activity in relation to "my study of books":

> But my serious study could not be much, by reason I took great delight in attiring, fine dressing, and fashions especially such fashions as I did invent myself, not taking that pleasure in such fashions as was invented by others. Also I did dislike any should follow my fashions, for I always took delight in a singularity, even in accoutrements of habits.[44]

In her autobiography, Cavendish imagines a direct and explicit link between the serious "study of books" and her "delight in attiring," one that suggests the ways in which young women of her privileged class channeled the energies that might have been directed into the former into the latter instead.

In Cavendish these dual energies express themselves in a very similar fashion, for the love of invention and singularity that characterize her "attiring" distinguish her writing as well, an aesthetic consistency not lost on her contemporaries. When Dorothy Osborne heard about the publication of *Poems, and Fancies*, she requested a copy from her fiancé, William Temple, expressing herself precisely as Cavendish imagined when she feared that "I shall be censur'd by my owne Sex": "For God sake if you meet with it [*Poems, and Fancies*] send it mee, they say tis ten times more Extravagant then her dresse. Sure, the poore woman is a little distracted, she could never bee soe ridiculous else as to venture at writing book's, and in verse too."[45] Years later, when John Evelyn and his wife met Cavendish in London during the spring of 1667, he, too, responded to her "extraordinary fancifull habit, garb, & discourse," her "extravagant humor & dresse, which was very singular."[46]

Cavendish clearly cultivated the outré in both the domestic and literary arts, the extravagant and the fanciful at the heart of her artistic self-fashioning. In a culture that more often associated exemplarity—rather than singularity—with fame, Cavendish's "delight in a singularity" suggests her distance from the conventional aesthetics valued by her society. Her attention to both literature and fashion was marked by her dedication to the rare and extraordinary, and, as the following passage from *The Philosophical and Physical Opinions* reveals, she apprehended one art in terms of the other, imagistically establishing an equivalence between writing and fashion: "our sex takes so much delight in dressing and adorning themselves, as we for the most part make our gowns our books, our laces our lines, our imbroderies our letters, and our dressings are the time of our studie" (B2). This formulation proceeds by recognizing a common complaint about the female sex—their essential triviality in consuming time and money to adorn themselves—admitting the truth of the criticism, and then inverting its significance by affirming the cultural importance of fashion through its alignment with writing, its masculine counterpart. Cavendish engages the male stereotype in order to subvert it, the normally frivolous activity of dressing transformed into a form of cultural literacy, its importance established by a rhetoric that allows female fashion to appropriate the values of the male art of writing.

Cavendish never pretends that she possesses the slightest interest or talent in the domestic arts that normally define woman's work: "needle-works, Spinning-works, Preserving-works, as also Baking, and Cooking-works, as making Cakes Pyes, Puddings, and the like, all which I am Ignorant of."[47] However, not only in this, her first volume, but throughout her career, she makes a concerted attempt to recuperate those female arts, and in her own attention to dress and fashion to use them as a sign of her aesthetic originality. At a time when, as Ann Rosalind Jones and Peter Stallybrass remind us, clothes were still "bearers of identity, ritual, and social memory," when they embodied "the materiality of memory," Cavendish's scrupulous regard to her mode of dress represents a second manifestation of her concern for cultural memory.[48]

Finally, the triadic movement from "Spinning with the Fingers" to "Spinning with the Brain" to "Spin[ning] a Garment of Memory," privileges the third term, for memory distinguishes between the first two in so far as it articulates Cavendish's recognition that in the conventional binary between sewing and writing a woman's relationship to memorial processes must be different from that of a man. Here the verb "lapp"—"To enfold in a wrap or wraps, to enwrap, swathe," according to the *Oxford English Dictionary*—takes on a more specific meaning when used with "up": "to attach or fix on with a lapping of thread." Cavendish wants her name fixed within the "garment" of memory, images of spinning, sewing, and knitting throughout the volume signaling her concern for the nature of memory and how the individual can achieve a life within it.

Unlike conventional architectural images for memory and futurity, Cavendish's textile metaphors here emphasize process rather than fixity, transformation rather than stability: at the center of her hopes for becoming part of the "Garment of Memory" stands her desire that "my Name...might grow to after Ages." Although buildings, tombs, statues, and triumphal arches remain, of course, subject to restoration, revision, and especially decay, architecture normally promises not just permanence but immutability. As we shall see, Cavendish found such images attractive and used them often as figures for her memorial aspirations. Still, at the very start of her literary career, textile images that suggest the fragility of the domestic employments women normally pursue carry the burden of her dreams of monumental fame. Twice in her dedication to Sir Charles she depicts herself unclothed by the "Garment of Memory," with nothing "to keep me from the cold," where she might even "dye with cold." Finding herself without the protection of memory promises only death for Cavendish, whose "Name"—the name she so assiduously affixed to the title pages of her many books—must somehow find a place within the warp and woof of cultural memory: "I had rather my Name should go meanly clad, then dye with cold." To find herself outside of memory, for Cavendish, signifies extinction.

In a letter addressed "To Poets," Cavendish admits "that Women have seldome, or never, (at least in these latter Ages) writte a Book of Poetry, unlesse it were in their Dressings, which can be no longer read then Beauty lasts" (121–22). Cultural prohibitions have forced women to forgo those arts that might defeat mortality and allow them to live in memory; instead, household arts such as dress command their attention and doom them to memorial extinction. Cavendish's use of domestic imagery here and throughout the volume represents not simply a calculated attempt on her part to disarm male criticism of her writing by presenting it in terms of traditional female avocations, but also her recognition that the conventional patterns of gender proscription work to keep women from those male arts that alone confer immortality.

<h1 style="text-align:center">V</h1>

The prefatory matter to Cavendish's first published book reveals what not just the rest of that volume but her entire oeuvre confirms: that her literary career was founded on the hard rock of her desire to achieve cultural immortality.[49] Cavendish never tired of reiterating her obsession with and addiction to how she would be remembered: "my Hopes fall to a single Atome agen: and so shall I remaine an unsettled Atome, or a confus'd heape, till I heare my Censure. If I be prais'd, it fixes them; but if I am condemn'd, I shall be Annihilated to nothing: but my Ambition is such, as I would either be a World, or nothing" ("To Naturall Philosophers," A6); "If Fortune be my Friend, then Fame will be my Gaine, which may build me a Pyramid, a Praise to my Memory. I shall have no cause to feare it will be so high as Babels Tower, to fall in the mid-way; yet I am sorry it doth not touch at Heaven: but my Incapacity, Feare, Awe, and Reverence kept me from that Work" ("To the Reader," A7ᵛ). A reader of *Poems, and Fancies* has not yet even encountered Cavendish's poetry—for the volume's introductory prose letters contain both of these confessions—and already the author has located her work between the poles of oblivion and immortality, annihilation and creation, gibberish and divine speech.

The reference to Babel that concludes her final letter suggests the difficulty of negotiating the dilemma defined by the confrontation between cultural expectations and individual aspirations: nothing less than the Tower of Babel will satisfy her grandiose desire to live in the collective memory, yet even as she recognizes the self-defeating nature of such a need—for that tower fell "in the mid-way"—she can only lament that her "Pyramid" will "not touch at Heaven." In such an image, she admits, with an uncharacteristic humility, both her plentiful inadequacies and her outsized desires by evoking a human architecture infamous for its presumption rather than famous for its achievement. Babel, as we shall see in the next chapter, figured prominently in Milton's memorial imagination as well, for the gulf between its pretensions to futurity and its sudden and terrible end make it one of the most potent symbols of an architecture of monumental failure and hubris.

Cavendish's fears of failure and punishment, and hopes of fame and transcendence, mark the three prefatory poems that follow the six letters: "The Poetresses Hasty Resolution," "The Poetresses Petition," and "An Excuse for so Much Writ Upon My Verses." These poems veer back and forth between the images of transgressive ambition and shameful incapacity that we have just examined. The weight of these conflicting fears and desires falls squarely on her book and its entrance into the public world, for in the Manichaean universe described by these extreme oppositions only the printed book can address Cavendish's desire to "be a World" rather than "nothing." In "To the Reader" Cavendish first employs the conventional metaphor of her book as a child in order to articulate her fears: "my Book coming out in this Iron age, I feare I shall find hard Hearts; yet I had rather she should find Cruelty, then Scorne, and that my book should be torn, rather then laught at" (A7ᵛ). Fears of derision, in which her female child, "harmlesse, modest, and honest," must hazard the dangerous public, make the book's printing an experience fraught with doubt, laughter rather than violence or even violation her greatest fear. In "The Poetresses Hasty Resolution," Cavendish confronts Reason, who argues that she must "the Printer spare, / Hee'le loose by your ill Poetry, I feare / Besides the World hath already such a weight / Of uselesse Bookes, as it is over fraught." When Reason advises that she burn her book, however,

> I to the Presse it sent,
> Fearing Perswasion might my Book prevent:
> But now 'tis done, with greife repent doe I,
> Hang down my head with shame, blush, sigh, and cry. (A8)

This abject posture, its blushes and tears, shame and grief, suggests the sexual and moral vulnerability of the woman scorned and betrayed, seduced and abandoned. The fragile girl-child that is her book perfectly reflects the poet's own frailty, her anxiety that her child will be an object of derision very much a comment on her fears for herself. The moment of publication overwhelms Cavendish in the paratextual introduction to her first volume, for it exposes her to public scorn and punishment while at the same time allowing her the chance to participate in memorial processes, normally reserved for men, which govern the achievement of a place in a society's cultural heritage. At the very beginning of her authorial career, Cavendish presents herself to her audience through an "anxious artifact," a tremulous textual body that both courts and fears the processes of memorialization.

While it would be inaccurate to claim that a volume as diverse and loosely structured as *Poems, and Fancies* possesses a single subject, it invariably and repeatedly returns to the concern for cultural memory engaged by all nine of its prefaces. The power of memory, the nature of its institutional and cultural manifestations, and particularly the relationship between women and memorial practices, form a leitmotif that runs throughout the volume, as Cavendish attempts to articulate a conception of memory that can resolve the fears, uncertainties, and confusions that mark the opening to *Poems, and Fancies*. To the question "why do I make public what should be private," An Collins could provide a list of answers structured by her relationship to the divine. In "An Epistle to Mistris Toppe," Cavendish raises the same question when she asks if in "this Action of setting out of a Book" she has "behav'd my selfe in *dishonourable* and loose carriage," or if she has brought "a *dishonour* to the *Family* I am link't to." Cavendish's emphasis on family and dishonor reveals that, like Collins, in making herself a public spectacle she cannot help but feel the weight of her decision to abandon the private, domestic sphere that defines the proper woman; this particularly disturbs Cavendish given the nobility and prominence of "the Family I am link't to." Unlike Collins, however, Cavendish, writing a very different volume of poetry, has no recourse to the divine and must instead answer her question in secular terms: "I have an Opinion, which troubles me like a conscience, that tis a part of Honour to aspire towards a Fame." Cavendish's answer looks not toward God but to fame, for in *Poems, and Fancies* that force alone can confront the gendered distinction between honor and dishonor that allows only men to participate in the realm of text, discourse, and print. Cavendish can clear her conscience because memory replaces God in the secular world of *Poems, and Fancies*. In Cavendish's formulation here, aspirations to fame not only ennoble all individuals irrespective of sex, but are demanded of them. In accepting the traditional female role, in not attempting to fulfill memorial desires normally reserved for men, Cavendish suffers a specifically ethical dilemma, something "which troubles me like a conscience."

Cavendish later asserts—in an address near the conclusion of the volume directed "To All Writing Ladies"—that society's memorial processes, and her gaudy conception of fame, must include women, "for they are poore, dejected spirits, that are not ambitious of Fame." Cavendish doesn't hesitate to admit that "we be inferiour to Men," but this subordination must not lead women "to eate, and drink, and sleep away our time as [Beasts] doe." Cavendish assures her female compatriots that the age is particularly favorable to women writers, who need not "turne into forgotten dust. But let us strive to build us Tombs while we live, of Noble, Honourable, and good Actions, at least harmlesse." For Cavendish, this desire for memorial permanence motivates all people; for women as well as men, the ultimate object of human ambition remains the achievement of a life in memory that need not end at the grave. As the third of her "Moral Discourses"—"Of Ambition"—puts it,

> Give me a Fame, that with the World may last,
> Let all Tongues tell of my great Actions past.
> Let every Child, when first tis taught to speak,
> Repeat my Name, my Memory for to keep. (94)

In *Poems, and Fancies*, the height of human ambition lies not primarily in the achievements that mark an individual's mortal life—although these are obviously a necessary precondition for fame—but in the transcendence of that mortality through the memorial processes that animate human generation and society.

Cavendish understands those processes, moreover, in a specifically gendered fashion in which society's memory depends on generational succession;

she imagines and locates a future life in the stories taught to and repeated by children. This is not the type of succession described by Kate Lilley as a typical feature of the male elegy, which remains "encoded in, a persistent concern with vocation, the creation of heroic genealogies and lines of apostolic succession."[50] In her genealogical imagery, Cavendish figures collective memory not in pompous public rites, but in the child, who represents both a realm of private, domestic transactions enacted within the family, and a link between that family and the wider life of society. In emphasizing specifically the speaking child she presents what the Popular Memory Group has described as "a common sense of the past...[that] may circulate, usually without amplification, in everyday talk and in personal comparisons and narratives."[51] In recognizing the complicated relationship between private and public, family and state, the childish acquisition of language and its articulation by "some deathlesse Muse," Cavendish insists on the dynamic interplay between the establishment of the individual memory and the formation of a collective memory that formalizes fame and a life lived in social time. She locates the child at the intersection of that relationship between individual and collective memory, and to the extent that Cavendish plays in the opening paratextual matter with the image of her book as a child, we can apprehend another way in which *Poems, and Fancies* tried to assert her memorial dreams.

VI

In an important essay on Cavendish and authorship, Sandra Sherman writes that "the self, which in Cavendish's oeuvre is always Margaret Cavendish, is always aware of and promoting an aesthetic of englobement. Cavendish appears in her works as an audience of one. She instantiates herself in writing about herself writing."[52] The truth of this insight will, I trust, be recognized by every reader of Cavendish, whose solipsistic self-absorption often overwhelms the reading experience. Rarely does one encounter a writer willing to admit that "my ambition is not onely to be Empress but Authoress of a whole World," and Cavendish's insistence on dominating completely her literary universe creates a textual landscape that can sometimes seem devoid of other human presence.[53] If, as we have seen, her paratextual practice forbids others—except for her husband—from contributing to her books, her claim that as a writer "All the materials in my head did grow, / All is my own, and nothing do I owe" would also banish previous writers and literary influences, as if Cavendish sprang full-grown from the head of Zeus.[54] Late in her career she even asserts, in a letter addressed "To the Readers" of her volume of *Plays, Never before Printed* (1668), that she writes and publishes "only for my own pleasure, and not to please others: being very indifferent, whether any body reads them or not; or being read, how they are esteem'd."[55] Although the terrible anxiety revealed by the prefatory matter in *Poems, and Fancies* may give the lie to her later expressions of contempt, her disdain for the criticism she received, and refusal to fulfill conventional literary expectations, demonstrates a profound distance between the writer and her contemporary audience. Barren of other contributors, and ostensibly divorced from not only other literary influences but even readers, Cavendish's books sometimes appear to be speaking to an audience of one, the putative "Authoress of a whole World."

At the same time, however, Cavendish's paratextual practices in *Poems, and Fancies* and throughout her career reveal a genuine attentiveness to both readers and their responses to her work. Milton, of course, strove to construct his elite status by appealing to a "fit audience...though few," but Cavendish's sometimes endless addresses to her readers suggest a much more "democratic" muse. Particularly in her first volume, where she singles out "Naturall Philosophers," "Morall Philosophers," "Poetts," "Writing Ladies," "Noble and Worthy Ladies," and even "Souldiers," Cavendish attempts to cultivate a diverse contemporary audience, to win particular segments of a growing population of readers to her side. In *The Fame Machine* (1996), Frank Donoghue investigates how the print trade created readers with the power to confer fame upon authors, and from the very start of her career Cavendish seems aware of and alive to changes in the reading habits of her era[56]; her use of paratext demonstrates her desire to dominate and channel these transformations in ways favorable to herself. In 1653 the community of "Writing Ladies" may not have been extensive, but Cavendish clearly wants to enlarge and empower, even to produce, a female readership sympathetic to her achievements.

Caught between a studied indifference to a contemporary readership, a defensive disdain for an audience she imagines as derisive or actively hostile, and paratextual practices that assume a diverse readership that she can anatomize and then cultivate, Cavendish betrays an underlying conflict in her relationship to her readers. Her indefatigable thirst for fame and celebrity, her admission in *A True Relation* that "I am so vain (if it be a vanity) as to endeavour to be worshipped, rather than not to be regarded" (177), suggests her intense desire to possess a public voice and persona, to forge a meaningful relationship with her reading public. At the same time, however, Cavendish remained throughout her career most empowered by and attentive to the Self, rather than a readership that rarely assumes a substantial form in her works. For all of her paratextual addresses to specific groups of readers, Cavendish never fully commits to, or concretely imagines a contemporary reader with whom she can engage her energies. Cavendish rarely provides the intense involvement with individual readers that can be such a large part of the reading experience in Jonson, for instance, who imagines a reader whose "wit reach no higher but to spring/Thy wife a fit of laughter."[57] The reader in Cavendish is normally an abstraction, a disembodied presence, for, in spite of countless paratextual addresses to her readers, Cavendish's most profound engagement is always with herself.

Cavendish's paratextual practices also stem, at least to some extent, from her great productivity, and the responses, often negative, generated by her oeuvre. Bradstreet's paratextual opening to her volume may imagine the critical voices that it might have raised, but Cavendish confronted actual criticism, charges of plagiarism, literary inadequacy, and scientific incompetence. Cavendish can even be said to have welcomed such criticism, her desire for cultural significance not always averse to vulgar fame or mere notoriety. While the paratextual matter that opens *Poems, and Fancies* reveals a terrible fear of ridicule and scorn, she nonetheless dreaded even more the possibility of silence and indifference. Although she speaks in the following of a general "some," I believe that Cavendish refers to herself when she explains that "Some love the life of their Memory so well, that they would chuse...rather to live in *infamy*, than to dye in *obscurity*. For *Infamy* is a loud *Reproach*, whereas *Fame* is a loud *Applause*; yet neither of them are got by ordinary means, but by Extreams."[58]

A lasting life in cultural memory could begin simply with a loud noise, as she suggests in "To All Noble and Worthy Ladies" at the start of *Poems, and Fancies*: "For all I desire, is *Fame*, and *Fame* is nothing but a *great noise*, and *noise* lives most in a *Multitude*; wherefore I wish my *Book* may set a worke every *Tongue*" (A3). Although fascinated and even preoccupied by the complexities of fame, the transmission of a cultural heritage, and the nature of collective memory, Cavendish rarely proves as analytical or fastidious as Milton or Pope; her overwhelming desire for attention renders her sometimes curiously indiscriminate in her appreciation of celebrity, fame, and memory, as if she were incapable of distinguishing between them. Milton, of course, casts an exceedingly cold eye on the promiscuous and unthinking pursuit of renown, the rebel angels in *Paradise Lost* characterized precisely by a rash commitment to glory and indifference to the distinction between fame and infamy. For Milton, *vainglory* is the term that describes those not attentive enough to the ethical responsibilities and demands of memorialization, as when Jesus in Book 3 of *Paradise Regained* rhetorically asks, "Shall I seek glory then, as vain men seek / Oft not deserv'd?" (105–06).

Cavendish, on the other hand, possessed no such moral dilemmas in her relationship to fame. In *A True Relation*, in fact, she proudly confesses that "I fear my ambition inclines to vain-glory, for I am very ambitious; yet 'tis neither for beauty, wit, titles, wealth, or power, but as they are steps to raise me to Fame's tower, which is to live by remembrance in after-ages" (177). Cavendish subordinates everything to the achievement of "remembrance in after-ages," the desires for power or wealth that conventionally drive people to succeed valuable to her only when in service to her thirst for a place on the monumental edifice of "Fame's tower." Cavendish did not shy away from "vain-glory" but actively cultivated it, the celebrity she created for herself in Restoration England a testimony to her shrewd manipulation of her image as an aristocratic, an author, a scientist, an exemplar of fashion.

During April and May of 1667, for instance, a stay in London that culminated in Cavendish's famous visit to the Royal Society, Pepys' *Diary* contains numerous references to the duchess, whom he is wild to see: "The whole story of this Lady is a romance, and all she doth is romantic. Her footmen in velvet coats, and herself in an antique dress, as they say." Pepys here discloses the way in which Cavendish's sense of fashion helped to construct her "romance." Pepys didn't have an easy time observing Cavendish, on one occasion "she being fallowed and crowded upon by coaches all the way she went, that nobody could come near her," but when he finally did he pays tribute to the way in which her flamboyant mode of dress both created and governed responses to her mystique:

> in the way met my Lady Newcastle, going with her coaches and footmen all in velvet; herself (whom I never saw before) as I have heard her often described (for all the town-talk is nowadays of her extravagancies), with her velvet-cap, her hair about her ears, many black patches because of pimples about her mouth, neck naked, without anything about it, and a black juste-au-corps; she seemed to me a very comely woman.[59]

The references here to the contrast between naked female flesh and male modes of dress (the cap and juste-au-corps, a knee-length coat worn by men) suggest that both her literary and fashion aesthetic exploited a gender hybridity that to a large extent defined her singularity and extravagance.[60] Yet by the time she visited the Royal Society on May 30, Pepys clearly had had enough of Cavendish, for although he still thought her "a good comely woman," he had decided that "her dress so antic and her deportment so unordinary, that I do not like her at all, nor did I hear her say anything that was worth hearing, but that she was full of admiration, all admiration."[61] Pepys now finds the various and diverse elements of her aesthetic and celebrity too discordant to admire. In less than two months romantic mystery has become antic behavior, Cavendish's deliberate cultivation of vainglory and notoriety leaving her open to disdain and even ridicule.

Nonetheless, derision, laughter, and infamy do not describe the responses Cavendish courted; to the extent that they characterized her reception by first Interregnum and later Restoration readers, Cavendish assiduously cultivated a second audience, always writing to those outside of both herself and her time, for "I regard not so much the present as future Ages, for which I intend all my Books."[62] Cavendish makes no attempt in any of her works to disguise her memorial ambitions, obscure her desire for fame, or forget that her ultimate audience consists not of a present reading public but a future posterity: "I verily believe, that ignorance and present envie will slight my book; yet I make no question, when envy is worn out by time, but understanding will remember me in after ages, when I am changed from this life; but I had rather live in a general remembrance, than in a particular life."[63] As we shall see, early in his career Milton also attempted to separate and protect himself from a present world of detraction by imagining a future of understanding and judicious readers, in whose memories the disappointments and failures of the individual life could be buried and forgotten. Cavendish's subordination here of her "particular life" to one lived "in a general remembrance" illuminates the importance she attributed to collective memory, which often in her works seems more substantial and "real" than the mundane, transitory world she inhabited. Privileging a future realm of "general remembrance," Cavendish necessarily alienates herself from current readers, one reason why they rarely assume tangible form in her writing.

Cavendish's insistence on calling herself a poet and inaugurating her career in print with a book of poems, stems from her conviction that above all else poetry dominates that collective human memory, the poet's cultural power unsurpassed in determining the judgments of future audiences. In her poem "The Elysium" poets possess a special place and role in society, for "Poets as great Gods do record all. / The souls of those that they will choose for blisse, / And their sweet number'd verse their pastport is." Without the poet's verse, the lovers, heroes, spirits, and ghosts who inhabit Cavendish's Elysium would cease to exist, for her Elysium is no conventional, classical afterlife but the individual consciousness and the cultural memory that it keeps alive: "The Brain is the Elysian fields; and here / All Ghosts and Spirits in strong dreams appeare. / ...But those that strive this happy place to seek, / Is but to goe to bed, and fall asleep." In this poem, the individual consciousness determines perception, our understanding of the outside world governed by internal mental processes. In "The Elysium," that individual consciousness dictates the cultural memory that allows the souls of great heroes to live and thrive.

For Cavendish, fame depends on the relationship between a collective memory that shapes the dreams individuals share, and the power of poetry to transform the merely mortal into the stuff of dreams. In such a world creation depends on "the God-head Wit," for poets preside over memorial processes that represent the second life we might live. Poets mediate memory, their textual representations the very ground of collective, memorial survival. In "The Elysium," Cavendish presents the "thread" spun by the Fates not as our physical lives—as in classical mythology—but as fame itself, the figurative life that we enjoy in memory. The poem concludes by assuring us that "Those that care not to live in Poets verse, / Let them lye dead upon Oblivions Hearse." Without the intervention of the poet, the individual's thread will "in knots, and snarles intangeled be," her spirit exiled from the memorial afterlife that represents the poem's dream of ideal fulfillment.

Cavendish's volume, moreover, advances these memorial processes as fundamental to what it means to be human:

> Man, as he hath a transcending Soule to out-live the World to all Eternity; so he hath a transcending desire to live in the Worlds Memory, as long as the World lasts; that he might not dye like a Beast, and be forgotten; but that his Works may beget another Soule, though of shorter life, which is Fame; and Fame is like a Soule, an Incorporeall Thing. (52)

Cavendish didn't possess the intellectual structures or psychological context that would allow her to define a concept like "collective memory," but in phrases such as "general remembrance" and "Worlds memory" she clearly attempts to create a way to talk about memorial structures that link the individual life to a collective human experience that separates us from and privileges us above the beasts. Our memorial practices, the construction of tombs, the honoring of individual names, even the thirst for war, all acknowledge the supreme importance of fame, for a secure place "in the Worlds Memory." Genesis may remind us that "dust thou art, and unto dust shalt thou return," but for Cavendish only the beasts need suffer that penalty, for fame allows us the possibility to "live as long as the World lasts." Cavendish would certainly agree with Steven Rose's assertion that what distinguishes the "specific human from non-human memory" is "our social existence, and the technological facility which has created a world in which memories are transcribed onto papyrus, wax tablets, paper . . . a world of artificial memory . . . which means that whereas all living species have a past, only humans have a history."[64]

In her third book, *The Worlds Olio* (1655), Cavendish elaborated on this distinction between the bestial and the human, using collective memory to distinguish the human from the natural world:

> Beasts, when they are dead, the rest of the Beasts retain not their memory from one posterity to another, . . . But the difference betwixt Man and Beast (to speak naturally, and without any relation to Divine Influence) is, that dead Men live in living Men; whereas Beasts dye without Record of Beasts. So that those men that dye in Oblivion, are Beasts by nature. (4)

This passage suggests the seriousness with which Cavendish tried to understand what she regarded as the unique place of the human in the natural world.[65] For Cavendish the supreme importance and immense cultural power of the book rests on its status as the most powerful "Record" that society can produce of itself; it is primarily through books that "dead Men live in living Men," that human society possesses its own past. Cavendish here registers the paradoxical nature of the book, its movement between the material and the spiritual, its ability to transcend its corporeal shape and link "one posterity to another." Although collective memory must ultimately take an immaterial form, defined by the presence of the dead in the living, the book is the material, cultural artifact that best represents our ability to retain generational continuity. Today some scientists possess a more plastic and expansive definition of collective memory: in a series of books on the relationship between biology and consciousness, Gerald M. Edelman has argued that "memory is an essential property of biologically adaptive systems," that (more directly put) "memory underlies meaning."[66] But the great sympathy for animals that Cavendish expresses throughout her poetry stems to a large extent from her empathy for what she regards as their lack of memory and history, their inability to master time and possess what she considered any genuine "posterity."

VII

Cavendish's contempt for those individuals who cannot secure their place in time, and never rise above a bestial oblivion, helps to explain her own desperation to achieve an authorial prominence, to attach her name to the book, and to place her books in the libraries that preserve our cultural heritage. Cavendish's obsession with memory displays itself most dramatically in two "Dialogues. Of Fame" that follow her address "To Morall Philosophers." Both short poems stage a debate between two voices speculating about the disposition of the soul or mind after death, in which one voice argues that "Alas, when Men do dye, all Motion's gone, / If no Motion, no thought of Fame hathe one," while another posits a world in which "Who knows, but that Mans Soule in Fame / delights / After the Body and It disunites?" These poems reach, of course, no conclusion about such matters, but both clearly privilege the voice that argues for an immaterial part of humankind that remains concerned with the individual's life in cultural memory even after the body dies. Cavendish plays with, and appears fascinated by, the possibility of an afterlife in which "the Mind delight / To heare its Fame, and see its Pyramid; / Or grieve, and mourne, when it doth see, and know, / Her Acts and Fame do to Oblivion go" (53).

In these poems, Cavendish imagines a life after death characterized not by conventional fears about heaven or hell, but by the poles of memory or oblivion.[67] Good Christians may aspire to enjoy God's grace after death, but for Cavendish acting as a voyeur of one's own fame describes the most satisfying of immortal pleasures. Cavendish invariably subordinates conventional morality to an economy of remembrance; the primary ethical imperative in Cavendish's world is determined not by the individual's relationship with and obedience to God, but by the individual's responsibility to ensure his or her memorial survival. At a time, according to Paula McDowell, when religious or religio-political works defined the largest category of printed matter available to the public, and when the vast majority of women wrote works of this character, one measure of Cavendish's uniqueness is her almost complete indifference to religious solutions to the questions that most concerned her.[68] Christian consolation hardly participates in Cavendish's attempts to understand how memory gives meaning to human mortality.

Poems, and Fancies links memory and humanity in an indissoluble relationship, the individual memory, and its participation in a more expansive collective memory that endures through time, a constituent part of what defines the human. In the course of *Poems, and Fancies*, poetry, both as a recording practice and cultural office, becomes central to that relationship, a fundamental part of both the desire for and realization of a second life in collective memory. Given the weight Cavendish places on the poet's vocation in society's memorial processes, her own assumption of this role necessarily generates tremendous anxiety in the fledgling poet, which marks not just the opening of her volume, with its extensive paratextual apparatus, but the concluding pages of the book, which ends with a short prose address followed by an untitled sixty-eight lines of poetry divided by printer's devices into five stanzas or untitled poems. The address and verses present themselves as a type of coda or conclusion, for they follow but are in no way connected to the last substantial piece in the volume, "The Animal Parliament."

She begins, in the prose address, by exploiting the link between poetic creativity and fashion, already established in the opening pages of the volume, in order to mitigate her weaknesses as a conventional poet and to elaborate her own ideas about what poetry should be. Here she emphasizes the importance of looking beyond ornament and *"glistering Shews,"* pleading with her readers not to mistake "a rich Hood" and *"Silver Lace"* for "the Golden Calf." This emphasis on clothing continues in a return to the imagery of spinning with which her book began:

> The *worst Fate Bookes* have, when they are once read,
> They're laid aside, forgotten like the *Dead*:
> Under a heap of *dust* they buried lye,
> Within a *vault* of some small *Library*.
> But *Spiders* they, for honour of that *Art*
> Of *Spinning*, which by *Nature* they were taught;
> Since *Men* doe spin their *Writings* from the *Braine*,
> Striving to make a lasting *Web* of *Fame*,
> Of *Cobwebs* thin, *high Altars* doe they raise,
> There offer *Flyes*, as sacrifice of *praise*.

The assiduousness with which Cavendish cultivated libraries throughout her life makes these lines especially poignant, for they suggest the fears and doubts that lay behind her constant self-promotion and confident projections of a future audience attentive to her fame. The act of publication, and even admission into the archive, cannot guarantee memorial success; books, as well as men, die, returning here in their own fashion to dust. This "small Library" preserves not memory but death, the ambitious memorial spinning of mankind (their "Art") mocked by the instinctual behavior of the spider, whose cobweb altars and insect sacrifices stand in stark contrast to the substantial life in memory that authorship promises and with which *Poems, and Fancies* began. The *"Web of Fame"* that might refer back to "The Elysium," and its confident celebration of poetry's memorial power, now registers instead the spider webs that undermine and mock human, artistic pretensions. This vision represents the *"worst Fate"* that books can suffer, the future audience of appreciative readers that Cavendish courts transformed into a heap of dust, forest of cobwebs, and graveyard of flies. Her reiterated idealization of the library returns here in the shape of its frightening doppelganger, in which slow decay and musty death sink her book and memorial aspirations into the oblivion she so feared and that Virginia Woolf famously consigned her to in *The Common Reader*: "But the last echoes of that clamour have now all died away;...her poems, her plays, her philiosophies, her orations, her discourses—all those folios and quartos in which, she protested, her real life was shrined—moulder in the gloom of public libraries."[69]

Other fates, however, remain possible for book and author; these lines never specifically characterize Cavendish's book, and the final two poems or

stanzas provide a recuperative vision of her poetic future when they introduce Cavendish's husband:

> A *Poet* I am neither *borne*, nor bred,
> But to a *witty Poet* married:
> Whose *Braine* is *Fresh*, and *Pleasant*, as the Spring,
> Where *Fancies* grow, and where the *Muses* sing.
> There oft I leane my Head, and *list'ning* harke,
> To heare *his words*, and all his *Fancies* make;
> And from that *Garden Flowers* of *Fancies* take,
> Whereof a *Posie* up in *Verse* I make.
> Thus I, that have no *Garden* of mine owne,
> There gather *Flowers* that are *newly blowne*.

In Cavendish's rather astonishing poetic debut, this represents perhaps the
most surprising moment of all, for at the conclusion of a volume that has
insisted throughout on her ambitions as a poet, Cavendish unexpectedly
lays her bays at her husband's feet. A poet neither born nor bred, Cavendish
affirms her husband William as the source of her creative inspiration, explicitly confessing to her readers that she possesses "no Garden of mine owne"
but must gather her poetic blooms from his fecund fields. *Poems, and
Fancies* has in no way prepared its readers for this final revelation, although
Cavendish had alluded to William earlier, in her letter "To Poets," when she
claimed that her verses "are like Chast Penelope's Work, for I wrote them
in my Husbands absence, to delude Melancholy Thoughts, and avoid Idle
Time" (122).

To a certain extent, her turn to her husband and Penelope surely represents a calculated attempt on Cavendish's part to disarm male criticism of
her poetic ambitions. This latter-day Penelope wants to assure us that her
volume does not represent the lawless or the naughty, that, like her classical predecessor's famous tapestry, it remains both chaste and sanctioned
by masculine authority, that however unusual it may appear it nonetheless
conforms to proper female standards of behavior.[70] This final reference to
William, however, possesses more than strategic importance, for it suggests
the centrality of his influence on her creative development, a subject that her
books rehearse frequently. One of the seven paratextual elements that introduce *The Worlds Olio* in 1655 is a letter from Margaret to William explaining that although she has yet to dedicate one of her books to her husband,
"when I have writ all I mean to print, I intend, if I live, to Dedicate the
whole summe of my Works unto you, and not by Parcells: for indeed you are
my Wits Patron." Margaret continues, trying more fully to rationalize the
creative relationship between them:

> though I do not write the same way you write, yet it is like Nature which
> works upon Eternal matter, micning [*sic*], cutting, and carving it out into sev-
> eral Forms and Figures; for had not Nature Matter to work upon, She would
> become Useless; so that Eternal Matter makes Nature work, but Nature makes

> not Eternal Matter. Thus she is but as a labouring servant; and as in Eternal
> Matter there lives Spirit and Motion, which is Life and Knowledge, so in your
> Discourse lives Sense and Reason.[71]

The difficulty a reader experiences in following this passage stems from
the confusion raised by its problematic analogical logic. At the beginning
it seems to equate William with "Nature," who "works upon" Margaret or
"Eternal matter" in order to generate the different forms that matter takes;
nature actively manipulates passive matter, mincing, cutting, and carving it.
But the passage concludes by explicitly identifying William as Eternal matter,
whose "Sense and Reason" is likened to the "Spirit and Motion" of matter,
and Margaret as Nature, "a labouring servant."

The passage founders on its inability to define the active principle or
primary mover in this relationship, which seems at first to be Nature, but,
by the end, has become Eternal matter. This confusion arises not simply
from an uncertain science, or the complexity of their unusual relationship,
but from Margaret's sensitivity to the charges, particularly at the start of
her career, that William's name rather than her own should be affixed to
her work. The passage after all is introduced by her insistence that "I do not
write the same way you write," which emphatically distinguished her work
and agency from his. As much as the passage wishes to credit William for his
inspiration, it also wants to assert both Margaret's creative individuality and
independence, and to declare her own poetic authority. Such assertions seem
necessary because the analogy suggests a passivity on her part that cannot
have pleased her, and which at every turn she struggles against.

As Margaret's career and confidence grew, and as her continued productivity disarmed assertions that William was the genuine author of her works,
attempts to rationalize her creative relationship to her husband become less
tendentious. In the 1662 edition of her *Playes*—her first foray into dramatic
literature—Margaret seems to have little difficulty acknowledging that
William has provided her with an occasional scene or song:

> My Lord supplied that defect [for I being no Lyrick Poet] of my Brain with the
> superfluity of his own Brain; thus our Wits join as in Matrimony, my Lords
> the Masculine, mine the Feminine Wit, which is no small glory to me, that we
> are Married, Soules, Bodies, and Braines, which is a treble marriage, united in
> one Love. ("To the Reader," A6)

Here the image of a "treble marriage" provokes far less anxiety for Margaret
than her earlier attempt to negotiate between the competing claims of Nature
and Eternal Matter. Here she seems willing to accept, rather than to scru-
tinize, an implicit distinction between male and female wit, and to feel free
to celebrate, rather than constrained to justify, "the superfluity of his own
Brain." Here his excess does not imply any sort of lack in her.

There seems little doubt, however, that contemporaries could only read
Margaret's poetic superfluity as William's lack, and the ways in which he

supported and enabled Margaret's career as an author made little sense to many of her Restoration readers. In his diary, for instance, Pepys records his reaction to Margaret's biography of William in terms that dismiss both author and subject: the book "shows her to be a mad, conceited, ridiculous woman, and he an asse to suffer [her] to write what she writes to him and of him."[72] According to Pepys, William has abandoned his responsibilities as a man and husband in allowing Margaret to write, such a failure transforming him into an ass. The sexual significance of this failure is made explicit in the anonymous "Session of the Poets":

> 22.
> Newcastle on's horse for entrance next strives,
>   Well stuff'd was his cloakbag and so were his breeches,
> And unbutt'ning the place where Nature's posset-maker lives,
>   Pulls out his wife's poems, plays, essays, and speeches.
> 23.
> "Whoop!" quoth Apollo, "What the de'il have we here?
>   Put up thy wife's trumpery, good noble Marquis,
> And home again, home again take thy career,
>   To provide her fresh straw and a chamber that dark is."[73]

Predictably, Margaret's creative excess can only be understood as William's sexual lack, her books replacing his penis. Although William, well horsed—as befits one of the most famous and expert riders of his day—appears also to be well-hung, his manhood has in fact vanished, the substitution of her books for his penis an indication that his status as a male has been obliterated by her identity as a poet. Yet neither husband nor wife can be considered for Apollo's prize, her "trumpery" merely a sign of her madness—for both Pepys as well as the anonymous author of this satire—and his neutering. Although the word trumpery doesn't become fully gendered until the mid-eighteenth century, when it could be applied especially to women, here it indicates that her poetry is not simply worthless trash or rubbish, but even a type of fraud and imposture. In such a formulation neither Margaret nor William can be allowed a poetic "career," for both have transgressed the proper seventeenth-century gender roles within which literary creativity and poetic self-fashioning can assume a legible shape.

William's refusal to understand "work" strictly in its conventionally gendered form represents to Margaret his ability to enable her literary career; at the same time, this refusal marked for his contemporaries his own failures as a man, husband, and writer. Indeed, if Margaret's career as a writer began in the early-1650s with charges that William bore the responsibility for her works, not even fifteen years later the Restoration public began to attribute his works to her. When his play *The Humourous Lovers*, which had been published anonymously, was performed in London during March and April of 1667, Pepys not only assumed that it was hers, but overcame his distaste for "the most ridiculous thing that ever was wrote" solely in order to understand her celebrity: "did by coach go see the silly play of my Lady Newcastle's called *The Humourous Lovers*, the most silly thing that ever came upon a stage; I was sick to see it, but yet would not but have seen it, that I might the better understand her."[74] Not only William's manhood but his entire public identity was subsumed by his wife's notorious career and work. Pepys' admission that he "was sick to see it" in order to "better understand her," even though he regards "her" play as contemptible, suggests not just how successfully she had cultivated her aesthetic persona and created, during her lifetime, the "*great noise*" that signified fame, but how fully that fame had devoured her husband, leaving him without a coherent authorial identity.

VIII

Sixteen years after Cavendish's death in 1673, Aphra Behn published a poem in broadsheet entitled "A Pindaric Poem to The Reverend Doctor Burnet, on the Honour he did me of Enquiring after me and my Muse." The poem represents a sardonic celebration of William of Orange's triumph over James II in which Behn pays homage to Burnet not only as one of William's chief supporters, but also as one of the most effective engineers of the new king's victory:

> 'Tis you that to Posterity shall give
>   This Ages Wonders, and its History.
> And great NASSAU shall in your Annals live
>   To all Futurity.
>   Your Pen shall more Immortalize his Name,
> Than even his Own Renown'd and Celebrated Fame.[75]

Behn's ironic praise of William—whose cause she refuses to embrace in the course of the poem—recognizes the immense power wielded by the "Pen" of a consummate propagandist like Burnet. The poem concludes here by insisting that not simply "Fame" and "Futurity," but "Posterity," "History," and even immortality will be determined by the "Annals" composed by Burnet.

Behn's poem appears to suggest that she can have no place in the production of such "Annals." The narrator bewails her "careless Muse," who is "out of an inferiour Metal wrought," insisting that she "never durst, like Cowly, tune her Strings,/To sing of Heroes and of Kings" (37–38). Yet Behn's poem is not simply another lament for the insufficiencies of a female Pen. Although the poem pays lip-service to the conventional inadequacies of the woman poet, the occasion of its composition rests on Burnet's solicitation of Behn in William's cause and the refusal of her "stubborn Muse" to betray James' doomed kingship. Behn might, in fact, have wielded her pen and quill in William's service, but her political sympathies and poetic integrity do not allow her to betray "every Notion, every Principle." Behn's pen is simply not for sale.

Behn's very public response to Burnet provides a fascinating glimpse into both politics and gender during the last decades of the seventeenth century.

In terms of England's turbulent politics, it acknowledges the way in which printed propaganda had become an indispensable part of the political process. Although its assertion that "The Sword [is] a Feeble Pow'r . . . / And to the Nobler Pen subordinate" (74–75) might perhaps strike us as an amusing example of wish fulfillment on the part of the race that writes, it nonetheless attests to the importance the pen had attained in complex political processes that since the print explosion of the 1640s could no longer separate themselves from textual representation and public scrutiny. The fate of England's throne and succession of the monarchy would no longer be decided entirely or even primarily on the battlefield, but would depend as well on intricate negotiations carried out in print for the hearts and minds of a nation of readers. As for gender, Behn's utterly conventional and entirely cynical allusions to her poetic inferiority only acknowledge the serious and important role she already plays in the writing of Restoration politics. The narrator takes for granted her place in the historical processes described in the poem, her refusal to participate on this occasion having nothing to do with female insufficiency but with her political conscience and literary ethics.

Published eleven years before Astell's comments on the gendered Pen in *Reflections upon Marriage* with which I opened this chapter, Behn's ironic use of the same trope suggests how the symbolic constructions that represented gender and authorship were being used in diverse and sometimes contradictory ways during the latter half of the seventeenth century. A customary vocabulary of female insufficiency was open to exploitation and manipulation from a variety of gendered subject positions, aristocrat as well as middling rank, gifted amateur as opposed to Grub Street professional, sexual innocent contrasted to the knowing leer and wink. Indeed, so complex and uneven is the development of seventeenth-century "feminisms" that, as Paula McDowell explains, the very public success of women like Cavendish, Astell, and Behn may have actually contributed to the consolidation of a "sexual division of literary labor" that undermined the position of other women in the print trade:

> While the gendered subjectivity of an Astell or a Cavendish became an important base for a new kind of proto-feminist 'political' writing, modern notions of the self as gendered and unique may have worked to reduce less privileged women's conviction of their own agency and involvement in national and local politics.[76]

Far less flexible than Behn in her ability to assume multiple subject positions, and lacking both Behn's irony and sexual sophistication, Cavendish nonetheless shared in Behn's desire to wield a pen that could insure fame and futurity, successfully compose history, and guarantee immortality. Even after her death, her husband carried on a campaign to ensure her posterity and secure her reputation. As we have seen, three years after Margaret's death William published a tribute volume of *Letters and Poems In Honour of the Incomparable Princess, Margaret, Duchess of Newcastle* in order to provide a testimony and witness to her achievements as an author. A poem included in the volume, "To her Excellency the Lady Marchioness of Newcastle, on Her Incomparable Works," even imagines just the type of literary futurity that Cavendish coveted, in which "the Learned strive / Whose Margin should strut biggest with your Name / Who raise up highest Pyramids of Fame."[77] Although in these tributes the monumental pyramids of fame built to her memory remain merely metaphoric, the Cavendishes' grand and ornate tomb in the north transept of Westminster Abbey does all it can to make literal her identity as an author. While William is represented through his martial virtues, Margaret's effigy rehearses her intellectual prowess. With books at her feet, and a book and inkhorn in hand, she is, as Peter Beal suggests, "in effect, reading—with the implication of also writing—into eternity...the monument...represents her immortality through writing—exactly, we may suppose, as she would have wished."[78]

Yet Cavendish is not the first to demonstrate the difficulty of trying to stage-manage history, a frustrating and often futile undertaking that Milton dramatizes in the confrontation between Samson and Dalila in *Samson Agonistes,* and which I will examine in the next chapter. Cavendish's place in literary history has fluctuated far more than the other, male authors who I will consider in the rest of this book, and even twenty years ago one would have been justified in considering her a mere curiosity of English literary history for most of the last three hundred years. As we have seen, even Woolf demonstrated little desire to save Cavendish from oblivion, the twentieth-century modernist more interested in recuperating Shakespeare's anonymous sister than the prolific and formidable duchess. In the last twenty years, however, Cavendish's obscurity and marginalization have been reversed, and, at least within the academy, literary criticism has rediscovered Cavendish's oeuvre.

This reevaluation remains as yet incomplete, and, as Alice Fulton impatiently notes, "historically, 'eccentric' is what female poets get to be instead of 'original.'" Even three-and-a-half centuries after the publication of Cavendish's *Poems, and Fancies,* we are only beginning to read it in terms that go beyond a celebrity fashioned from equal parts of aristocratic nonconformity, literary madness, and female alterity. Fulton believes that "Cavendish's role as designated whipping girl of English literature is frightening. The fearful derision directed at her...should be retargeted toward the literary culture that created her reception."[79] Cavendish, to be sure, must assume some responsibility for her memorial plight, her deliberate cultivation of singularity during her lifetime, her refusal to acknowledge any literary forebears, female as well as male, and her almost complete isolation from the world of professional letters making it easy to read her conspicuous individuality as freakish eccentricity.

In the rest of my book, however, I will argue that the literary culture castigated by Fulton is in fact built upon not simply the erasure of female creativity, but its defamation. In Milton, Pope, and Richardson, we will see how modern cultural memory takes its shape from a struggle in which female creativity must be constructed as infamous in order for men to privilege their creativity and secure their own cultural immortality. The scene of memorial inscription always involves a variety of contested objects, motivations, and values; inevitably, gender is implicated in the struggle to achieve memorial authority. According to the Popular Memory Group, processes of domination and contestation are central to the establishment of a collective memory: "Dominant memory is produced in the course of these struggles and is always open to contestation. We do want to insist, however, that there are real processes of domination in the historical field. Certain representations achieve centrality and luxuriate grandly; others are marginalized or excluded or reworked." Their insistence that "memory is, by definition, a term which directs our attention not to the past but to *the past-present relation*,"[80] suggests that for female poets of the seventeenth century, the politics of memory govern not simply their claims to poetic and authorial legitimacy, but the way in which their place in literary history has been remembered by succeeding generations. Until the last half century, representations of masculine literary immortality and memorial hegemony have "luxuriated grandly," the erasure, marginalization, or ridicule of female writers an important structural component of the construction of the English literary canon. As Jennifer Summit argues, "the idea of loss has served as a powerful fiction that shaped the cultural place of the woman writer as well as the abstract model of a literary history that excluded her...producing the woman writer as 'lost' from literary history was part of the process of conceiving what literary history was in a fundamental way."[81] The derision directed at Cavendish must therefore be understood as a necessary condition of male attempts to build literary monuments that will triumph over time and oblivion.

Although, as we have seen, Cavendish could occasionally ignore or confuse the differences between fame and infamy, she nonetheless fashioned her literary efforts and publishing career aware of both the intimate relationship between oblivion, infamy, and fame, and the difficulty of attaining a durable form of the last while avoiding the first two. She recognized that a woman's commitment to achieving a place in memory made her vulnerable to the ridicule of others, to a fate that promised infamy rather than fame. Memory represented a double-edged sword to Cavendish, who textualizes herself because of her intense desire to incorporate herself within cultural memory, even as she fears the infamy that may likely be her fate. She knew just how ludicrous and futile the pursuit of literary immortality appeared in a woman: "the Lady M. L. spoke of me, saying, I liv'd a Dull Unprofitable, Unhappy Life, Imploying my time onely in Building Castles in the Air." What sustained her belief in herself, her career, and her books, however, was the certainty that "the Minds Architecture," the "Airy Castles" of literary creativity, could triumph over both time and present detraction to secure a second life in memory: "neither doth the Builder need any other Monument or Tomb, than his Own Airy Works, which...[if] carefully Written and Printed, are more Glorious, Stately, and Durable, than Tombs or Monuments of Marble" (*CCXI Sociable Letters,* 226–28). The Lady M. L. derides Cavendish's monumental aspirations, "Building Castles in the Air" a representation of the futility of female authorship, which can never overcome the abyss that separates the intangible, immortal essence of the book from its material form. Cavendish, however, believed in the subtle alchemy that transforms the "Airy" into the "Durable," assured that the careful printing of her books could monumentalize the airy castles of the literary imagination and resolve the memorial mysteries that govern our lives in time.

CHAPTER 2

"A SPACE FOR NARRATION":
MILTON AND THE POLITICS OF
COLLECTIVE MEMORY

I

My last chapter argues that much of the power of Cavendish's *Poems, and Fancies* stems from the inaugural drama that it enacts between a fledgling poet and her audience. Throughout the volume, Cavendish's self-presentation reveals both the pressures that attend her first public assumption of the mantle of author-ship, and the ways in which she constructs her authorial self in order to engage her projected readers, who comprise the complex object of her desires and fears, her memorial hopes, aspirations, and anxieties. The last volume published in Cavendish's lifetime—a second edition of *The World's Olio*—appeared in 1671, and while much changed over the course of her almost twenty-year career, particularly in her science, her first book provides an accurate representation of a concern for and understanding of fame, memory, and posterity that evolved very little from her first volume to her last. These sentiments expressed in "To the Readers"—one of fourteen introductory elements accompanying her final original volume, *Plays, Never before Printed* (1668)—could have appeared (and often did) in any of the books she published during her lifetime: "their malice [of her detractors] cannot hinder me from Writing, wherein consists my chiefest delight and greatest pastime; nor from Printing what I write, since I regard not so much the present as future Ages, for which I intend all my Books." Cavendish's insistence on the relationship between publication and futurity never wavered, her belief in the desirability and importance of an enduring cultural memory remaining constant from first to last. Distinguished by a combination of debili-tating shyness and aristocratic hauteur, and an intellectual commitment to an ideal of aesthetic and authorial singularity, Cavendish remained throughout her career relatively isolated from her literary peers, and aloof from many of the influences that normally force a writer to change and evolve.

In attending to Milton's *Paradise Regain'd. A Poem. In IV Books. To which is added Samson Agonistes* (1671)[1] I will describe a very different authorial drama, one of endings rather than beginnings, of a long and tumultuous literary and political career reflecting back on itself, imagining its memorial future not through the excited and anxious innocence of the virgin author, but through the sometimes bitter knowledge derived from a lifetime of personal, political, and cultural triumphs and defeats. Published three years before Milton's death, this volume rehearses what Stanley Fish describes as "a characteristic Miltonic strategy: to think through a problem by revising and complicating an earlier treatment of it. Milton is continually in dialogue with himself."[2] Although I will conclude with the two poems published in the 1671 volume, in this chapter I will examine that Miltonic self-dialogue in a number of works that deal with the relationship between history, memory, and authorship, including *Lycidas* (1638), *Areopagitica* (1644), the Latin ode "To John Rouse" (1647), and the Latin prose masterpiece *A Second Defence of the English People* (1654). Measuring Milton's public career from its first decade to its last, these texts suggest his passionate investment in considerations of the nature and durability of collective memory, and demonstrate that such concerns were central to the ways in which he imagined his life as the author of controversial prose pamphlets, as secretary for foreign languages, and as a poet. The internal regulation of the bourgeois subject, the formation of a national identity, the proper definition of "active virtue," and the necessity to apprehend and seize the opportune moment—topics fundamental to Milton's literary career and cultural ideology—all intersect in his fascination with the paradoxical weakness and resilience of human memory and the ways in which fictions and narratives generate and sustain collective memory.

The arc that describes Milton's progress from *Lycidas* and *Areopagitica* to *Paradise Regained* and *Samson Agonistes* moves from the youthful uncertainty of the pastoral elegy, through the triumphant assurance of *Areopagitica* and *A Second Defence*, to the terrible doubt and frustration of the dramatic poem, from authorial innocence and self-confidence to struggle and even despair. Early in his career, Milton has little doubt that history will vindicate his life and writings, for he sees himself as one of those upright custodians of memory who alone can defeat time and preserve what otherwise would be forgotten. The collapse of the Cromwellian settlement, however, and Restoration of the Stuart monarchy undermine such certainties, forcing Milton to confront the dialectical bond between memory and forgetting, the tension between fragility and monumentality in the preservation of writing and culture, and the problematic relationship between truth and fable in the recovery of history.[3]

Both Jesus' resounding triumph in *Paradise Regained* and Samson's ambiguous one in *Samson Agonistes* must be read in light of a confrontation, developed throughout Milton's career, between martial and intellectual virtue, and his conviction that cultural labor is essential to the establishment of a national identity and the collective memory that depends upon it. Milton returns to this confrontation frequently, always attempting to resolve the same pressing issues that generated what has become the most enduring poem to emerge from the English civil war:

> The forward Youth that would appear
> Must now forsake his Muses dear,
>   Nor in the Shadows sing
>   His Numbers languishing.
> 'Tis time to leave the Books in dust,
> And oyl th' unused Armours rust.[4]

These opening lines from Marvell's "Horatian Ode" envision a moment of national crisis that both demands sacrifices of those who would actively participate in the processes of history, and provides special opportunities to those ambitious for recognition and fame. The devaluation of the arts suggested in these lines is perhaps not as extreme as might first appear: in its assumption of a periodic rhythm to the cycles of national history the poem anticipates times when the "Muses" will triumph over warfare, and "Books" will reign rather than "Armour." Indeed, the poem's cynical conclusion, which suggests the inability of armed might to legitimate itself except through an inevitable and continued force, questions and even subverts the military opportunism that it initially celebrates.

Nonetheless, the poem begins with a very conventional insistence on the irrelevance of books, art and cultural labor at moments of historical crisis. The normative power of such sentiments in early modern Europe, which "governed" itself through an almost perpetual state of military crisis, is most famously dramatized in the opening of *An Apologie for Poetrie*, where Sidney cannot mount his defense of poetry without acknowledging, in the words of John Pietro Pugliano, that "Souldiours were the noblest estate of mankinde." Sidney certainly mocks Pugliano's "strong affection and weake arguments," but in choosing to begin with Pugliano he nevertheless acknowledges the cultural and ideological authority of Pugliano's orthodox wisdom.[5] Statesmen of all stripes have ever been eager to damn "the inglorious Arts of Peace" when young men (and now women) must be recruited in the service of the gods of war and the politicians who exploit them. Even the unorthodox Cavendish confirms customary wisdom when she insists that "Those *Fames* that are gotten in the Warrs, sound louder than those that are gotten in Peace, by reason Warr is a disturber, and causeth a violent motion, like a Tempest at Sea, or Storm at Land" (*The World's Olio* [1671] 5).

In the works I will consider in this chapter, Milton challenges and attempts to overthrow the elevation of the military over the artistic by insisting that the creation of national history and collective memory depends on writers as well as soldiers, poets as well as conquerors, the book as well as the sword. Milton certainly responds to the cultural prestige that normally distinguishes military prowess, and betrays a measure of guilt and even shame over his failure to participate in the battlefield triumphs that brought down the monarchy. But, like Marvell at the conclusion of his poem, Milton articulates—in this case through God in *Paradise Lost*—a belief that in violence "no solution will be found: / War wearied hath perform'd what War can do" (6.694–95).[6] "Active virtue" reveals itself not only in those thousands who "post o'er Land and Ocean without rest," but in the writer who bears witness. For Milton, bearing witness is not a passive activity, but instead participates in a process of contestation fundamental to the formulation of a national identity and cultural heritage. Milton delineates a poetics of memory that positions the author as the privileged witness of history.[7]

In his insistence on the centrality of the writer to collective memory, Milton abrogates powers and responsibilities previously held by others. Michael Schudson's perception that modern intellectuals "are often the agents of instrumentalizing the past" is given historical specificity by James Fentress and Chris Wickham, who argue that "the bearers of national memory since the arrival of capitalism in each country are the upper middle classes and the intelligentsia who have inherited the mantle from the aristocracies, lawyers, and clergy of previous epochs."[8] Both Milton's political activism and his dedication to the aesthetic imperatives of his art embody this new dispersal of political, literary, and cultural power. As both poet and propagandist, the writer of prose pamphlets addressing the most timely political, social, and religious issues of his day, and the literary "genius" dedicated to the cultivation of a thoroughly classical model of authorship, Milton participated in what Jacques Le Goff has described as the conflict to achieve power over the new sites of memory that accompanied these cultural and historical changes: "to make themselves the master of memory and forgetfulness is one of the great preoccupations of the classes, groups, and individuals who have dominated and continue to dominate historical societies."[9]

In this chapter I will survey Milton's struggles to formulate conceptions of memory that can sustain his poetics and politics within this new order. Even in his earliest works, Milton distinguishes between mere fame, the individual desire for immortality that motivates the poet, "That last infirmity of Noble mind" according to *Lycidas*, and collective memory, which should bind and nourish entire communities within a coherent and meaningful identity. By the end of his career, Milton's turbulent public and political careers have inscribed themselves on his evolving sense of the relationship between writing and history, as he struggles to envision a conception of collective memory that can transform the experience of defeat occasioned by his blindness and political reversals. In the apocalyptic conclusion to *Samson Agonistes*, Milton contemplates the nature and significance of memory for those defeated and apparently betrayed by history and abandoned by God, and considers what type of heroic victory over one's enemies can secure a place in national history and the collective memory that it validates.

II

Milton's poetic career began two decades before the publication of Cavendish's *Poems, and Fancies*, his introduction to the public suggesting a very different paradigm of authorship from that adopted by the duchess, one that supports Robert J. Griffin's contention that "anonymity does not simply disappear with the emergence of a commercial culture."[10] Milton's first English publication, "An Epitaph on the Admirable Dramatick Poet W. Shakespear," was printed anonymously in 1632 along with other commendatory poems prefixed to the Second Folio of Shakespeare's plays. A Mask Presented at Ludlow Castle followed five years later in 1637, also presented without Milton's name. In 1638 Lycidas, followed by the initials I.M., appeared as the last poem in a volume of memorial verses dedicated to the memory of Edward King. Even four of Milton's five anti-episcopal tracts, his first prose pamphlets, appeared anonymously in 1641–1642, when the meeting of the Long Parliament transformed the print industry's participation in the nation's political upheaval.

Although the reasons for choosing anonymity in the political and religious controversies of the early 1640s would have differed from those governing the commencement of a poetic career, taken together they suggest that Stanley Fish correctly identifies one of the central conflicts that inspire Milton's writings when he insists that Milton "wants at once to celebrate humility and to be celebrated as the celebrator of humility. He is the poet of submission and corporate identity...and he is also the poet who would write something the world will not willingly let die."[11] Milton's entire career reveals a struggle between his understanding that God's service precludes the necessity to thrust oneself forward in a variety of ultimately futile and selfish heroic poses and his determined and aggressive desire to assert his self-importance as an immortal author divinely inspired, a tension between Milton's wish to appeal only to a select, elite audience and eagerness to speak to and for an English nation separating itself from, and then falling victim to what he regarded as a corrupt and degenerate monarchical government. Milton dramatizes these conflicting desires and needs in his very first attempts to court the muse, particularly in Lycidas, where he demonstrates the ambition not simply to engage in public speech but to assume the voice of prophetic utterance. Such an aspiration takes on a special urgency and ambivalence through the poem's concomitant development of fame and literary immortality as dangerous and potentially morally debilitating objects of desire.

Memorializing a young man who died before he could realize any of the achievements that normally bring fame, Milton's Lycidas undoubtedly remains one of the most enduring early-modern literary considerations of the relationship between poetry, authorship, and cultural memory. Part of a memorial volume that is itself now valued almost entirely because it includes Milton's elegy, the poem represents not only a profound and historically significant meditation on cultural immortality and literary production, but illuminates as well some of the paradoxes that make this relationship a source of continued fascination and mystery. In the poem, the capricious nature of poetic renown stems from the disjunction between the mortal and the divine that the poem structurally realizes by juxtaposing the narrator's reflections on fame to those of Phoebus Apollo, the first of the voices who wrest control of the poem from the inexperienced, nervous, and anonymous "I" who opens the poem with his "forc'd fingers rude" (4):

> *Fame* is the spur that the clear spirit doth raise
> (That last infirmity of Noble mind)
> To scorn delights, and live laborious days;
> But the fair Guerdon when we hope to find,
> And think to burst out into sudden blaze,
> Comes the blind *Fury* with th'abhorred shears,
> And slits the thin-spun life. "But not the praise,"
> *Phoebus* repli'd, and touch'd my trembling ears;
> "Fame is no plant that grows on mortal soil,
> Nor in the glistering foil
> Set off to th'world, nor in broad rumor lies,
> But lives and spreads aloft by those pure eyes
> And perfect witness of all-judging *Jove*;
> As he pronounces lastly on each deed,
> Of so much fame in Heav'n expect thy meed." (70–84)

The movement of this passage from narrator to pagan god, from authorial desire to divine correction, rests on the disparity between a mortal fame that represents "That last infirmity of noble mind," and a heavenly fame that "is no plant that grows on mortal soil." Unlike Cavendish, Milton invariably questions the ethics of and desire for literary immortality; visible here in the poem's refusal to fully endorse the pursuit of fame are a scriptural tradition that distinguished between earthly and heavenly fame as part of the doctrine of redemption, as well as a literary tradition, alluded to in my introduction, that linked fame to rumor and personified both as inextricably part of the fallen world. While fame does impel "the clear spirit" and "noble mind" to rise above itself, it remains an "infirmity," not necessarily antithetical to nobility, but a frailty or want of moral strength, a weakness of character or failure to maintain moral standards nonetheless.

To the narrator's credit, his youth and inexperience do not prevent him from recognizing the insufficiency of fame. He is, perhaps, too attracted for his own good to the sudden "blaze" of glory that represents the transitory and superficial nature of fame, but he understands as well the work necessary to pursue a poetic career, the acts of temperance, self-discipline, and labor that must define "the homely slighted Shepherd's trade." Here the textile imagery that in Cavendish indicates the strength of memorial desires, and the way in which poetry can help construct the garment of memory, symbolizes the opposite, "th'abhorred shears" of "the blind *Fury*" representing the fragility of "thin-spun life" and the untimely death of the narrator's friend that has precipitated the narrator's spiritual and literary crisis, giving rise to the poem in the first place. The narrator stands in a perilous moral position at this point in the poem, aware of the ways in which fame can undermine his poetic integrity, but not yet proof against its temptations. He still possesses a sense of entitlement, a conviction that fame represents a just, earthly reward or recompense for his poetic endeavors.

Apollo's touch, which follows the fatal action of Atropos, and moves us from this inadequate mortal understanding of fame to its divine counterpart, is an apparently simple gesture freighted with a number of meanings. Within the Virgilian context established by the poem's literary genre, the action clearly alludes to Eclogue VI and a rebuke delivered to the overly ambitious shepherd. Within the political and religious context of Laudian England, the touch certainly functions as either a threat or a warning, for John Leonard has convincingly linked the poem to the brutal punishment suffered by John Bastwick, Henry Burton, and William Prynne on June 30, 1637, when all three men had their ears cropped for "seditious libel." Such scenes of punishment were enacted not infrequently during the years of Charles I's personal government and within a month of Bastwick's, Burton's, and Prynne's judicial torture a Star Chamber decree of July 11, 1637 further extended the power of the Stationers' Company to control and regulate the press. Anonymity possessed a genuine value for a poet tempted to rail against those in the church who might "scramble at the shearers' feast, / And shove away the worthy bidden guest" (117–18).

But Leonard suggests as well that Apollo also offers "comfort and consolation," and, for all of the negative associations that it carries, Apollo's gesture here provides a moment of reassurance, a comforting touch in the midst of the narrator's despair over his friend's death.[12] At this moment Apollo, even as he warns and rebukes the narrator, sympathizes with him as well, aware of both the narrator's grief and frustrated poetic ambition. In whichever register Apollo's ambiguous touch functions, it reminds the narrator of the demands and responsibilities of the muse, and suggests that the virtues of anonymity go far beyond the perhaps necessary acts of self-preservation required during a time of political crisis; anonymity also represents an ethical and spiritual posture recommended by the recognition that genuine fame does not and indeed cannot live "in the glistering foil" and "broad rumor" of this our earthly world. To the extent that "perfect witness" is found only in heaven, fame on earth is at best a distraction and may even represent a trap and snare, a fruitless and misdirected pursuit of the "glistering foil" that deludes our sight and perverts a writer's attention to the ethical demands of his craft.

Apollo's intervention "changes everything," as Stanley Fish notes, for it marks the initial moment when the narrator loses control of his own poem and finds himself dislodged "from center stage." But Fish's assertion that "Apollo poses a threat to the speaker"[13] is only half of the truth, for if Apollo's touch represents comfort as well as rebuke, his lesson on the nature of fame is an important first step in the narrator's education as a poet. Until its conclusion, *Lycidas* reveals a powerful tension in the narrator's struggle to maintain control of his poem, to "build the lofty rhyme" that pays tribute to his friend's unseasonable death. In the periodic changes of narrative voice that remain such a distinctive feature of the poem, it may be difficult to determine whether the earnest but insecure and anonymous poet who opens the poem voluntarily relinquishes his place to a variety of authority figures who tutor and educate him, or finds himself repeatedly thrust aside by a series of more assertive and powerful speakers who appropriate his poem. Although the hesitancies visible in the first fourteen lines do not impede the poet from attempting to "build" his monument to a friend whose own memorial hopes were blasted by an untimely and premature death, the other narrative voices that erupt throughout the poem clearly disrupt the narrator's search for consolation, even as they simultaneously broaden, extend, and further his attempts to understand the ultimately Christian context within which the achievement of poetic renown takes legitimate shape.

Apollo's interruption, for example, provides a "higher mood" than the narrator on his own can achieve, but at the same time the classical god cannot resolve the pressing questions that occasioned the poem. Grounded only in a pagan context, without reference to either Christian salvation or redemption, Apollo's pronouncements can provide at best an incomplete answer to the problems raised by the narrator's attraction to fame. While the classical consolation Phoebus provides is not rejected as definitively and shockingly as the classical heritage represented by Athens is denied by Jesus in the penultimate temptation in book four of *Paradise Regained*—which I will examine later—*Lycidas* nonetheless moves quickly beyond, and renders irrelevant the "witness of all-judging *Jove*." "The Pilot of the *Galilean* lake" also moves the poem into a different tonal and moral dimension; and while he doesn't directly address the questions concerning fame and immortality that occupy the first half of the poem, he nonetheless reiterates the ethical imperatives that must motivate anyone seriously interested in pursuing "the faithful Herdman's art" (121), the "flashy songs" and "scrannel Pipes" of those with "Blind Mouths" as antithetical to poetry and virtue as the "glistering foil" that Apollo earlier dismissed.

Lycidas enacts a drama of poetic and ethical maturation, the inexperienced and unnamed narrator both tutored and marginalized, educated and interrupted by a succession of classical and Christian teachers. This education, moreover, is almost exclusively male, the lines leading to the narrator's initial consideration of fame concerned precisely with the gender boundaries that define poetry and authorship:

> Alas! What boots it with uncessant care
> To tend the homely slighted Shepherd's trade,
> And strictly meditate the thankless Muse?
> Were it not better done as others use,
> To sport with *Amaryllis* in the shade,
> Or with the tangles of *Neaera's* hair? (64–69)

Milton doesn't simply debar women from the memorial power of literature, but he presents them as the very antithesis of literary fame, as the transient "delights" that would seduce men from the rigorous discipline demanded by the life of poetry. This famous passage doesn't simply oppose women to poetry, implicitly denying them the perseverance necessary to cultivate the "thankless Muse" and "live laborious days," but to fame itself, to which they remain mindlessly indifferent. Working within a very conventional gendered binary, Milton delineates an aesthetic and moral economy in which men represent the realm of mind—striving relentlessly toward spiritual perfection and transcendence—while women, unable to rise above the dark and corrupt world of matter, epitomize the pleasures that the poet must renounce if he would perfect his art.

Such gender exclusions, however, are not as absolute as they appear in these lines, and the poem betrays a certain confusion in its gendered depiction of literary creativity. Both the Muse and Fame, of course, were conventionally represented as female figures, and the poem invokes both the "Nymphs" and "the Muse herself," Calliope, in lines 50–60, although unsuccessfully, for they remain unable to save either Lycidas or Orpheus. Earlier, the narrator begs inspiration from "Sisters of the sacred well" (15), although here too the poem invokes female invention only to abandon it almost immediately, for, when the narrator follows his request that they "loudly sweep the string" (17) by asking for some "gentle Muse" to favor "my destin'd Urn," he imagines a male and not a female muse: "And as he passes turn,/And bid fair peace be to my sable shroud" (20–23). As Elizabeth Hanson notes of this unusual substitution, the narrator "displaces the female muses with a male muse, expunging the feminine from his poetic. The masculinity and immortality of the poet's voice are simultaneously asserted in an act which imaginatively costs him his life."[14] Milton struggles throughout his literary career to articulate the association between creativity and the feminine, the confrontation between Samson and Dalila in *Samson Agonistes* his final attempt to understand and rationalize the relationship between gender and cultural production.

By the conclusion of *Lycidas* both the gender uncertainties and authorial hesitations of the poem's opening have been, if not resolved, at least transcended, when, in the final eight lines, the narrative "I" who opens the poem is replaced or supplanted by the anonymous "uncouth Swain." Whether this figure represents what Stanley Fish presents as the triumph of the anonymous, or what J. Martin Evans describes as "a transformation so profound that by the end of the poem [Milton] has become, quite literally, another person,"[15] the calm, assured demeanor and "eager thought" of the poem's new singer suggest that the crisis that gave rise to the poem has passed. However arbitrary and inexplicable the poem's sleight of hand in conjuring a heretofore invisible third-person narrator, his confidence and self-assurance demonstrate that the intervention of "him that walk'd the waves" (173) has provided sufficient resolution to the poem's concern for the ethical ambiguities of fame and the possibilities of cultural immortality. The swain's "warbling" here points to the mature Milton's conviction in book three of *Paradise Lost* that "Harmonious numbers"—figured in "the wakeful Bird/ [Who] Sings darkling, and in shadiest Covert hid/Tunes her nocturnal Note" (38–40)—represent genuine poetic inspiration. While Lycidas, once "sunk low" but now "mounted high," has become "the Genius of the shore," the narrator himself has been transformed, no longer out of season but looking forward "to fresh Woods, and Pastures new" (193).

III

The self-confidence visible at the end of the poem that concluded the volume *Justa Edouardo King Naufrago* flourished during the early 1640s as Milton's authorial engagement with the revolution became more profound. Milton provides one indication of his growing power as a writer by including *Lycidas* in the 1645 *Poems of Mr. John Milton*, where, in a different setting, the new headnote can explicitly claim prophetic speech for "the author": "In this Monody the author bewails a learned Friend, unfortunately drown'd in his passage from *Chester* on the *Irish Seas*, 1637. And by occasion foretells the ruin of our corrupted Clergy then in their height." "Then," in 1637, the "dread voice" that "shrunk thy streams" did not belong to the narrator but to the "the Pilot of the *Galilean* lake"; now, eight years later, Milton can make that voice his own, assuming, according to Michael Dietz, a power "doubly prophetic": "the explanatory headnote...answers not merely the new political circumstances but the new demands of publication...it also advertises Milton's authority as a seer to his new audience in his new historical moment. With the headnote *Lycidas* becomes a prophetic poem doubly prophetic."[16] Later in this chapter I will consider *A Second Defence* in order to see how Milton himself portrayed and understood his relationship to England's civil strife during the 1640s, but I first want to examine *Areopagitica* and "To John Rouse," two works from the mid-1640s, which, taken together, provide a dual perspective on Milton thoughts regarding literary production and the place of the book in the new political and religious order he hoped to help establish and celebrate.

I have argued elsewhere that part of the genius of *Areopagitica*, Milton's response to the June 14, 1643, "Ordinance to prevent and suppress the license of printing," resides in its ability to appropriate the rhetoric of press censorship, developed for over a century by a succession of monarchs, for very different purposes.[17] From the first royal proclamation containing a list of prohibited books, Henry VIII's "Enforcing Statutes against Heresy; Prohibiting Unlicensed Preaching, Heretical Books" in 1529, through the Charter of Incorporation granted by Mary and Philip in 1557 to the Stationers' Company, to the "Decree of Starre-Chamber, Concerning Printing, 1637," a language of infection, fragmentation, and uncontrollable growth had served to stigmatize print and its effects on what successive royal governments had portrayed as a giddy, unruly, and irresponsible populace. In *Areopagitica*, Milton exploits this derogatory language in order to celebrate the power of the printed word, to advance alternative models of memorial inscription, and to enfranchise a mature citizenry of readers eager to understand the truth.

Milton's respect for the book, in fact, has misled many readers into misrepresenting his stance toward censorship, his soaring rhetoric in this prose masterpiece often obscuring his conviction that books must be threatened with "fire and the executioner" should they prove "mischievous and libel-lous" (569). Milton's post-publication censorship demands that the com-monwealth maintain "a vigilant eye how Bookes demeane themselves" (492) precisely because books "are not absolutely dead things." Because books cannot be considered mere objects, "dead things," Milton holds them to a strict accounting, wary of their power, suspicious of their ability to pervert the commonwealth, scornful (as we shall see) of their life within a vulgar and dirty world of commercial transaction:

> For Books are not absolutely dead things, but doe contain a potencie of life in them to be as active as that soule was whose progeny they are; nay they do preserve as in a violl the purest efficacie and extraction of that living intellect that bred them. I know they are as lively, and as vigorously productive, as those fabulous Dragons teeth; and being sown up and down, may chance to spring up armed men. (492)

This famous spiritualization of the book that opens *Areopagitica* extends a number of the decorporealizing themes that underlay considerations of the book in the seventeenth century. Visible here, for instance, is Bacon's notion that books "cast their seeds into the minds of others"; like Bacon, Milton attempts to explain how books can erase the disparity between the material and the spiritual, can, as apparently simple, inanimate objects, dead things, nonetheless represent the "soule" and "living intellect." Markus Klinge sug-gests that Milton's contradictory imagery here portrays books as "incongru-ous composites, [which] as mediators contain elements both of the human and of the divine."[18] Milton employs a generative vocabulary to explain this mystery, metaphors of breeding and sowing establishing the book's ability to live through time, to "preserve" for future ages the "potencie of life" that moves between one generation and the next. Like Cavendish, Milton under-stands that the apparently "Airy Castles" represented by the book "are more Glorious, Stately, and Durable, than Tombs or Monuments of Marble."

Visible too is the vocabulary of censorship employed by both Tudor and Stuart governments. Incorporating the imagery of the very type of legislation he would oppose, Milton transforms into wonder and awe a legal language of condemnation, prohibition, and suspicion that feared the

> corrupt and pestilent teaching as hath of late secretly crept in by such printed books...So as now the purging of that which is noisome and hurtful cannot, without taking away some part of that being tolerable, be put in execution, being the books increased to an infinite number, and unknown diversities of titles and names, whereby specially to revoke, annul or condemn the same, the King's majesty is enforced to use his general prohibition, commandment, and proclamation.[19]

Milton's "armed men" who "spring up" from his classical landscape perfectly realize both the language of uncontrollable replication and fragmentation in these lines from Henry VIII's proclamation "Prohibiting Heretical Books," as well as the threat and danger that the "corrupt and pestilent" book represents. Milton uncovers the disquiet that occasioned such legislation, and even the violence that it both fears and promises, the necessity for "purging," for "condemnation," perhaps for "execution." Milton's armed men are "lively" and "vigorously productive," representative of a "fabulous" world of books and letters, but in a different context, that provided by governmental statute and regulation, they take on a very different demeanor.

Areopagitica adopts and revitalizes the conventional language that heralded the book's early-modern reception, which included great excitement as well as fear and trepidation. Nowhere is Milton more successful in doing this than in his exhortations to a populace that he imagines in the most heroic of postures: "Methinks I see in my mind a noble and puissant Nation rousing herself like a strong man after sleep, and shaking her invincible locks: Methinks I see her as an Eagle muing her mighty youth, and kindling her undazl'd eyes at the full midday beam" (557–58). Nothing could be further from the way in which royal proclamations concerned with controlling the book trade constructed the people and nation; in these legal documents books become the avatars of destruction and anarchy, those objects that would "stir and incense them [the people] to sedition and disobedience against their princes, sovereigns, and heads, as also to cause them to contemn and neglect all good laws, customs, and virtuous manners, to the final subversion and desolation of this noble realm."[20] The precipitous movement here from "disobedience" to "desolation," from the reading of books to the "subversion...of this noble realm," reveals both the terrible fear of and great power attributed to the book, which can overthrow all rank and hierarchy, all that custom and good government represent. Milton's vision in *Areopagitica*, on the other hand, remains fixed on truth and reason, and the way in which the book can not only help the individual reader participate in the divine task to "bring together every joynt and member" of the "virgin Truth" (549), but employ "the gift of reason to be his own chooser" (514). "Reason is but choosing," according to *Areopagitica*, which, with only a few important exceptions, banishes a vocabulary of punishment and enforcement, arbitrary authority and the compulsion of law, in order to imagine a state where "the great art lyes to discern in what the law is to bid restraint and punishment, and in what things perswasion only is to work" (527).[21] In Milton's thought the book becomes one of the primary tools through which such a nation can found and sustain itself.

The gender confusions apparent in Milton's attempt to rouse this "noble and puissant Nation" look back to the equivocations of *Lycidas*, although here, in the "Nation rousing herself like a strong man" and allusion to Samson "shaking her invincible locks," they seem even more bewildering and inexplicable. At the very height of his rhetorical powers, Milton appears unable to control or rationalize the gender implications of his vision of the heroic, which moves erratically between feminine pronouns and masculine images. These contradictions are epitomized in his famous image of Juno, which he uses to denigrate the practice of pre-publication book licensing: "Till then

Books were ever as freely admitted into the World as any other birth; the issue of the brain was no more stifl'd then the issue of the womb: no envious *Juno* sate cros-leg'd over the nativity of any mans intellectual off spring" (505). Here, as in the image of the nation and evocation of Samson, Milton shifts erratically from masculine to feminine, "the nativity of any mans intellectual offspring" inextricably linked to the female womb. The juxtaposition in this complex and startling passage between "the issue of the brain" and "the issue of the womb" reveals another attempt to depict and understand the book's ability to unite the physical and the intellectual through an image of reproduction; and it might even remind us of Cavendish's attempt in *Poems, and Fancies* to privilege female invention by the figurative link between "Spinning with the Fingers" and "Spinning with the braine." But while Milton represents male creativity through female generation, at the same time his female Juno functions as an emblem of intellectual frustration, her envy preventing male creativity from fulfilling itself. Female sexuality is at once a figure for male creativity, and that which prevents it from being born; it provides a figurative escape from the restraints of the merely corporeal and at the same time embodies the fleshly, physical world that would itself frustrate spiritual transcendence.

To the extent that the Stationers' Company remained central to governmental efforts to control the press in the 1643 ordinance—as they had through the century preceding the revolution—they, too, and the world of commerce that they exemplify, become another figure for the material world that would stand in the way of intellectual growth and fulfillment. Without attacking them by name, *Areopagitica* rails against the Stationers' Company's economic power and political might, arguing famously that "truth and understanding are not such wares as to be monopoliz'd and traded in by tickets and statutes, and standards. We must not think to make a staple commodity of all the knowledge in the Land, to mark and licence it like our broad cloath, and our wool packs" (535–36). Like female sexuality, the unclean world of commerce, monopolies, and licenses would prevent the intellectual flowering that Milton looks for in the new political order his prose wants to call into being. Milton refuses to locate the book in the economic world of the commodity; it cannot be a mere object, one of the dead things like broad cloth or wool, which are antithetical to the spiritual transcendence that the book seeks to effect in its readers.

Markus Klinge argues that Milton's depiction of England as the triumphant eagle presents itself as an inspired vision—"Methinks I see in my mind"—through which the author claims for himself the role of a "poet–prophet": "by relating visions of the ideal, the poet-prophet can encourage and exhort the Commonwealth (and its people) not to forebear in their search for truth, and to continue in their striving toward this ideal...his function is not to suggest practical legislation, but to refine and civilize the minds of his readership."[22] In *Areopagitica* books provide the conduit between the poet–prophet and reader that makes this search for truth possible; Milton must reject a monopoly "most injurious to the writt'n labours and monuments of the dead" (535), for as living monuments books are fundamental to the establishment of a society's collective memory. In the lofty rhetoric of *Areopagitica*, Milton seeks to depict a world unlike that of John Weever, who mourns for a society that has allowed its monumental past to disappear and crumble; Milton, on the other hand, imagines a new political dispensation that can correct the abuses of England's royalist past and save the printed monuments that best preserve the dead for the living, that in some fashion preserve the dead in the living.

IV

Milton's "To John Rouse," the librarian of Oxford University, provides a portrait of what such a world might look like, although it does so in a fashion quite different from that of the deeply committed and civically engaged *Areopagitica*; in the process, it reveals some of the conflicts and contradictions that marked Milton's assumption of the public mantle of the poet–prophet. While *Areopagitica* apparently revels in Milton's immersion in the political and intellectual turmoil of England's mid-century crisis, "To John Rouse" suggests his discomfort with acting on the public stage and his desire to retreat to precincts more rarified. Milton's ode certainly acknowledges the terrible years of civil war, asking for some "god or god-begotten man" to "sweep away these accursed tumults among the citizens," some "deity…who will use the arrows of Apollo to transfix the foul birds whose claws menace us, and will drive the pest of Phineas far away from Pegasus' river."[23] Milton's poem is confident, witty, and even at times light-hearted, but it nonetheless registers the violence disfiguring England, and communicates the urgency of the nation's plight. Yet the poem rather quickly turns away from the political, religious, and military crises that beset the kingdom in order to consider how to reestablish the arts within a nation that has, during the years of civil war, found it necessary "to leave the Books in dust, / And oyl th' unused Armours rust." Countering the inevitable rejection and banishment of the arts that accompanies civil strife, Milton asserts the centrality of their cultivation: "What deity will summon our fostering studies home and recall the Muses who have been left with hardly a retreat anywhere in all the confines of England?" (30–32). This poem never doubts the value of culture or the importance of those who labor in its precincts. The arts and their study nourish and sustain, particularly in times of crisis when Rouse's library alone guarantees the durability of cultural memory: "a new hope shines that you may avoid the depths of Lethe and be carried on soaring wing to the courts of Jupiter on high" (44–46).

The "you" addressed by Milton here is his "little book"—the *Poems of Mr. John Milton* published in 1645—which will avoid the oblivion threatened by "the depths of Lethe" precisely because Rouse's library will assure its survival. Milton had sent the book to Rouse after its publication, along with a collection of the eleven prose pamphlets that he had by that date published. The volume of poems, however, either stolen or lost, failed to negotiate the trip from London to Oxford, and Rouse had requested another copy. The manuscript of "To Rouse"—not apparently in Milton's hand—accompanied the replacement volume, strategically placed between the English and Latin poems.[24]

Milton structures his poem around a simple and stark contrast between the order, security, and serenity of Oxford and its library, and the disorder, uncertainty, and tumult of the rest of England. This ode represents the latter not simply through the civil war, but also in the commercial realm of print, commodity, and consumption that so disturbed him in *Areopagitica*. When Milton contemplates the fate of his lost "little book," he imagines it polluted by filth and the unclean hands of a despicable commerce: "whether some den or some dive imprisons you now, where perhaps you are scraped by the dirty, calloused hand of an illiterate dealer" (40–43). And when he imagines the future of the replacement volume, he emphasizes instead the "quiet rest" it will enjoy, "the alert protection of Rouse," and the exclusivity that marks the "blessed retreats" of Oxford, "where the insolent noise of the crowd never shall enter and the vulgar mob of readers shall forever be excluded" (78–80).

The choice of Latin, of course, reinforces the poem's distance from that "illiterate dealer"—who perhaps cannot even read, and, ignorant of letters or literature, certainly cannot appreciate the wares in which he deals—and the "vulgar mob of readers," just as its rigorously classical imagery and vocabulary emphasize its interest in a select, educated audience.[25] The poem addresses and imagines an ideal community of readers, rather than a contemporary, partisan, political audience; it contains no stirring declamations to a heroic readership. Oxford, for instance, had surrendered to Fairfax in June of the previous year when Charles had given himself up to the Scots. But the poem scrupulously avoids reference to the city's recent liberation; instead, it celebrates Oxford as "the nursery of the Thames—blue father Thames—where the limpid fountains of the Muses are found" (18–21). Milton doesn't use Oxford and the Thames to glorify parliamentary success, British nationalism, or a valiant citizenry but to evoke a timeless, classical world of learning and study.

Rouse and his library best represent for the poem the temporal triumph of this world divorced from the present strife of civil war. Creating such an ideal version of the library represents just one of many evasions in the poem, which in this case simply ignores the widespread destruction of the monastic libraries that accompanied the Reformation in England: Milton can assert the "timelessness" of Rouse's library only by disregarding its history, which, in its current form, began hardly a half century before Milton composed his ode. While the first university library at Oxford, for instance, founded by Thomas Cobham, bishop of Worcester, dates back to the fourteenth century, it had been almost entirely destroyed during the Dissolution of the Monasteries, and the modern history of the library began only in 1598, when Thomas Bodley offered in a letter to the vice chancellor to restore it to its former glory.[26]

During the first half of the seventeenth century, London contained a number of important private collections to which Milton probably had access through his father's and his own connections, most notably the Cottonian, established by Sir Robert Cotton in the decades preceding and following the turn of the century. But until the founding of the British Museum and Library in 1753, the Bodleian would have served as the equivalent of a national library, which here represents a timeless world of past greatness and future promise firmly divided from present demands and responsibilities, current political and martial crises. Milton's poem ends not with the rousing exhortations of *Areopagitica* that attempt to rally and construct a concerned and committed reading public, but with "our distant descendants and a more sensitive age...when envy has been buried, [and] a sane posterity will know what my deserts are" (81–86). Like Cavendish, Milton in this poem projects the proper appreciation of his work onto a distant future where a difficult and capricious present can be recast in a simpler and more sympathetic mode. Both writers reveal that the uncertainty generated by Jonson's commitment to an unknowable and perhaps untrustworthy contemporary reader can be relieved by the creation of an imaginary, prospective reader, upon whose futurity the author can inscribe whatever he or she desires.

The alienation from his own age that Milton articulates here, and his idealization of a future audience, objective, sensitive, and rational, depends on his certainty that Rouse's library, a "sacred sanctuary," can survive the present chaos and preserve Milton's writings. Milton celebrates Rouse as "warden" and "custodian" of "immortal works," the librarian's power realized in his collection's distance from present strife and ability to preserve the present for the future. "On Rouse" thus both acknowledges and ignores a present historical crisis, just as it both celebrates and denigrates the act of publication that in some measure occasioned it. But publication, birth into a contemporary world of conflict and filth, envy and detraction, remains a dirty and even shameful act in the poem, an attitude that Ann Baynes Coiro has demonstrated characterizes the entire volume:

> public exposure of the private cabinet was, for Milton, a political act, one still further complicated by money and the marketplace—forces that politically, socially, and intellectually defined the public...The political act that the *Poems* of 1645 performs is the choice, at last, to let go of class privacy and turn to openness.[27]

"To Rouse" suggests that Milton's "turn to openness," his willingness to enter the world of print and the public exposure it entailed, depended on a calculus that opposed marketplace to library, public to archive, present notoriety to future memory.

These simple binaries suggest the limited nature of the accommodation that Milton reached with his contradictory desires early in his public career. It depends on what Peter Burke has described as "the traditional view of the relation between history and memory" in which "the historian's function is to be a 'rememberer,' the custodian of the memory of public events."[28] Such a formulation assumes an ideal correspondence between history and memory, the custodian assuring the survival of an objective record for an appreciative future that, according to the ode, "will render a more nearly just judgment of things out of its unprejudiced heart" (83–84). The way in which "To Rouse" honors the archivist and his archive, the institution that it insists can alone preserve memory and truth, leads to what Eric Hobsbawm has called "a curious, but understandable paradox: modern nations and all their impedimenta generally claim to be the opposite of constituted, namely human communities so 'natural' as to require no definition other than self-assertion"; as Frances Dolan more bluntly insists, "what one finds in whatever 'archive' survives is rumor, disputation, missing documents, contested authority."[29]

Milton's ode, however, staunchly refuses to recognize the constructed nature of cultural and national history, and the doubts this raises about the ideal system it erects. The poem's concluding emphasis on a just posterity that will properly judge the poet arises out of its recognition of the controversy that he now arouses. Milton needs posterity precisely because in the present his just desserts are not recognized. Indeed, the lost book that occasioned the poem suggests the fragility of institutional memory, the vagaries and mere accidents that can effect and transform the relationship between history and memory. In "To Rouse," Milton wants to pretend that Rouse's Oxford library can guarantee his published works a secure future, a timeless moment within which an objective audience will recognize and applaud the unambiguous truth of his oeuvre. But the poem can maintain such a fiction only by ignoring the occasion of its own composition, the complex political realities that condition its reception, the tumultuous history of the library as an institution, and even Milton's own intimate relationship to a print trade that he here affects to disdain. The conception of collective memory articulated in "To Rouse" remains too simplistic to illuminate the political uncertainty it recognizes, the cultural labor it celebrates too limited to contribute to the healing of the nation's wounds.

V

Published in Latin in 1654, Milton's *A Second Defence of the English People* would seem to have little in common with "To Rouse" except for their shared language. The latter originates as a private, manuscript communication to a sympathetic individual, generated by an insignificant, personal accident; the former, on the other hand, represents a very public response to a national challenge, designed and commissioned for a large and important European audience as a justification for a government, a people, a nation. Yet both works are occasioned by a book—the loss of Milton's *Poems* in the first instance, and the publication of the anonymous *Regii sanguinis clamor ad coelum adversus parricidas Anglicanos* in the second—and both seek, among other issues, to understand the place of the book in history, to contemplate the role a writer of books might play in a moment of national drama and crisis. In *A Second Defence*, Milton transforms the general and archetypal moment of choice imagined by Marvell—when "the forward Youth" must leave his poetry and abandon books for armor—into the personal recollection of, and justification for his own conduct at the outbreak of civil war.

Milton's extended autobiography, one of the most remarkable features of *A Second Defence*, illuminates Marea Teski's view of memory as a "culturally specific field, a meeting ground between individual and culture... It is a dialogue with limitations between cultural templates and individual and group experiences and interpretations. In this view, memory is neither a cultural given nor an individual creation, but something between the two."[30] Milton's memories of his own behavior during the years 1641–1643, and the narrative he constructs from it, constitute an alternative to the "template" contained in the opening lines of "An Horatian Ode"; in *A Second Defence*, Milton fashions a commitment to cultural labor grounded on his conviction that the creation and preservation of a society's memory depends on the writer rather than the soldier.

From the opening, Milton's presentation of self in relationship to national history struggles against the glorification of martial youth. Milton's initial celebration of a people who have "put slavery to flight" is immediately followed by his admission that he played no part in that military success: "Although I claim for myself no share in this glory, yet it is easy to defend myself from the charge of timidity or cowardice, should such a charge be leveled. For I did not avoid the toils and dangers of military service without rendering to my fellow citizens another kind of service that was much more useful and no less perilous" (552). Answering a "charge" not actually made and formulating that answer as a confession suggest Milton's defensiveness here, and the normative power possessed by the cultural stereotypes visible in Marvell's evocation of "forward Youth."

Milton must assure both reader and self that he has undertaken tasks "much more useful and no less perilous," for he recognizes that times of national crisis inevitably subordinate cultural to military prowess; throughout *A Second Defence* Milton shows himself extraordinarily sensitive to his failure to "share in this [military] glory." Milton's articulation of his own form of "service" suggests again his discomfit in the face of cultural maxims that subordinate the pen to the sword: "I concluded that if God wished those men to achieve such noble deeds, He also wished that there be other men by whom these deeds, once done, might be worthily praised and extolled, and that truth defended by arms be also defended by reason—the only defence truly appropriate to man" (553). In distinguishing between the achievement of "noble deeds" and their praise, Milton creates a role for himself that, in reminding us of the conventional superiority of the mind over the body, can subvert the intense pressure to subordinate the cultural to the military in times of public need. What elevates "man" in the creation is not physical superiority, but the mind, "reason," and therefore the "truly appropriate" response to crisis is the intellectual rather than the military. Milton's soaring rhetoric here attempts to convert defensiveness into confidence, lack into plenitude.

In *A Second Defence*, Milton struggles to redefine masculinity, to dignify cultural and intellectual labor by insisting that "he alone is to be called great who either performs or teaches or worthily records great things" (601). Praising and recording become as important as performance, the deed itself not sufficient to establish its own preeminence or permanence. Such a formulation suggests how intricated teaching, performing, and recording have become in Milton's thought. Like Marvell at the conclusion of his "Horatian Ode," Milton suggests the inability of action and force to escape their own limitations and the ravages of time; only by being joined to the works of reason can they fulfill their true potential and become successfully incorporated in a society's collective memory.

Milton designed his self-portrait in *A Second Defence* to ratify the work's celebration of cultural achievement, for when he recounts his reactions to "the sad tidings of civil war from England [that] summoned me back" from his European travels, he never suggests that he contemplated abandoning books for armor. Although he left Europe because "I thought it base that I should travel abroad at my ease for the cultivation of my mind, while my fellow-citizens at home were fighting for liberty" (619), upon his return he "blissfully enough, devoted myself to my interrupted studies." In seeking "a place to become established" (621), Milton locates himself firmly among his books, his "talents and all my active powers" expressing themselves publicly for the first time when "I addressed to a certain friend two books on the reformation of the English church" (622).

Milton's memory of these "upset and tumultuous times" (621), and the narrative he constructs about his response to them, turns on his commitment to "active virtue" and its achievement by an intellectual and a writer. For all of his ambivalence toward the dirty world of publication that *Areopagitica* and "To Rouse" reveal, *A Second Defence* recognizes and insists upon the writer's necessary participation in that world, for publication alone allows an author a significant role in the historical moment. Here Milton suggests that recording is a mode of performance, the writer an active participant in history rather than simply a passive auditor.

Milton's autobiography strives to present a man assured of his intellectual mastery, one who recognizes the centrality of his cultural mission, and who stands poised to intervene in the processes of history at precisely the right moment. Achieving a life in the collective memory is never a matter of simply acting, whether one is a military man or a writer: "I had learned to hold my peace, I had mastered the art of not writing...for it was not fame, but the opportune moment for each thing that I awaited" (608). As in *Lycidas*, mere fame remains in itself insufficient for the poet committed to his craft, which here Milton implies is not simply to respond to a history already made, but to make history. In *A Second Defence*, Milton's celebration of authorship depends on his recognition that the "art of writing" doesn't simply keep collective memories alive, but generates the narratives that allow a society to transform those memories into a coherent and meaningful history. Milton ratifies the values exemplified by his autobiography in his brief biography of Cromwell, where he presents Cromwell's soldiership not primarily as a military virtue, but as one grounded in self-discipline and knowledge: "he was a soldier well-versed in self-knowledge, and whatever enemy lay within—vain hopes, fears, desires—he had either previously destroyed within himself or had long since reduced to subjection" (667–68). Milton's own victories over self suggest that he too shares in the rare soldiership that distinguishes Cromwell.

Indeed, when it comes time to recount Cromwell's strictly military victories, Milton metaphorically equates his own task with that of the man he would praise: "Such deeds require the grand scope of a true history, a second battlefield, so to speak, on which they may be recounted, and a space for narration equal to the deeds themselves" (668). Milton fights on this "second battlefield," the achievement of a "true history"—one that will live in and through time—as rare, valuable, and hard-fought as those won through blood and arms. Milton designed *A Second Defence* to create this "space for narration," to forge its equality with the deeds of illustrious men, to link narration and memory so that the writer alone possesses the keys to "true history" and time. As the sociologist Michael Schudson has written, "to pass on a version of the past, the past must be encapsulated into some sort of cultural form, and generally this is a narrative, a story...Reports of the past observe certain rules and conventions of narrative."[31] In *A Second Defence*, Milton attempts to change those rules and compose a new narrative of heroic action, one that replaces military with intellectual glory.

I don't mean to suggest that in *A Second Defence* Milton repudiates violence or denigrates the military. He rehearses Cromwell's victories over the Royalists, the Irish, and the Scots, celebrates Fairfax as a modern Scipio Africanus, and evokes the courage of Overton at "the unforgettable Battle of Marston Moor...amid dense slaughter on both sides" (676). As Michael Lieb insists in *Milton and the Culture of Violence* (1994), Milton participates in "a sparagmatic mentality" in which "destructive violence has the potential for becoming generative violence."[32] Indeed, throughout *A Second Defence*, Milton employs metaphors that allow him to appropriate military prowess for intellectual endeavors: "I have not borne arms for liberty merely on my own doorstep, but have also wielded them so far afield" (684).

Milton particularly frames the presentation of his blindness within a martial context, issues of fame and obscurity, civic obligation and cultural memory, understood through a succession of military metaphors. Dramatizing himself as a latter-day Achilles, Milton converts that warrior's choice between long life and immortality into this writer's choice between sight and duty: "Either I must necessarily endure the loss of my eyes, or I must abandon my most solemn duty." Milton sacrifices his sight just as Achilles sacrificed his life, and while Milton recognizes that he was "offered a greater good at the price of a smaller evil," he nonetheless pointedly disparages the classical hero's choice of mere fame: "As duty is of itself more substantial than glory, so it ought to be for every man more desirable and illustrious" (588).

The conclusion of *A Second Defence* thus represents a ringing defense not only of England, but of the rare individual "who could rightly counsel, encourage, and inspire, who could honor both the noble deeds and those who had done them, and make both deeds and doers illustrious with praises that will never die" (685–86). England's place in history, its triumph over time, depends on the cultural labor of the writer who can alone secure the nation's place and identity in the collective memory. Bearing witness becomes central to *A Second Defence*, where England's historical triumph depends on the cultural achievement of its spokesman and narrator: "I have borne witness, I might almost say I have erected a monument that will not soon pass away" (685). Milton's movement from bearing witness to erecting a monument reveals the intricate relationship between memory and history, the process by which the latter converts the narratives of the former into institutionalized fact. Milton here captures the complexity of the writer's task, its curious mixture of the passive and the active, the way authorship both preserves history and memory while at the same time transforming the latter into the former. He also reveals the way in which the monumentality he seeks memorializes both the country he would celebrate and himself. Visible here is both the humility of the individual who seeks to incorporate himself in the whole, to become an anonymous voice within the larger choir, and the pride of an author who would secure his own place in history and without whose voice that history could never even be written.

VI

Milton's rhetoric in *A Second Defence* certainly betrays a significant measure of doubt and uncertainty, revealing the tensions that problematize his relationship to the revolution he celebrates and the nation he would vindicate. His defensiveness about both his military inactivity and his blindness suggest some of the difficulties raised by his very public role as England's spokesman and defender. Yet the work's conversion of loss into triumph does not seem to mark a particularly difficult passage. Whatever doubts Milton possessed about himself in 1654, or harbored about the direction of the Cromwellian settlement, for the most part *A Second Defence* swaggers with confidence and even arrogance. When, near the conclusion, Milton compares himself to an epic poet, proud "to have celebrated at least one heroic achievement of my countrymen" (685), he reveals his conviction that in this prose work at least he is not writing with his left hand. *A Second Defence* attempts to create history on a grand scale, its "space for narration" rivaling the classical epics in its fulfillment of civic duty and aspirations to national celebration and cultural preeminence. *A Second Defence* emphatically presents itself as history written by a victor, its prose and rhetoric secure in its triumph over its enemies, time, and memory.

When that certainty gives way, as in *The Readie and Easie Way*, for example— published early in the year of Charles II's Restoration and triumphant return to England—one can glimpse the anguish that accompanied the recognition that history might belong to Milton's enemies. His pride in *A Second*

Defence, which in *The Readie and Easie Way* he designates as "a written monument, likely to outlive detraction" (421), is converted into despair for a nation that has constructed only a "tower of *Babel*; and have left no memorial of thir work behinde them remaining, but in the common laughter of *Europ*" (423). As we have seen, the Tower of Babel figures in the introductory paratext to Cavendish's *Poems, and Fancies,* where it represents the anxieties of authorship, the tower's equivocal, monumental status emphasizing the disconcerting gap between ambition and its realization, genuine fame and mere infamy, linguistic mastery and a chaos of unintelligible tongues.

In Milton, the Tower possesses an even more powerful moral significance, for *Paradise Lost* links it to the demonic creation of Pandaemonium through the discovery by Nimrod and his "crew" of "a black bituminous gurge/Boils out from under ground, the mouth of Hell" (12: 41–42). With bricks formed from this discharge, they design their Tower specifically without regard for the ethical dimension of fame, concerned simply with the selfish and trivial desire to secure their names in mortal memory: "And get themselves a name, lest far disperst/In foreign Lands thir memory be lost,/Regardless whether good or evil fame" (12. 45–47). For Milton the Tower represents not just the "common laughter" of other men, but the disjunction between the divine and the mortal, for in *Paradise Lost* the "derision" occasioned by the Tower comes from heaven:

> Great laughter was in Heav'n
> And looking down, to see the hubbub strange
> And hear the din; thus was the building left
> Ridiculous, and the work Confusion nam'd. (12. 59–62)

As in *Lycidas,* the desire here for fame must finally be understood and evaluated by the disproportion between the earthly and the heavenly. Babel represents a memorial architecture without an ethical foundation, a human construction doomed to failure because it can only parody a divine understanding of those values that alone assure fame.

The reference to Babel in *The Readie and Easie Way,* and the way in which that Tower may supplant or repress Milton's own memorial structures, suggests the despondency with which Milton faced the failure of the republican experiment. On the one hand, in his fear of ridicule Milton reveals the bitter knowledge that the meaning of such monuments depends on a larger historical context determined by struggles for the control of political authority and cultural supremacy. The energy and power of *The Readie and Easie Way* stem from its unwilling recognition that Milton's cause might shortly lose those struggles, history and collective memory becoming the possessions of a royal power once defeated but now apparently triumphant. Republican England and its champion have become laughingstocks, Milton's carefully crafted prose, "a written monument" that once promised to conquer time and construct history, transformed into a babble of confusion and impotence, a site of despair, and occasion for the laughter and mockery of others.

On the other hand, the Tower also points to Milton's fear that the republican failure represents a divine judgment and indictment of the moral bankruptcy of the government for which he spoke and to which he was committed. The Plain of Shinar dominated by Babel, a ruined and degenerate world of "jangling noise" and "hideous gabble," is a potent symbol not simply for the loss of memorial hopes that must accompany a language that no longer communicates or possesses meaning, but for the ethical confusion and doubt that results from the apparent withdrawal of God's favor.

The volume containing *Paradise Regained* and *Samson Agonistes*, published a decade after the Restoration, engages and inhabits just such a desperate and blasted landscape—literally, in the first poem, where Jesus' battle with Satan takes place in the "pathless Desert" and "waste Wilderness" where temptation and trial often prove biblical virtue; and figuratively, in the dramatic poem, where the blind hero, "Eyeless in *Gaza*," must confront his existence, like republican England in *The Readie and Easie Way*, as "the scorn and gaze" of his enemies. The relationship between these two poems has long engaged critics, formal parallels and inversions, as well as linguistic echoes, signifying that their appearance in a single volume places them in a context of mutual critique, qualification, and amplification; interpretations of the one seem to depend, to at least some extent, on interpretations of the other. This has proven particularly true during the last two decades, when new historical modes of analysis have increasingly focused scholarly attention on the oppositional culture of the 1660s and 1670s, placing Milton within a range of Puritan experiences and nonconformist contexts that situate the models of behavior enacted by Jesus and Samson in alternative rather than necessarily oppositional relation to each other.[33]

Within the context of the issues raised by considerations of fame, history, and memorialization, the relationship between the two poems is indicated by the title of the volume, which firmly privileges *Paradise Regained* over *Samson Agonistes*: *Paradise Regain'd. A Poem. In IV Books. To which is added Samson Agonistes.* The former is presented not simply as the first but as the primary object of the volume, its genre and length tersely but accurately described; the latter, on the other hand, represents what is added, the supplement, a mere name given no substantial form. In terms of the marketing of the volume, such a title-page makes perfect sense. *Paradise Lost. A Poem Written in Ten Books* had been published four years earlier in 1667, and the heralding of the sequel is the most important task performed by the title-page of the 1671 volume. If either had been responsible for the composition of the title-page, the printer of the volume, probably John Macocke, or the publisher and bookseller, John Starkey, would have wanted to capitalize on both the celebrity and most recent poetic performance of their notorious author.[34]

Given the vagaries of the trade, however, we cannot know whose intentions the title-page represents. But even if Milton himself were responsible, I suspect that this hierarchical relationship between the two poems would still apply, although the grounds for that ranking would probably have shifted from the economic and commercial to the ethical and moral. The privilege accorded *Paradise Regained* in this context stems from its depiction of the relationship between "true glory and renown," and "false glory" and a mere "blaze of fame," a distinction developed repeatedly by Jesus in books three and four. *Paradise Regained* concerns itself with the divine and the ideal, presenting a drama in which "a man / Of female Seed" (1.150–51) emerges from his ordeal, "By proof th'undoubted Son of God" (1.11). Jesus' triumph in the poem is complete, his final knowledge of himself absolute, his achievement of immortal renown assured and transparent. Few critics nowadays would suggest that *Samson Agonistes* provides such certainties. Firmly fixed in the mortal, mundane human world, Samson, Dalila, Manoa, and the Chorus strive to discern the true lineaments of history, and their attempts to achieve memorial certainty are mocked and rebuked by the opacity of the theater within which they pursue their dreams of a second life in time.[35] The juxtaposition of *Paradise Regained* and *Samson Agonistes* does not pit "true glory and renown" against "false glory," but a divine world in which the former can be both fully realized and perfectly understood against a mortal world, obscure and impenetrable, in which distinguishing between the two frustrates the sincere but puny efforts of its human inhabitants.

Insofar as *Paradise Regained* depicts its protagonist as "one man" or "th' exalted man," Jesus certainly shares the frustration suffered by those with memorial aspirations in *Samson Agonistes*; like Samson, Jesus begins in a state of profound uncertainty, "Musing and much revolving in his breast, / How best the mighty work he might begin" (1.185–86). But his status as the "beloved Son," in whose face "glimpses of his Father's glory shine" (1.92–93), suggests the unique nature that will privilege his pursuit and understanding of how to best "Publish his Godlike office now mature" (1.188). John Rumrich has labeled the body of Jesus "Milton's *theanthropos*," reminding us that Jesus as "godman" participates in a classical mythological tradition concerned with union between the divine and the human.[36] Within such a pagan context, exemplified by figures such as Achilles and Hercules, the achievement of immortality remains always a primary concern, its centrality to the figure of the godman dramatized in that moment when the hero must explicitly and consciously choose between the two paths that lead in opposite directions, one to happiness, long life, and oblivion, the other to conflict, premature death, and an immortal second life in time.

Jesus' perfect achievement of that second life depends on the way in which his unique nature allows him typologically to complete and perfect the conception of fame articulated early in Milton's career by Phoebus Apollo in *Lycidas*. Lycidas' unseasonable death generates anxiety in Milton's early poem precisely because it may extinguish the memorial hopes that for the classical godman depend on his untimely and even premature death. This temporal juxtaposition between poetic and martial fame is part of Milton's life-long endeavor to rationalize the difference between the two and to provide a way to privilege the former. With Jesus at its center, however, *Paradise Regained* can securely relocate Apollo's understanding of fame in a Christian context, and its success in doing so helps to explain both the completeness of Jesus' triumph and, in the companion poem, the uncertainty of Samson's.[37] In *Paradise Regained* the reader is privy to the judgments of that "perfect witness" who alone can measure and reward fame, not Jove but "the Eternal Father," whose "Angelic Choirs" demonstrate the perfection of his judgment in their celebrations of Jesus at both the beginning and end of the poem. The Chorus in *Samson Agonistes* also attempts to render such judgments, but without unmediated access to "the most High" they remain a mere parody of their divine counterparts.

Both poems situate their protagonists before an audience: the action in *Paradise Regained* begins with God making a spectacle of Jesus' trial to Gabriel "and all Angels conversant on Earth" (1.131), while the Chorus of Danites observes Samson almost from the opening of *Samson Agonistes*, "bear[ing] thee witness" (239) long before his climactic spectacle in the "spacious Theater" of the Philistines. As types of actors, both Jesus and Samson suggest Donne's reading of 1 Corinthians 4:9, where he insists that "*Spectaculum sumus*, sayes the Apostle; *We are made a spectacle to men and angels*. The word is there *Theatrum*...And therefore let us be careful to play those parts well, which even the *Angels* desire to see well acted."[38] The victory "Anthems" and "Celestial Food" that greet Jesus' triumph leave no doubt about his success; but the "horrid spectacle" of Samson's simultane-ous triumph and self-slaughter cannot be so easily applauded, particularly by a Chorus absent from the dramatic poem's decisive moment and dependent on the Messenger as an "Eye-witness of what first or last was done" (1594). The Chorus's irrelevance at such a crucial moment exemplifies the difficulty of comprehending true fame in the earthly *Theatrum* of *Samson Agonistes*. Dependent on "broad rumor," the Chorus's final insistence that god has turned his "face" toward Samson and "Bore witness gloriously" (1749–52) can hardly be regarded as definitive.

The initial claim by Apollo in *Lycidas*—that "'Fame is no plant that grows on mortal soil'"—is powerfully affirmed by *Paradise Regained*, which culminates its opening invocation by insisting that it will celebrate a deed genuinely heroic although at the same time thoroughly obscure:

> to tell of deeds
> Above Heroic, though in *secret* done,
> And *unrecorded* left through many an Age,
> Worthy t' have not remain'd so long *unsung*.
>
> (1. 14–17; emphasis added)

Each of these three lines emphasizes that the most important action in human history, the recovery of Eden and defeat of "the Tempter," has remained throughout that history unremarked, although the obscurity of Jesus' achievement will now be reversed not only by the narrative voice—the "I" with which the poem begins—and the "great Proclaimer," who opens the action and plot of the poem, but by "the Father's voice," which publicly "pronounc'd [Jesus] his beloved Son" (1. 31–32). The poem opens, in short, with a dramatic juxtaposition between obscurity and fame, anonymity and glory, the unexpressed and invisible contrasted to that which must be heard and witnessed. The poem's invocation constructs a tension between a past silence and a present dramatic clamor in which song, proclamation, pronouncement, "a voice / More awful than the sound of Trumpet" (1. 18–19), a baptismal dove, and an "assembly fam'd" all attest to the glory, visibility, and public prominence of the trial that humankind will shortly witness.

After these first thirty-two lines, however, a stillness falls on earth, the extended duel between Satan and Jesus occurring "far from path or road of men" (1.322). Although the heavens twice will echo with "Celestial measures" and "Heavenly Anthems," on earth all remains still. While this drama may not be hidden from him, even the narrator vanishes, making only a brief reappearance at the beginning of book two. The powerful narrative "I," privy to secrets disclosed to no other mortal, exhibits the terrible temptation fame presents for the poet who claims divine inspiration for "my prompted Song, else mute." The singer who first brings this tale to human ears, the individual narrative voice whose repetition of "sung" and "sing" insists on the intimacy of his relation to that "Spirit" whose "prosperous wing" will "bear [him] through height or depth of nature's bounds" (1. 12–14), must himself disappear, his perfect witness in this poem proving itself in his invisibility. Having opened with a very public blaze of glory, the poem resolutely turns its back on its mortal audience. Jesus' triumph is "Set off to th'world" for only a moment, his true heroism and fame otherwise understood and appreciated only in heaven.

N.H. Keeble has emphasized the way in which Jesus "adheres to another model of renown: to be 'singularly good' (3.57) is to be singular, that is, alone, impoverished, marginal, neglected, 'Outlandish,' without the insignia of earthly success, fame, or glory." And Laura Lunger Knoppers has argued that *Paradise Regained* reappropriates "the arts and learning in service of a radical Protestant inwardness" that emphatically rejects both the civic pageantry that distinguished the court of Charles II, and the external shows of an imperial Papacy.[39] In the poem Jesus fully develops this conception of an unknown and even fugitive fame in book three, where he and Satan clash over the nature of empire, glory, and, predictably, martial virtue. Satan cannot understand why Jesus will "hide" his "Godlike Virtues, "Affecting private life, or more obscure" (3.21–22). Blinded and dazzled by the "glistering foil" of common fame, Satan proceeds to tempt Jesus with a catalog of great classical warriors, Alexander, Scipio, Pompey, and finally Caesar. Insofar as Satan comprehends Jesus as the "forward Youth" of Marvell's "Horatian Ode," here he can offer only the conventional path of military success; and Jesus has little difficulty in rejecting such "Conquerors, who leave behind / Nothing but ruin whereso'er they rove" (3.78–79), explicitly grounding "true applause" and "true glory" among the "few" who might merit God's approbation. The anonymity that for Satan describes only failure stands as one of the primary marks of memorial success for Jesus.

Paradise Regained thus presents a radical Christian reformulation of fame and the ethics of memorialization: anonymity becomes renown, obscurity replaces notoriety, while true fame asserts itself, in the words of God, "By Humiliation and strong Sufferance," for "weakness shall o'ercome Satanic strength" (1.161–62). Such a conception of fame necessarily indicts and debases the "martial equipage" of "the Parthian King" (3.299–305), and the "grandeur and majestic show" of Rome, but in book four it also calls into question the significance and authority of the intellectual and aesthetic virtues that Milton had previously presented as the genuinely heroic alternative to the "glistering foil" and "broad rumor" of war. In *Paradise Regained*, the "forward Youth" of Marvell's "Horatian Ode" suddenly finds his choice between Books and Armour irrelevant; neither proves sufficient to the challenges presented by the historical moment. Satan's response to Jesus' long denunciation of Athens demonstrates just how puzzling it is when neither "arms nor arts" provide a legitimate mode of memorial aspiration: "What dost thou in this World?" (4.372), he despairingly cries, his question indicative of just how hard it will be to appraise the nature of true fame, and to understand the relationship between memory and history, in the unredeemed world of *Samson Agonistes*, not only for the blind warrior but for a poet who longs "to tell of deeds / Above Heroic."

VII

In *A Second Defence*, Milton could confidently assert that it is "not blindness but the inability to endure blindness [that] is a source of misery" (584). In *Samson Agonistes*, the protagonist finds himself unable to endure his blindness precisely because it calls into question his place in history, and leads him to reflect on "restless thoughts" that "present / Times past, what once I was, and what am now" (19, 21–22). Samson's life in time reveals not triumph but defeat, his place in the collective memory lost to his enemies. Samson describes himself as his own "Sepulcher" (102), entombed within himself and unable to claim an active role in the national history that his birth seemed to promise.

Samson is tormented by the belief that God had chosen him for a special task, "some great work" that would live in memory, and the chorus articulates the wrenching disparity between this sense of election and his current plight:

> Nor do I name of men the common rout,
> That wand'ring loose about
> Grow up and perish, as the summer fly,
> Heads without name no more remember'd,
> But such as thou hast solemnly elect'd
> With gifts and graces eminently adorn'd
> To some great work, thy glory. (674–80)

Samson's shame stems from the possibility that he might now be numbered among "the common rout," those "heads without name" unable to claim a place in history, the collective memory that he once thought to construct now possessed utterly by his enemies. Not to be remembered, to be "loose" and unfixed in time, torments the man who expected to dominate the processes of history through heroic deeds.[40] Like Satan in *Paradise Regained*, Samson and the chorus apprehend anonymity as failure.

Dalila's appearance, however, shortly after the chorus' intervention here, reveals the inadequacy of their formulation that not to be remembered is to be forgotten. The argument between Samson and Dalila turns not on the simple binary between historical glory or marginalization, but on the cruelty of memorial processes that can bring fame to some and infamy to others; worse than erasure is ignominy. Their bitter debate focuses on the relationship of history to memory, and the way in which the socially constructed activity of remembering will doom one of them to historical obloquy or oblivion.

Like Samson—and Milton in *A Second Defence*—Dalila understands her choices and actions in terms of a national identity that can alone give them meaning, significance, and a genuine place in the collective memory. Solicited by "the Magistrates / And Princes of my country," "Adjur'd by all the bonds of civil Duty" (850–53), Dalila finds it impossible to resist the force of arguments that subordinate love to duty, personal satisfaction to public good. Placed in the mouth of Dalila, of course, such sentiments are meant to sound parodic, for Samson's sarcastic response affirms conventional early modern beliefs that women—subject to the authority of a husband rather than a country—were incapable of fully participating in the public sphere.[41] Samson dismisses Dalila as a hypocrite, a heathen, and a woman, but her rejoinder—"In argument with men a woman ever / Goes by the worse, whatever be her cause" (903–04)—illuminates and questions the gender biases that dictate his arguments. Dalila's insight may not be quite as powerful as the Wife of Bath's assertion that women suffer marginalization and erasure because men write history, but it shares in the Wife's bitter sense that male culture contains no legitimate place for women. At such a moment, Milton, like Chaucer, presents an ironic view of the gendered nature of narrative and cultural memory, and recognizes the ways in which women are normally excluded from or ridiculed by male history. While I would not go as far as Ann Baynes Coiro, who maintains that "it can be argued that Dalila is the voice of Milton the Author," Dalila's concern for a second life in cultural memory links her in fundamental ways to Samson, Milton, and Jesus in *Paradise Regained*.[42]

Samson fears, of course, that his own place in history has been lost, but Dalila reminds us that in *Samson Agonistes* women represent the truly dispossessed. Samson makes this all too clear when he threatens Dalila with a cultural history that will condemn her as an icon of female misdeeds: "to make thee memorable / Among illustrious women, faithful wives" (956–57). Dalila, in other words, will take her place in Jankyn's "book," her memory and cultural significance limited and defined by the ideology of an oppressor: "Tho redde he me how Sampson loste his heres: / Slepynge, his lemman kitte it with hir sheres; / Thurgh which treson loste he both his yen."[43] In many ways her plight is Samson's, and like him she struggles to secure a "space for narration" that will celebrate her place in her nation's heroic past:

> My name perhaps among the Circumcis'd
> In *Dan*, in *Judah*, and the bordering Tribes,
> To all Posterity may stand defam'd,
> With malediction mention'd, and the blot
> Of falsehood most unconjugal traduc't.
> But in my country where I most desire,
> In *Ekron*, *Gaza*, *Asdod*, and in *Gath*
> I shall be nam'd among the famousest
> Of Women, sung at solemn festivals,
> Living and dead recorded, who to save
> Her country from a fierce destroyer, chose
> Above the faith of wedlock bands, my tomb
> With odors visited and annual flowers. (975–78)

Dalila is not oblivious to the vulnerability of our lives in memory, for she understands that "Fame if not double-fac't is double-mouth'd, / And with contrary blast proclaims most deeds" (971–72); Dalila disdains the "glistering foil" and "broad rumor" of a vulgar fame. Thus her final speech here strives to distinguish between mere fame and complex memorial practices that can produce and protect a vital life in a society's collective memory. In her vision of the future, memory depends fundamentally on national integrity, political victory and defeat governing the life in time of competing civic fictions. Dalila satisfies herself that the infamous memory of her circulated among "the Circumcis'd" will be countered by her glorious memory "in my country where I most desire," songs, festivals, and "annual flowers" keeping her deeds and memory alive. Her vision of cultural practices emphasizes the involute and multilayered nature of the way in which communities generate and sustain the memories that knit them together. Dalila places her tomb at the center of acts of commemoration that emphasize change and performance; while her body will decay, cultural processes of formalization and ritualization will reinvigorate her memory and its symbolic value for Philistine society. Dalila leaves Milton's dramatic poem convinced that competing national histories assure her at least some measure of memorial power and justice: "I leave him to his lot, and like my own" (996).

Dalila's belief in her future vindication, and recognition of the constructed nature of social memory, reveals a tolerance and breadth of vision, a willingness to accept what Marea C. Teski and Jacob J. Climo have described as "a concept of negotiated memory, in which various interest groups living in a pluralistic present are aware of and tolerate their differences."[44] Manoa and the chorus, however, have little but contempt for the virtues of pluralism and forbearance, for the apocalyptic understanding of history that they articulate after Samson's destruction of the Philistines leaves no room for dissent or otherness. They describe an historical process in which the memorial practices of one people survive only at the expense of those of another. Competing histories, they suggest, can coexist for only so long, cultural and historical memory determined ultimately by the victors and the dominant ideology that underwrites their triumph. Manoa implicitly derides Dalila's hope that her "solemn festivals" and annual flowers can live along side the memorial practices of "the Circumcis'd," for her "tomb" will be silenced by the "Monument" he will build to Samson at "his Father's house":

> there will I build him
> A Monument, and plant it round with shade
> Of Laurel ever green, and branching Palm,
> With all his Trophies hung, and Acts enroll'd
> In copious Legend, or sweet Lyric Song.
> Thither shall all the valiant youth resort,
> And from his memory inflame thir breasts
> To matchless valor, and adventures high. (1734–40)

This "Monument," and not Dalila's "tomb," according to Manoa, determines history and memory. The narratives that preserve Samson's heroism— the "copious Legend" and "sweet Lyric Song"—will breed martial virtue in other young men, the "valiant youth" who attend his monument here much like the "forward Youth" of Marvell's "Horatian Ode." Samson's memory will live on in "thir Breasts," kept alive in the hearts of those young men who fulfill his military traditions.

But Samson has much to teach women as well:

> The Virgins also shall on feastful days
> Visit his Tomb with flowers, only bewailing
> His lot unfortunate in nuptial choice,
> From whence captivity and loss of eyes. (1741–44)

Samson's ascendancy depends not on Dalila's erasure but on her eternal infamy, for she becomes the object lesson of his tale, the "ideal" image of the perfidious and fallen woman. In the narratives constructed from Samson's life, Dalila lives on only as the woman who proves the necessity of male authority and female subjection:

> Therefore God's universal Law
> Gave to the man despotic power
> Over his female in due awe,
> Nor from that right to part an hour. (1053–56)

The monument built to Samson emphasizes not change, but permanence. It possesses a powerfully tutorial function, meant to enforce strict ideological lessons about gender roles, martial virtue, and sexual morality; and it insists that male domination of collective memory depends on the corresponding subordination of women, whose attempts to rewrite male models of heroism, fame, and memorialization must be silenced or held up to ridicule if men are to achieve their second lives in time.

Manoa's imaginary construction of Samson's monument reveals the tensions that frustrate Milton's attempts in *Samson Agonistes* to reconcile the disparities between military achievement and aesthetic, literary, and intellectual endeavor. The "Laurel ever green" with which Manoa's description begins refers, of course, to the poet's laurel crown, to the opening line of *Lycidas*, and to Samson's own attempts to recreate himself as a spiritual rather than a strictly military leader. Mary Ann Radzinowicz has made perhaps the strongest case for Samson's moral regeneration, arguing that in Samson, "Milton's strategy . . . to reconcile action with patience and good deeds with sound beliefs is the most complex he ever employed."[45] In memorializing Samson, the archetypal hero as a man of violence rather than words, Milton complicates the simpler polarities between the intellectual and military that he sets out in "To John Rouse" and *A Second Defence*.

Joseph Wittreich, however, delineates three different interpretive traditions concerning Samson that were available to Milton, the recuperative ideal sponsored by the Epistle to the Hebrews undermined by readings of the Book of Judges, Genesis, and Revelation.[46] While Manoa's vision of Samson's monument begins with the "shade / Of laurels ever green," it concludes by enforcing military and gender values that the poem has earlier questioned and revealed as inadequate. Manoa's description ends by reminding us of "captivity, and loss of eyes," the spiritual insight that should have replaced Samson's loss of physical sight displaced by what Stanley Fish describes as "a walled-in (monumental) fortress that refuses the dissolving touch of female power"; and what Dayton Haskin denigrates as an interpretative practice that rejects patience and freedom in favor of premature closure.[47]

This masculine, interpretative, and memorial sterility is only emphasized by the historical irony that unites and undermines both Samson's monument and Dalila's tomb. In *Samson Agonistes*, Milton demonstrates a profound awareness of the inevitable tensions that accompany competing representations and interpretations of the past. The juxtaposition of Samson's monument and Dalila's tomb represents the inevitably contestational nature of collective memory, and Milton's understanding that commemorative practices represent the constructed nature of national identity and collective memory. But historical victory belongs to neither Samson nor Dalila, nor either of their memorial sites. Samson brings ruin to Philistine society, when the destruction of "Thir choice nobility and flower" means that "the vulgar only scap'd" (1654 and 1659), the political, social, and intellectual leaders lost who, in this elite vision of cultural production, alone can create the images and narratives that determine social memory. Although Philistia ruled until the period of the Kings, Samson's apocalyptic act of destruction foreshadows both their eventual historical oblivion and the triumph of his version of Dalila's perfidy. At the same time, however, Milton and his readers knew that Samson's final act did not lead the Isrealite youth to rise up against their oppressors, and that it is Samson's own tribe of Dan that disappears from history. In *Paradise Regained*, Satan even tempts Jesus with the possibility of bringing "deliverance" to "those ten Tribes," although Jesus emphatically rejects them as communities "Who wrought their own captivity, fell off / From God to worship Calves," singling out for his contempt the "Unhumbl'd, unrepentant, unreform'd" tribes "Of *Bethel* and of *Dan*" (3.415–31). For all of their undeniable energy and power, neither Samson nor Dalila can finally dictate the judgments of posterity. An awful futility mocks their struggles, the memorials designed to guarantee their lives in memory powerless to determine the shape of history.

This powerlessness becomes even more disturbing when Hugh MacCallum reminds us that in *Samson Agonistes* "Milton is presenting a society in which the sacred texts are locked up in the ark of the covenant, and the past is kept alive primarily by oral tradition."[48] Milton finds particularly threatening a world in which memory is sundered from the written and dependent principally on oral tradition, and we can measure his unease more precisely by moving for a moment from a distant biblical past to the history of his own country. Milton concludes the first book of his *History of Britain* with a palpable sense of relief, pleased to have "travail'd through a Region of smooth or idle Dreams" and arrived "where day-light and truth meet us with a cleer dawn, representing to our view, though at a farr distance, true colors and shapes" (37). Milton rejoices to leave behind pre-Roman Britain, an age "either wholly unknown, or obscur'd and blemisht with Fables" (1), whose lack of written record makes it impossible for the judicious historian to determine the truth.

Britain before Rome, this world of "idle Dreams," of "story," "fiction," and "reputed Tales" (3) that the historian can neither confirm nor deny, disturbs Milton even as the reasons for its historical silence fascinate him, the opening of his *History* marked by intense speculation about the absence of "the monuments of more ancient civility." Did the original inhabitants of the island not possess the "use of Letters"? Was there a superstition forbidding them "to write thir memorable deeds"? Milton even wonders if those wise men "of best abilitie" had "forborn to write the Acts of thir own daies, while they beheld with a just loathing and disdain,... how below all History the persons and thir actions were" (1–2).

The dark, savage, and apocalyptic world of *Samson Agonistes* bears a compelling resemblance to the fantastic, prehistoric landscape of Britain before the coming of the Romans. From the perspective of seventeenth-century England, both are known primarily through "Legend" and "Fable," their monuments and memorials lost in the abyss of time. Milton, however, lives securely in a new dispensation, characterized in *Paradise Regained*, according to MacCallum, as a world in which " 'it is written' is a phrase of power and authority."[49] The authority of that written word belongs to Milton, whose juxtaposition of *Samson Agonistes* and *Paradise Regained* in his 1671 volume emphasizes the contrast between the heroism of the violent and destructive warrior and that of the "meek / Sung Victor" who disdains the "ostentation vain of fleshly arm / And fragile arms" (IV. 387–88).

But that juxtaposition suggests as well the fragility and vulnerability of our lives in history and memory, particularly for a poet who, in his two great epics, attempts to "see and tell / Of things invisible to mortal sight" (*Paradise Lost* 3.54–55); and "to tell of deeds / Above Heroic, though in secret done, / And unrecorded left through many an Age" (*Paradise Regained* 1.14 16). At such moments, Milton portrays himself as the privileged witness of both divine and human history, his sometimes shameful and belligerent claims for intellectual and literary priority over military achievement suggestive of the unique heroism he would claim. Milton is neither Samson nor Dalila, although he certainly shares their desires to achieve a heroic monumentality. But he shares as well their fears and uncertainties, and, near the end of his long literary and political career, recognizes more fully than either of his characters that neither participation in a collective, national identity, nor a final act of apocalyptic violence can assure one's survival in time, particularly when, like Milton, living under a government he despised and among a people who had betrayed their revolution, one has witnessed "with a just loathing and disdain,...how below all History the persons and thir actions were."

VIII

Milton's lifelong engagement with the subject of memorial continuity and survival is visible even in his first English publication, "On Shakespeare," which accompanied the Second Folio (1632) as "An Epitaph on the Admirable Dramatick Poet W. Shakespear." This sonnet explicitly presents itself as an act of memorialization that celebrates Shakespeare as the "Dear son of memory," and considers how a poet can create "a livelong Monument" to his literary art. Here the young Milton addresses issues concerning literary succession and change, cultural memory and its preservation in the face of death and decay. These concerns converge in the image of monumentality, an important conceit because the poem raises its questions about literary immortality in terms of which monument best represents a poet to, and saves a poet for the future; what type of monument bears witness to aesthetic achievement and preserves the living memory of the poet?

The poem begins, conventionally enough, by announcing its scorn for pompous memorials of "piled Stones" and "a Star-ypointing Pyramid," the vain architectural constructions represented at the end of Milton's career in the tomb of Dalila and monument of Samson. The poem dismisses such "weak witness" within its first six lines, moving on to the "livelong Monument" of "our wonder and astonishment" in lines seven through fourteen, where Milton asserts that a poet's life within individual readers represents the only true measure of literary immortality. Literature works on "each heart," which receives "deep impression" from "the leaves of thy unvalu'd Book." Cavendish, in contrast, situates memory in the brain, invariably concerned with the human mind when she strives to imagine posterity and memorial triumph: "Memory is a future Life; and so many Friends as

Remember me, so many Lives I have, indeed so many Brains as Remember me, so many Lives I have."[50] Milton, however, locates our triumph over time in the heart; this is the place where the dead inhabit the living and achieve their second lives in time. Milton's poem demonstrates this process of internalization in its shift of pronouns from "my Shakespeare" in line one to "our wonder and astonishment" in line seven. In the course of the poem, the narrator succeeds in submerging himself within an anonymous, general audience whose hearts have "deep impression took," his initial insistence in line one on his own individuality, on his "ownership" of the object of his tribute—"my Shakespear"—giving way to a collective narrative voice transformed by the experience of reading: "Then thou our fancy of itself bereaving,/Doth make us Marble with too much conceiving" (13–14).[51]

The publication of "On Shakespeare" as part of the Second Folio is crucial in terms of its memorial significance, for the power attributed to Shakespeare's book anticipates Milton's later celebration of books in *Areopagitica*. Milton's poem also anticipates, like Jonson's in his memorial contribution to Shakespeare's First Folio, the extraordinary impact these two books would have on the literary and cultural memory of England. Although neither Jonson nor Milton could have imagined that Shakespeare would eventually form the cornerstone of English literary history, with his first two folios achieving a canonical status unequaled by almost any other volumes written in English, both authors acknowledge his preeminence and actively contribute to its establishment with their tributes; indeed, the memorial convergence of Jonson, Milton, and Shakespeare must mark one of the most unique moments of canon formation in English literary history.

I conclude with Milton's early poem "On Shakespeare," because in the lifelong self-dialogue about fame, memory, and cultural immortality that Milton held with himself this process of internalization, the magical transformation of the human heart, became a foundational trope in his cultural and religious ideology. Milton's emphasis on the heart of each reader in "On Shakespeare," for instance, should remind us of Jesus in *Paradise Regained*, who twice insists that his ministry on earth will become manifest when "winning words...conquer willing hearts" (1.222), when the "Spirit of Truth" that he represents shall "dwell / In pious Hearts, an inward Oracle / To all truth requisite for men to know" (1.462–64). In contrast, the mere "blaze of fame" cannot penetrate the heart, cannot engender a living or animating presence in a "miscellanous rabble"; it can merely "live upon thir tongues, and be thir talk" (3.47 and 54).

Such formulations almost certainly take their shape from Paul's pronouncement in 2 Corinthians 3:3 that "Ye are our epistle written in our hearts, known and read of all men: Forasmuch as ye are manifestly declared to be the epistle of Christ ministered by us, written not with ink, but with the Spirit of the living God; not in tables of stone, but in fleshly tables of the heart." The replacement of ink by the Spirit, "tables of stone" with "fleshly tables of the heart," and the transformation of writing on the heart into a divine, living presence, forms the religious paradigm through which Milton came to understand the mystery of the book, the magic of its participation in the act of cultural transmission, and its conversion of the material into the intellectual. This spiritual power cannot be counterfeited and is certainly unavailable to the conventional monuments that people erect to memorialize their achievements. Manoa intends for Samson's "Monument" to ennoble "his [son's] memory," inflaming the breasts of "valiant youth...To matchless valor, and adventures high," but only the book can genuinely imitate Cadmus's "fabulous dragon's teeth" and fill our mortal world with "armed men."

This living presence of the book plays an important role in the climactic moments of books eleven and twelve of *Paradise Lost*, which are profoundly concerned with the form and content of postlapsarian memory and the transmission of human history. In the Garden, Adam fondly imagines, memory would have naturally inhered in the prelapsarian landscape, the presence of God memorialized by Adam in every pine and fountain where He "Stood visible" to man:

> So many grateful Altars I would rear
> Of grassy Turf, and pile up every Stone
> Of luster from the brook, in memory,
> Or monument to Ages. (11. 323–6)

Although Michael assures Adam that God dwells everywhere in his creation, even in what Adam calls "yonder nether World," His presence in the fallen world must now be read in "many a sign," no longer visible or clear to the eyes of mortal men. The perfect correspondence between memory, monument, and God that Adam envisions remains only an unrealized fantasy, fallen history characterized by humankind's repeated failures to remain true to God, "Justice and Temperence, Truth and Faith forgot" (11. 807). According to Michael, the long and dispiriting account of life within this fallen world of an invisible but all-seeing God will begin to achieve its spiritual denouncement only with the coming of Jesus, the Comforter

> who shall dwell
> His Spirit within them, and the Law of Faith
> Working through love, upon thir hearts shall write,
> To guide them in all truth. (12. 487–90)

Even then, of course, a corrupt and degenerate man will disregard and forget, taint and pervert "the sacred mysteries of Heav'n," and the truth will remain "only in those written Records pure, / Though not but by the Spirit understood." This truth can only be realized by "what the Spirit within / Shall on the heart engrave" (12. 509–524).

Divorced from this spiritual context in which God's Law is written on the heart, and only God's Book can represent "written Records pure," the books of man cannot but maintain an ambiguous relationship to truth and salvation. Throughout his life Milton reveals an intractable ambivalence to visual forms, his Puritanism making it difficult for him to overcome an iconoclastic distrust of the printed book that he most often articulates in his contempt for the dirty, commercial print trade that would pollute and commodify the spiritual and intellectual essence of the written word. Cavendish's unaffected and single-minded pursuit of fame thus has little in common with Milton's equivocal attempts to justify his attraction to "That last infirmity of Noble mind," her desire to fix either her name or works in cultural memory at a far remove from Milton's need to locate his works within a spiritual context defined in *Areopagitica* by the attempt to discover the "thousand peeces" of "the virgin Truth" and "bring together every joynt and member, and shall mould them into an immortall feature of lovelines and perfection" (549).

Throughout his life and career, Milton labors to establish the ways in which not heroic actions but the apparently simple acts of reading and writing can help achieve this monumental task that will be perfected only in "her Masters second comming." For Milton both reading and writing constitute dynamic processes, ones that work on the individual sensibility to excite the "wonder and astonishment" that can alone produce "a livelong Monument." Represented by images of sowing and reaping, by the "leaves" of a book, the activity of reading is one that maintains life, that achieves its own form of potency and progeny, that participates in the natural processes of life, growth, death, and rebirth. Books bear a living witness to Truth's work in ways that memorials of stone cannot.

The deeply allusive nature of Milton's "On Shakespeare," for instance, which looks to both Horace's Ode 3:30 and Shakespeare's sonnet 55, realizes this dynamic process of reading—and the active nature of collective memory that it represents—for the poem's meditation on monumentality proceeds through its understanding of how both earlier poets addressed the same subject. Milton holds a "conversation" with his illustrious predecessors that Fentress and Wickham regard as crucial to the distinction between textual and oral modes of memory: writing figures "memory in textual forms which evolve in ways quite unlike those of oral memory...It is this sense of texts 'talking' to texts that explains why the syntax of a legal document bears so little resemblance to the syntax of either speech or thought."[52] Although they use legal texts as their example, literary "documents" reveal similar textual echoes, the "living" presence of both Horace and Shakespeare in Milton's poem paradigmatic of the active nature of literary language and cultural memory, of the dynamic relationship between remembering and representation. Indeed, Cavendish's willful originality, her refusal to acknowledge either her literary predecessors or contemporaries, may account in some measure for her exclusion from the literary canon, for it exacerbates her tendency to speak only to herself, effectively removing her from any commerce with the living tradition of literary representation.

The nature of literary representation and cultural remembering was to be fundamentally altered by the printed book, whose mass production transformed the relationship between patron and author, author and reader, and the reader with his (and increasingly her) literary artifact. Milton's relationship to the book and the commercial, London print industry that produced it in the middle of the seventeenth century was, as we have seen, complex and ambivalent. Milton was certainly not unaware of, or immune to the immense cultural and political power possessed by ritual and theater, public displays and civic dramatizations.[53] *Samson Agonistes* in particular demonstrates a sophisticated awareness of how a people's collective memory depends on a complex and interrelated network of dramatic cultural rituals. The rival feasts and festivals, funereal and nuptial rites that define the confrontation between Samson and Dalila speak to the ways in which ritual performances generate and sustain a society's knowledge of the past. They remind us that "the orchestration of festivity," in the words of David Cressy, was an important part of the seventeenth-century English calendar, and essential to the struggle for memorial hegemony between competing political and social factions before, during, and after the Restoration.[54] Milton did compose a masque, describe a number of his prose works as speeches, and conceive of *Samson Agonistes* as a dramatic poem; as an historian, according to David Loewenstein, Milton even depicted history as a series of "competing spectacles and performances," aware not just of "the theatricality of history...[but of] his own active performance in the process."[55] Yet Milton never delivered his speeches or intended *Samson Agonistes* for the stage, the "space for narration" that he cultivated throughout his career resolutely determined by the printed and published word. Milton achieves his victories in that narrative space where textual mastery strives to establish cultural authority, the "space for narration" that he cultivated fundamental to the modern state and the dynamic collective memory that sustains it.

CHAPTER 3

"OH GRANT AN HONEST FAME, OR GRANT ME NONE!": THE ETHICS OF MEMORIALIZATION IN POPE'S ARCHIVES OF DULNESS

I

Unlike Milton, who suffered throughout his creative life from a terrible sense of belatedness, Pope was one of the most precocious of English poets, not simply finding a place in literary society while still a teenager and being celebrated as an author in his early twenties—as magisterial a work as *An Essay on Criticism* was published in his twenty-third year—but self-consciously experimenting with the drama of a poetic career from the moment he first thrust himself onto the London stage. Pope's wary and ambivalent conclusion to *The Temple of Fame*—"Unblemish'd let me live, or die unknown, / Oh grant an honest Fame, or grant me none!"[1]—seems to register an apprehension of danger and temptation remarkably similar to that found in Milton's declaration that "Fame is the last spur that the clear spirit doth raise / (That last infirmity of noble mind)," and it dramatizes Pope's incessant struggles as a literary careerist to avoid moral contamination. Yet Pope insists on the possibility of an authorial purity that Milton's lines emphatically deny: the desire for fame may be the *last*, or, in the example provided by the *Oxford English Dictionary*, the *only remaining* "infirmity of noble mind," but in Milton's rigorous formulation infirmity and nobility, like good and evil, cannot be separated: "Good and evil we know in the field of this World grow up together almost inseparably."[2] Pope, however, attempts to have his ethical cake and eat it too, to locate a privileged position from which moral deformity can be cast out and "an honest Fame" exemplified by the upright poet.

Pope's distance from Milton can also be measured by the very different paths each negotiated in order to define the "honest Fame" that would
allow them to claim literary immortality. Milton, as we have seen, invariably
described cultural achievement by distinguishing it from military success, the
humane arts displacing the martial by demonstrating the final inadequacy of
the soldier to achieve his conquest over time without the witness provided
by the writer. This dynamic between author and soldier, however, plays a
relatively insignificant role in Pope's poetry. His translation of Homer's *Iliad*
early in his career certainly placed military prowess at the center of his poetic
imagination for a time, his famous parody of Sarpedon's speech to Glaucus
in the five-canto revision of *The Rape of the Lock* a good example of how
nimbly he could move between a classical age that celebrated a male heroism
achieved through warfare and his own cosmopolitan, urban society in which
a professionalized army saw to the global expansion of the future empire
upon which the sun never set. Pope's practice of translation both created and
preserved a transnational cultural memory in which military virtue possessed
an important place.

Yet even in an early work such as *Windsor-Forest*, Pope subordinates the
spectacle of successful British military adventurism to the climactic moment
when a female monarch puts an end to bloodshed and violence: "great ANNA
said—Let Discord cease! / She said, the World obey'd, and all was *Peace*!
(327–28). In *The Temple of Fame* Pope may pay homage to Alexander and
Caesar, and acknowledge those "Heroes who thro' loud Alarms / In bloody
Fields pursu'd Renown in Arms" (149–50), but when lesser warriors crowd
Fame's throne seeking her blessing they receive, in a scene with no precise
parallel in Chaucer, only rebuke and historical erasure rather than praise.
At work here is not simply the absence of an equivalent in Pope's historical
imagination for the battles of the English civil war that played such a forma-
tive role in Milton's understanding of heroic achievement, but Pope's Roman
Catholicism and physical infirmity, his status as both a despised religious
minority and physical cripple, that effectively removed him from a world in
which military activity was ever a possibility.

Although critics have long recognized that Pope's distance from conventional society had a profound influence on his poetry, in the last two decades
commentators have focused in particular on how his Roman Catholicism and
deformity forced Pope, in the words of Catherine Ingrassia, "to use poetry
and textual production in a complicated compensatory strategy to overcome
his fears of social and sexual inadequacy and to fulfill (if only discursively)
his culture's construction of masculinity."[3] Given his religious and physical
"deformities," conventional military values hardly possessed any normative
value for Pope, whose attempts to define an honest Fame, and demonstrate
in his own person the heroism necessary to achieve it, inevitably led him to
experiment with varied, ambiguous, and unusual gender roles. The assumption of a conventional, masculine heroism was never a satisfactory option
for Pope, whose attempts in his twenties to adopt the carriage of a young
rake proved notoriously unsuccessful, and led to some of the most vicious

and demeaning attacks on the poet during his lifetime. Libertine culture's concern with celebrity and self-replication certainly explains Pope's youthful infatuation with its airs and poses, but Cibber's publication of *A Letter from Mr. Cibber to Mr. Pope*, and the illustrations that sprang from it, depicting a dwarfish, deformed, diminutive Pope plucked from the lap of a prostitute by a Cibber concerned to "save Homer," suggest just how untenable were Pope's attempts to portray himself through the familiar tropes of libertine self-assertion or martial valor.

In this chapter I will examine the way in which Pope's gender anxieties intersect with both his desire to achieve a permanent form of literary monumentality, and his involvement in the early-eighteenth-century print trade, a complex relationship in which a consummate professional writer invests tremendous energy and resources to deny his professional identity and traduce the emergence of a literary professionalism that brought him fame and wealth. Contemporary academic scholarship presents Alexander Pope not simply as the foremost poetic genius of his age, but as a Machiavellian businessman of formidable craft and vision who publicly derided the skills and energies that brought him success.[4] In the last two decades, scholarship concerned with the cultural and literary significance of Alexander Pope's life and work has increasingly portrayed him as a reluctant modern.[5] Temperamentally conservative, his face set rigidly against many of the cultural changes overtaking his society, Pope nonetheless reveals not only his fascination with what he ostensibly disdained, but his participation, however reluctant and sometimes unwitting, in a host of modern practices that he publicly reviled.[6]

For all of his business acumen and economic prosperity, the unprecedented transformations in the print trade that Pope had to negotiate, as well as the ironies that undermined his stance as a simple, unambitious amateur, generated great anxieties in the poet. However secure he may have been in his poetic abilities, and however much he may have dominated his commercial rivals, Pope reveals a genuine concern for how literary history would be written in the new age of the book, and memorials constructed that might succeed in representing a poet to posterity. In November of 1708, while anticipating the appearance of his first publication, *The Pastorals*, the virgin poet explains to Henry Cromwell, "That Poet were a happy Man who cou'd but obtain a Grant to preserve His [Fame] for Ninety nine Years; for those Names very rarely last so many Days, which are planted either in Jacob Tonson's, or the Ordinary of Newgate's, Miscellanies."[7] For all of his posturing before an older friend, Pope nonetheless reveals, in his association between collections of contemporary poets and sensational biographies of condemned criminals, publishing ventures both made profitable by the expanding book trade, a shrewd and cynical understanding of the relationship between modern poetry, financial profit, and enduring fame. The almost four decades that Pope spent planting and working that particular field only darkened his suspicions about modernity and literary history. As he expressed it to Warburton near the end of his career, "I hope Your Friendship to me will be then as well known, as my being an Author, & go down together to Posterity; I mean to as much of posterity as poor Moderns can reach to."[8]

Engaged from his earliest years by classical ideals of the literary vocation and its relationship to poetic immortality, Pope nonetheless recognized that a new age had rendered these inherited models unsustainable, and that his identity as both a deformed outsider and "poor Modern" undermined his ability to emulate them. I will argue that Pope specifically fashioned *The Dunciad* as a response to his anxieties concerning masculinity and modernity and the unprecedented challenges presented by the new age of the book to a poet ambitious for "the second Life, he receives, from his *Memory*."[9] To do so I will concentrate on what Paul Connerton has described as "the storeroom of collective memory: museums, libraries, and academies," because these institutions are central to the narrative of cultural destruction portrayed in *The Dunciad*.[10]

In focusing particularly on the book and the library, I want to historicize the poem, situating it more precisely in its specific intellectual milieu, while at the same time locating it within the larger project of this book, the formation and evolution of a particularly modern conception of memory. David McKitterick establishes the dimensions of the former when he argues that the "essentials of modern book collecting" were established in England during the years 1660 and 1753, between the foundation of the Royal Society and the passage of the British Museum Act.[11] According to Raymond Irwin, the decades following the Restoration were crucial to the development of the English library: both the rapid accumulation of printed books and pamphlets in private collections, as well as "the impulse given by the accessibility of these collections and by the more scientific approach of the new age, to carry out systematic research and to analyse and collate the wealth of material now for the first time available to the student," transformed the idea of the library and the principles directing its use and organization.[12] Composed during the last quarter of this century-long process, *The Dunciad* reveals Pope's powerful ambivalence toward the "storehouse" and "archive" as the sites of a new collective memory. The poem represents an anguished protest against the breakdown in traditional structures of memory, a bitter condemnation of the feminization of elite culture, and a sustained critique of the new (or newly redesigned) institutions—library, museum, and academy—that print culture helped to erect in their place. At the same time, Pope's successive revisions of the poem transform it into the very type of textual archive that he despises, for it memorializes and preserves the print industry that Pope both vilifies and exploits.

The monumental aspirations of Pope's poem, which attempts to immortalize the poet even as it portrays the apocalyptic extermination of literate civilization, reveal the involute and problematic nature of our modern memory, its paradoxical richness and poverty. *The Dunciad* moves from the triumph of memory to its defeat, from the promise of a plenitude that can frustrate the encroachments of modernity to a recapitulation of modernity's most deplorable excesses. In *The Dunciad* Pope both contemplates and duplicates the effects of the first two-and-a-half centuries of a print revolution whose innovations in the storage and transmission of knowledge fundamentally altered the nature of collective memory. The print trade so carefully depicted and obsessively archived by the poem and its elaborate critical apparatus represents the paralyzing modern condition in which the creation and preservation of a collective memory signals but a new bondage to a past from which we can never escape.

II

Before considering *The Dunciad*, I want to examine briefly Pope's *Temple of Fame*, for this early treatment of "hostile Time" and "Fame's high Temple"—published when Pope was twenty-seven and written when he was perhaps only twenty-two[13]—indicates how the young man conceived of the processes of memorialization that would concern him as a poet, and suggests just how far his youthful, classical understanding of fame, derived to some extent from the medieval poem he imitated, would be transformed by his experiences within the busy London marketplace that would in starkly material ways mediate his desires for literary renown.

The bulk of the poem consists of two central sections of almost equal length, the first a description of Fame's temple and the worthies celebrated in it, the second a depiction of Fame on her throne and the jostling crowds eager to receive her favor. In this fashion the poem illuminates classical and medieval understandings of fame's dual nature, the first section paying tribute to a goddess who can grant a reputation "ever new, nor subject to Decays" (51), the second recognizing that Fame's "blind Sister, fickle Fortune reigns, / And undiscerning, scatters Crowns and Chains" (296–97). When the three shorter sections of the poem—the opening depiction of the landscape surrounding the temple, the description of the Mansion of Rumour, and the closing dialogue with the poet/narrator—are considered, the weight of the poem falls squarely on the second of the two central sections, privileging the cynical conception of Fame that it emphasizes. In this Pope clearly follows his Chaucerian model: although Chaucer's unfinished *House of Fame* lacks both the symmetry and narrative closure of Pope's much shorter poem, it nonetheless provides a wary and distrustful portrait of the relationship between Fame and Fortune.[14]

In Pope, just as in Chaucer, Fame, Fortune, and Rumour appear to work in concert, distinguished one from the other, of course, but nonetheless generative of a similar noise, uncertainty, and ethical confusion:

> And all the Nations, summon'd at the Call,
> From diff'rent Quarters fill the crowded Hall:
> Of various Tongues the mingled Sounds were heard;
> In various Garbs promiscuous Throngs appear'd.
> <div style="text-align:right">(<i>The Temple of Fame</i>, 277–81)</div>

Given the relationship between the three deities who control The *Temple of Fame*, the ease with which Pope would later fold the apparently assured classical model of Fame into the iconography of *The Dunciad* should not surprise us, the architecture and choreography of *The Temple of Fame* transformed seamlessly through inversion or imitation into the Cave of Poverty and Poetry and court levee before the Throne of Dulness.[15] Fame's high Temple appears indestructible, but not even fifteen years would pass before in Pope's imagination Dulness replaces Fame on the "Imperial Seat" of cultural empire, both personifications avatars of the Tower of Babel that so disturbed Cavendish and Milton when they contemplated the relationship between memory, poetry, and cultural production.

The problematic nature of Pope's own relationship to the literary and cultural marketplace marks the conclusion to *The Temple of Fame*, where the narrator of the dream-vision confronts the blandishments of an inseparable "Truth and Lye" that "whisper'd in my Ear." This echo of Satan's first attempt on Eve in *Paradise Lost* suggests the extent of the temptation "rash Ambition" presents to the "fond Youth" who admits to being "not void of Hopes" for a "second Life in others' Breath" (501 and 505). Chaucer's original poem suggests little of the seductive power presented to Pope's dreamer by his vision, for Geffrey is confronted not by a satanic tempter but by a fellow bystander, whose simple question "Artow come hider to han fame?" elicits only a brief declaration of authorial independence. Pope's narrator, on the other hand, feels called upon to deliver an earnest, pious, grandiloquent speech that defines in detail what an honest Fame looks like, and how it can be distinguished from "the guilty Bays" that he scorns. Certainly the sentiments expressed here remained a staple in Pope's repertoire throughout his career, extended and refined in the early 1730s, for example, in *An Epistle to Dr. Arbuthnot*, where Fame is once more juxtaposed and subordinated to Virtue, and flattery "ev'n to Kings,...held a shame" (338).

In conventional satiric apologia such as *Arbuthnot*, where Pope could polish relentlessly his classical model of the Virgilian career, the power of these portraits of authorial virtue and incorruptibility cannot be denied.[16] But as guides to Pope's satiric practices and cultural authority in a work such as *The Dunciad*, they remain hopelessly insufficient. The youthful narrator in *The Temple of Fame* may proudly assert that "if no Basis bear my rising Name, / But the fall'n Ruins of Another's Fame: / Then teach me, Heaven! To scorn the guilty Bays" (519–21); but such a boast can only be undermined by the bitter and aggressive poet who spent over fifteen years reworking *The Dunciad* in order to traduce and abuse as many of his enemies as possible, the ruins of their fame the very foundation of his. Even at this early date in his career, Pope seems to recognize, even in his denial, that satire would be his métier, and that attacks on other poets would constitute a fundamental part of his authorial identity. Indeed, the failure of this version of poetic virtue in *The Temple of Fame* to explain Pope's own satiric practices can be demonstrated not only by looking back from the vantage point of the later poem, but in the way the portrait follows immediately from the narrator's recognition that "inseparable now, the Truth and Lye; / The strict

Companions are for ever join'd, / And this or that unmix'd, no Mortal e'er shall find" (494–96). Such an understanding of the impurity of earthly morality must call into question the simple ethical binaries that inform the narrator's easy distinctions between "Fame," "Folly," "Vice," and "Praise" in his concluding speech. The dream-vision dramatizes a mortal realm as ethically confused, uncertain, and difficult to interpret as that of Milton; the dreamer, on the other hand, insists that he can exemplify a moral purity and honest Fame unsullied by the "lust of Praise" or desire to follow "where Fortune leads the way." The dreamer apparently has not fully understood his own dream, articulating a poetic and cultural heroism at odds with the prophetic vision he has just received.

This cultural heroism, moreover, is gendered in ways that both reveal Pope's very conventional attitudes toward female achievement, and resemble the sexual politics of *The Dunciad*, where a cultural world populated almost entirely by men worships at the throne of a (perverse) female deity. It goes without saying that not a single woman finds a place within Fame's temple, the political, military, and cultural elites recognized by Pope, and his Chaucerian model, presented as exclusively male.[17] Pope himself reveals the gender proscriptions that underlie his literary aesthetics and ambitions in the epigram inscribed in the copy of the poem he presented to Martha Blount, "To a Lady with the Temple of Fame":

> What's Fame with Men, by Custom of the Nation,
> Is call'd in Women only Reputation:
> About them both why keep we such a pother?
> Part you with one, and I'll renounce the other.

Like Rochester in his famous song entitled "Womans Honour," Pope demonstrates how a male virtue is diminished and demeaned when applied to women. "Fame" in Pope's poem and "Honour" in Rochester's become mere "Reputation" in the former and "mean mistrustfull shame" in the latter, such transformations reminding us of Margaret Cavendish's unhappiness with how male society excludes women from the artistic and ethical endeavors that deserve a genuine place in cultural memory. Women are absent from Pope's poem precisely because they waste their time pursuing reputation rather than fame, just as their failure to achieve "reall Honour" in Rochester's poem stems from their concern with the reputation upheld by the false idols of pride and shame. For both Rochester and Pope this occasions a witty variation on a conventional poem of seduction, in which the gendered substitution of terms betrays the insignificance of reputation, revealed now as an arbitrary formulation of "Custom" in Pope's poem and "pride" in Rochester's. Both poems remain quite knowing and self-conscious about the gender games they play, and although Pope's amused offer to trade his fame for Martha Blount's virtue is hardly serious, it nonetheless demonstrates Pope's gendered understanding of literary immortality and memorial authority. Both poems provide commentaries on a society in which men actively strive to secure their fame through positive action, while women can only hope to preserve their precarious rank and status through negation.[18]

The gender inequalities on display in both *The Temple of Fame* and the epigram appear not quite as severe as those previously examined in *Lycidas*, where Milton represents women not simply as indifferent to artistic excellence, but as the very temptations that might disable male achievement. Indeed, Pope's own uncertain masculinity and position as a scorned outsider made him particularly sensitive to the needs and vulnerabilities of his female friends, and suggest that Valerie Rumbold correctly identifies as "one of the characteristic paradoxes of Pope's writing on Women, the combination of uncommon delicacy with all too common prejudice."[19] This critic has shown that Pope provided artistic encouragement to a number of female poets, including Lady Mary Wortley Montagu (at least for a time), Judith Cowper, and Anne Finch, countess of Winchilsea; nonetheless, *The Temple of Fame* and the epigram it occasioned exemplify the casual male assumption that the memorial issues raised by the poem can have nothing to do with women, who are hardly even an afterthought in a world primarily concerned with "Th'Estate which Wits inherit after Death" (506).

Yet in both *The Temple of Fame* and *The Dunciad*, that estate can only be secured by pleasing, placating, or confronting a powerful female deity who dictates the processes and outcomes of literary memorialization from an unchallenged and apparently unassailable throne. Though women were themselves excluded from inheriting such estates, in the former poem Pope had no choice but to enthrone Fame and Fortune, both his classical and medieval models dictating their gender identity. In the latter work, however, Fame's transformation into Dulness, "The Mighty Mother," reveals Pope's own fantasies about the transmission of cultural memory, his greatest fears about his place in literary history projected onto personifications of female power, instability, and indifference.

III

Pope's attempts to confront the powers that in his imagination governed the disbursement of cultural immortality are evident in his concern for monuments and monumentality. Over the course of his career, Pope composed over two dozen epitaphs, the first, on John Lord Caryll, written in 1711 when he was twenty-three, the last, to Nicholas Rowe, probably written in 1743, the year before he died. In the late 1730s and early 1740s Pope even penned two for himself, both emphasizing his literary independence, and expressing his disdain for contemporary judgments of his life. A number of these epitaphs are comic, like the three devoted to John Hewet and Sarah Drew, the Stanton-Harcourt lovers killed by lightning, who represent "two poor Lovers, who had the mishap / Tho very chaste people, to die of a Clap." But many were occasioned by the death of prominent friends and reveal Pope's concern for how "this Marble" ("Epitaph. On John Lord Caryll"), or "this sad Shrine" ("Epitaph on Mr. Rowe"), or "The sacred Dust below" ("Epitaph. designed for Mr. Dryden's Monument") could secure for cultural, political, or ethical achievement a place in an enduring collective memory. As Philip Connell argues, Pope was "actively committed to a civic conception of monumental statuary,...as an ennobling public art ideally suited to the patriotic commemoration of virtue and genius."[20]

The obelisk that Pope built in his garden to memorialize his mother remains the most emphatic gesture of his desire to enshrine memory in stone or marble, while the careful cultivation of that Twickenham estate reveals his continuing commitment to give material form to his ideal aesthetic and ethical self-image.[21] But there can be little doubt that as a poet the creation of textual monuments represents Pope's most serious, determined, and characteristic mode for memorializing his own life. Both the 1717 and 1735 *Works* self-consciously present themselves as monuments to Pope the author, and James McLaverty has shown how in the former, a single volume produced when the author was yet in his twenties, Pope attempts to define his own canonical status: "The major, if not pervasive, theme of the volume is fame. This is a classical theme, but for Pope it had strong contemporary resonance: authorship was entering a new sphere of publicity and, from this point on, his concern was to exploit its potentialities while avoiding its dangers."[22]

The Dunciad embodies Pope's most ambitious and radical attempt to define and exploit this new conception of authorship. This work, appointed, in a letter to Swift, Pope's "Chef d'oeuvre,"[23] occupied the last two decades of his creative life and went through successive alterations that transformed it in ways that went far beyond those visible in *The Rape of the Lock*, for example, an early work that also underwent a significant refinement and enlargement. In the bizarre, fantastic, and multiform world of *The Dunciad*, which took shape over the fifteen-year period from 1728 through 1743, Pope redefines fame for the modern poet, removing it from the classical contexts provided by *The Temple of Fame* and 1717 *Works* and refashioning it in a form that might meet the challenges provided by the new commercial print industry within which his career flourished. In *The Dunciad* Pope attempts to create a poem and a book that can guarantee the triumph of his vision of the literary marketplace and secure his place in his society's collective memory.

It may seem perverse to talk of the triumph of memory in a poem that celebrates the power of Dulness, for "Wits have short Memories, and Dunces none" (4. 620). The cultural and historical oblivion to which *The Dunciad, in Four Books* inexorably moves depends on Dulness' successful appropriation of the resources and potential of the modern library, museum, and academy. The fourth book in particular contains a powerful and sustained critique of the eighteenth-century academy, in which the schoolmaster's ability to "hang one jingling padlock on the mind" (4. 162) relies to some extent on the trivialization of memory. When Busby boasts that "We ply the Memory, we load the brain" (4. 157), the note scoffs that "By obliging them [students] to get the classic poets by heart, [a teacher] furnishes them with endless matter for Conversation, and Verbal amusement for their whole lives." Here a bankrupt educational system undermines the classical heritage that it should sustain, reducing memory to a mere parlor trick.[24]

In the figures of Annius and Mummius, and the collectors of flowers and butterflies, book four also savages the private collections that led to the establishment throughout Europe of the great public museums during the eighteenth and nineteenth centuries. Even before 1683, when the "Museum Ashmoleanum" first opened its doors to the public, the term "museum" was evolving from its primary designation as a private, scholar's study or building dedicated to the pursuit of learning to its modern meaning as an "institution in which objects of historical, scientific, artistic, or cultural interest are preserved and exhibited."[25] For Pope, however, such miscellaneous and promiscuous objects reveal themselves not as treasure but excrement, a random collection of nasty, trivial, and meaningless oddities: "Each with some wond'rous gift approach'd the Pow'r, / A Nest, a Toad, a Fungus, or a Flow'r" (4. 399–400).[26]

In book one, Pope portrays even collections of books in such a light, the library of first Theobald, in the 1728 *Dunciad*, and then Cibber, in the 1743 version, mere conglomerations of "learned Lumber," "The Classics of an Age that heard of none." Collectors of books, Pope's note to line 120 in the 1729 *Dunciad Variorum* insists, base their libraries not on rational principles of selection and evaluation, but on "one of these three reasons . . . that they fitted the shelves, or were gilded for shew, or adorned with pictures." This, sadly, explains Cavendish's inclusion in both libraries, the care and attention she lavished on her volumes now but a mark of her poetic insignificance: "Here swells the shelf with Ogilby the great: / There, stamp'd with arms, Newcastle shines compleat" (1. 121–22). Pope's verse not only ridicules her aristocratic eminence—suggesting the disjunction between her social and poetic rank—but in his note describes her as a mere amateur, an enthusiastic poetaster "who busied herself in the ravishing delights of Poetry." This note to line 122 continues by mocking both her productivity and memorial aspirations: "leaving to posterity in print three *ample Volumes* of her studious endeavours. Winstanley, *ibid. Langbaine* reckons up eight Folio's of her Grace's; which were usually adorn'd with gilded Covers, and had her Coat of Arms upon them." Given her attentive cultivation of the library as an institution, the care with which she prepared presentation copies of her books, and her appreciation for the archival power of colleges and universities, this is not the library that Cavendish would have wanted to inhabit.

Historians of the book generally agree that in Britain the rise of modern book collecting and the establishment of the "new age of libraries" took place during the late seventeenth and early eighteenth centuries. By modern standards, medieval libraries, normally part of a cathedral or monastery, were extremely small, and even the establishment of English universities in the thirteenth century did not at first lead to larger library collections. Most of the Oxford colleges opened without formal libraries; New College, founded in 1380, was the first to begin life with a library of its own.[27] Only during

the Elizabethan period did systematic book collecting begin to create libraries of any appreciable size. Even the original Cottonian collection, whose
importance was discussed earlier, numbered only about one thousand volumes at the turn of the seventeenth century, and the famous libraries of
Robert Burton and John Donne numbered only a few thousand volumes.
But between the Restoration and the first decades of the eighteenth century,
much larger collections of books came into existence; numerous private
collections of books were established during these years—Pepys' among
them—and many scholarly working libraries as well. Even more significantly,
designs for public and national collections began to take serious shape. In
1694 Richard Bentley published his *Proposal for Building a Royal Library*,
while the first proposal for a national library was put forth in 1697; the
first union catalog of manuscripts in Britain was published in 1697–1698;
the first book clubs were organized in 1725; the first circulating library in
1726.[28] The foundation of an English national library did not take place
until the 1750s, but Pope's *Dunciad* registers the excitement occasioned by
the evolution of modern library science.

In both the 1728 *Dunciad* and the 1729 *Dunciad Variorum*, the
library emerges as one of the most powerful symbols of Dulness' triumph,
its corruption and eventual destruction by her minions a measure of her
approaching cultural hegemony. In book one, Pope introduces Theobald
"with all his books around, / Sinking from thought to thought, a vast
profound." Here, within this "Gothic Vatican," the hero of the poem
assembles his altar, prays for inspiration, and receives his first visit from
Dulness. The note to line 120 in the 1729 edition describes a "library
divided into two parts," containing both "polite learning," from which
Theobald steals his poetry, and what "the author calls solid Learning,
old bodies of Philosophy, old Commentators, old English Printers, or
old English Translations; all very voluminous, and fit to erect Altars to
Dulness." Age does not automatically confer cultural value, however, and
the "old" books housed in the hero's library efface cultural memory rather
than sustain it.

When Pope determined to replace Theobald with Cibber in the 1743
version of the poem, he revised extensively in order to provide his new hero
with a library suitable for a dramatist rather than a scholar. Indeed, critics
have complained that a library is hardly appropriate to the poem's new hero,
but Pope was loathe to abandon a cultural institution that since antiquity
had represented the progress of learning. The library, in fact, figures prominently in the parodic progress of Dulness contained in book three, where
the institution merely corrupted by the laureate in book one is now utterly
destroyed:

> Heav'ns! what a pyle? whole ages perish there:
> And one bright blaze turns Learning into air.
> Thence to the South extend thy gladden'd eyes;
> There rival flames with equal glory rise,

From shelves to shelves see greedy Vulcan roll,
And lick up all their Physick of the Soul. (69–74)

As the notes to the 1729 *Dunciad Variorum* reveal, Pope refers to two different book burnings here, the first committed by Chi Ho-am-ti, the emperor
of China who both built the Great Wall and "destroyed all the books and
learned men of that empire," the second by Caliph Omar I, who "caus'd
his General to burn the Ptolomaean library, on the gates of which was this
inscription, Medicina Animae, The Physick of the Soul." When the laureate
burns an altar of books in book one as a pious sacrifice to Dulness, Pope
does not ask the reader to lament the loss; these are volumes, "Redeem'd
from tapers and defrauded pyes," that deserve their fate. But the burning of
books and entire libraries in book three possesses a whole other meaning,
the destruction of a society's cultural heritage instrumental in Dulness' ability to preserve only "the dulness of the past," to create "A Lumberhouse of
Books in ev'ry head, / For ever reading, never to be read" (3. 186, 189–90).
As the note to these lines suggest, Dulness' servants represent in miniature the perversion of the cultural value of the library, for their "heads were
Libraries out of order."

The question of order within the modern library, what came to be
called "library economy," was almost exactly a century old when Pope
published the first version of his *Dunciad*, Naudé's 1627 *Advis pour
dresser une bibliothèque*, as we have seen, establishing in France some of
the basic principles of modern library science. Naudé succeeded in putting
his ideas into practice when he became Mazarin's librarian in 1643 and
went on to assemble, and open to the public, the collection that became
the Bibliothèque Mazarine. In England, John Drury, the deputy director
of the King's Library in London, had published *The Reformed Librarie-
Keeper* in 1650, arguing that

> A fair Librarie, is not onely an ornament and credit to the place where it is; but
> an useful commoditie by it self to the publick; yet in effect it is no more than
> a dead Bodie as it is now constituted, in comparison of what it might bee, if it
> were animated with a publick Spirit to keep and use it, and ordered as it might
> bee for publick service.

Drury proposed that the fundamental principles of that order include "a
Catalogue, of the Treasurie committed unto his [the keeper's] charge,"
a ranking of books "in an order most easie and obvious to be found," and
a system in which "all the Books are divided into their subjectam materiam
whereof they Treat."[29] Drury's unhappiness with current library practices,
his sense that in 1650 the English library represents little more than "a
dead Bodie," cannot diminish his enthusiasm for the triumphant future
he envisions, in which a properly regulated library will welcome and serve
the public, the new library science an essential part of a new intellectual
order.

IV

Paradoxically, the library in *The Dunciad* exemplifies both the virtue of a civilized society and the triumphant progress of Dulness, the "publick service" provided by Drury's institution representative of the forces that both ensure civilized society and hasten its apocalyptic end. The metamorphosis of the library into the "Lumberhouse," the ease with which an institution that since antiquity had preserved literary history could be used to destroy that history, reveals Pope's intense anxiety about the ability of cultural memory to sustain itself in the modern world. During the seventeenth and eighteenth centuries, the transformation of the academy, the evolution of the museum, and the formation of new types of libraries to house and circulate the printed book represent significant challenges to the traditional institutions and structures that English society employed to preserve and remember its past. Indeed, as early as the sixteenth century, according to Frances Yates, "the printed book is destroying age-old memory habits," the classical "art of memory" undermined by the modern book and its mechanical reproduction.[30] For Pope, the new forms taken by the academy, museum, and library embody the uncontrollable and perverse growth of modern culture, and the inability of genuine culture to sustain itself in the face of modern methods of reproduction and preservation. Laura Brown has described the "primary poetic effect" of *The Dunciad* as "pure numerousness, an inexhaustible and indistinguishable accumulation,"[31] the material manifestations of these poetic effects exemplified by the rote learning of the academy, the assiduous collection and preservation of trivial artifacts, and, especially, the proliferation and indiscriminate assemblage of bad books.

When Dulness' "Anointed" visits the underworld at the opening of book three, he observes "poetic souls…Demand new bodies, and in Calf's array / Rush to the world, impatient for the day" (21–22). Pope's note to these lines insists that it glosses the obvious: "The Allegory of the souls of the Dull coming forth in the form of Books, and being let abroad in vast numbers by Booksellers, is sufficiently intelligible." The libraries of Theobald and Cibber that preserve this promiscuous rout of books embody the "indistinguishable accumulation" that Brown describes because, as we have seen, they fail to demonstrate any rational principles of selection, evaluation, or organization. The order that Drury regarded as vital to a genuinely useful library is nowhere apparent in libraries designed to house "Volumes, whose size the space exactly fill'd" (Theobald's library, 1. 117), or books that "serve (like other Fools) to fill a room" (Cibber's library, 1. 136). Naudé, like Drury, has nothing but contempt for collections of books that possess no transparent organizing principles: "without this Order and disposition, be the collection of Books whatever, were it of fifty thousand Volumes, it would no more merit the name of a *Library*, than an assembly of thirty thousand men the name of an *Army*."[32] For Naudé, an agglomeration of books, no matter how extensive, is not a library. Without a structural raison d'être and a series of organizational axioms, what Theobald and Cibber have created does not even deserve the name of a library; their miscellaneous accumulation of books, distinguished only by the meaningless difference between "polite" and "solid Learning," describes nothing more than a "vast heap" of books.

In regard to the book and the library, in fact, Pope's slighting references to William Caxton demonstrate his unwitting insight into the evolution of the modernity he so despised. Today, of course, scholars celebrate Caxton as a seminal figure in the English print revolution. In the early eighteenth century, however, Caxton's importance remained generally unregarded, and Pope places him in both Theobald's and Cibber's libraries—"There Caxton slept, with Wynkin at his side, / One clasp'd in wood, and one in strong cow-hide"—only as an example of the antiquated rubbish that an indiscriminate culture has kept, "like mummies," uselessly intact.

Yet in the 1729 *Dunciad Variorum*, Pope himself preserves Caxton's remains by including "A Copy of Caxton's Preface to his Translation of Virgil" among the many appendices that he added to the original poetic text. In doing so, he not only extends his satiric attack on Caxton, providing what he thought a compelling example of useless, fusty knowledge, but transforms the poem itself into an exemplar of the modern excesses he so deplores. Pope's emphasis on sheer numbers and endless accumulation, the nightmarish propagation of "nameless Somethings" and "momentary monsters," finds its perfect realization not only in the triumph of Dulness chronicled in the poem, but in the poem itself, whose successive transformations from 1728 through 1743 generate a textual artifact that faultlessly mimics the cultural depravity of a modernity unable to escape from the narcissistic and self-referential contemplation of its own unruly and promiscuous growth.

Although *The Dunciad* casts a very jaundiced eye on the archival dimensions of modern culture, other contexts—as well as the poem's own archival gestures—reveal that Pope was himself interested in utilizing the potential of the library to preserve his own works and poetic memory. From the very beginning of his career, Pope recognized how transitory that memory might be, modernity in *An Essay on Criticism* defined precisely by its memorial insecurities:

> Short is the Date, alas, of *Modern Rhymes*;
>
> . . .
>
> Now Length of *Fame* (our *second* Life) is lost,
> And bare Threescore is all ev'n That can boast:
> Our Sons their Fathers' *failing Language* see,
> And such as *Chaucer* is, shall *Dryden* be. (476, 480–83)

Employing a language whose linguistic transformations make antique even his recent forebears, Pope laments the iron age in which he now lives and writes; even the achievement of fame secures a poet a second life no longer than his first, a "bare Threescore." In the context of a *"failing Language"* that possesses none of the memorial power of the classical languages, fame becomes merely a brief coda to a modern literary life that cannot hope to emulate that life in time achieved by the *"Patriarch-Wits."*

Indeed, Pope's letters disclose a conviction that for "poor Moderns" the library constitutes a necessary resource for determining the meaning and even the content of literary history and cultural memory. In 1728 Pope donated his published works to the public library established by the New England Historical Society. During this same period, Pope's friend Robert Harley, the earl of Oxford, was completing the construction of his library, and the publication of the posthumous works of William Wycherley provided an occasion for Pope to request Oxford's help in "responding" to the way in which these poems brought discredit to the reputation of himself and his friend: "you would suffer some Original papers & Letters, both of my own and some of my Friends, to lye in your Library at London...Something will be necessary to be done, to Clear both his & my reputation, which the Letters under hand will abundantly do." Someone has played Pope and Wycherley "some dirty Trick," and "certain it is, that no other way can Justice be rendered to the Memory of a Man."[33] Here "reputation" and "Memory" depend on textual archives where, Pope insists, the truth about the present can be made available to the future.

A year after this exchange, Pope again avails himself of Oxford's help, anxious now to present him with some poems from Swift, who "has promisd me some Verses, not to be printed, which however may increase the Collection in the Harley Library, where I look upon all good papers to have a sure retreat, safe from all Present & future Curlls. I rejoice at the finishing your New Room, the Palace of Learning."[34] In these letters, Pope implies that the library represents a powerful corrective to the transitory productions of the commercial world of publication. Such sentiments sound much like those expressed by Milton in "To John Rouse," although Pope replaces the anonymity that Milton uses to dismiss "an illiterate dealer" with the individual name of a contemporary who comes to particularize the cultural, aesthetic, and economic sins of the industry. Pope's use of the proper name was crucial to his satiric process, and later in this chapter I will consider its effect on his attempt to create in *The Dunciad* a memorial to his own genius.

Pope must erect his own memorial because, controlled by cultural vandals such as Curll, the print trade cannot secure the reputation or memory of authors who depend on the productions of their pen. The act of publication is no longer sufficient to establish the just measure of a writer's stature. The cultural depredations of publishers such as Curll can be corrected only by the archive, which represents the true "Palace of Learning." Pope even used Oxford's library as part of a joke when he published separately the fourth book of *The Dunciad* in 1742 as *The New Dunciad*: in an appendix, "Advertisement to the First Edition, Separate, of the Fourth Book of the Dunciad," Pope pretends that the new book "was found merely by accident, in taking a survey of the Library of a late eminent nobleman." Harley had died in June of 1741, his library here used as the alleged preserver of Pope's manuscript. This collection, in fact, the child of both the first and second earls of Oxford, was even more extensive than that of Sir Hans Sloane, which became the core of the English national library when Sloane directed in his 1753 will that its 40,000–50,000 volumes be sold to the government. Estimates at the death of Pope's friend put the Harlian collection at about 50,000 printed books, and it included as well 350,000 pamphlets, 7,639 volumes of manuscripts, with 14,236 charters, rolls, and deeds, and an additional 41,000 prints.[35] Pope's desire to secure his own reputation and "Memory" in Harley's extraordinary library suggests his understanding that "the archive is primarily the product of a judgement, the result of the exercise of a specific power and authority...The archive is, therefore, not a piece of data, but a status."[36]

Yet even the status granted and assured by Harley's extensive archive cannot necessarily protect a writer's memory and present his true preeminence to future generations. In a 1729 letter to Pope and Bolingbroke, Swift admits that "I hate a crowd where I have not an easy place to see and be seen. A great Library always makes me melancholy, where the best Author is as much squeezed, and as obscure, as a Porter at a Coronation."[37] A crowd of books, like a crowd of people, inevitably produces a leveling effect, reducing its individual members to a common and melancholy anonymity. A library may save the past and present for the future, but those preserved in the archive remain powerless to assert their unique status.

One of the curses of modernity, for both Pope and Swift, lies in the difficulty of separating oneself from the promiscuous rout who clamor for the attention and rewards of posterity. The urban landscapes of both Pope's *Dunciad* and Swift's *Tale of a Tub* represent nightmarish visions of enforced anonymity, where crowds, stink, and the claustrophobic press of humanity make genuine distinction almost impossible to achieve: "Whoever hath an Ambition to be heard in a Crowd, must press, and squeeze, and thrust, and climb with indefatigable Pains, till he has exalted himself to a certain Degree of Altitude above them."

This opening to *A Tale of a Tub* points to the desire to distinguish oneself from the rabble, and the hack continues by describing the three mechanical aids that generations have erected to achieve preeminence: "the Pulpit, the Ladder, and the Stage-Itinerant."[38] In the versions of *The Dunciad* after 1728, Pope adds a fourth machine to this list, the book itself, attaining the hack's hard-won "Altitude" by claiming the authority in his textual monument to construct cultural memory and literary history. As Leo Braudy argues, "By the end of the seventeenth century the book was defining itself as a prime new place of fame, not (like the stage) tied to the world of political and military action, but somehow hovering above it, judging it, and finding it deficient."[39] After 1728, Pope's obsessive concern for *The Dunciad*'s textual apparatus, his conscription of friends and colleagues in the task of writing, collecting, and providing references for the notes, suggests his intuitive understanding of the new status of the book. James McLaverty, in fact, argues that Pope strove to achieve a book-like quality even in his manuscripts, and that for Pope "making a poem usually implied making a book."[40] In the new dispensation it was the book and not the poem that possessed genuine economic and memorial power. Early in his career, Pope made his fortune by the canny manipulation of the book format through which his translation of a poem, the *Iliad*, was marketed; in the latter half of his career, he just as carefully prepared his literary monument by transforming one poem into a number of separate books.

V

By the late 1720s Pope could exercise almost complete control over the way in which his poems assumed book form because, according to McLaverty, "from the publication of the *Dunciad Variorum* in 1729 onward he had dealt mainly with a printer and a bookseller he had set up in business, John Wright and Lawton Gilliver. Together they constituted a sort of 'House of Pope.'"[41] Even early in his career, Pope had played a major role in the production of his books, his contract with Lintot for the *Iliad*, by way of example, allowing him to oversee the design of the volumes. By the time he wrote *The Dunciad*, however, he had achieved an unprecedented authorial ascendancy over the printing of his works, and the successive editions of the poem reflect this. The holding of *The Dunciad* copyright by Gilliver, for instance, attests not to Pope's economic or editorial subservience to the bookseller, but to Pope's ability to manipulate ownership of the poem to his own advantage and for his own protection: when the poem first appeared, and might have occasioned legal difficulties for the poet, the copyright was assigned to the earl of Oxford, earl of Burlington, and Lord Bathurst.[42]

Because of the significance I attach to the "bookishness" of the poem, I want to proceed by momentarily examining facsimiles of both *The Dunciad* of 1728 and *The Dunciad Variorum* of 1729. Although James Sutherland's decision to organize his authoritative Twickenham edition of *The Dunciad* around the 1729 variorum and the four-book version of 1743 cannot be faulted, it has nonetheless obscured some of the important differences that separate Pope's original version of the poem from what it was eventually to become. Even a brief examination of the two facsimiles can reveal much about the expansion and elaboration of Pope's memorial ambitions, and explain a fundamental distinction between *The Dunciad* of 1728 and the many versions of the poem that followed its original publication.

When studied together, these facsimiles suggest that Pope's first version presents itself as a relatively simple and clearly defined literary text in ways that the second does not. Indeed, the title page of the 1728 version explicitly and fully identifies the object before us: *The Dunciad. An Heroic Poem. In Three Books.* The 1729 version, on the other hand, reveals its more ambiguous status not simply in the title, *The Dunciad, Variorvm. With the Prolegomena of Scriblerus*, but in its now distended and unwieldy length. Though the number of verses remains about the same, 918 in the first, 1016 in the second, the fifty-one pages of verse and six pages of prefatory matter in the 1728 edition have multiplied prodigiously, becoming in the 1729 *Variorum* seventy-nine pages of verse—swollen by the addition of copious "Remarks" and "Imitations" at the foot of each page—framed by ninety pages of new textual apparatus. Although the poem itself has changed little, Pope's archival ambitions have transformed the work, the unity and coherence of his original design compromised by what a newly added "Advertisement" refers to as the poem's now more problematic status as "too much a Cento" (4). A "patchwork" or composition formed by joining scraps from other authors, *The Dunciad Variorum* of 1729 announces itself as new not primarily by virtue of revisions to the poem, but because a series of archival gestures has linked the verse to a host of other works, a preface from Caxton, for instance, "Testimonies of Authors, Concerning our Poet and his Works," and "A Parallel of the Characters of Mr. Dryden and Mr. Pope, as Drawn by Certain of Their Contemporaries." Earlier in his career Pope had capitalized on the success of *The Rape of the Lock* by extending a brief two-canto poem into a more serious and weighty five-canto mock epic; he transforms the *The Dunciad*, however, by embedding the verse within a massive repository of contemporary documents and scholarly commentary.

This material survey of these two facsimiles raises important questions about what we mean when we refer to the work conventionally designated as Pope's *Dunciad*. Such a comparison suggests that after 1728 Pope's *Dunciad* cannot simply be considered a poem, that the poetic text cannot be understood apart from its relationship to the extensive and varied critical apparatus that came to surround it. When Emrys Jones, for instance, in his classic essay "Pope and Dulness," insists that "the poet at once succumbs to and defies the power of Dulness; and what destroys the world completes the poem,"[43] he forgets that what destroys the world may indeed complete the poem, but after 1728 it does not complete the work. In the 1728 version of *The Dunciad* the "FINIS" that follows the last verse marks the conclusion of the poem, the work, the volume. In the 1729 version, however, that "FINIS" marks merely the end of the verse, for the work itself continues, completing itself only in a bewildering array of appendices, indices, and addenda. After 1728 the poetic text loses its primacy, and attempts to understand its significance must take into account its status as part of a much larger work.

Embedding his initial publication over a fifteen-year period in an increasingly extensive, self-referential, and labyrinthine architecture of contemporary documents, gossip, and (mis)information, Pope converts a relatively simple mock-epic poem into a repository devoted to the reconstruction and preservation of the early-eighteenth-century print industry. In 1728 and 1729 Pope's decision to do so would have been daring but certainly not novel, since the archival ambitions that underlay *The Dunciad*'s transformation define an important dimension of contemporary attempts to organize the republic of letters and engage the increasingly diverse productions of its citizens. A concern for the archive, repository, and storehouse marks the era, and I want to briefly examine two works published at about the same time as *The Dunciad* in order to further explore the archival impulse in early-eighteenth-century Britain and its implications for our modern articulations of memory and literary history.

The first, Ephraim Chambers' *Cyclopaedia*, was published in the same year as *The Dunciad*, 1728. Issued by subscription, its two handsome and expensive folio volumes (four guineas) occupied the high end of the literary marketplace, the "List of the Subscribers" as glittering as that affixed to Pope's translation of the *Iliad* thirteen years before. The dedication embodies Chambers' belief that his undertaking participates in modernity's heady and inevitable eclipse of the past: "Indeed, the Time seems at hand, when we are no longer to envy Rome her AUGUSTUS and AUGUSTAN Age, but Rome in her turn shall envy ours."[44] Hanoverian England can surpass Augustan Rome because Chambers sees himself as "Heir to a large Patrimony, gradually rais'd by the Industry, and Endeavours of a long Race" of academicians, dictionarists, and lexicographers. Moderns can elevate themselves above the ancients because their forebears have made Chambers "rich enough not only to afford Plenty, but even Profusion" (i). His own work, he assures us, is "what it ought to be, a Collection; not the Produce of a single Brain, for that would go but a little way; but of a whole Commonwealth" (xxix). Chambers prides himself, therefore, not on his knowledge of particulars, but on his ability to organize and structure the diversity of knowledge and information that he has inherited; Chambers has organized "a confused Heap of incongruous Parts" into "one consistent Whole," proud that his work is "as different from theirs, as a System from a Cento" (i). The specter of the "Cento" bothers Chambers as well as Pope, both men aware, in spite of the very different nature of their undertakings, that the archival dimensions of their projects threaten to undermine their authorial integrity.

Chambers' belief in his "System," however, protects him from doubt. So grand is his conception for the *Cyclopaedia* that he can assure us "that half the Men of Letters of an Age might be employ'd in it to advantage" (ii), for his volumes represent no less than a distillation of all knowledge, both past and present: "a Work accomplish'd as it ought to be, on the Footing of this, would answer all the Purposes of a Library, except Parade and Incumbrance; and contribute more to the propagating of useful Knowledge thro' the Body of a People, than any, I had almost said all, the Books extant" (ii). In his two volumes Chambers imagines an entire library, a quintessence of knowledge—purified from the physical inconveniences of a real library and its multitudinous volumes, the dross of "Parade and Incumbrance"—that can reveal the essential truth contained in "almost" all books.

The first issue of *The Gentleman's Magazine, or Trader's Monthly Intelligencer*, dated January 1731 (and appearing early in February), announces no such grand ambitions, its price of sixpence and monthly publication placing it at a very different stall from Chambers' in the literary marketplace. Although the periodical publication does not aspire to replace entire libraries, its title-page nonetheless asserts its own archival virtues by claiming that it contains "More in Quantity, and greater Variety than any Book of the Kind and Price."[45] Designed to evade both the 1710 copyright law and stamp taxes imposed in 1712 and 1725—because it primarily reprinted news and extracts from daily and weekly papers—*The Gentleman's Magazine* presented itself, in the "Advertisement" that introduced the first edition, as a way for the educated individual to confront the impossible demands of the periodical press: "This may serve to illustrate the Reasonableness of our present Undertaking, which in the first Place is to give Monthly a View of all the Pieces of Wit, Humour, or Intelligence, daily offer'd to the Publick in the News-Papers, (which of late are so multiply'd, as to render it impossible, unless a Man makes it a Business, to consult them all."[46]

Capitalizing on the class-coding of print, the stigma of writing as a "business" that so marks a poet such as Pope, Edward Cave, founder and editor of *The Gentleman's Magazine*, provided a decorous way for his audience to sample and enjoy the chaotic outpouring of the contemporary print trade. For a modern reader this "Advertisement" can almost suggest the witty pen of Pope or Swift, for it communicates a powerful sense of the overwhelming numbers produced by the trade, of the sheer mass of material "thrown from the Press," of the many "loose Papers, uncertainly scatter'd about." But its accents remain earnest not satirical, its energies devoted not to a critique of the periodical press but to its celebration: "many Things deserving Attention...are seen by Accident, and others not sufficiently publish'd or preserved for universal Benefit and Information. This Consideration has induced several GENTLEMEN to promote a Monthly Collection, to treasure up, as in a Magazine, the most remarkable Pieces on the Subjects abovemention'd."

Throughout the seventeenth century, the chief meanings of the term "magazine" had referred to a storehouse or repository for goods or merchandise, a victualing ship, or a military building protecting particularly gunpowder, ammunition, or explosives. Late in the century, however, examples of its figurative use in titles are provided by *The Mariners Magazine* (1669) and *The Penman's Magazine* (1705). Cave, however, deserves credit for the establishment of the modern meaning of the word, the enormous success of his publication transforming "magazine" into a generic term for a periodical publication intended for a general readership.

That readership may have differed profoundly from the worthies contained in the impressive "List of the Subscribers" that accompanied Chambers' *Cyclopaedia*, but both publications are nonetheless marked by the insistence that only as archives can they bring order to and make sense of the increasingly chaotic contemporary world of letters and print. Chambers complains, using an image we've examined in Cavendish and Milton as well as Pope, that because of the multiplication of dictionarists and lexicographers "all the Confusion of Babel is brought upon us" (xxi), while Cave figures this Babel in the illustration that highlights his title-page: in the center a stone structure titled "St JOHN's GATE"—the actual location of Cave's London press—is flanked on both sides by a difficult-to-read jumble of small print representing, on the left, the titles of a host of London publications, on the right those of the provinces (beginning with York and Dublin and ending with Jamaica and the Barbados). Out of this confused heap of publications, *The Gentleman's Magazine* will "preserve those Things that are curious," its single voice a way to "treasure up" and "preserve" the best of an otherwise promiscuous and chaotic literary culture.

Pope certainly would have regarded the efforts of Chambers and Cave to organize and preserve contemporary culture with some contempt. The former's insistence on elevating the moderns above the ancients placed him on the other side of that quarrel from Pope, although Chambers finds a place in neither Pope's letters nor poetry. While the 1731 establishment of Cave's magazine protected it from the 1728 and 1729 versions of the poem, his efforts did not escape Pope's censure in the 1743 *Dunciad*, where in the first book Pope replaces "Hence the soft sing-song on Cecilia's day" (40) with "Hence Journals, Medleys, Merc'ries, Magazines" (42). A note to the line only emphasizes Pope's contempt for Cave's extraordinarily popular formula for success: "These [Miscellanies in prose and verse] were thrown out weekly and monthly by every miserable scribler; or picked up piece-meal and stolen from any body...equally the disgrace of human Wit, Morality, and Decency." That by 1743 *The Dunciad* itself had become a collection of extracts from a host of other works seems to have escaped Pope's notice.

VI

Pope's blindness in regard to the ways in which *The Dunciad* as an archive participates in cultural imperatives that he ridicules elsewhere undoubtedly stems from the elaborate acts of satiric negation that define his project. Pope can only locate his work and reputation in the "ancient" or (in his mind) "timeless" context of enduring literary value by simultaneously asserting its preeminence in the "modern" context of a Grubstreet that he affected to despise. To conceive of *The Dunciad* as a memorial is to recognize that Pope's own survival as a poet is inextricably bound up with those he mocks, for much of its archival energies are devoted to preserving the biographies of contemporaries whose work Pope disdained. In her book on Pope, Helen Deutsch asserts that "If this poet lives forever he will do so by himself and by negation,"[47] and while *The Dunciad* certainly attests to the validity of her latter proposition, it belies the former. *The Dunciad* immortalizes its poet by firmly grounding him within the mundane and transitory reality of his time, surrounding him, indeed overwhelming him with the writers, booksellers, printers, and publishers who populated the early-eighteenth-century book trade.

The Dunciad asserts Pope's own preeminence by providing the dense cultural context within which to judge what he confidently assumed to be the insignificance of his contemporaries; their unworthiness to achieve enduring fame provides a measure of Pope's own triumph over time. Such a project, which seeks to memorialize Pope's own antimodern literary genius, is obviously profoundly contradictory, both because it utilizes an ideology of archival comprehensiveness that Pope scorned, and because it depends on individuals whom Pope deemed unworthy of literary immortality. The 1728 version of the work registers the problem of the insignificance of the dunces in "The Publisher to the Reader," the only textual apparatus to accompany the poem, where the "publisher" claims that he would have done the author a wrong "had I detain'd this publication: since those Names which are its chief ornaments, die off daily so fast, as must render it too soon unintelligible" (v). The joke here, to be sure, remains something of a scriblerian commonplace, utilized as early as 1704 by Swift in *A Tale of a Tub* when his hack narrator, in "The Epistle Dedicatory, To His Royal Highness Prince Posterity," laments that contemporary writers, "altho' their Numbers be vast, and their Productions numerous in proportion, yet are they hurryed so hastily off the Scene, that they escape our Memory, and delude our Sight."[48]

Even the modern library, with its ambitions toward archival inclusiveness, cannot preserve the memory of writers so insignificant and transitory. In "A Letter to the Publisher"—signed by William Cleland though written by Pope—affixed to the 1729 *Dunciad Variorum*, the obscurity of the dunces and their literary efforts again emerges as a significant concern: "as for their writings, I have sought them (on this one occasion) in vain, in the closets and libraries of all my acquaintance...[these writings] themselves will be so soon and so irrecoverably lost. You may in some measure prevent it, by preserving at least their *Titles" (8–9). Without the help of Pope's poem, his enemies cannot hope to survive, and the note here assures us that at least their titles have been saved "in a List in the Appendix, No. 2." This "List of Books, Papers, and Verses, in which our Author was Abused, Printed Before the Publication of the Dunciad: With the True Names of the Authors" was constructed from the bound volumes of attacks on himself and his poetry that Pope had busily and compulsively collected over the years. Its inclusion in the poem reveals not simply Pope's thin-skinned bitterness, his inability to forget or forgive an insult, but his recognition that his own literary memory depends on the preservation of those he despises. Their obscurity, however, cannot be allowed to undermine his immortality. As "A Letter to the Publisher" puts it when comparing Pope to Boileau, they were "equally abus'd by the ignorant pretenders to Poetry of their times; of which not the least memory will remain but in their own writings, and in the notes made upon them" (13).

The transitory nature of modern authorial fame is not simply noted in *The Dunciad Variorum*, but becomes the primary rationale for the enlargement of the work's critical apparatus. "The Publisher's Advertisement," which replaces the earlier "Publisher to the Reader," explains: "Of the Persons it was judg'd proper to give some account: for since it is only in this monument that they must expect to survive,...it seem'd but humanity to bestow a word or two upon each, just to tell what he was, what he writ, when he liv'd, or when he dy'd" (3). The term "monument" possesses great resonance in such a context, its meaning for a poet such as Pope always inflected by Horace's claim that "I have finished a monument more lasting than bronze and loftier than the Pyramids' royal pile,...I shall not altogether die, but a mighty part of me shall escape the death-goddess. On and on shall I grow, ever fresh with the glory of after time."[49] Emphasizing the tremendous disparity between the materials of fame available to emperor, conqueror, and poet, Horace's ode impressed itself on the literary imagination precisely because it insists that insubstantial texts may outlive the adamantine memorials erected by the rulers of this world. *The Dunciad* represents Pope's attempt to memorialize himself at the expense of his contemporaries, to present an archive that would distinguish between their dross and his precious metal.

The calm certainty of Horace's vision of poetic immortality, however much it served as a powerful classical model that grounded Pope's own dreams of lasting fame, must also have rebuked his attempts to achieve the monumental in the age of the printed book. While the 1729 *Dunciad Variorum* begins with an explicit avowal of its monumental ambitions, it recognizes as well the modern condition that undermines such aspirations:

> We shall next declare the occasion and the cause which moved our Poet to this particular work. He lived in those days, when (after providence had permitted the Invention of Printing as a scourge for the Sins of the learned) Paper also became so cheap, and printers so numerous, that a deluge of authors cover'd the land. ("Martinus Scriblerus, of the Poem," 23)

This "deluge" of authors threatens to recapitulate Noah's flood, the history and memory of civilization erased not this time by the waters of God's ire, but by the promiscuous productions of the vile Grubstreet press. *The Dunciad Variorum* is marked from the start—even before the poem itself begins—by the poles of memory and oblivion, its monumental status mocked by the extinction toward which modernity rushes. For Pope the waters have not receded, but continue to rise, literary and cultural survival a matter of building his own ark.

Pope populates that ark not with the many creatures of God's creation, but with the miscellaneous hordes of Dulness, that "vast involuntary throng, / Who gently drawn, and struggling less and less, / Roll in her Vortex, and her pow'r confess" (4. 82–84). *The Dunciad* contains many such scenes, in which Dulness manifests her power over the numberless, anonymous mobs that populate her kingdom. At the same time, however, the poem insists on individualizing those who pay tribute to Dulness, juxtaposing mass and anonymity against particular individuals and the specific name.

The power and significance of *The Dunciad* in particular depends on its willingness to hazard and even court its unintelligibility to posterity through its insistence on the importance of names that do not deserve to endure. By "naming names," of course, Pope asserts his own power, for as Deutsch insists, the "power to name is also his power to judge."[50] In this guise, Pope assumes the status not simply of a Noah who will preserve what might otherwise be lost, but of Adam, who demonstrates his unique and superior place in the creation by his ability to name the rest of God's creation. At the same time, Pope's use of names recalls the magical origins of satire, when to name was to curse, the satirist's invective, abuse, and violence designed to commit symbolic murder.[51]

The power that Pope claims through his decision to eschew general satire depends on his instinctive recognition that print, the book, and the library would transform the nature of modern memory. According to Pierre Nora, that memory "is, above all, archival...Memory has been wholly absorbed by its meticulous reconstitution. Its new vocation is to record...What we call memory is in fact the gigantic and breathtaking storehouse of a materialist stock of what it would be impossible for us to remember."[52] From such a perspective, the insignificance of the dunces is precisely the point, the "virtue" that gives them their value. Doomed to extinction without Pope, their very anonymity demonstrates his triumph.

Pope's victory over his trivial and anonymous enemies depends on his ability to control the mechanisms and content of collective memory, the archival nature of *The Dunciad* after 1728 refining and augmenting its ideological determination to act as an instrument of power as well as a form of conquest. Pope's off-hand remark to Thomas Sheridan in a letter of 1728, in which he refers to the care he takes in *The Dunciad* of "branding none but our own Cattle," suggests precisely this sense of power and conquest in its assertion of property rights and ownership.[53] The issue of ownership is obviously crucial here, for Pope must elevate himself not simply over rival writers, but over the booksellers and printers who control the print trade. The "high, heroic Games" of book two begin with the race between Lintot and Curll, "persons, whose names being more known and famous in the learned world than those of the authors in this Poem, do therefore need less explanation" (note to line forty-nine). The latter's economic power makes him an irresistible target to Pope, for as the note to line fifty-four explains, "he possest himself of a command over all authors whatever; he caus'd them to write what he pleas'd; they could not call their very names their own." This is precisely the power that Pope's *Dunciad* attempts to wrest from those who dominated the trade: Pope makes the dunces his own, and in doing so he claims the power to determine their place in literary history and memory. In *The Dunciad* Pope employs the names of others to forge his own memorial, commemorating his memory through their "Monumental Brass." In this mock-heroic archive, Pope joins "a range of institutions including libraries, museums, local records and special collections all designed to create a particular vision of society."[54]

In such an archive, Pope both presents a history of the early-eighteenth-century book trade, and distorts that "history" in order to present himself in the most favorable light possible. William Kinsley has noted that "the *Dunciad* as book has useful real notes, and as mock-book it has ludicrously inept and overgrown mock-notes." But he also reminds us that "recent critics who quite rightly emphasize the fictional role of the notes sometimes tend to ignore their quite straightforward complementary role of elucidating a poem that was obscure even to Swift."[55] In a letter to Swift after the poem's 1728 publication, but before its revised appearance in 1729, Pope asks that his friend "read over the Text, and make a few [Notes Variorum] in any way you like best, whether dry raillery, upon the stile and way of commenting of trivial Critics; or humorous, upon the authors in the poem; or historical, of persons, places, times; or explanatory, or collecting the parallel passages of the Ancients."[56] Pope delineates here five different classes of notes, and while the first and second clearly possess a satirical purpose, numbers three, four, and five fulfill a historical and explanatory function.

The work's intrusive textual apparatus, which physically dominates the poem and on the page can at times reduce the verse to the status of a mere footnote, exists as an immense and unwieldy hodgepodge of miscellaneous information, some of it true, some false, some faithfully reporting current gossip—which may have been accurate or not—some creating that gossip. In his book on individual memory, John Kotre suggests that "the remembering self...has the temperament of a librarian, a keeper of memory's most important archives. It can be fastidious in that role, guarding its original records and trying to keep them pristine...But memory's archivist by day has a secret passion by night: to fashion a story about itself...a personal myth...a different kind of reality than a librarian knows."[57] The Dunciad's textual apparatus functions in a similar fashion, both preserving a historical record and distorting that record in order to generate a personal narrative that consolidates Pope's own position as literary and moral exemplar.

VII

Part of the success of Pope's Dunciad has manifested itself in its ability over the last two-and-a-half centuries to help govern how literary history has in fact judged those consigned to the "Grubstreet race." Very few of those dunces "branded" by Pope have escaped the stigma of his aesthetic judgment. As Fentress and Wickham remind us, "the social meaning of memory, like its internal structure and its mode of transmission, is little affected by its truth; all that matters is that it be believed"; "social memory is not stable as information; it is stable, rather, at the level of shared meanings and remembered images."[58] Pope's misshapen, eccentric, and unique masterpiece has, like few other literary works of the eighteenth century, shaped those "shared meanings" and provided the "remembered images" that have constructed our literary past. The Dunciad, as Brean Hammond reminds us, "was an act of canon formation,"[59] and even an abbreviated history of the poem's critical reception will suggest the extent to which Pope's readers have acquiesced in his critical conception of his age and of his place within it.

Johnson completed his Life of Pope, the last biography he wrote for his Lives of the English Poets, early in 1781, not forty years after Pope's death. Johnson considers The Dunciad "one of his [Pope's] greatest and most elaborate performances," worthy "to claim the praise of an original." Although he recognizes the "petulance and malignity" that motivated Pope's attacks on his contemporaries, he confesses that "I cannot think it very criminal," for "an author places himself uncalled before the tribunal of criticism, and solicits fame at the hazard of disgrace." Johnson has, in fact, little to say about the individual verdicts that Pope hands down from his "tribunal of criticism," but Johnson's commonsensical pronouncement that "upon bad writers only will censure have much effect" suggests that he saw Pope's enemies not as an undifferentiated mob of dunces, but as individual authors of diverse talents who enjoyed various degrees of literary and intellectual success: "The satire which brought Theobald and Moore into contempt, dropped impotent from Bentley, like the javelin of Priam."[60]

Thomas De Quincey, in the mid-nineteenth century, displays a similar judiciousness in his evaluation of Pope's dunces, although in refusing to accept uncritically Pope's formulations he reveals that others have already ceded to Pope the aesthetic field. In his 1837 contribution on Pope to the seventh edition of the *Encyclopaedia Britannica*, De Quincey had declared *The Dunciad* the "very greatest" of Pope's works, a "monument of satirical power the greatest which man has produced."[61] Perhaps because of his high regard for the poem, De Quincey was particularly troubled by Friedrich Christoph Schlosser's charge, contained in his eight-volume *History of the Eighteenth Century and of the Nineteenth till the Overthrow of the French Empire, with Particular Reference to Mental Cultivation and Progress*, that Pope's "satire only hit such people as would never have been known without his mention of them." In his 1847 review of the first six volumes of Schlosser's work, De Quincey insists that such a charge "is the grossest of blunders," and attempts to prove it by reevaluating and praising a number of the "Grubstreet race," including Bentley, Dennis, Cibber, Aaron Hill, and Samuel Clarke. Although he recognizes that such a reassessment "impeaches the equity, and sometimes the judgment, of Pope, at least it contributes to show the groundlessness of Schlosser's objection that the population of the 'Dunciad,' the characters that filled its stage, were inconsiderable."[62] De Quincey willingly questions Pope's judgment here in order to aggrandize Pope's enemies and thus expand the power and scope of what he regards as the satirist's masterwork. De Quincey can affirm the greatness of Pope's *Dunciad* only if the objects of Pope's satiric attack can justify the work's pretensions.

This correlation between the importance of the mock-epic and the stature of the duncies is abandoned in De Quincey's contemporary Thackeray, who includes Pope, along with Gay and Prior, in his fourth lecture on *The English Humourists of the Eighteenth Century*. This series of six lectures, first delivered in London between May 22 and July 3, 1851, and published in both Britain and the United States in 1853, represented a major financial and critical success for Thackeray, and offered an important reassessment of Augustan literature for Victorian audiences.[63] Thackeray regards Pope as "the greatest name on our list—the highest among the poets, the highest among the English wits and humourists with whom we have to rank him." His examination of Pope proves remarkable for Thackeray's willingness to accept, essentially at face value, the heroic poses that Pope struck in his assumption of satiric gravitas. For the most part, Thackeray simply buries Pope's rivals under the generic category of "the dunces"; the following extract is a characteristic example of how for Thackeray even the most important of Pope's contemporaries had difficulty emerging from anonymity:

> The tastes and sensibilities of Pope, which led him to cultivate the society
> of persons of fine manners, or wit, or taste, or beauty, caused him to shrink

equally from that shabby and boisterous crew which formed the rank and file of literature in his time:...when Pope's triumph passed,...it was natural for Dennis and Tibbald, and Webster and Cibber, and the worn and hungry pressmen in the crowd below, to howl at him and assail him.

Thackeray's insistence on adopting Pope's satiric name for Theobald, as well as his use of an image that reduces Theobald and company to howling beasts, indicates the unthinking contempt with which he contemplates Pope's rivals, and his unquestioned belief in Pope's critical and aesthetic pronouncements. Although Theobald, along with Dennis, Webster, and Cibber, emerge briefly here as individuals, all four remain otherwise sunk within the "shabby and boisterous crew," the undifferentiated mass of "worn and hungry pressmen," "the rank and file of literature" in Pope's time, which Thackeray understands in ways fully invested in Pope's own version of literary history.

Thackeray reserves his greatest praise for the concluding lines of the fourth book of *The Dunciad*, "astonishing lines...the very greatest height which his [Pope's] sublime art has attained," which elicit this final portrait of the poet surrounded by his enemies: "It is heroic courage speaking: a splendid declaration of righteous wrath and war. It is the gage flung down, and the silver trumpet ringing defiance to falsehood and tyranny, deceit, dulness, superstition. It is Truth, the champion, shining and intrepid, and fronting the great world-tyrant with armies of slaves at his back."[64] Such a confrontation presents Pope as a veritable Horatius at the bridge, the fate of civilization itself dependent on his ink-stained fingers. In this vision of cultural apocalypse, Pope alone attains an individual subjectivity, his nameless foes leveled within a promiscuous and seething mob of slaves. Slightly more than a century after his death, Pope has found his perfect reader and champion, the most idealized and narcissistic memorial hopes that Pope could have harbored publicly articulated by one of the foremost literary figures of the mid-nineteenth century.

Compared to such hyperbole, Leslie Stephen's *Alexander Pope*, published in 1880 as part of John Morley's English Men of Letters series, seems positively restrained. Indeed, Stephen's provides a relatively prudent assessment of *The Dunciad* in his chapter entitled "The War with the Dunces," but he nonetheless affirms that "Bentley is, I think, the only man of real genius of whom Pope has spoken in terms implying gross misappreciation. With all his faults, Pope was a really fine judge of literature, and has made fewer blunders than such men as Addison, Gray, and Johnson." Stephen, for all of his thoughtfulness, provides a ringing vindication of Pope's judgment, reifying the title of "dunce" and privileging Pope's use of the term in a universalizing fashion: "Though Gildon and Arnall are forgotten, the type 'dunce' is eternal."[65]

The full measure of the memorial triumphs that Pope enjoyed by the first decade of the twentieth century can be appreciated not by attending to one of his supporters, but by registering the tone of resignation that characterizes Thomas R. Lounsbury's attempts to rescue Theobald from the scrapheap of history in *The Text of Shakespeare* (1906). Lounsbury spent over thirty years at Yale beginning in 1870, a significant voice in the establishment of English studies in its modern form in the United States. His book examines editions of Shakespeare up to and including those of Pope and Theobald, most of it devoted to the rivalry and quarrel between the two earliest editors of the dramatist. Lounsbury is no friend to Pope, and he attempts to rehabilitate the reputation not only of Theobald, but of many of those attacked by Pope: "The truth is that nearly all the writers satirized in 'The Dunciad' had either distinguished themselves or were to distinguish themselves in some particular field of intellectual effort. The position they held in the eyes of the public furnishes presumptive proof that they were not dunces." Lounsbury takes pains to salvage the careers not simply of Defoe, Dennis, and Bentley, but of men like Theophilus Cibber, Ambrose Philips, and Eustace Budgell. He has little doubt that "no flimsier structure has ever been built upon more insecure foundations than the belief in the special intellectual inferiority of the men attacked in 'The Dunciad.' "

Yet Lounsbury recognizes that, in regard to Pope's satiric masterpiece, he is tilting futilely at windmills: "The legendary past has handed down nothing more mythical than some of the beliefs which have grown up about this satire...they have been and are so universally accepted that to doubt or deny them will seem to many as being of the nature of a blow aimed at the foundations of all accredited literary history."[66] Lounsbury has no doubt that Pope and his allies have determined the definitive shape of literary history, "for a century and a half" their version of culture, having attained a "mythical" stature, privileged and legitimated above all others.

In the century since Lounsbury's attempt to rehabilitate the dunces, Pope's reputation has waxed and waned, but there can be little doubt that he still bestrides the field of eighteenth-century studies like a colossus. The revolution in literary studies of the last thirty years has certainly empowered theoretical modes of criticism that, in emphasizing the ideological contradictions that characterize Pope's work, have allowed scholars to reassess the cultural importance of a number of Pope's enemies.[67] Nonetheless, the vast majority of Pope's dunces remain at best marginalized and at worst forgotten. In his 1929 facsimile edition of *The Dunciad Variorum*, Robert Kilburn Root recognizes the completeness of Pope's memorial triumph over his foes by noting that "only four of the persons lampooned in the *Dunciad* of 1729 have been thought worthy of inclusion in Mr. D. Nicol Smith's admirable *Oxford Book of Eighteenth Century Verse*."[68] For all of the significant changes in the criticism of the past thirty years, that situation has changed little, only a handful of those Pope scorned in *The Dunciad* part of *The Norton Anthology of English Literature*.

Methodologically, this anthology is a direct descendant of Chambers' *Cyclopaedia*, Cave's *Gentleman's Magazine*, and even Pope's *Dunciad*, its desire "to contain many of the most remarkable works written in English during centuries of restless creative effort," to meet "the challenge of representing, justly and in only two volumes, the unparalleled range and variety of English literature,"[69] participating in the same archival ambitions that were taking modern form during the early eighteenth century. *The Dunciad*, of course, cannot be held directly responsible for the eighteenth-century authors excluded from this anthology, although what Lounsbury refers to as its "mythic" stature suggests how close the poem has come to fulfilling its ambition to function as a transcendent cultural artifact that might recreate posterity in its own image. But insofar as Pope's satiric poem represents and articulates an aesthetic perspective that has remained remarkably stable for over two hundred and fifty years, it remains an important component in the ideology that determines the content as well as the form of *The Norton Anthology*.

VIII

Significantly, two of the figures who have survived Pope's ridicule are women, Lady Mary Wortley Montagu and Margaret Cavendish, the latter represented in the seventh edition of *The Norton Anthology* by two poems from *Poems, and Fancies*, as well as short selections from *A True Relation of My Birth, Breeding, and Life*, and *The Description of a New World, Called The Blazing World*.[70] Until the recovery of a feminist literary history in the last three decades, generations of scholars and readers, who for the most part shared Pope's suspicions concerning woman writers, would have had little reason to challenge or even investigate the gender politics of the literary past depicted in *The Dunciad*. Pope most famously expresses the conventional understanding of women that defines their diminished status in his literary and intellectual marketplace when he asserts in the second of his *Moral Essays*, "To a Lady. Of the Characters of Women," that "Woman and Fool are two hard things to hit, / For true No-meaning puzzles more than Wit" (113–14), and "good as well as ill, / Woman's at best a Contradiction still" (269–70). The latter in particular may help to explain the singularly contradictory nature of Dulness, who manifests her female power by displaying a wide range of paradoxical behaviors and conditions. Dulness represents at once an inert and passive lack of energy along with a furious and uncontrollable motion; soporific silence interrupted by mind-shattering noise; an unresisting sea of anonymous, indistinguishable dunces and a narcissistic mob in which individual accomplishment cries out for recognition; a world of dark, deformed, intellectual endeavor and a realm of ebullient, unselfconscious juvenile play. The considerable energy of the poem partially stems from the way in which it moves frequently between these diverse poles of duncical deportment.[71]

If the contradictory manifestations of female nature provide the characteristic mode of Dulness's majesty and her minion's erratic behavior, the "true No-meaning" that women represent describes the much more frightening conclusion toward which the poem ultimately and inexorably moves. Meaning in Pope's literary world is granted primarily by the movement of literature through time; even in *The Dunciad*, the normative understanding of poetry rests securely in the conventional, assured belief that the arts can conquer time: "Now Night descending, the proud scene was o'er, / But liv'd, in Settle's numbers, one day more" (1. 90–91). Poetry grants futurity, and even Settle's verse provides a new day that can triumph over the oblivion of night. But as the "Daughter of Chaos and Eternal Night" (1. 12), Dulness seeks to reestablish a kingdom in which time, posterity, and memory come to an end, a quiescent state of "true No-meaning" in which the poet becomes "the tall Nothing" won by Curll for his victory in the footrace against Lintot, and where the unfortunate who drinks from the Wizard's cup near the conclusion of book four "forgets his former friends, / Sire, Ancestors, Himself" (4. 518–19). Those who drink from the cup lose both history and self, the memories that preserve genealogy and identity forfeited in the attempt to secure the favor of Dulness' chief political agent, Walpole.

From such a perspective, the fundamental contradiction represented by Dulness lies in her paradoxical desire to find and celebrate an heir while at the same time perfecting a world in which "Universal Darkness buries All." Dulness is at once obsessed with establishing the proper succession that can affirm her preeminence and also with the creation of a kingdom that will bring an end to all succession. In this poem, the "true No-meaning" associated with women takes its final and most terrifying form in a world in which time defeats poetry and the poet loses his individual identity in the "vast involuntary throng" who gather round "their dusky Queen" (4. 77–84).

The Temple of Fame concludes with the youthful, male poet's attempts to negotiate with a female Fame an ethical mode of behavior that would allow him to succeed to "Th'Estate" represented by "that second Life in others' Breath." In *The Dunciad*, however, that estate, and the images of succession that govern its descent, all lead to the same place, the grotesque, female body of Dulness that would engross all and make succession impossible. The "long Posterity" of Dulness, of course, must end in oblivion, marking the end of any posterity whatsoever, and at the conclusion of book four the male poet who sings *The Dunciad* has nothing left to negotiate; like everyone and everything else he can but capitulate to the end of days: "In vain, in vain—the all-composing Hour / Resistless falls: The Muse obeys the Pow'r" (4. 627–28). The note to line 620 suggests the finality of this surrender, for "the Muses…as the Daughters of Memory, are obliged not to forget any thing." In *The Temple of Fame*, the intimate relationship between Fame, Fortune, and Rumour suggested the instability of the memorial processes that might allow a poet to hope for a life in time. In *The Dunciad* a range of debased female figures collude with Dulness in order to secure her triumph: Cloacina and the Mud-nymphs in book one, the "Harlot form" of Italian opera in book four, among others. But when even the Muses find their powers appropriated by Dulness, the poet who would sing, as Scriblerus recognizes in the conclusion to the note to line 620, is finally silenced: "But our Poet had yet another reason for putting this Task upon the Muse, that all besides being *asleep*, she only could relate what passed." When the Muse herself obeys Dulness, poetry ends in sleep, the poet's song in a yawn, and literary history in oblivion. In a world ruled by Dulness, the "Poet's vision of eternal Fame" becomes merely a debased, stock illusion, like "The air-built

Castle, and the golden Dream, / The Maid's romantic wish, the Chemist's flame" (3. 10–12)

Although the poem certainly savages a number of female writers, as Valerie Rumbold suggests, "attacks on women writers are neither particularly numerous nor unambiguously focused on a notion of female publication as intrinsically offensive."[72] The satire directed against women writers in *The Dunciad* seems no more harsh or unfair than that directed against men in the poem, and Pope does not seem particularly exercised by having to share with individual women such as Eliza Haywood or Elizabeth Thomas a literary marketplace growing ever more receptive to products of a female pen. According to both Richard Terry and Jonathan Brody Kramnick, that marketplace proved receptive, within limits, to the integration of both female writers and readers. Terry argues that during the eighteenth century we can discover the first attempts to create a coherent female literary canon, and even the initial efforts to place women within the established canon of male writers, while Kramnick shows how representations of the cultural community changed in response to the incorporation of women and a female taste that might educate and refine a wider reading public. Both insist that the reception of women was necessarily complex and ambivalent, the successes women could achieve far different from those available to men, and their presence within the republic of letters blamed for a commodification of culture that threatened established conceptions of masculine virtue.[73] Nonetheless, symbolic constructions of female writers and readers during the eighteenth century point the way to important changes in how the cultural marketplace was imagined and understood.

In Pope's poetry these gendered changes in the literary community appear as but another unremarkable corruption of modernity, Pope apprehending them, for the most part, through the utterly conventional and time-honored misogyny honed by centuries of satiric practice, in which women represent the physically squalid and the sexually insatiable, a human substance and personality infirm, unstable, erratic, and weak. But this impure and enervated substance does threaten Pope's ability to create the monumental, Dulness in book four reveling in her power to undermine all the traditional gestures of literary futurity, "printing *Editions* of their [distinguished Writers] works with impertinent alterations of their Text . . . [or] setting up *Monuments* disgraced with their own vile names and inscriptions" (note to line 119). As Pope's verse insists, none of the materials that normally possess memorial power can overcome the transformative effects of the fantastical and unnatural female body:

> 'Leave not a foot of verse, a foot of stone,
> A Page, a Grave, that they can call their own;
> But spread, my sons, your glory thin or thick,
> On passive paper, or on solid brick. (4. 127–30)

No matter what type of memorial one contemplates—the "page" and "grave," "paper" and "brick," representing the poles of intellectual and material commemoration—the heirs of Dulness will destroy or pull it down. Monuments, whether literary or architectural, will be unable to transmit to posterity a culture worth saving. The fundamental mystery and power of the monument, dependent on its inexplicable movement in time between the material and the spiritual, will be disrupted, futurity itself undermined and then annihilated.

Against such a power, which eventually silences even the Muses, the poet struggles in vain to maintain his individual voice and dreams of immortality. Eric V. Chandler recommends that we take some solace in the infantilized degradation of Pope's enemies, and the evidence that "Dulness's new world must be sterile in its self-proliferation."[74] But for Dulness this sterility is precisely the point, because it cuts off the possibility of futurity or growth. Under the reign of Dulness, her loyal followers remain indifferent to fame or their potential lives in time, the "satanic" temptation represented in *The Temple of Fame* by the whisper in the ear heard no longer: "No more, alas! The voice of Fame they hear, / The balm of Dulness trickling in their ear" (4.543–44). Indeed, within the imagined world of the poem, no form of masculine self-assertion can resist this liquid balm, impede or reverse Dulness' triumph.

Such a world mocks the ethical pretensions, heroic aspirations, and memorial dreams of the youthful poet in *The Temple of Fame*. However forcefully he may assert his virtue, or articulate new and more unusual conceptions of manly behavior, he cannot bend Dulness to his will. Dulness can be defeated only by turning the world she would create against her, employing the excesses of modernity that define her triumph in the service of the poet himself. Except in the act of actually writing the poem, Pope does not imagine a heroic confrontation between himself and Dulness; he does not structure *The Dunciad* around a dramatic encounter between the opposed forces of female depravity and male virtue, as Milton, for instance, does in *Samson Agonistes*. In Pope's poem, in fact, the poet himself disappears, his absence a necessary condition of his eventual triumph, for no masculine pose can succeed in dominating Dulness, her "Force inertly strong" proof against all representations of masculine power. Dulness, in fact, loves to appropriate the traditional gestures and signs of male superiority, the "vigour and superior size" that Curll exhibits during the pissing contest, and Olmixion's "naked majesty" in the diving contest, moments that dramatize how the normally triumphant male body has become no more than an obedient servant to her commands.

The Dunciad represents Dulness' triumph over the world of culture, and her apparently effortless domination over the male body, in the tableaux of Cibber asleep on the goddess' lap throughout book four. The long note to line twenty, attributed to both Scriblerus and Bentley, emphasizes the justness of imagining him asleep and able to "have very little share in the Action of the Poem." Although his succession remains crucial to Dulness' triumph, and forms the very action of the poem, the joke is that once chosen he becomes completely irrelevant, present throughout the demonstration of her victory in book four, but asleep, unconscious, absent. Ironically, Pope's response to the specter of female power takes a similar form, the poet at once absent from the poem, having withdrawn from a direct confrontation with the Goddess, but at the same time everywhere present. Pope, as Pat Rogers has recognized, played a very cagey and knowing game about assuming responsibility for *The Dunciad*: "he was able to exploit his technical anonymity: no separate edition of the poem issued before his death carried his name, though by that time nobody was asking about the identity of the author."[75] Pope succeeds in both withdrawing from the fictive landscape of the poem—never placing his name on the title-page, creating a narrative voice that cannot be his, and employing multiple factotums such as Scriblerus and Bentley to compose his notes—while at the same time dominating its textual universe, by implication always available as the transcendent authorial presence who alone can provide meaning in a cultural order gone mad. Pope, as Peter Stallybrass and Allon White suggest, attempted the impossible: "In the absence of any guarantee of higher authority Pope's obsessive negation drew attention inevitably to the arch-negator himself, who was no more able than those whom he attacked to climb outside or above the marketplace."[76] Pope endeavors to climb outside of the marketplace by exploiting his anonymity, making an issue of his lack of a name in order to make that name even more powerful.

The issue of names, as I've already discussed, is crucial to the poem, and Pope plays with names in all sorts of ways, suppressing his own in order to make it even more powerful, and highlighting the names of his rivals in order to diminish theirs. Pope's own name comes to represent a figure who, as it were, "needs no introduction," while the extended biographical introductions in the notes to other writers merely emphasize the futility of preserving the names of poets of no distinction or importance. Pope practices an impressive sleight of hand here, using his tactical anonymity to illuminate the genuinely anonymous state of the Grubstreet race. In this fashion Pope succeeds, as James McLaverty recognizes, in presenting himself "as a historical figure...a figure distanced in time." Pope perfects his monument to himself by managing "to think of himself as dead and to interpret himself to future generations."[77] In the textual archive that goes by the name of *The Dunciad*, Pope anticipates, stages, and celebrates his own death in an attempt to transform Dulness' triumph into his own apotheosis. This strategy looks backward to *The Rape of the Lock*, in which Belinda's supposed victory over time really signals that of the poet, her "lock" having been transformed into his text: "*This Lock*, the Muse shall consecrate to Fame, / And mid'st the Stars inscribe *Belinda*'s Name" (5. 149–50). Although Belinda has her name inscribed in the heavens, it is Pope's *Lock* that achieves cultural currency; fame and futurity now belong to the poet and his poem, not the individual woman who may have inspired the poem. *The Dunciad* represents an even more ambitious attempt to determine collective memory by textualizing the entire cultural world, utilizing new technologies to "MAKE ONE MIGHTY DUNCIAD OF THE LAND" (4. 604). Pope's archival text has overwhelmed its cultural landscape, *The Dunciad* having become "the land" itself.

As archives, libraries have always possessed a special status and significance for the civilizations whose texts they have protected, whose memories they have preserved. In the classical world they were associated with temples and shrines; the library at Alexandria was accounted one of the Seven Wonders of the World. During the seventeenth and eighteenth centuries, as the library took its modern form, it represented a specifically modern fantasy of inclusion, created by moveable type, the printed book, and the specific effects generated by the print revolution, which presented an unprecedented opportunity to codify, systematize, and periodicize a new world of learning. *The Dunciad* represents Pope's unusual and ungainly attempt to realize the promise of the print revolution and modern library, to create the one (or in Chambers' case, two) volume(s) that represents the key to all knowledge, to perfect a self-contained literary artifact that could present his greatness to the future. But the oblivion toward which Dulness hurries her minions is not, finally, defeated or even arrested by a textual apparatus that attempts to preserve memory and literary history within its byzantine ziggurat of notes, appendices, and addenda. The universal library remains a hopeless dream that rebukes and mocks modern aspirations to the perfect and exhaustive knowledge that the print revolution seems to promise.[78] Anyone who has attempted to teach *The Dunciad* recognizes that its obsessive self-referentiality does not help to better understand it, but positively hinders students, who become lost and frustrated within the bewildering landscape of early-eighteenth-century London. Although the poem's textual apparatus attempts to function like a street map, the ubiquitous *A–Z*, for instance, that both residents and tourists depend on to make London navigable, finally it recapitulates the effects of Dulness rather than counteracting them. In preserving the bewildering and miscellaneous details of contemporary literary history, the poem's notes present not an alternative vision to the forces that in the fourth book silence a narrator who asks for "yet a moment, one dim Ray of Light / Indulge, dread Chaos, and eternal Night" (4. 1–2), but another version of the oblivion that overwhelms the created world.

CHAPTER 4

"Graven with an iron pen and lead in the book for ever!": Paper and Permanence in Richardson's *Clarissa*

I

At the conclusion of *The Dunciad*, the transformation of the world into a text resembles a satiric device that Pope employs frequently in his mock epic: the substitution of a material object for the human identity it represents. Most often Pope uses the book or its individual pages for this satiric substitution, as when book three portrays an underworld in which poetic souls "Demand new bodies, and in Calf's array / Rush to the world, impatient for the day." This representation of the human by the material, and specifically the movement from book or paper to author, is most famously rehearsed in Dryden's *Mac Flecknoe*, as news of Shadwell's coronation spreads throughout London:

> No *Persian* Carpets spread th' Imperial way,
> But scatter'd Limbs of mangled poets lay:
> From dusty shops neglected authors come,
> Martyrs of Pies and Reliques of the Bum.
> Much *Heywood*, *Shirly*, *Ogleby* there lay,
> But loads of *Sh*— almost choakt the way.[1]

Here Dryden figures Shadwell's admirers as the pages of their own neglected books, no longer read but used instead to wrap greasy pies and wipe filthy bums. That which should nourish the mind becomes instead an image of bodily abjection and the physical processes that represent digestion, decay, and corruption. In the final line, Dryden's relentless satiric logic moves a reader from the bum to what issues from it, the "scatter'd limbs of mangled poets" altered into loads of shit. Pope would later utilize this association between paper and shit more indirectly in book two of *The Dunciad*, when Curll bests Lintot in their footrace after slipping in the "evening cates" dropped by his own Corinna in front of his rival bookseller's shop.

During the seventeenth and eighteenth centuries, this associative and metonymic link between paper and excrement looks toward both the material production of paper, as well as to the anxiety generated by paper's centrality to authorial identity. In the first instance, the manufacture of paper depended quite literally on the decomposition of rags into fiber. Cotton and linen fabric were fermented, sometimes with the addition of lime, until fungi appeared and high temperatures, beating, and stamping reduced the rags to a frothy pulp. Thomas Churchyard, in a 1588 poem celebrating the paper mill established by John Spilman at Dartford, Kent, expresses a naïve wonder at a process of manufacture that can transform "rotten ragges" into paper "white as snowe":

> And most to prayse, because of trifling toyes,
>   so great a wealth, our worthy world enioyes,
> Of drosse and rags, that serues no other meane,
>   and fowle bad shreds, comes Paper white and cleane.[2]

Linking the pages created by Grubstreet's minions with shit is not difficult when those pages were themselves the product of a trade that transformed rags, "drosse," and "fowle bad shreds," into paper.

Yet the association of paper and excrement depended as well on an anxiety that stemmed from the apparent fragility of the material early modern authors depended on for the preservation of their literary immortality. Churchyard refers to the rotting rags that eventually become paper as "nought" (D2), but, compared to other material substances, paper itself appears insubstantial and unreliable. Ancient civilizations had tried to preserve important historical records on metals, brass, copper, bronze, and lead, all employed to lend permanence to treaties, laws, and alliances.[3] Churchyard surveys the history of writing by looking back to a time when societies "wrote in stones, and barks of trees for shift." Placed besides such materials, the "Paper and the Pen" appear as "trifling toyes." Both classical and early modern poets, of course, explicitly recognized the futility of depending on the apparently indestructible materials of nature to preserve memory, and the dismissal of the pompous memorial of stone is a standard poetic trope, as we have seen. Nonetheless, the ability of paper to endure in the face of time when more substantial materials fail remains a source of both puzzlement and anxiety to early modern authors who participated in a print trade that consumed and produced an apparently endless supply of a substance, according to Churchyard, "Without whose helpe, no hap nor wealth is won, / and by whose ayde, great workes and deedes are done."

For writers who dream of immortality, a significant mystery attaches itself to the material reality of paper. Pope captures this perfectly in his *Moral*

Essays "Epistle III: To Allen Lord Bathurst," when he laments the invention of "blest paper-credit," which "lends Corruption lighter wings to fly":

> A single leaf shall waft an Army o'er,
>
> ...
>
> A leaf, like Sibyl's, scatter to and fro
> Our fates and fortunes, as the wind shall blow:
> Pregnant with thousands flits the Scrap unseen. (69, 75–77)

In this poem no material substance can mimic the power of paper, which, however airy and insubstantial, possesses the ability to move armies and determine the fate of nations. At one extreme, paper is shit, the foul remains of the processes of physical corruption and decay; at the other extreme it is impalpable, flimsy, a weightless substance whose power seems shadowy and unreal. This unstable movement between the excremental and the ethereal represents the most radical manifestation of the material/spiritual binary that for the early modern exemplifies the mystery and power of the printed book. In either register, paper provokes disquiet in authors who wish to construct literary monuments that will assure their place in cultural memory.

No writer in eighteenth-century England more fully evokes the material culture of the act of writing, and particularly the centrality of paper to the writing process, than the printer Samuel Richardson. His insistence on "writing to the moment" in *Pamela, Clarissa*, and *Sir Charles Grandison* means that each of these novels privileges writing above action, the latter always refracted through and dependent on the physical activity of putting ink on paper. As Carol Houlihan Flynn observes, "In all of his novels, Richardson makes his readers aware of the physical nature of correspondence. His letters become real objects of weight, taking up actual space."[4] Not only paper, but ink, quills, penknives, and seals figure prominently in his fiction, their material functioning and physical presence inseparable from the scenes of writing out of which Richardson constructs his plots.

In this chapter I will focus on *Clarissa*, because in this novel more than any other Richardson links his fascination with the act of placing ink on paper to the circulation and fate of the letters out of which his narrative emerges. For Pope in "To Bathurst" paper-credit flits unseen through the corridors of power, the magical power of paper figured precisely in its rarefied and intangible movement; in this poem paper possesses an ability to motivate and determine human behavior denied even to gold, a metal that itself has long occupied an important place in the human imaginary.[5] In *Clarissa*, on the other hand, how letters, placed under bricks, or written in the rain, hidden in stays, a wainscot box, pocket, or letter-case, are transported by messengers or post is always a matter of the greatest concern. Confined and forbidden to write from almost the beginning of her novel, Clarissa must continually attend to the material circuits that will allow her letters to reach their proper destination. And by the end of the novel, the ultimate fate of the immense correspondence initiated by her battle with Lovelace comes to concern almost every character in the novel. The 537 letters that compose their story must be accounted for, collected, archived, and preserved, rather than allowed to disappear into Pope's airy nothingness.

II

It is both predictable and ironic that what is generally regarded as one of the longest novels—if not THE longest—written in English should be haunted by the specter of its own insubstantiality. Questions regarding the fate of the correspondence that composes the novel—both of whether it will survive and how it will be interpreted—become increasingly important to more and more characters as the novel progresses. First Clarissa and Lovelace, then Anna Howe and John Belford, and finally both Clarissa's and Lovelace's families become consumed by the desire to preserve and control the collection of letters from which the novel takes its shape.

Such desires, however, are not just a fictional concern, but very much a consideration for Richardson himself, as well as the fictional form that he helped to create. The novel, according to Christopher Flint, is "perhaps the literary genre most closely allied with the development of print culture,"[6] and it remains, therefore, more than any other modern literary form, absorbed by issues of futurity and monumentality. Michael McKeon argues that the novel develops during a century and a half when Europe undergoes

> a major cultural transition in attitudes towards how to tell the truth in narrative...[when] empirical attitudes in the study of history and practice of law helped stimulate an unprecedented dedication to the collection of records, and validated both the first-hand 'evidence of the senses'...and the 'objective' testimony of documentary objects.[7]

Questions concerning the nature of truth, the status of history, and the transmission of cultural memory are fundamental to the generic evolution of the novel, just as they were to the institutional development of the early modern print trade, which helped in corresponding ways to transform conceptions of modern memory.

As a printer and publisher as well as an author, Richardson was embedded in mid-century print culture, especially sensitive to the memorial ambitions of both print and the distinctive fictional form he helped pioneer.[8] Christopher Flint insists that "the paradox of Richardson's technique is not that he enhances the story's realism by making us forget its printed nature but that he underscores the printed nature of the text as part of its documentary realism and its manufactured artifice within the public realm."[9] From his privileged position, in which the figures of printer and author coalesce, Richardson registers with particular clarity the tension between "documentary realism" and "manufactured artifice" that concerned not just the print trade, but an entire economic culture taking shape through the formation and early capitalist evolution of banks, credit, a national debt, and stock manipulations like the South Sea Bubble. Paper money, more useful than gold—as Pope recognized—precisely because it possessed no intrinsic value in itself, functioned as a "general equivalent" and "standard measure" in an economy dependant on circulation and fungibility.

Representations of that economy, moreover, possessed a distinctly gendered dimension; according to J.G.A. Pocock,

> in that Augustan journalism concerned with evaluating the impact of public credit upon society,...Credit is symbolized as a goddess having the attributes of the Renaissance goddess Fortune, and even more than she equated with fantasy, passion and dynamic change. She stands for that future which can only be sought passionately and inconstantly, and for the hysterical fluctuations of the urge towards it.[10]

Fortune and Credit share an inconstancy and dynamism that comes to characterize the new economy, and, in Pope's goddess Dulness, the print trade that played such an important role in its evolution. The magic and mystery of paper, fundamental to new forms of credit and the new novel, both underwrote and undermined economic as well as authorial stability and certainty.[11]

The archival growth of *Clarissa* documents Richardson's unease about the "insubstantiality" of his massive novel, and the intellectual difficulties that mark its desire to achieve realism. Although *Clarissa* does not undergo an archival proliferation quite as extraordinary as that of *The Dunciad*, it nonetheless became a textual object that continued to evolve for as long as its author lived. Thomas Keymer even argues about *Clarissa*—as I did in the last chapter about *The Dunciad*—that "the novel notoriously resists simple textual definition. Between 1744, when Richardson began to circulate the first handwritten copies, and 1761 (the year of his death), when he seems to have planned a new revision, its text was in a state of recurrent flux, each version bringing together elements from the total set of Clarissa material in significantly different forms and combinations."[12] Such materials include *Hints of Prefaces for Clarissa* (1749), *Meditations Collected from the Sacred Books* (1750), both introductory matter and the "Postscript" to the third edition (1751), *Letters and Passages Restored from the Original Manuscripts of the History of Clarissa* (1751), and *A Collection of Moral and Instructive Sentiments, Maxims, Cautions and Reflections Contained in the Histories of Pamela, Clarissa and Sir Charles Grandison* (1755).[13] Like *The Dunciad*, *Clarissa*, marked by its diverse constituent parts and self-archiving growth over time, challenges some of our conventional assumptions about the status of a literary text and the physical reality of a printed work.[14] The way in which Pope and Richardson transform their most important works into archives suggests both the power of material production, as well as the tendency of literary texts to undermine the more serious epistemological claims of the technology whose powers they appropriate; both Pope's poem and Richardson's novel emphasize the conditional status of the object and its objectivity. Both privilege and celebrate the memorial power of the archive, even as they reveal, as James E. Young insists, that "the motives of memory are never pure," and that "both the reasons for memory and the forms memory takes are always socially mandated."[15]

In joining Pope and Richardson in this fashion, I don't mean to obscure the great differences between them, or to claim that both shared a similar understanding of the relationship between literary fame and memorial power. Pope's turn to and dependence on the archive stems from his determination to populate his satiric world with real individuals, and to confront the problem of literary survival when surrounded by a multitude of competing contemporaries. Richardson's letters, on the other hand, demonstrate that he possessed no appreciation for the unusual satiric strategies and memorial aspirations of *The Dunciad*: "Methinks, Sir, Mr. Pope might employ his Time, and his admirable Genius better than in exposing Insects of a Day: For if these Authors would live longer, they should not be put down as Dunces." A year later, in 1743, Richardson, writing to Aaron Hill, was even more dismissive about Pope's apparently endless revisions of the poem: "I have bought Mr. Pope over so often, and his Dunciad so lately before his last new-vampt one, that I am tir'd of the Extravagance; and wonder every Body else is not.... Has he no Invention, Sir, to be better employ'd about? No Talents for worthier Subjects?"

Ironically, Richardson here ridicules Pope for the archival growth of a text whose excesses he would soon imitate, and even during the late 1740s, while the first edition of *Clarissa* was still being published, his contempt for the unsettling extravagances of *The Dunciad* is hardly modified by his appreciation for Pope's desire to dictate interpretations of his work, and the more general question of how the knowing "Few" must educate "the Tastes" of the "Many":

> a Son of Thunder is wanted to rouse the Public out of its Stupidity, and tell it what it should, and what it should not, approve of. Mr. Pope in the Height of his Fame, tho' he had made himself, by Arts only He (as a Man of Genius) could stoop to, the *Fashion*, could not trust his Works with the Vulgar, without Notes longer than the Work, and Self-praises, to tell them what he meant, and that he *had* a Meaning, in this or that Place. And thus every-one was taught to read with his Eyes.[16]

Richardson presents Pope's "Arts" as morally suspect, detrimental to the ethical interests of a reading public whose moral education the proliferation of *Clarissa*'s text was designed to protect. Considering the reception of *Pamela*, and the very public division between "Pamelists" and "Anti-Pamelists," the problem of enforcing authorial meaning particularly concerned Richardson, who struggled to develop a new prose form whose protocols during the mid-century remained as yet unformed and uncertain. Sarah Fielding thought that Richardson's use of "familiar letters to relate a compleat Story...is a Method so intirely new...that the Author seems to have a Right to make his own Laws."[17] For Richardson such "Laws" were necessary if he were to transform the letter into a literary artifact, the "novel" into a "history," his status as "a plain writer: a sincere well-wisher: an undesigning scribbler; who admire none but the natural and easy beauties of the pen" into an author who could claim the power to control interpretations of his own pen and press.[18]

Both the fictional Clarissa and Lovelace, like the printer Richardson, identify themselves as scribblers,[19] and all three are equally disingenuous in trying to pretend that their writing is careless or illegible, hastily written, meaningless, or even the product of a petty author or worthless writer. Richardson, in fact, turns to the archive—turning his novel into an archive—precisely for the same reasons as his two main characters: he wants to ensure the survival in cultural memory not only of his own fiction, but of his interpretation. Like Clarissa and Lovelace, Richardson becomes consumed by the task of transforming *story* and *tale* into *history*, of controlling the text, its preservation, reception, and meaning in time. Like his fictional protagonists, Richardson wants the record to endorse his authority, the compulsive collecting and proliferation of texts both within the novel and around it dedicated to the effort to achieve cultural and memorial mastery. In paraphrasing "these sacred books" in her "Meditation" in letter 364, Clarissa captures the ultimate ambitions that drive the three scribblers who give the novel its shape: "Oh that my words were now written! Oh that they were printed in a book! that they were graven with an iron pen and lead in the book for ever!" (1125). Clarissa here evokes a transcendental model of memory that reflects an ideal of permanence functioning within, between, and finally, in its aspirations toward the divine, beyond the printed word.

From paper and words, writing and printing, to iron and lead and the assumption of a sacred authority that will never end, this quotation touches on the extraordinary range of meanings that animate the activity of writing, which moves from the most mundane and material to the most exalted and sublime. In what follows I want to trace the circuits that link the former to the latter, and in so doing demonstrate that however imbricated *Clarissa* is in the materiality of writing, that materiality cannot guarantee the mastery over narrative, time, and memory that Clarissa, Lovelace, and their creator Richardson wished to possess. All three cannot escape the fundamental irony of *Clarissa*: memorial mastery's incommensurability with material forms of representation.

III

Before turning to the novel itself, and the fictional struggle between Clarissa and Lovelace for memorial supremacy, I want to look briefly at contemporary receptions of the novel, for they can suggest how the battle waged between his fictional creations resembles the one Richardson himself fought with his readers, as well as the important convergences between the interpretative communities depicted in the novel and the ones that received and in effect immortalized Richardson's work in mid-century Britain.

Although a major success, the publication of *Clarissa* did not occasion the enormous public furor and debate that ensued after the appearance of *Pamela* on November 6, 1740. While Fielding's *Shamela* and *Joseph Andrews* remain the most famous of contemporary responses to Richardson's first novel, Richardson's distinguished rival represents but one voice in a large, raucous chorus, what Thomas Keymer and Peter Sabor in *Pamela in the Marketplace* (2005) label a "Grubstreet grabfest," which transformed the novel's appearance into an astonishing commercial, as well as aesthetic and moral phenomenon: "to write about Richardson's novel was not only, and sometimes not even, to enter a high-minded debate about style and technique, gender and rank, or religion and ethics; it was also, or often simply instead, to enter a bustling forum...in the larger project of selling print."[20] And sell print it did: *Pamela* itself went through five authorized editions within a year of its initial publication, perhaps twenty thousand copies printed and sold.

Clarissa did not replicate this type of success, either in terms of sales—four authorized editions printed in three and a half years—or responses: Sarah Fielding's *Remarks on Clarissa* (1749) appears to be the sole pamphlet occasioned by Richardson's second novel.[21] Yet *Clarissa* did generate a great deal of interest, and the debate it occasioned breathes a more "high-minded" air than that of its predecessor. While the serial publication of the novel—which appeared in three installments in December 1747, April 1748, and December 1748—may have helped to increase sales by whetting the interest and curiosity of readers, it was even more significant in its creation of an unusual space within which serious debate about the novel could flourish, particularly in Richardson's own correspondence. Just a few weeks before the first installment was published, in November of 1747, Richardson is already complaining to Edward Young about "What contentions, what disputes have I involved myself in with my poor Clarissa, through my own diffidence, and for want of a will! I wish I had never consulted any body but Dr. Young, who so kindly vouchsafed me his ear, and sometimes his opinion."[22] Although Richardson undoubtedly flatters his friend here, one of his chief literary advisors, he also acknowledges the intense pressures on him to mitigate Clarissa's harsh fate that would only increase as the novel appeared over the course of the year; in the months preceding the appearance of the final three volumes, while advanced copies circulated among his friends, he faced repeated requests for mercy.[23] Responses to the novel in Richardson's correspondence present a rare opportunity to examine the relation between an author and his early modern readers.

If, as I suggested earlier, Ben Jonson's decisive turn from the theater to the book inaugurated a fragile pact between a mysterious and anonymous reader and the early modern author, Richardson's correspondence concerning *Clarissa* demonstrates how profoundly the marketplace within which that relationship took shape had changed in almost a century and a half, and just how much more familiar that reader had become. Many of those readers, of course, were Richardson's friends, whose advice he sought—and rarely followed—before the novel was published, during its publication, and in the years after its first appearance, while he was still revising both the text and the paratextual matter that would accompany the novel. As late as April 24, 1751, the Reverend Patrick Delany promises that "I will observe your directions about Clarissa, and write my impertinent observations in the margin" (4: 37). Yet many offering advice and criticism were not known to Richardson, and Henry Fielding, in his praise for *Clarissa* in *The Jacobite's Journal*, which appeared in early January of 1748, shortly after the publication of the first two volumes of the novel, reacts with high authorial disdain to adverse judgments of Richardson's work: "With what Indignation do I therefore hear the Criticisms made on this Performance...Do, pray, Sir, now and then lay aside your Politics, and take upon you to correct our Critics. Advise these Snarlers, of both Sexes, to improve their Heads a little, before they venture to sit in Judgment on the Merit of an Author."[24] For Fielding, anonymous critical readers can only be "Snarlers," unfit to sit in judgment on an author, who possesses sole responsibility for the literary text.

However much Richardson may have shared this opinion—and the letter in which he desired "a Son of Thunder...to rouse the Public out of its Stupidity" suggests that he, like Fielding, privileged the author far above his reader—he nonetheless shaped his fiction with his readers very much in mind, particularly in regard to the novel's conclusion. Thomas Keymer even insists that in *Clarissa* "the roles of text and reception are peculiarly intertwined. It is the text, in its final instalment, that responds to its readers, as much as vice versa. It gives voice to their desires, challenges the legitimacy of these desires, and eventually denies them the comfortable resolutions they had sought."[25]

Nowhere is this dynamic more visible than in Richardson's unusual relationship with Lady Dorothy Bradshaigh, who, when she first wrote Richardson on October 10, 1748, as "Belfour," was unknown to him, driven to initiate a correspondence because she had "too much reason to apprehend a fatal catastrophe" (4: 178) in the final three volumes of Clarissa, which were to appear in December of that year. Although her curse remains the most famous part of this letter—"May the hatred of all the young, beautiful, and virtuous, for ever be your portion!" (4: 181) if he makes Lovelace and Clarissa unhappy—what strikes me as most remarkable is Belfour's attempt to write, or rewrite, Richardson's text for him. "Belfour," herself a fictional creation, doesn't simply ask Richardson to change his ending, but to explain the transformation by writing "a little excuse to the reader, 'that you had a design of concluding so and so, but was given to understand it would disappoint so many of your readers, that, upon mature deliberation and advice of friends, you had resolved on the contrary'" (4: 180). Here she attempts to imitate Richardson's voice in penning an excuse to his readers that can make room for her own version of his ending.

Intrigued by this first letter, Richardson offered to send "Mrs. Belfour" the fifth volume—"if you will favour me with a letter upon it" (4: 193)—which she read with trepidation and unhappiness: "dear Sir, it is too shocking and barbarous a story for publication. I wish I could not think of it. Blot out but one night, and the villainous laudanum, and all may be well again" (4: 201).

Shortly after, however, she sent him another response, much more fully developed, in which she proposed "another scheme, which came into my wild head; and, for my life, I could not help transmitting it to paper...Suppose Clarissa..." (4: 202–03). For three pages, Belfour spins a predictable fantasy in which "the compassionate Clarissa," restored to health, visits Lovelace, who, overwhelmed with grief and remorse, lies on his deathbed. She promises marriage should he recover and, when his disorder takes "an unexpected turn," he returns to health and redeems her promise: marriage, happiness, "tender scenes"—"with what pleasure could I sob, and dedicate a deluge of tears to those scenes" (4: 203–05). Belfour ends her letter to Richardson explaining that "You are in love with your image as it is, and you will still be more so, by giving it additional and enlivening graces" (4: 206).

The friendship that grew out of this exchange of letters lasted until Richardson's death, and it suggests just how enmeshed author and reader might become in the modern literary marketplace, and how a literary text might be shaped by the tension between their diverse desires.[26] Richardson certainly never let what Belfour calls "your image" out of his own control, resisting the "additional and enlivening graces" that she only too happily put forward, but there is no doubt that the form the novel took in its successive printings responded to his readers' desires, even as he denied them. Richardson never capitulated to the chorus of readers calling for Clarissa's earthly triumph and Lovelace's redemption, but the archival growth of his novel embedded such voices in his text through his unremitting attempts to challenge and resist them.

Moreover, this struggle between rival conceptions of the novel was often carried out in the form of competing fictions. Belfour, as we have seen, kindly provides Richardson with the outlines of an alternative ending; later in their correspondence, after they had met and she had assumed her real name as Dorothy Bradshaigh, she sends him "a pity-moving case" that relates the "tragic story" of a young lady wed to a man she hated. But Bradshaigh wasn't the only one who sought to rewrite Richardson's novel: her sister, Lady Elizabeth Echlin, admitted to Richardson in 1754 that she had, unlike her sister, not simply imagined an alternative ending, but actually written it: "I...contented myself with supposing that I had discovered some mistakes in Clarissa's story, which were owing to your being mis-informed...I cannot, without blushing, confess that I weakly attempted to imitate an eminent pen" (5: 20). In his reply, the "misinformed" author kindly requests that Lady Echlin favor him with the "different turn" she has given his story: "I wish you not to have it transcribed; I ever admired the first flowings of a fine imagination" (5: 24).[27]

Richardson could resist such fictions, revisions, and "fine imaginations" because, like his heroine, fixated on words that might be "graven with an iron pen and lead in the book for ever," he "was willing to do something in this way, that never before had been done":

[I] Cannot consent, that the History of Clarissa should be looked upon as a
mere Novel or Amusement—since it is rather a History of Life and Manners;

the principal View of which, by an Accommodation to the present light Taste of an Age immersed in Diversions, that engage the Eye and the Ear only, and not the Understanding, aims to investigate the great Doctrines of Christianity, and to teach the Reader how to die, as well as how to live.[28]

Richardson certainly doesn't claim a divine warrant for his work here; he isn't quite a Milton, proud to "see and tell / Of things invisible to mortal sight." Nonetheless, like his heroine, he has nothing but contempt for the "Diversions" of a shallow, fashionable world, and looks in his writing for a type of permanence that will outlast the "light Taste of an Age." He insists that his book represents that which "never before had been done," its religious dimension essential to its unique status.

Yet such an achievement, as Richardson's negotiations with his correspondents suggests, depends not just on the author but on his readers as well. In *Critical Remarks on Sir Charles Grandison, Clarissa and Pamela*, published in 1754, Richardson found himself ridiculed by an anonymous "Lover of Virtue" who opined that "if ever a good taste universally prevails, your romances, as well as all others, will be as universally neglected": "Such, Sir, must be the fate of all works which owe their success to a present capricious humor, and have not real intrinsic worth to support them."[29] Richardson, of course, shared this contempt for a "capricious" age, which is one reason why he insists that *Clarissa* is not a "mere Novel or Amusement." His emphasis on the proper Christian understanding of and appreciation for death is precisely his attempt to embed "real intrinsic worth" in his work, to achieve literary futurity through the moral as well as aesthetic power of his fictions. But Richardson recognized, I suspect, that such a project is doomed to failure: "intrinsic worth" alone cannot save a literary work for the future. As Edward Young wrote to Richardson in 1749, the year after *Clarissa*'s publication, "How long was *Paradise Lost* an obscure book? Authors give works their merit; but others give them their fame" (2: 27). Richardson's many years of perfecting *Clarissa*, and his willingness to engage so many attempts to rewrite his novel, suggest his reluctant agreement with Young's pronouncement. Nothing an author writes can, in and of itself, guarantee immortality; that gift, perversely enough, only readers can bestow.

IV

In order to understand writing in *Clarissa*—the physical act of putting ink on paper, as well as the memorial aspirations that this apparently mundane act embody—a reader must begin with the letter, for almost all writing in Richardson's world concerns the writing of letters. There are, of course, important exceptions in the novel—wills, marriage settlements, and other legal documents come immediately to mind, and I will address these later in the chapter—but for the most part to write in *Clarissa* means to write a letter. That the letter should prove so important to the formal evolution of the novel should not surprise us, because few forms of writing in the West have as complex and rich a history. Moreover, as Philip Beale reminds us, "To put your hand on a letter, to see its address panel and seal, to read the text and signature, is to come as close as we can to the essence of our history."[30]

Beale's idealized image of the letter—his evocation of how letters put us in touch with both an individual life and a sense of collective history—stems from the way in which the letter has moved, historically, quite dizzyingly between the poles of public and private, from the rhetorical and political to the familiar and intimate. Terry Eagleton refers to "the Janus-faced letter, at once nature and artifice," while Howard Anderson and Irvin Ehrenpreis explain that "the letter is bounded on one side by the essay—in which the substantive element takes over—and on the other by the confession, in which awareness of the reader is subordinated to preoccupation with self."[31] In the West the letter has functioned as both the most public of forms, used by governments to provide a documentary record of historical fact, or, particularly during the latter half of the seventeenth century and first half of the eighteenth, by citizens as a forum for the discussion of political and religious issues, and the most private, in which individuals are called upon to reveal their personal lives to their closest friends and family while privileging, at the same time, everyday, material life.

In Richardson's novel, the letter functions in both fashions. Clarissa's fateful correspondence with Lovelace begins, we should remember, as a public and not a private exchange, when Clarissa's uncle Hervey desires from Lovelace a description of the Grand Tour for a young man entrusted to his care. Lovelace is to write letters, in response to queries from Clarissa, to a young gentleman (who it appears he doesn't even know); and these letters are first designed to be read aloud to her whole family as "agreeable amusements in winter evenings" (47). A sort of "winter's tale," these letters begin as a wholly public event, designed—at least by Clarissa's family—to educate a youth about a conventional form of travel, and to amuse the family on otherwise unoccupied evenings.

Yet even at this very early stage in the novel, before she has the least suspicion of Lovelace's predatory nature, Clarissa apprehends a certain danger in her situation that depends on the radical instability of the letter as a form, its ability to move promiscuously from the "full assembly" to a "particular address." Clarissa recognizes that however formal and public its nature, "a kind of correspondence [was] begun between him and me" (47). While she may struggle to keep their "kind of correspondence" entirely in the public domain, Lovelace, of course, has designed something quite different, and has little difficulty in transforming their letters into the personal, furtive, and prohibited.[32] Within just a few months, the baleful influence of Lovelace has altered not only his correspondence with Clarissa, but Clarissa's correspondence with her friend Anna Howe, into something not just private but clandestine, with letters hidden under bricks and searched for in the pockets and stays of Clarissa's servant. The surreptitious transportation of incriminating and dangerous letters occupies Clarissa, Anna, and even Lovelace for much of the novel.

By its conclusion, however, the hundreds of letters generated by the original but now forgotten description of the Grand Tour have become again a very public property. Clarissa's will stipulates that two copies be made of the correspondence Belford has collected, and that these copies be used to vindicate her actions to her family. Later, Lovelace even relates his fear that "Miss Howe threatens to have the case published to the whole world" (1437). Clarissa articulates many reasons for refusing to take Lovelace to court, but it becomes increasingly clear that the letters she asks Belford to collect are designed as an alternative site where she can more fully protect her reputation and memory. Both the courts of law and the print trade, because of their public natures, could be very dangerous places for women in the seventeenth and eighteenth centuries, their honor and reputation always at risk of public exposure. Clarissa, like Margaret Cavendish, attempts to utilize the archive as a new public forum where her memory might be protected, preserved, and vindicated. The "archival turn," according to Ann Laura Stoler, stems from a special relationship to documentary evidence, a new understanding of "how people imagine they know what they know and what institutions validate that knowledge," and both the aristocratic rake and scribbling heroine endeavor to manipulate the archive in order to validate their lives and memories.[33]

The public to private trajectory of the letter in *Clarissa* to some extent recapitulates the form's history in England, where, according to M.T. Clanchy in *From Memory to Written Record* (1979), the evolution of the letter played a crucial role, even before the change from script to print, in the process that transformed England from a country that relied on oral wisdom and the authority of age to one that depended on books, charters, and governmental writs. The "original" impetus to archive, collect, and preserve, according to Clanchy, belongs not to the seventeenth and eighteenth centuries, but to the eleventh and twelfth, when English kings first began to construct bureaucracies and administrative structures that depended on the accumulation of written records: "The primary records most commonly met with are letters of one sort or another. They are here collectively described as 'statements issued by individuals' because the generic term 'letters' is ambiguous and can mislead." What we primarily think of as *the letter*, a private and privileged communication between two individuals, only gradually came into being:

> The documents considered so far are not "letters" in the modern sense of missives. Charters, chirographs and certificates were not usually sent by the writer to a recipient who is addressed in the document; instead they were addressed to the public and handed to the beneficiary at the time they were written. They were primarily intended to be records rather than communications...The habit of sending missives, conveying ephemeral information about day-to-day matters, developed slowly.

Distinctions between the ephemeral and the historic are built into the evolution of the letter as a form, which proliferated in medieval England not as correspondence between individuals but as "writs" and "*brevia*." According to Clanchy, what we think of as "real missives were introduced by Henry II in the form of letters close. A letter close was sealed on the tie that kept it rolled up, so that it could be opened only by the addressee."[34] It is in this form that the letter migrated from the narrow world of public records and documentary evidence to the private realm of correspondence and "mundane" news.

Private letters do survive from the thirteenth century, but a flourishing, national correspondence depended not just on an increasingly literate population, but on specific advances in both the manufacture of paper and the collection and distribution of mail. An increase in the production of paper, more affordable for large numbers of people than either parchment or vellum, meant that by the late fifteenth and early sixteenth centuries extensive collections of private letters begin to take shape. But the establishment of a postal system that could deliver letters to private individuals throughout the country took another two centuries to develop: "while persons of wealth and power have always had messengers to carry their scrawls, it took the development of a convenient, reliable postal service to provide less exalted correspondents with an equivalent amenity. Only after the Glorious Revolution did the English post office give that kind of service."[35] Richardson's career as a writer of fiction famously begins with a book that provided epistolary models for those unfamiliar with this burgeoning form, and *Clarissa* is especially sensitive to the role played by the letter in eighteenth-century England, registering the changes taking place in both the manufacture of paper and the administrative evolution of the mail service.

V

At only one moment in *Clarissa* must the protagonist confront a writing surface not made of paper, and her response to the novelty is one of horror: "And then to my great terror, out she drew some parchments from her handerchief, which she had kept (unobserved by me) under her apron and, rising, put them in the opposite window. Had she produced a serpent, I could not have been more frighted." What Aunt Hervey produces here, of course, are the marriage settlements between Solmes and the Harlowes, "engrossed, and ready for signing, and have been for some time."

Clarissa's fear of "those horrid parchments" (339) stems primarily from what they represent, her enforced marriage to a man she disdains. But the material is itself significant, because although parchment predates paper as a writing material, by the eighteenth century it was normally used only for documents of great importance because of its relative indestructibility compared to paper. When, later in the novel, Lovelace provides marriage settlements with which to tempt Clarissa, nothing in their description suggests the use of parchment, and the difference between Solmes' proposals and Lovelace's emphasizes the falseness of the latter's promises compared to the frightening finality of the former's. Should Clarissa allow herself to marry Solmes, her fate would be fixed, for they would be married forever. His parchments represent the durable and permanent, the unchanging and inviolate.

Parchment is made from the skin of sheep, and vellum, the finest parchment, from calfskin.[36] Originally invented and used in Asia Minor as a substitute for papyrus, it became "the principal writing material in medieval Europe. Illuminated manuscripts...epitomize the achievements of the Middle Ages as much as great churches in stone. Like stone, parchment was a durable material which demanded of its users an awareness of form and a consciousness of posterity."[37] The attention to time and memory that parchment demanded—and which accounts in the novel for Clarissa's horror—was even reinforced by the difficulty of writing on parchment with a quill, which made writing a special skill that demanded its own discipline. Utilizing a range of instruments and materials—the knife or razor, quill, and ink—the writer on parchment participated in a practice that, because of the specialization demanded by its sheer difficulty, accentuated the intimate relationship between writing and memory.

The replacement of parchment by paper marks therefore a significant material transformation in early modern Europe, one involved not only in increases in literacy, as well as matters of manufacture and cost—because paper is cheaper to produce than parchment—but one that depended on the relationship of paper to the printing press: "the first bookprinters of Europe had to make their work conform to paper that had been made primarily for writing."[38] The complex material calculus that links writing to parchment, parchment to paper, and paper to printing provides an explanation for some of the anxieties of Clarissa, Lovelace, and Richardson, who employ technologies that call into question what often presents itself as the direct, straightforward, and idealized relationship between writing, printing, and memory.

This was particularly true of paper, not simply because it lacked the durability of parchment, but because its manufacture and trade bound it to some of the most pressing economic and social issues in early modern England. An anonymous eighteenth-century lyric suggests the centrality of paper to the cultural, social, and economic systems of early capitalism:

RAGS make paper,
PAPER makes money,
MONEY makes banks,
BANKS make loans,
LOANS make beggars,
BEGGARS make RAGS.[39]

I have already touched on the almost contradictory system of circulation encompassed by the first three lines of this verse, whose movement from rags to paper to money links paper at one extreme to excrement and at the other to the immaterial. But it is worth examining these associations in greater detail, for they perform an important role in the novel, particularly because they are rarely articulated in any explicit fashion, but play instead at the margins of the text.

The linen rags needed to make paper, for instance, connect paper directly to clothing and what Jones and Stallybrass in *Renaissance Clothing and the Materials of Memory* (2000) have discussed as one of the primary "bearers of identity, ritual, and social memory" in Renaissance Europe. Clothing, unlike money, was made of "material that was richly absorbent of symbolic meaning and in which memories and social relations were literally embodied."[40] Richardson's novel demonstrates that this symbolic system remained very much alive in the eighteenth century, for the circulation of clothing punctuates key moments in the narrative. One of the first bribes used by the Harlowes to persuade Clarissa to marry Solmes involves the "patterns of the richest silk" with which they try to tempt her, "the newest, as well as richest, that we could procure; answerable to our station in the world" (188). The relationship of clothes to rank and identity figures largely in Clarissa's successful attempt to escape Lovelace, when—in Lovelace's absence—she fools the ladies of Mrs. Sinclair's establishment by pretending to give to Mabel "a brown lustring gown...with some alterations to make it more suitable to her degree" (966). While Mabel tries on this gown, Clarissa uses Mabel's "upper petticoat" to disguise herself and affect her escape. The relationship between clothing, particularly linen, and paper is visible throughout the novel. Clarissa not only spends much of the novel hiding her letters within her stays or clothing, but, when she contemplates her escape from Harlowe Place, prepares parcels that include "all the letters and papers you would not have them see," and parcels of "clothes, linen, &c" (279; see also 283). For Clarissa, the bare essentials demanded by flight include paper on the one hand, and clothing on the other, the former created from the remains of the latter.

The intimate relationship of rags to the manufacture of paper was economically recognized and legally formalized as early as 1589, when John Spilman's patent for his papermaking facilities at Dartford, Kent, granted him a monopoly over both papermaking and the collection of rags.[41] The dependence of papermakers on rags had important consequences for English trade, a 1640 petition requesting a patent for the manufacture of white writing paper asking also "for the prohibition of the export of linen rags."[42] By the first half of the eighteenth century, the explosion of print in England had led to a tremendous increase in the demand for both paper and rags, a demand that England could not meet without depending on imports from other European countries, particularly France. During the latter half of the seventeenth century, the Stationers' Company licensed ships specifically to import paper from France; the 1690 Act of Parliament entitled "An Act for encouraging and better establishing the manufacture of white paper in this kingdom" laments that "the trade with France is found to be of pernicious consequence to this kingdom, much of the treasure of this nation having been exhausted by the importation of vast quantities of the commodities of the earth and manufactures of France, and particularly of white writing and printing paper."[43] Although the English manufacture of paper increased over tenfold from the 1690s to 1720s, securing good quality paper remained an issue throughout Richardson's life as a printer.

The novel glances at trade with France in the figure of Mrs. Townsend, Anna Howe's friend, "a great dealer in Indian silks, Brussels and France laces, cambrics, linen, and other valuable goods; which she has a way of coming at, duty-free." Mrs. Townsend, in other words, is a smuggler, a "contraband trader" as Anna Howe reluctantly admits, even as she urges Clarissa to seek the protection of Mrs. Townsend's "principal warehouse" in Deptford and her "two brothers, each master of a vessel" (621–22). Even the upright Mrs. Howe and her scrupulously moral daughter find themselves slightly tainted by their association with the clandestine trade in luxury goods that marked England's relationship with Europe, and particularly France, during the development of early capitalism.

Paper's association with cloth and clothing, as well as its relative scarcity and the subsequent English dependence on foreign manufacture that it fostered during the late seventeenth and early eighteenth centuries, provides this very indirect link with smuggling in the novel. But paper had also long been tainted by a wide range of associations with unhealthy smells, flooding, infection, and plague, as well as a host of contentious issues involving hierarchy, rank, and station. The complaints of Jack Cade to Lord Say in Shakespeare's *2 Henry VI* are only the most famous expression of a long-held distrust of important changes that linked technology and literacy:

> Thou hast most traitorously corrupted the youth of the realm in erecting a grammar school. And whereas before, our forefathers had no other books but the score and the tally, thou hast caused printing to be used, and, contrary to the King, his crown, and dignity, thou hast built a papermill. (4.7. 36–42)

This passage is a tissue of anachronism and untruth, since this Lord Say would have had nothing to do with paper mills—the first paper mill in England was not built until very late in the fifteenth century—and Cade's rebellion predates as well the establishment of Caxton's first printing press in England. Nonetheless, it suggests the contentious history of transformations in literacy, technology, and manufacture that dispossessed some elements of the population while privileging others. "The score and the tally" represent a world eclipsed and overthrown by the printing press and archive, books, paper, and a new literacy.

During the plague year of 1636 it was even thought that the infection had been brought to England by the linen and cotton rags imported by papermakers.[44] In September, Peter Heywood, justice of the peace for Westminster, ordered that all rag shops be burned in order to prevent their merchandise from being transported or used to make paper; later in the month an order mandated the closing of all paper mills in the county. A petition to the Privy Council from people living near paper mills in Buckingham and Middlesex provides a dramatic sense of the myriad ills that could be laid at the door of the papermakers: the petitioners "allege" that landlords "by converting their corn mills into paper mills have advanced their rents," that papermakers "have brought many poor and indigent persons into their parishes," that they pay "double wages in comparison with other labourers," that paper mills "have flooded the country" and "killed the fish," and that "the noisome smells of the rags spread an infection."[45] The manufacture of paper is here linked to a host of social and economic evils, from industrial pollution to wage disparities, from food shortages to the greed of landlords. Behind the whiteness of the best writing paper that Clarissa, Anna, and Lovelace use so promiscuously, lies a history of manufacture that associated paper with infection, pollution, smuggling, and class rivalry and even warfare.

VI

In Richardson's novel the single juxtaposition between parchment and paper suggests the potential fragility and physical corruptibility of the medium to which the imprisoned heroine, the vicious rake, and the master printer have entrusted their memorial aspirations. In contrast, the novel is continually concerned with the circulation of paper, and specifically of the letters that are paper's primary form in Richardson's world. As early as letter nine, Clarissa must begin to devise elaborate procedures in order to secure her correspondence to Anna Howe. After this first reference to "clandestine correspondences" (67), Clarissa's attention to the safe delivery of her letters never wavers: even on her deathbed, on the very night before she dies, she initiates the following conversation with Belford:

> —'Tis time to send the letter to my good Mrs. Norton.
> Shall I, madam, send my servant post with it?
> Oh no, sir, I thank you. It will reach the dear woman too soon (as she will think) by the post.
> I told her this was not post-day.
> Is it Wednesday still? Said she. Bless me! I know not how the time goes: but very tediously, 'tis plain. (1352)

Here, the reference to the post—which left London on Tuesdays, Thursdays, and Saturdays—serves to fix the day of Clarissa's death, and to remind us as well that most letters in the novel are not sent via the postal service, but by a veritable host of servants, bearers, and messengers. Such a reference, in other words, points both to the institutionalization of the postal service—whose invariable schedules have already begun to measure time—as well as to its as yet marginal status: the economic privileges enjoyed by the Harlowes, Lovelaces, and Howes allow them alternative modes of delivery whenever they deem it necessary.

The development and evolution of the postal service in England took place over centuries, and, as Christopher Browne argues, "was one of the pioneers of the Industrial Revolution. It forged new trading links, created a national news network."[46] The Post Office and the print trade, in fact, can be linked as part of "a coordinated system for circulating both private messages and public works."[47] Together they helped forge the modern information age and even the industrial state. A little more than two hundred years after Clarissa's death, a very different English hero, Ian Fleming's James Bond, attests to the way in which the Post Office has become synonymous with the power of the state it represents when he wins $15,000 playing blackjack at the Tiara in Las Vegas and "put the three big bills in the envelope...Then he bought stamps at the desk and slipped the envelope down the slot marked 'U.S. Mail' and hoped that there, in the most sacrosanct repository in America, it would be safe."[48]

In the mid-eighteenth century, the postal service in England had yet to achieve this measure of trust. Indeed, in letter 341, Lovelace laments that he has not the access Belford enjoys to two letters between Clarissa and Anna Howe: "Thou hadst the two letters in thy hand. Had they been in mine, the seal would have yielded to the touch of my warm finger (perhaps without the help of the post-office bullet)" (1085). Here the reference to the "post-office bullet" emphasizes the common knowledge that letters sent through the government's postal service could be opened as a matter of course by government order. Even when the government was not suspected of abusing the privacy of its own postal service, the post did not inspire confidence. After Clarissa finally escapes from Lovelace she suggests to Anna that she will "send my letters by the usual hand (Collins's), to be left at the Saracen's Head on Snow Hill: whither you may send yours (as we both used to do, to Wilson's), except such as we shall think fit to transmit by the post" (1016). Clearly, the postal service represents the least trusted method for delivering letters.

Although the Post Office was officially established and named in 1635, when Charles I passed an act of parliament opening the royal post to all members of the British public, for those who could afford it the private messenger remained the preferred mode of delivery: "the method of delivering letters by a messenger who took mail from a sender to the recipient continued to be used until modern times. Speed was not the main consideration; it was the certainty of arrival and security of the letter that mattered most. The conversation between the messenger and the recipient of the news was an essential part of the process."[49] At no point in the novel is the interaction between messenger and recipient more important to Clarissa's fate than the interview involving the simple, country messenger who Anna Howe sends to her friend after Clarissa has escaped to Mrs. Moore's house in Hampstead. Mrs. Bevis' impersonation of Clarissa, and Lovelace's interception of the letter, protects the latter's plots while dooming Clarissa's attempted escape. Ironically, the most trusted form of mail delivery in the novel—in which the written communication can be verified and supplemented through the personal intervention of a messenger—proves vulnerable to Lovelace's plots and leads most directly to Clarissa's downfall.

But Lovelace doesn't normally need to depend on such extreme measures in order to compromise Clarissa's vital communication with Anna Howe.

Because of the necessity of keeping her hideaway a secret from her family, Clarissa recognizes the importance of securing a third party or forwarding agent in order to safeguard her communications. Such an agent was a normal part of postal delivery before the official Post Office achieved its monopoly on the circulation of letters: "Delivery could be a problem when the whereabouts of the recipient was not known and it was necessary to send mail to some forwarding agent. The major inns would send on letters knowing that the messenger would be well rewarded."[50] As soon as Clarissa finds herself settled in London after her escape from her family, she informs Anna Howe of Lovelace's consideration in providing an agent through which they can write: "If, my dear, you *will* write against prohibition, be pleased to direct, *To Miss Laetitia Beaumont; to be left till called for, at Mr. Wilson's in Pall Mall*. Mr. Lovelace has proposed this direction to me, not knowing of your desire that our letters should pass by a third hand." As always in such matters, Lovelace remains far too subtle and devious for Clarissa and Anna, having anticipated their conviction that Clarissa would need a "third hand"—rather than trust her correspondence to him—and determined that in broaching the subject before Clarissa did he could emphasize his honesty and attentiveness.

The history of the letter as a form, and evolution of the post as a significant administrative arm of the modern state, is central to the way in which Clarissa and Lovelace duel for dominance in Richardson's novel. Their battle for pre-eminence is figured in the collision between private and public, ephemeral and permanent, story and history. To each of these binaries, the circulation of paper remains crucial, the power to forge memory manifest in the control of the material substances utilized by the writer, or by the bureaucratic systems that govern their propagation, diffusion, and preservation. Both Clarissa and Lovelace possess personal memories of some power, but the struggle between them in the novel turns not on their individual memories, however powerful, surprising, or infallible, but on their success in determining the collective memory of the society in which they live. The conflict over the fate of their correspondence assumes more and more importance as the novel progresses, for the memorial aspirations of both Clarissa and Lovelace eventually rest on how their letters will be read and interpreted after their death, circulated and preserved by the archive that the novel comes to represent.

VII

One of the fundamental goals of the archive, according to Bhekizizwe Peterson, is its institutional commitment to organize the past as inheritance, and one of the primary mechanisms for determining collective memory in early modern Europe was its system of inheritance, which, as Jones and Stallybrass note, "is both about the ownership of the future and about the control of memory." Moreover, this ownership and control belonged almost exclusively to men, since "legally women were excluded from the dominant memory system of inheritance."[51] The gendered nature of the struggle to master a society's memory makes the material culture within which the act of writing is embedded even more important, for control of the pen comes to define cultural and memorial dominance in the novel. The ability to write a will, a letter, or a history confirms power in Richardson's world.

Although letters remain the central cultural and memorial artifact in the novel, the contest between Lovelace and Clarissa takes place between a pair of testaments, both of which attest to the importance of inheritance in the determination of history, memory, and the preservation of cultural preeminence.[52] The novel begins with the will of Clarissa's grandfather, the postscript to the very first letter in the novel highlighting its significance: "Will you oblige me with a copy of the preamble to the clauses in your grandfather's will in your favour; and allow me to send it to my aunt Harman?...she assents to the preference given you in it, before she knows his reasons for that preference" (40–41). The novel insists from the very first that the preference given to Clarissa by her grandfather is remarkable, extraordinary, almost unimaginable. By writing a woman into his will—placing her before her father, uncles, and brother—the patriarch of the Harlowe family generates the tremendous resentments that result in Clarissa's isolation within the family she has heretofore ruled.

The will that ends the novel, of course, is Clarissa's, "her last will and testament; contained in seven sheets of paper, all written with her own hand, and every sheet signed and sealed by herself" (1420). Clarissa is not a lawyer, and her anxiety that the conditions of her will be fulfilled to the letter explains both its parodic imitation of legal discourse and its obsessive concern with its own materiality. Her will represents one "letter" that will NOT go astray, each sheet of paper attesting to its authenticity, written, signed, and sealed by the woman who insists twice that she composed this document while of "*sound mind* and *memory*," "of sound and perfect mind and memory" (1412). From its preamble, "written on a separate paper [and] stitched with black silk," to its final list of three witnesses, her will seeks in minute particularity to determine how everyone connected to her will remember both her and her fate. It concerns itself with land and money, certainly, but with a host of other material objects as well—plate, jewelry, musical instruments, clothes, paintings, books—which it attempts to embed within a memorial context that will secure Clarissa's history and identity. Letters represent one of the most important of these repositories of memory, and we should not be surprised to learn that Clarissa has acted as a self-archivist even before the novel opened: "in the middle drawer of my escritoire at Harlowe Place," she has saved many of the letters (and copies) of the correspondences she has carried out "ever since I learned to write" (1417). These letters contain "many excellent things," and Clarissa wants them all saved for her most faithful correspondent, Anna Howe.

The importance of these letters, however, pales next to two other collections of letters that she has prepared, both of which act as important supplements to her will. The first collection represents one of the most important bequests contained in her testament, those letters that Belford has assiduously gathered as a "compilement to be made of all that relates to my story" (1418). Clarissa had helped Belford begin this collection almost two months before her death, when in late July she gave him "a parcel sealed up with three seals" that contained all of Lovelace's letters (1127). Her will specifies that two copies must be made of this collection, one given to Miss Howe and the second kept by Belford himself, made available when necessary "for the satisfaction of any of my family" (1418). The archiving of the letters that compose the history of her relationship with Lovelace—that is, the novel we are reading—is essential to the proper preservation of her memory, for, as she wrote Belford when asking him to act as the executor of her will, "it will be an honour to my memory" (1176).

The second collection, which Clarissa also prepared before her death, is contained in a parcel "sealed up with three black seals," and consists of "no less than eleven letters, each sealed with her own seal and black wax" (1367). These posthumous letters, as a number of critics recognize, allow Clarissa to speak from the grave, to control both the lives of her family and friends as well as the shape her memory will take for those she has left behind.[53] Clarissa's letters act almost like the ghost of Hamlet's father, visitations from the spiritual world of the dead that would enforce their memorial expectations on the material world of the living. Clarissa's will, like Pope's *Dunciad* and Richardson's novel itself, becomes a textual object that generates its own supplements, the bare will, like the 1728 poem and 1747–1748 novel, not sufficient to enforce its meaning without the addition of further textual apparatus. Clarissa's will cannot encompass her memorial aspirations without becoming embedded in three collections of letters that extend, clarify, and empower its intentions.

The weight of Clarissa's memorial expectations for this will and its three complementary sets of letters reveals itself in a concern for seals that could be regarded as obsessive if not for Lovelace's rape of her correspondence. We have already seen her warning to Anna Howe that her friend "look carefully to the seals of my letters" (529), a caution justified by Lovelace's erotic sense that "the seal would have yielded to the touch of my warm finger" (1085). The triple seals that protect two of the collections of letters, and individually sealed pages of her will, describe a justifiable response to Lovelace's persistently searching finger, although Lovelace's close examination of her letters once Clarissa has become his captive reveals that she has always taken great pains to safeguard her correspondence: "She wafers her letters, it seems, in two places; pricks the wafers; and then seals upon them…And she always examines the seals of the letter before she opens them" (570–71). In her extreme caution Clarissa resembles no one more than Lovelace, who twice explains to Belford that "I am always careful to open covers cautiously and to preserve seals entire" (754 and 811).

Clarissa's insistence on using both wafers and seals suggests the special significance of the latter. The former, a thin disk of dried paste—made of flour, water, and gum—performed the practical and mechanical duties of the latter in sealing letters and fastening documents. But the seal itself possesses a long and important history connected to rank, literacy, and even printing. M.T. Clanchy argues that "in some ways sealing was as significant a step towards extending literacy as Gutenberg's subsequent invention of printing...Because seals reproduce script, they enabled people to sign their names in an acceptable form without labor or skill."[54]

If, as a technology capable of exact reproduction, the seal suggests the printing press, it also points to the postal service, for "once conveyances began to be made or messages to be sent in greater numbers, some method of reproducing authenticating objects was required, if the custom were to continue. From this point of view, seals in wax were standardized and mass produced symbolic objects."[55] In England, as we have seen, the prototype of the modern letter was Henry II's "letter close," which was sealed on the tie that kept it rolled up so that the addressee could rely on the integrity of the correspondence. In the evolution of modern correspondence, the letter and the seal go hand in hand.

When affixed to a letter, the seal assures the genuineness of the communication we hold in our hand. But its history also reveals that when the seal is part of a document, it promises incorruptibility as well. Medieval charters, according to Clanchy, contain thousands of variations on the following formulae: "And so that this gift of mine may be permanent, stable, and unshaken, I have esteemed it worthy to be strengthened with my seal"; "And so that this gift and grant of mine and confirmation of my charter may last in perpetuity, I have reinforced the present writing with the impress of my seal."[56] The seal functions not just as an important symbolic object, but even as a magical one, durability and constancy its promise. The multiple seals that Clarissa obsessively attaches to her will and the packets of letters that it collects and archives reveal her need to believe that her legacy can guarantee both its own authenticity and permanence.

The strength of her desire in this regard stems not just from her sense of the wrongs done her, but her recognition that combat with Lovelace has necessarily involved her in a struggle to control the transmission of collective memory. Even at the novel's opening, Clarissa's desire "of sliding through life to the end of it unnoted"—which Anna Howe connects to her friend's motto, "Rather useful than glaring"—has already been compromised by Lovelace, for, according to Anna in her very first letter, "My mama, and all of us, like the rest of the world, talk of nobody but you on this occasion" (40). As the novel progresses, Clarissa grows more and more concerned that she is becoming a public object, her revulsion for the sexual stigma attached to such a label revealing itself (after the rape) in her first meditation: "Oh that Thou wouldst hide me in the grave! That Thou wouldst keep me secret...He hath made me a byword of the people" (1192). The biblical resonance of a phrase like "byword of the people" is echoed in the novel, once by her uncle Antony, who insists that the "shameless daughter" has transformed her family into "a laughing-stock to thine enemies" and "a reproach among the people" (1196), and a second time by Clarissa when writing to her uncles John and Antony: "I was betrayed, fell, and became the byword of my companions" (1375). Uncle Antony's fear of being made a "laughing-stock," like Milton's shame in *The Readie and Easie Way* when he imagines "the common laughter of Europe," reveals the anxiety of men apprehensive about the verdict of history. For Clarissa, however, like Dalila, the sexual context within which women are judged promises infamy as well as scorn or erasure.

Clarissa's concern for wills and letters, signing and seals, reveals her need for documentary evidence that can transform her sad story and tale into history. Early in the novel, Clarissa responds with contempt and condescension to "These men, my dear, [who] with all their flatteries, look forward to the PERMANENT" (134), when speaking of the legacy from her uncle. By the end of the novel, however, her fall has made Clarissa attentive to just what will be permanent in her story, and she recognizes, like Cavendish, that the advantages men enjoy in wielding the technologies of writing and reproduction may doom her. Particularly after the rape, when Clarissa fears for her own memory and begins to make "minutes of everything as it passed, in order to help my memory" (926), she becomes obsessed with achieving the permanence that she once scorned.

VIII

In the novel, the permanence and documentary efficacy promised by the seal is continually threatened by Lovelace's "warm finger," not simply because he can so dexterously and erotically remove seals but because of his ability to counterfeit what the seal protects. In a letter to Belford, Lovelace reminds his friend "that an adroitness in the art of manual imitation was one of my earliest attainments" as he explains how he can make Lord M "write a much more sensible letter than this he has now sent me" (700). While Lovelace's confederate Patrick McDonald, who plays the part of Captain Tomlinson in the plot against Clarissa, was expelled from Dublin University because his "ingenious knack of forgery" (696) was detected, Lovelace possesses far greater skill and succeeds in the course of the novel in imitating not just his uncle's hand, but Clarissa's and Anna Howe's as well.

His facility, and the delight he takes in it, is vividly displayed when he sends to Belford the crucial intercepted letter from Anna Howe that contains her discovery of Lovelace's "forgery": as he reads her revelations concerning the true nature of both "Tomlinson" and the house within which Clarissa has been imprisoned, he threatens Anna for her interference: "I am always careful to open covers cautiously, and to preserve seals entire. I will draw out from this cursed letter an alphabet. Nor was Nick Rowe ever half so diligent to learn Spanish, at the Quixote recommendation of a certain peer, as I will be to gain mastery of this vixen's hand" (754). The tale of Rowe's futile attempt to obtain preferment from the earl of Oxford—who enjoined the dramatist to first learn Spanish and then dismissed him with the consolation that he could at least read *Don Quixote* in the original language[57]—is transformed into Lovelace's celebration of his mastery of both other tongues and other hands. Lovelace understands that his prowess in both depends on his attention to the letter, to his ability to "draw out from this cursed letter an alphabet." In one of the longest novels written in English, one moreover that consists almost entirely of 537 letters, the pun on *letter* returns the reader to Richardson's attention to the material conditions of writing. Richard Kroll has written of the Augustan fascination with the "plastic quality in language," its delight in "the concreteness of the page impressed by visible marks, ascending atomically from letters to words, to sentences, to entire discourses."[58] *Clarissa*'s concern for pen, ink, paper, and seals is here refocused on the most minute element in the construction of literary artifacts and memorials, the alphabet and individual letters that comprise it. The act of writing begins here, when an individual takes pen in hand, puts pen to paper, and begins to draw the individual letters of an alphabet.

In the printing house, each letter, each character, is a separate piece of type, and, like the seal, capable of an exact duplication that provides a guarantee of authenticity. Lovelace's facility in forging the handwriting of others, in both writing their *letters* and sending *letters* that appear to be theirs, however, undermines the very notion of the authentic, his ability to appropriate the *hand* of another a reflection of his protean nature, his desire to play many parts and slough off the limitations of a single self; Lovelace lives and thrives in a world of unchecked proliferation and counterfeit. Clarissa, on the contrary, defines herself in stark opposition to such a conception of *character*; her search for an essential self, which can be preserved against all forgeries and impermanence, describes one of her primary endeavors throughout the novel. When Anna Howe finally penetrates Lovelace's forgery, the puns on both *hand* and *letter* fix our attention on the act of writing, its material components, and the relation between the individual character and authenticity: "The letter you sent me enclosed as mine, of the 7th of June, is a villainous forgery. The hand, indeed, is astonishingly like mine; and the cover, I see is actually my cover: but yet the letter is not so exactly imitated but that (had you had any suspicions about his vileness at the time) you, who so well know my hand, might have detected it" (1014). In forging Anna's letter, and imitating her letter and letters, Lovelace has stolen her hand and identity. Clarissa "might" have detected Lovelace's forgery, might have seen through to the essential character beneath the forgery, might have recognized the hand she supposedly knew so well, but she did not.

Yet Lovelace himself, for all of his skill and artifice, fears the appropriation of his own hand, and in letter 246, which he writes to Belford, he imagines a scene in which his own conscience—gendered female—"had stolen my pen...and thus *she* wrote with it, in a hand exactly like my own; and would have faced me down, that it was really my own handwriting" (848; emphasis added). This important letter, which I shall look at shortly for its gendering of cultural memory, has been extensively analyzed by Deanna Kreisel, who recognizes its unusual material construction: the scene in which Lovelace confronts and then murders his conscience is "*Wafered on, as an after-written introduction to the paragraphs which follow*" (847). This rare act of revision "ruptures the seamless fabric of Lovelace's art...It is one of the few moments where Lovelace's art, his *control* over his art, is exposed and denaturalized."[59] For all of their efforts, neither Clarissa nor Lovelace can guarantee the genuineness of their hands, their authority over their own pens, and the regulation of their own letters.

Lovelace's failure in this regard even manifests itself at the very moment when he sends to Belford Anna Howe's intercepted letter and his triumph seems most secure. While letter 246 exposes a remarkable moment of self-revision, the letter from Miss Howe reveals a singular moment in the revision of another's letter, for Lovelace crowds the margins of her original letter with "indices" that "mark the places devoted for vengeance" (743). This intercepted letter thus represents not simply a crucial moment in the novel's plot, but perhaps the most unusual typographical moment in the novel, the repetition of this printer's ornament a vivid indication of Lovelace's fury, obsession, and loss of control. The ornament that Richardson the printer chose for this mark was the human hand with a pointed index finger, a conventional figure of moralistic writing in works such as Bunyan's *Grace Abounding*. Here Lovelace appropriates and parodies a typographical feature of a spiritual discourse that he despises. Yet this printer's device represents an ideal figure for Lovelace, who loves to appropriate the hands of others, and whose warm finger constantly threatens Clarissa. The ninety-two separate hands that Lovelace draws reveal, according to Christopher Flint, "the degree to which the fiction is enmeshed in its mode of production":

> In printed form, Lovelace's display of emotional, physical, and discursive mastery is itself undermined by the very conventionality he exploits...Lovelace's aggressive typographical acts only accentuate his failure to possess the objects of his desire or to control the significance of his writing in the public sphere.[60]

Lovelace's ability to forge the hands of others and appropriate their identities is perfectly realized, but also undermined, in the repetition of a printer's ornament that uses the human hand to signal print's ability to duplicate and authenticate the individual character and letter in ways that the human hand cannot.

The physical inscription of individual letters, *Clarissa* demonstrates, can be broken down even further than this, for the novel's inclusion of Lovelace's and Belford's interest in shorthand reveals the way in which the elements of our standard alphabet can be deconstructed by another alphabet, collapsed and reassembled in even smaller units. Mowbray refers to Lovelace's shorthand as a "cursed algebra" (1382), reminding us that other symbolic systems compete with the one we regard as "natural" and complete. In this other alphabet, Lovelace is, not surprisingly, a master, as Belford readily admits: "I pretend to be (now by use) the swiftest shorthand writer in England, next to yourself" (1332). In the mid-eighteenth century, Belford and Lovelace would have had many competitors for this title, for Henri Talon has described the period as "shorthand-minded": "To us, stenography is one of the dull necessities of modern life. To Byrom and his friends it was a source of fun and an art that could be described—in a thoughtful gradation of epithets—as "'the most easy, concise, regular, and beautiful manner of writing English.'" Talon refers here to John Byrom (1691–1763), who in May of 1742 was granted by an Act of Parliament "the sole right of publishing for a certain term of years the art and method of short-hand invented by him."[61] Byrom, a poet and diarist, was elected a Fellow of the Royal Society in 1724, and published two papers on shorthand in their *Transactions Philosophical*.

In a speech recorded in Byrom's journal for February 28, 1726, which he delivered at the inaugural meeting of the Shorthand Society that he helped to found, he provides a history of shorthand, in which Caesar—"no one could write swifter than himself"—plays an important role: "His ambition did not hinder him, nay, perhaps it prompted him to invent more commodious and expeditious methods of writing." According to Byrom, Caesar possessed "a Shorthand for secrecy as well as swiftness," and "he died with that instrument of glory by which he thus subdued us, his graphium, in his hand."[62] Caesar, as we shall shortly see, plays an important role in the gendering of cultural memory in the novel, and here Lovelace's and Belford's use of shorthand begins to suggest how unequal educations make it impossible for women to properly attend to the act of writing, which Byrom explicitly presents as Caesar's "glory," the pen and not the sword the measure of his true conquests. At a time when, as both Astell and Cavendish lament, control of language and writing defined a fundamental male prerogative, the ability to write shorthand was a legitimately masculine pursuit. At the same time, according to Leah Price, shorthand was also "a tool used by individuals not organizations, to encrypt not to transmit." Only at the end of the nineteenth century, when Pitman and Gregg had succeeded in establishing a standardized model for shorthand, did its mastery become an undervalued female skill, the mark of a mere secretary or stenographer, "one of the dull necessities of modern life" according to Henri Talon.[63] The use of shorthand by Lovelace and Belford reveals their commitment not to communication but to secrecy, not to transparency but to obscurity and the opaque.

In the mid-eighteenth century, while Belford and Lovelace are masters of a number of alphabets, Clarissa complains—in a letter to Belford in which Anna reminisces about her friend—that women "are generally too careless in their orthography (a consciousness of a defect which generally keeps them from writing)." The often haphazard nature of women's education in the eighteenth century tended to make women poor spellers, and generally precluded them from an expertise in both shorthand and the attainment of foreign languages. Both Fielding and Smollett use the orthographically challenged female to great comic effect in *Joseph Andrews* and *Humphry Clinker*, where even ostensibly educated women display an orthographical incompetence every bit as shocking as that which characterizes the uneducated woman. Clarissa, to be sure, is herself a master of orthography, and Anna goes on to describe "the admirable facility she [Clarissa] had in learning languages: that she read with great ease both Italian and French...that she had begun to apply herself to Latin" (1468). Clarissa's skill in languages may rival that of Lovelace, but the novel provides no indication that she was skilled in shorthand as well. While the latter employs a shorthand that allows him, like Caesar and other male conquerors, to both disguise his communications and compose them "swifter" then others, Clarissa writes laboriously letter by letter. If the novel's insistence on Lovelace's and Belford's skill in shorthand is also a gesture toward verisimilitude, an attempt, however unconvincing, to explain how two men of the world can live active lives and still manage to maintain such extensive correspondences, it provides an explanation from which Clarissa is excluded, both by skill and temperament: Clarissa writes no shorthand, takes no shortcuts, tries to express herself as fully and openly as possible, her laborious honesty distinguished throughout the novel from Lovelace's intoxication with secrets and desire to take the easy way out. A prisoner for much of the novel, increasingly isolated and kept from society, Clarissa does nothing but write, letter by letter, the letters that compose her story. And that story, ultimately, is a history of her writing.

IX

The gendered understanding of writing and history that characterizes male society in the novel is depicted in the letter from Lovelace to Belford where the former imagines the murder of his conscience, boasting about "what a figure shall I make in rakish annals" (846). From the start, Lovelace has seen himself in the heroic mold of Caesar: according to Anna Howe, Lovelace would "compare himself to Julius Caesar, who performed great actions by day and wrote them down at night" (74). In the novel—as in John Byrom's speech—Caesar's war commentaries become the model for male achievement, which consists of heroic actions accompanied by their own written history. The "rakish annals" that loom so large in Lovelace's imagination are the equivalent of the war commentaries that have guaranteed Caesar's memorial power, and which inevitability, as Anna Howe recognizes, write the history of the triumphant male self: "But supposing it to be true, that all his vacant nightly hours are employed in writing, what can be his subjects? If, like Caesar, his own actions, he must undoubtedly be a very enterprising and very wicked man" (74).

Female access to this memorial power, depicted later in Lovelace's letter, contrasts sharply with the rakish annals of male historiography: "Do not the mothers, the aunts, the grandmothers, the governesses of the pretty innocents, always, from their very cradles to riper years, preach to them the deceitfulness of men?—That they are not to regard their oaths, vows, promises?" (847). This circle of women describes a very different version of historical transmission, one that emphasizes the oral over the written, performance over print. Lovelace's letter juxtaposes his community of rakish males, linked through the compilation of historical record, to this family circle of women whose collective knowledge, orally transmitted, governs the passage from "cradles to riper years." Women "preach" to one another, the unchanging wisdom of "their preachments" describing a coherent body of knowledge passed from one generation to the next. Lovelace, however, expresses interest only in the novel, for "it is my intention in all my reflections to avoid repeating...so I would have thee reconsider the *old* reasonings...and add the *new* as they fall from my pen" (847). This male emphasis on the new, and on the triumph of the narcissistic self, stands very much at odds with the spiritual connotations of the female dependence on preaching and preachments, of the communication of invariable truths through the repetition of time-honored tales. Lovelace's attention here to how "new reasonings...fall from my pen" suggests the ways in which male power transforms material reality into ideology. This male pen is precisely the one feared, ridiculed, and coveted by Astell and Cavendish.

Such a traditional gendering of the scene of writing and historical transmission demonstrates that however literate Clarissa and Anna Howe prove, women in the mid-eighteenth century, compared to men, still possessed a secondary relationship to the act of writing. As Michael Warner reminds us, "nor is it the case that the gender barrier in letters dissolved when women took up pens to write...Insofar as written contexts entailed dispositions of character that interpolated their subject as male, women could only write with a certain cognitive dissonance."[64] Even *Clarissa* is marked by society's conviction that the woman who writes too much engages in an unnatural act. In the novel, the gendering of female writing is depicted through its relationship to needlework, the conventional binary construction of the needle to the pen suggested when Arabella sarcastically asks Clarissa for an "account of the disposition of your time? How many hours in the twenty-four do you devote to your needle? How many to your prayers? How many to letter-writing?" (192).

In my earlier reading of Margaret Cavendish's *Poems, and Fancies*, I delineated the complex gendering of the early modern juxtaposition of needlework to writing. Although in its most extreme form the opposition between sewing and writing acted as a prohibition against women writing, in practice certain forms of writing were thought proper for a woman: even Sir Edward Denny thought that the translation of "godly books" and composition of "heavenly layes" were appropriate exercises for a woman. Arabella's list, which moves from the needle, to prayers, to letter-writing, can be read as a sign that, like needlework and prayers, letter-writing represents an educational and moral activity that the proper lady can use to discipline herself and make good use of her time. Renaissance humanists had insisted that writing for women could prove, like needlework, an exercise both practical and moral.

But there remained, as Jones and Stallybrass argue, even into the eighteenth century, an opposition between the two activities: the "recommendation that women read and write rather than sew reverses a more usual opposition: the needle *versus* the pen. Text after text throughout Europe insisted on the division of these two kinds of labor: the useful industry of the private woman could save her from aspiring to the dangerous self-display of the woman in print."[65] Arabella's list, in other words, also suggests that of the three activities, letter-writing is by far the least appropriate for a woman, a sentiment that Clarissa recognizes when, for instance, she wishes to demonstrate her obedience to her mother by asking "to pursue my needleworks in your presence" (222). Even Clarissa can be successfully manipulated by the equation between female modesty, morality, and needlework. When Lovelace wishes to ingratiate Dorcas in her new mistress's favor, he has his duplicitous servant commended "for her skill in the needle" (524).

The cultural prejudice that privileges needlework over writing for women sometimes leads Lovelace to underestimate Clarissa. When exasperated by her resistance even after the rape, he rails at her as if she were a compliant "pretty little miss" who understood nothing but the polite forms of her society: " 'Tis true, this pretty little miss...who always minded her book and had passed through her sampler-doctrine with high applause; had even stitched out in gaudy propriety of colours an Abraham offering up Isaac, a Samson and the Philistines, and flowers, and knots, and trees, and the sun and the moon, and the seven stars, all hung up in frames with glasses before them for the admiration of her future grandchildren" (971). Here Lovelace parodies a second scene depicting the female conveyance of history, mocking the reduction of powerful biblical stories to the merely decorative. The proper, homemaking, eighteenth-century lady is here admired by her descendents for her pretty accomplishments, which trivialize even as they transmit the histories that are their subject. In this case, of course, those histories are thoroughly male, in the first instance, the sacrifice of the first-born son that seals God's covenant with Abraham, and, in the second, Samson's victory over the Philistines that also marks his triumph over Dalila. The lessons learned by the pretty little miss and transmitted through her domestic arts depict male triumphs that women can neither appreciate—thus their artistic diminishment—nor share.

Samplers, however, could resist the demeaning and repressive codes of early modern femininity, and Lovelace's ridicule remains blind to the often subversive evolution of women's needlework through the seventeenth and eighteenth centuries; he depicts in his imagination the dismissive male cliché rather than the complex material reality of the domestic arts. In *Clarissa*, the survival of female history, and specifically Clarissa's history, is continually threatened by Lovelace's articulation of the conventional, male understanding of cultural memory, which inevitably marginalizes female stories and their transmission. The ease with which this can occur is dramatically represented after Colonel Morden returns to England and visits Lord M. and Lovelace at the former's estate. Even Morden's decision to seek out Lovelace before visiting his cousin suggests the casual male fraternity that governs the dispersal of knowledge. During this visit, Lord M., who deals in old saws, proverbial wisdom, and the time-honored bromide, intervenes between the two rash young men by reminding them "in his phraseological way *that one story was good, till another was heard*" (1286). The relativity of truth, the fragility of narrative, and the freedom of interpretation that this platitude demonstrates places Clarissa's entire struggle to preserve her integrity at risk.

Lovelace proves the truth of his uncle's wisdom by fetching "all the letters and drafts and copies of letters relating to this affair." After a selective reading, Lovelace assures his correspondent Belford "that it is but glossing over one part of a story, and omitting another, that will make a bad cause a good one at any time" (1287).

Colonel Morden eventually penetrates Lovelace's distortions, and recognizes that the rapist of his cousin has provided only part of the story. Yet this parody of the relationship between "story" and "documentary" evidence suggests the vulnerability of narrative, and particularly female narrative, to both misrepresentation and misinterpretation. The letter in which Lovelace describes his encounter with Morden is immediately followed by a letter from the officious Reverend Brand to John Harlowe, in which self-satisfied male wisdom transforms Clarissa's blameless life at Mrs. Smith's into a tale of female moral corruption that "*looketh not well*" (1293). Brand's account is eventually overthrown—just like that of Lord M.'s and Lovelace's—but not before it prevents Clarissa from enjoying a reconciliation with her family.

The radical instability of textual representation portrayed in these two incidents leads directly to a fascination—displayed by both Lovelace and Clarissa—with alternative modes of memorial expression. Lovelace begins by literalizing Belford's sentimental notion that Clarissa has been "sent from heaven to draw thee after her": "I could not for an hour put thee out of my head in the attitude of Dame Elizabeth Carteret on her monument in Westminster Abbey." This famous monument, built to honor the widow of Sir Philip Carteret, might represent a memorial gesture that provides an alternative to the unreliability of the textual world within which both Lovelace and Clarissa live. Yet Lovelace introduces the sculpture only to mock its representational pretensions and failures, which entirely undermine its emotional potency. Lovelace has nothing but ridicule for the idea that "this dame in effigy" and her accompanying cupid—"one clumsy foot lifted up"—could possibly ascend (1302). The memorial power of this sculpture, housed, like the memorial to Margaret Cavendish erected by *her* husband, within England's most famous public shrine to the noble and famous dead, is thoroughly compromised by Lovelace's disdain for the illusion that stone can provide an adequate response to the human aspiration for permanence or remembrance; and by his conviction that a woman cannot achieve the memorial triumph depicted by the sculpture. Lovelace's thoroughly cynical reaction to this monument suggests that for him nothing can provide an alternative to the uncertain male world of textual reproduction and rakish annals.

Belford's response to this letter introduces Clarissa's famous coffin, which she presents as a direct challenge to Lovelace's cynicism and disdain. When Belford and Mrs. Smith profess shock at the arrival of the coffin, Clarissa asks them, "Why may we not be as reasonably shocked at going to the church where are the monuments of our ancestors, with whose dust we even *hope* our dust shall be one day mingled, as to be moved at such a sight as this?" (1304). The ridicule that Lovelace has just poured on one such monument is rebuked by Clarissa's emotional response to the "hope" that such memorials can generate in a pious audience. At this moment in the text, Belford becomes just such an audience, his dreams the night after he first hears about Clarissa's coffin a vindication of her conception of the memorial potency of the "monuments of our ancestors."

Clarissa recognizes the unusualness of what she has done, and her justification explicitly links her memorial gesture here to the needlework that describes one of the sanctioned activities of female culture and its transmission: "She excused herself to the women, on the score of her youth, and being used to draw for her needleworks, for having shown more fancy than would perhaps be thought suitable on so solemn an occasion" (1306). Clarissa's memorial imagination was formed by both her letter-writing and her needlework, two linked activities in the education of proper young women. Her coffin thus represents a further memorial adjunct to her will and collections of letters, one that uses both metal and cloth—"It was covered with fine black cloth, and lined with white satin"—to add to the power of paper in preserving her story. Together the will, collections of letters, and coffin, a material supplement to both, create a memorial that rebukes Lovelace's male hauteur and dismissive disdain for women's culture.

X

In *Clarissa*, the "Female Pen" that helps to generate Clarissa's memorial possesses more than just a rich figurative significance, for the novel's attention to the act of writing focuses not just on paper, but on pens and inks, penknives and standishes, on all of the other material accoutrements that the writer brings to the task of writing. As Jonathan Goldberg explains, writing is a discipline, control of the hand part of a "civilizing process" that institutionalizes social and cultural ideology: "with the instruments to hand—knife and quill, paper and ink—the instrumental hand is instructed to write." During the Renaissance, according to Goldberg, the teaching of such a discipline inevitably reproduced the exclusionary economies of both gender and rank: we can trace "the ideological functions of an educational apparatus bent on the formation of a class of intellectuals with power (in the court or in the schools), thereby also depriving women and the lower classes such access in the name of 'humanity.' "[66]

By the mid-eighteenth century such exclusions remain visible, precisely because a reader can observe them in the process of being overcome. Clarissa, for instance, requests a letter from her sick servant Hannah by hoping that "I shall see you have not forgotten the pretty hand you were taught, in happy days, by Your true friend, Clarissa Harlowe" (977). A few pages later, Judith Norton recalls "the death of a dear father, who was an ornament to his cloth (and who had qualified me to be his scribe and amanuensis)" (980). As in the conventional image of Milton's daughters, Judith Norton's skill with the pen serves primarily to reinscribe her subjection to male, parental authority. She has learned the requisite manual skills necessary to write, but remains a mere "scribe," true creativity identified with the father "who had qualified me," impressing his knowledge on his passive although mechanically proficient daughter.[67]

The figure in the novel who most clearly raises issues of gender and rank in regard to the act of writing is Dorcas, who ostentatiously both pretends and "laments her incapacity as to writing and reading" (570). Although, as we have seen, skillful with the needle, Dorcas is presented to Clarissa with "one great defect; which was that she could not write, nor read writing; that part of her education having been neglected when she was young" (524). Dorcas, however, reveals herself a writer of considerable skill, for she not only ferrets out Clarissa's letters, but copies and transcribes them as well.[68] Indeed, the novel connects Dorcas' writing ways with those of Clarissa, both women whose dedication to the act of writing betrays itself through the stain of "inky fingers":

> I [Clarissa] will go down and deposit this; for Betty has seen I have been writing. The saucy creature took a napkin, and dipped it in water, and with a fleering air: Here, miss; holding the wet corner to me. What's that for, said I? Only miss, one of the fingers of your right hand, if you please to look at it. It was inky. I gave her a look; but said nothing. (344–45)

> He [Lovelace] orders Dorcas to cultivate by all means her lady's favour; To lament her incapacity as to writing and reading;...to be always aiming at scrawling with a pen, lest inky fingers should give suspicions. And says that he has given her an ivory-leaved pocket-book with a silver pencil, that she may take memoranda on occasion. (570)

The interplay between servant and lady in both cases directs our attention to the act of writing, the hierarchies of rank and privilege that are inscribed in the "tools of the trade," and the necessity in both cases of hiding or disguising their considerable skills. Both women have reason to fear the taint of writing.[69]

The inky fingers that would betray them remind us that "the discovery of an oil-based printing ink by Gutenberg was just as important as his development of the use of moveable type and the press."[70] Without the appropriate paper and ink, Gutenberg's first bible would not have achieved its revolutionary impact, for the technological (as well as aesthetic) triumph that it represents depended on the development and evolution of a number of interdependent material elements. Advances in the manufacture and production of both ink and paper were essential to the print revolution and the spread of literacy throughout Europe, a process that was itself marked by inequalities of both rank and gender. Clarissa finds it "strange" that Dorcas' parents neglected her education, but not surprising that a female servant in the mid-eighteenth century should be unable to write, and regards Lovelace's encouragement of Dorcas' desire to "scrawl" as unexceptional, even if it involves a gift clearly above her station, "an ivory-leaved pocket-book with a silver pencil."

For at least part of the novel, in fact, Clarissa is reduced to employing writing implements as far beneath her station as Dorcas' are above hers. The scene in which the Harlowe family deprives Clarissa of her pen and ink represents a crucial moment in the process of her estrangement, for she describes "taking away my pen and ink" as an "act of violence, as I may call it." Betty had already given warning of the approaching prohibition, providing time for Clarissa "to conceal in different places pens, ink, and paper" (321). Even after cousin Dolly removes Clarissa's "standish and all its furniture," she consoles herself with the knowledge of "having half a dozen crow-quills which I had hid in as many different places" (324). Within a week of her family's "act of violence," Clarissa has left her parents' house.

Quills, like paper, suggest the complex economics of international trade within which the act of writing was inscribed: "the quills employed for pens were generally those of the goose . . . Each wing produced about 5 good quills, but the number thus yielded was so small that the geese reared in England could not furnish nearly enough for the demand, hence the importation of goose quills from the Continent was very large."[71] Clarissa presumably gives up her good goose quills to her family, keeping the inferior crow quills as her emergency supply. Later in the novel, when Lovelace intercepts and then forges Anna Howe's crucial letter of warning to Clarissa, Lovelace—who knows from the letter that Anna is also being watched for evidence of a prohibited correspondence—ends his forgery by providing a ready excuse for anything untoward that Clarissa may notice in the handwriting: "I have written all night. *Excuse indifferent writing. My crow-quills are worn to the stumps, and I must get a new supply*" (814; emphasis in the original).

Quills, whether crow or goose, needed constant attention and maintenance, their tendency to wear out the result of excessive use, the desire to write with more rapidity, and the necessity of frequent mending. The penknife therefore represented one of the chief tools of the early modern writer, and although it rarely makes its appearance in the novel, when it does so in what Lovelace facetiously entitles "The history of the Lady and the Penknife!!!" (952), the penknife takes us to the heart of the act of writing, which, as Goldberg insists, enacts a scene of violence:

> At a basic material level, then, writing begins with a tool of violence, the knife or razor, and it produces the point of the quill as another cutting edge. A material sphere is opened by these tools, one that circulates through the violence of the instrument, one that shapes the world . . . through violence.[72]

In *Clarissa*, the primary act of violence—Lovelace's rape of Clarissa—remains notoriously obscure, an absence at the very center of the text. But the dramatic scene in which Clarissa meets with her penknife Lovelace's continued attempts to reduce her to cohabitation is powerfully described by Lovelace, the moment when Clarissa turns her penknife against herself the point at which power in the novel decisively shifts from the one to the other: "To my astonishment, she held forth a penknife in her hand, the point to her own bosom, grasping resolutely the whole handle, so that there was no offering to take it from her" (950). After this Lovelace is clearly undone, the "hand" of Clarissa—the hand that writes, the hand that offers violence, the hand that is her writing—clearly ascendant: "This, this, Belford, was the hand I made of a contrivance I expected so much from!" (952). Within days, Lovelace laments his feminization, for, like Dalila, he has earned nothing more than "a title to eternal infamy and disgrace!" (957).

XI

It is apparently a commonplace among historians of paper "that the civilization of a country may be determined by the amount of paper used."[73] If we accept this judgment, then *Clarissa*'s prodigious length places it among the most refined and civilized productions of eighteenth-century culture. The struggle between Clarissa and Lovelace plays itself out amidst a correspondence firmly grounded in the material history of those products and resources requisite to early modern writing and printing, and, in the case of the postal service, one of the chief bureaucratic systems that governed their circulation. That struggle, and its extravagant consumption of paper and ink, may have been generated by Lovelace's obstinate and resourceful attempts to control Clarissa's body and mind, but it is extended and ultimately determined by Clarissa's unswerving resolution, even after her physical violation, to maintain her intellectual and emotional integrity and to assure her memorial triumph over the man who betrayed her. The letter for Lovelace contained in the collection of letters distributed after Clarissa's death—that is, her last letter to Lovelace—reminds him that "The triumphing of the wicked is short, and the joy of the hypocrite but for a moment. . . . Tremble and reform, when you read what is the portion of the wicked man from God. Thus it is written: . . . His remembrance shall perish from the earth; and he shall have no name in the streets" (1427). Employing a biblical language and rhetoric that in English carries the full weight of the most sacred textual authority—"Thus it is written"—Clarissa threatens Lovelace with the punishment feared by Samson in Milton's *Samson Agonistes*, being numbered among "the common rout," one of the "Heads without name no more remember'd."

Richardson reveals his awareness of these memorial issues from the very start of the novel, the "Preface" to his first edition beginning with the words, "The following history," and repeating these generic ambitions just a few paragraphs later: "the collection contains not only the history of the excellent person whose name it bears, but includes the lives, characters, and catastrophes of several others" (35). At the beginning of the novel, in fact, Richardson's insistence on the creation of history stands in stark contrast to Clarissa's desire, described by Anna Howe in the first letter of the novel, "of sliding through life to the end of it unnoted." But Clarissa has already become the object of "talk," because of which Anne asks her to "write in so full a manner" that "your account of all things previous to it will be your justification" (40). Clarissa's response ironically articulates the trajectory of her desires in the novel, the repetition of the term history central to the process by which her initial desire to remain anonymous becomes transformed into a fierce, single-minded, and compulsive determination to control the fate and meaning of her correspondence: "I will be as particular as you desire in the little history you demand of me. But heaven forbid that anything should ever happen which may require it to be produced for the purpose you so kindly mention" (41).

By the novel's end, Lovelace's rape has placed on Clarissa the burden of constructing a feminist history that, in displaying "the villainy of the worst of men, and the virtue of the most excellent of women" (1017), can invert the male interpretation of history contained in a canonical tale like that of Samson and Dalila. In fact, Terry Eagleton characterizes Clarissa's death as "that Samson-like act of self immolation by which she brings her enemies toppling to the ground,"[74] reminding us that Clarissa's memorial triumph depends on the way in which she both wills and orchestrates her death. After the publication of the first edition of the novel, Sarah Fielding suggested the importance of the relationship between Clarissa's death and her life in memory when she asked, "may her Memory be as Triumphant as her Death."[75] Lovelace himself measures his adversary's ultimate success when, after Clarissa's death, he indulges his grief after "poring over the affecting will, and posthumous letter. What an army of texts has she drawn up in array against me in the latter!—But yet, Jack, do they not show me that, two or three thousand years ago, there were as wicked fellows as myself?" (1473). Clarissa's letters sustain a textual history that spans centuries and privileges her memory while condemning his.

Given the gendering of memory in the seventeenth and eighteenth centuries, Clarissa's creation of an "army of texts" that can outface Lovelace's beloved rakish annals contains a terrible irony, for she begins the novel cherishing the memorial anonymity that Lovelace most abhors. Her fear after her rape that she has become "a byword of the people" contrasts with her threat that Lovelace "shall have no name in the streets," and reveals how her female modesty and desire "of sliding through life to the end of it unnoted" has been transformed in the course of the novel into a much more assertive and aggressive need to control precisely how textual authority will present her *history* to the future. Jerry C. Beasley may be correct in asserting that because Clarissa "dares to speak in defiance of the male center of power and authority...her author cannot allow her to have final control over her story," Belford as her executor and Richardson as her editor usurping the textual control that she has learned to covet.[76] But her metamorphosis from Lovelace's victim to his rival and even conqueror plays itself out in the memorial arena where textual mastery attempts to assure memorial success, and her ability to marshal an army of texts to defeat his rakish annals attests to her coup de maître in appropriating a masculine pen.

Yet however large the army of texts the novel brings to bear in Clarissa's defense, its emphasis on the material basis of Clarissa's triumph undermines the textual certainty for which it strives. Not only Clarissa and Lovelace, but Richardson as well must fail in the attempt to control one's hand, to establish the authenticity of a manuscript, to guarantee meaning. The archive that all three scribblers wish to construct cannot fix memory or stabilize history, for as Sarah Nuttall writes, the archive depends not only on the excision of texts, but also on "excess, as *unlimited*, in the sense of the endless readings to which it gives rise...A constitutive dimension of the archival object is that it lends itself to becoming the tool of the imagination. Thus it is capricious, inviting a promiscuity of meanings."[77]

In letter 183, Anna Howe insists that "words leave no traces; they pass as breath; and mingle with air, and may be explained with latitude. But the pen is a witness on record" (588). The insistence that writing can achieve documentary certainty, that it stands resolutely as an objective "record," is repeated throughout the novel; even Antony Harlowe, when he screws up his courage to propose marriage to Anna Howe's mother, insists that "I resolved to write: that my writing may stand, as upon record, for my upright meaning; being none of your Lovelaces" (625). In the seventeenth and eighteenth centuries, the claim that writing assures the integrity of memory was underwritten by the print revolution and strengthened, as Michael McKeon argues, by the privileging of the written over the oral: "Printed narrative, by contrast [to oral presentation], substitutes for this vulnerable sort of presence the incontestable factuality, the typographical 'fetish' of documentary objecthood."[78] Clarissa adapts Job when she comes to believe that her vindication lies in the correspondence collected by Belford: "Oh that one would hear me! And that mine adversary had written a book!—Surely, I would take it upon my shoulders, and bind it to me as a crown! For I covered not my transgressions as Adam, by hiding mine iniquity in my bosom" (1164). Clarissa possesses just such book, and in that, as Carol Flynn argues, rests her redemption: Clarissa "asks for salvation not from heaven, but from the edited collection of her seducer's letters."[79] The transformation of a collection of handwritten letters into a printed and published book stands as Richardson's triumph rather than Clarissa's, but in the fictional world Clarissa does as much as she can to "publish" her tragic history to the world by creating the textual archive that can vindicate and secure her memory.

Yet letter 183, in which Anna Howe proclaims the power of the written record, contains another sheet, an enclosure in which she announces the possible marriage of her mother to Clarissa's uncle Antony. Her contempt for what she perceives as her mother's weakness, and respect for "the memory of [her] father," leads Anna to express her anxiety in a language she fears Clarissa will find objectionable: "you'll think me faulty. So I won't put my name to this separate paper. Other hands may resemble mine. You did not see me write it" (589). Here the assurance of the first pronouncement is vitiated by the second; on one sheet of paper the pen may be "a witness on record," but on another that record is but a forgery, generated in a private act whose integrity, finally, no one can guarantee: "you did not see me write it."

In a novel in which people ceaselessly write, painstakingly copy, collect, seal, sign, and endlessly circulate letters, Anna's admission or confession calls into question the documentary edifice that represents at once the raison d'être of the novel and one of the most exalted projects of modernism. Carefully tucked away on an unsigned sheet and hidden within a letter, Anna's suggestion that no "ocular proof"—to quote the demand of a famous seeker of truth from the previous century—can ever definitively recover the originary moment of composition reminds us that our belief in the power of documentary evidence rests ultimately on an act of faith. However complete our archives, however imposing our libraries, the texts they scrupulously maintain may not be worth the paper on which they are printed.

CONCLUSION

FROM THE "GARBAGE HEAP" OF MEMORY TO THE CYBORG: THE EXHAUSTION AND REVITALIZATION OF MEMORY IN THE TWENTIETH AND TWENTY-FIRST CENTURIES

I

I want to take advantage of and even abuse the freedom offered by an unabashedly speculative conclusion to violate the strict protocols of periodicity and nationality adhered to in the preceding four chapters and not only leap forward two centuries, but consider a more geographically diverse range of authors in bringing this book to a close. In terms of time, I am aware of the risks in simply eliding the intervening history of the nineteenth century, particularly because the evolution of the novel, the form with which I have ended my survey of the seventeenth and eighteenth centuries, accompanied, figured, and, in many cases, celebrated the triumph of the British Empire, with all of its attendant monumental pomp and overweening visions of memorial hegemony. As Thomas Richards writes in *The Imperial Archive: Knowledge and the Fantasy of Empire* (1993), one strand of the Victorian novel imagined "an imperial archive holding together the vast and various parts of the Empire. This archive was neither a library nor a museum...rather...a fantasy of knowledge collected and united in the service of state and Empire."[1]

Yet this fantasy, like that of the universal library in the seventeenth and eighteenth centuries, was never realized, the imperial archive undermined and eventually doomed by the dissolution that awaited the Empire itself after World Wars I and II. In terms of nationality, the construction, evolution, and demise of a modern conception of memory were not alone a

British project, but a European and, certainly in the twentieth century, even global one. During the seventeenth, eighteenth, and nineteenth centuries, Western print culture, exported around the world by a triumphant capitalist and imperialist Europe, played a large role in determining the economic, colonial, and memorial structures that have governed nineteenth- and twentieth-century history. In three short stories by the Argentinean Jorge Luis Borges, two short stories by the Serbian Danilo Kiš, and a novel by W.G. Sebald, a German-born writer who lived most of his adult life in England, I want to describe some of the ways in which the last half of the twentieth century brings to a close the memorial hopes and ambitions articulated in England during the seventeenth and eighteenth centuries. Since World War II, the memorial dreams set in motion by modern print culture have been critiqued, dismantled, and even abandoned. In *On Longing* (1984), Susan Stewart suggests how the series of binaries and correspondences between matter and spirit, object and knowledge, material and idea, which celebrated the mystery and power of the printed book during the seventeenth and eighteenth centuries, can now be collapsed into volumes that call into question "our notion of [the] 'book.' " She surveys books so delicate that they must sit forever in glass cases, Dadaist books covered "by a forbidding configuration of needles," a book of black magic bound in human skin: "The volume is horrible in much the same way that the pyramids are horrible: it is a monument to death, ... The taboo here is the transformation of the living body into the merely material, the doubling of human labor moving spirit into matter. The book has murdered its content." In our century, we can imagine "the outer limits" of the transformations that govern the book's physical properties and modes of production.[2]

However great the anxiety of Cavendish, Milton, Pope, and Richardson as they confronted the challenges of a new technology and surveyed their state as "poor Moderns," they nonetheless communicate a vigorous belief in and enthusiasm for the book, library, and print trade, all of which seemed to promise so much for writers concerned about their lives in time. Without wanting to ignore or flatten the differences I have delineated between these four writers, their uncertainty, confusion, and even fear in response to a technological change whose consequences they can hardly imagine remain firmly balanced by the excitement all four share in a technology and marketplace that heralded the possibility of a triumphant futurity for the emerging figure of the modern author.

In Borges, Kiš, and Sebald, however, we witness the waning of that enthusiasm and the death of those hopes, the early-modern promises of memorial authority compromised and ultimately betrayed by a Western culture that has become increasingly opaque, self-destructive, and a prisoner of its own narcissistic desires. The twentieth-century authors I examine certainly share the transcendental dreams and impulses that characterize the early-modern appreciation of print culture, but they register the exhaustion of that tradition and the frustration that accompanies the discovery that such dreams are not simply illusions but nightmares. While the Holocaust and often violent end to European colonialism has led, in war crimes tribunals and reconciliation processes in countries such as Germany, South Africa, and Ireland, to a number of inspiring examples of collective remembering and memorializing, modern memory in the West, and even globally, more often seems overwhelmed by the task before it, the duty to remember unable to confront adequately the traumatic history that we have created. Although I examine an admittedly arbitrary and partial collection of contemporary materials to describe the exhaustion of modern conceptions of memory, the violent and genocidal history of our century has placed unprecedented demands on the ethical management of collective memory and the necessity to acknowledge past transgressions. By the end of the twentieth century, the collective and cultural memory underwritten by the print revolution often seems to guarantee little, except perhaps the continuing pain and horror of memories that one could only hope to forget.

Marianne Hirsch describes one powerful tool for understanding just what has been lost in the passage from the seventeenth and eighteenth centuries to the twentieth, and how profoundly the basic elements of our memorial constitution have been transformed, in her conception of "postmemory":

> Postmemory most specifically describes the relationship of children of survivors of cultural or collective trauma to the experiences of their parents, experiences they "remember" only as narratives and images with which they grew up, but that are so powerful, so monumental, as to constitute memories in their own right.[3]

Collective memory, to be sure, is always located in narratives and images, in representations through which one generation "remembers" events that it never experienced. To return to Jan Assmann, these representations form "the store of knowledge from which a group derives an awareness of its unity and particularity... Through its cultural heritage a society becomes visible to itself and to others."[4] For Assmann the movement from representation and narrative to memory constitutes the conventional manner in which collective memory engenders and invigorates itself.

Hirsch, however, attempts to explain specifically the memory of trauma, and particularly the wounds created by our century of mass murders and exterminations, which present an unbearable memorial burden to both the generations threatened with death, and the children of those who have survived:

> The term "postmemory" is meant to convey its temporal and qualitative difference from survivor memory, its secondary, or second-generation memory quality, its basis in displacement, its vicariousness and belatedness. Postmemory is a powerful form of memory precisely because its connection to its object or source is mediated not through recollection but through representation, projection, and creation... The work of postmemory defines the familial inheritance of cultural trauma.[5]

For Hirsch, postmemory defines a specifically twentieth-century phenomenon that characterizes an age in which we cannot escape the recognition or consequences of the traumatic history we have created.

The fine balance between anxiety and excitement in the early modern authors I examine is absent in the three twentieth-century writers, whose fictions register loss not triumph, cynicism rather than hope, and, although only Sebald responds directly to the Holocaust, a far more pronounced sense that collective memory and the history it validates can be neither interpreted nor trusted. Yet, at the end of the twentieth century, and in the first decade of the new millennium, that earlier combination of anxiety and excitement is evident once again, this time in response to a new technological revolution whose consequences, while still not fully understood, have already begun to transform both the material world in which we live, as well as the collective memory of our increasingly global community. I hope that the reiteration of this cultural response further justifies my movement forward in time, for it suggests the ways in which the computer has begun to compose a new chapter in the history of memory, and has already begun changing the memorial fantasies and aspirations of our culture. Like the printing press, the computer alters both the retrieval and transmission of information, as well as the fundamental activities of reading and writing.[6] Like the printing press in the seventeenth and eighteenth centuries, the computer in the twentieth and twenty-first seems poised to transform the world in ways that we can only begin to imagine, our response to this uncertainty a powerfully ambivalent compound of hope and fear, exhilaration and dread, celebration and disquiet.

I don't intend to repeat or endorse some of the rather hysterical contemporary warnings about the death of the book and print culture, which predict that the book as we know it is about to wither away and die. Just as the printing press did not signal the end of England's traditional oral culture, but in fact ushered in an era in which print and oral cultures worked together with a particular vibrancy, the electronic age will not put an end to a print culture that remains ubiquitous in postmodern society.[7] These admonitions concerning the end of print, in fact, primarily articulate the fears that have greeted the new electronic age in which we are being forced by the rapid pace of change to live. Yet those fears, evident throughout the electronic global community that the computer has already begun to create as well as transform, are countered by the often equally exaggerated hopes for the brave, new world that will evolve from the computer revolution. I want to balance my portrait of the end of modern memory with at least a brief consideration of the postmodern memory that may replace it, the figure of the cyborg, particularly in the works of Donna J. Haraway, central to at least one vision of a new and (possibly) triumphant memorial futurity. Moreover, her theorizing of the cyborg returns us to the questions of gender with which I began, for Haraway's insistence that our current "communications revolution means a re-theorizing of natural objects as technological devices properly understood in terms of mechanisms of production, transfer, and storage of information," has profound consequences not just for postmodern collective memory, but for what Haraway calls the "post-gender world," in which the fusion of animal and machine may refashion Man and Woman and the very structures of gender and sexual desire.[8]

II

In three of his spare, elegant, intellectual fictions, Borges reflects on the related trinity of memory, archive, and history, each story revealing the futility and emptiness of the memorial dreams generated by modernism. "Funes the Memorious," an austere contemplation of the mystery and potential of the individual memory, presents a despairing ode to what it considers "this sacred verb," *remember*. In their subtle variations on the simple statement "I remember," the first six sentences of the story perfectly capture the unsubstantial and tenuous nature of a linguistic formulation and human action that aspire to a certitude and precision they can never achieve: "I remember...," "I remember...," "I remember (I think)...," "I remember...," "I remember...," "I clearly remember..."[9] Juxtaposed to the four simple, repeated, declarative affirmations of an individual's power to *remember*, the qualifications of "I think" and even "clearly" insinuate the universe of doubt, the profound apprehension of uncertainty and instability, which must lurk just beyond the divine authority for which "this sacred verb" strives.

The fictional occasion for the story is a memorial volume celebrating Ireneo Funes, an obscure working-class Uruguayan of uncertain parentage who suffers a riding accident that both paralyzes him and unaccountably leaves him with an infallible memory. The story's narrator bears witness to the inspiring nature of his subject's mnemonic perfection. This narrator, whose uncertain memories of the single night he spent in conversation with Ireneo fifty years before manifest themselves in constructions such as "It seems to me" and "I believe I recall" (62), cannot help but provide an appreciative audience for Ireneo's unique and terrible talent, his ability to remember "not only every leaf of every tree of every wood, but also every one of the times he had perceived or imagined it" (65).

In admiring and idealized descriptions such as this, the narrator presents Ireneo as a type of superman worthy of a commemorative volume, for the ability to remember *everything* apparently allows Ireneo to achieve both a species of immortality and the opportunity to understand the sum of human knowledge. Ireneo himself shares the narrator's wonder, convinced that before his accident "he had been what all humans are: blind, deaf, addle-brained, absent-minded . . . he had lived as one in a dream: he looked without seeing, listened without hearing, forgetting everything, almost everything" (63). He cheerfully sacrifices his mobility for this rare gift, captivated by the singular new world that lies before him, tantalizing glimpses of which he allows the narrator to share.

Although Borges' story never loses its fascination with the apparently infinite possibilities that Funes' impossible gift discovers, it nonetheless resonates with scorn as well as awe, ridicule in addition to wonder. Borges' tale insists that the exalted powers Funes cherishes and that have occasioned his commemoration have also left him "hopelessly paralyzed" and "a perpetual prisoner" (61). Even Funes betrays the preposterous nature of his gift, his self-characterizations in the course of the evening spent with the narrator moving precipitously from the sublime to the ridiculous: "He [Ireneo] told me: 'I alone have more memories than all mankind has probably had since the world has been the world.' And again: 'My dreams are like you people's waking hours.' And again, toward dawn: 'My memory, sir, is like a garbage heap'" (64). The apparent opulence of Funes' memorial life remains only an illusion, his extraordinary ability, which seems to promise a new and dazzling world of knowledge and self-realization, in fact dooming him to a life of paralysis in the prison-house of an ever-increasing store of useless and burdensome memories from which he can never escape. The sum of all of an individual's memories, finally, is not infinity but zero, its ostensible and intolerable richness merely a sign of its own negation. As Suzanne Nalbantan writes, "in this ironic display…memory reaches its ultimate postmodern stage of chaotic disintegration."[10] Borges presents Funes' impossible talent as an object of both fascination and repulsion; like Swift in his description of the *struldbruggs* in part three of *Gulliver's Travels*, Borges reminds us that what we conventionally regard as a blessing is actually a curse, dreams of immortality, transcendent knowledge, and an infallible memory really a nightmare from which one can never awake.

Borges captures the same unusual combination of celebration and despair, wonder and anguish in "The Library of Babel," where the archive that should secure and preserve the sum of all human knowledge becomes instead a symbol of the biblical monument to human incomprehensibility and unintelligibility that Cavendish, Milton, and Pope imaginatively confronted when contemplating the nature of literary achievement and immortality. In this story, Borges imagines the universe as one vast, eternal library, its "atomic" units the twenty-five orthographical symbols: twenty-two letters, the comma, period, and the space. These individual characters, randomly assembled, constitute the building blocks of every book housed in the library. Each book contains four hundred and ten pages, each page forty lines, each line approximately eighty letters. These books are housed in the individual hexagonal galleries that represent the basic physical unit of the library.

Borges' library is perfectly organized, intolerably sterile, and hopelessly impenetrable, however desperately its human inhabitants attempt to generate meaning from its perhaps infinite collection of nonsensical books. Contemplating the promise of their library universe, the residents of this modernist archive move between the twin poles of enthusiasm and despair: "When it was proclaimed that the Library contained all books, the first impression was one of extravagant happiness. All men felt themselves to be the masters of an intact and secret treasure" (54–55). When this treasure refuses to yield its secrets, however, when people realize that in a library containing an infinite number of books wisdom remains inaccessible, "inordinate hope was followed by excessive depression," and various sects destroy millions of books. In Borges' library, the burning of books, a recurring modernist nightmare, can easily be rationalized, for "the Library is so enormous that any reduction of human origin is infinitesimal" (56). In this library that is the universe, the individual book loses its singularity and importance, the fear of an anonymous existence within the modern library that depressed Swift in the eighteenth century exactly realized in this twentieth-century collection of books so vast and unimaginable that any single one remains meaningless.

Yet at the same time, the Library is haunted by the specter of the particular volume or volumes that might make sense of its infinite collection of books, which might contain the key to the otherwise inaccessible knowledge lodged uselessly within its hexagons. Some, for instance, posit the existence of a "great circular book, whose spine is continuous and which follows the complete circle of the walls...This cyclical book is God" (52). Others imagine that "the faithful catalogue of the Library" can be found, although they must admit the existence of "thousands and thousands of false catalogues." Although the Library contains "all that it is given to express, in all languages. Everything" (54), without a catalog or index, key or god, the "everything" it promises must remain distant and withdrawn, unapproachable by those who contemplate the Library's sublime but indifferent magnificence. Somewhere in the Library, on a particular shelf in a specific hexagon, the equivalent of Chambers' *Cyclopaedia* must sit, only awaiting the reader who can use it to illuminate the perfect world of knowledge encompassed by the countless books that construct this mad universe. That, at least, represents one of modernism's most visionary ideals, as well as, according to Borges, one of its most self-deluding illusions.

In "The Library of Babel," Borges creates the universal library that, as we have seen, was a dream of the eighteenth century, and in doing so reveals the bankruptcy of the intellectual economy it represents. His story ends, appropriately enough for a fiction about an imaginary library, with a footnote to an imaginary source in which the equation between the macrocosm of the infinite library and the microcosm of a single volume realizes the futility of the modern preoccupation with the fullness of the archive:

Letizia Álvarez de Toledo has observed that this vast Library is useless: rigorously speaking, *a single volume* would be sufficient, a volume of ordinary format, printed in nine or ten point type, containing an infinite number of infinitely thin leaves...The handling of this silky vade mecum would not be convenient: each apparent page would unfold into other analogous ones; the inconceivable middle page would have no reverse.[11]

Borges' parodic meditation on religious disputation, the Einsteinian universe, and the modernist chimera of an intellectual utopia ends with the most mundane of scholarly devices—the footnote (so successfully travestied by Pope in his *Dunciad*)—which presents the absurd and oxymoronic image of a book "of ordinary format" that contains an "infinite number of infinitely thin leaves." Richardson's preoccupation with the material culture of print, paper, and ink concludes here, in a single, fantastic volume that represents an endless library, constructed of a paper so thin that it can hardly be said to exist. Borges' inconceivable volume takes its place among those curious twentieth-century books surveyed by Susan Stewart in which the tension between the material and spiritual dissolves into an impossible object that "tests the limits of the book's physical properties."[12]

In the "Theme of the Traitor and the Hero," Borges interrogates and questions the existence of history as a privileged and detached intellectual category. From the very beginning of this brief fiction, in which an unidentified "I" imagines writing the story that will follow, Borges plays with the narrativization of history, and the way in which the literary imagination determines historical form. The main characters are two, "the young, the heroic, the beautiful, the assassinated Fergus Kilpatrick" (72), who in 1824 was murdered on the eve of the successful Irish revolt that he led against England; and Ryan, his great-grandson, who, to celebrate the first centenary of the death, is writing a biography of his heroic ancestor. The identity of Kilpatrick's assassin has never been established, and, as Ryan probes his forebear's death, he becomes disturbed by a number of parallels that link the death of an Irish conspirator to the earlier assassination of Julius Caesar.

But Ryan then discovers other parallels that appear to link Kilpatrick's fate with Shakespeare's *Macbeth*: "That history should have copied history was already sufficiently astonishing; that history should copy literature was inconceivable" (73–74). The "inconceivable," however, becomes imaginable, for as Ryan studies "the historians," as he combs through "the archives," he learns that his ancestor's death was actually a coup de théâtre, that "Kilpatrick was killed in a theater, but the entire city was a theater as well, and the actors were legion, and the drama crowned by his death extended over many days and many nights. This is what happened" (74). The story that Ryan unfolds reveals that Kilpatrick in fact betrayed the revolt he captained, that his perfidy was discovered by his oldest friend and coconspirator Alexander Nolan, who then designed, with Kilpatrick's shamed compliance, a drama that would metamorphose the traitor into a hero by transforming his ignoble sentence of death into an inspiring assassination. The story ends with Ryan's decision not to reveal what he has learned, to publish, in fact, a book celebrating the glory of the hero.

This Borges story begins with a playful irony particularly visible in the opening two paragraphs, where the narrative "I" who self-consciously composes the fiction quickly places the tale in the hands of the imagined narrator, Ryan. The first narrator's insouciance about narrative detail emphasizes the arbitrary nature of fictional truth: this narrative "I" admits that "details, rectifications, adjustments are lacking; there are zones of the story not yet revealed to me." Indeed, the action can take place in any "oppressed and tenacious country: Poland, Ireland, the Venetian Republic, some South American or Balkan state." In the end, this narrator, who now leaves the story, launches the tale with a casual "Let us say (for narrative convenience)

Ireland; let us say in 1824. The narrator's name is Ryan" (72). The elaborate and studied carelessness of the first narrator is very much at odds with the search for historical truth that Ryan inaugurates, for he allows nothing arbitrary or random to intrude on his "investigation." Ryan's examination of published and unpublished documents proceeds with scientific rigor as he attempts to "decipher the enigma" and provide "irrefutable proof" for the history of heroism or treachery that he uncovers.

Yet Ryan concludes the story by publishing a book that affirms the lies he has penetrated, his historical truth not finally distinguishable from the apparently accidental narrative decisions of the original narrator. Everything in Borges' amused tale works quite deliberately to undermine commonplace distinctions between history and fiction, to assert the dependence of the former on the latter, to question the possibility of historical facts segregated from narrative invention, to insist, as Paul Ricoeur does, that "representation as narration does not simply turn naively toward things that happen. The narrative form as such interposes its complexity and opacity on...the referential impulse of the historical narrative."[13] The elaborate "drama" of Kilpatrick's death and transfiguration is both literal and figurative, history unable to remain aloof from the narrative logic of fiction.

In referring to the "hundreds of actors" who participated in Nolan's plot and Kilpatrick's death, we are told that "The things they did and said endure in the history books, in the impassioned memory of Ireland" (75). History and memory, in such a world, cannot be privileged above story and tale, for all share in the shaping power of fiction and narrative form. Borges' story suggests that "history" does not exist as a single, simple generic category, that between "the history books" and the "impassioned memory of Ireland" lie multiple "histories" that in the twentieth century would include popular history and historical fiction as well as "official" histories, like Ryan's, that pretend to rely on an objective examination of the archive. Borges' story reminds us as well that history began to assume its modern form during the seventeenth and eighteenth centuries, when, according to Donald R. Kelley and David Harris Sacks, "recognizably modern forms of historical research and writing took shape in relation to, and often in passionate conflict with, the narrative arts and new genres such as the novel."[14] Borges' story returns us to the writing of *Clarissa*, and the determination of Clarissa, Lovelace, and Richardson to transform story into history, fiction into Truth.

Milton, as we have seen, recognized some of the ways in which history depended on heroic narratives, and he sought throughout his career to change or at least qualify how that narrative would be understood and interpreted. But Milton nonetheless assumed that heroism was more than a narrative convention and that however difficult its achievement might be, it defined a genuine virtue that distinguished the writer from the soldier, Samson from Dalila, Jesus from his tempter. Borges' story questions this assurance, for Kilpatrick is at once both a traitor and a hero, a man who betrays the revolt he leads and a man who plays the part of the doomed, heroic Moses "who from the land of Moab glimpsed but could not reach the promised land" (73). The forms of heroism are multiple and diverse, but all conform to specific narrative conventions through which history and memory take recognizable shape. David Bakhurst argues that the "distinctive character of human memory is that it is mediated by symbolic means…it requires the ability to engage in the specific practice, social in origin, of the production and interpretation of narrative forms,"[15] and Borges' story insists that this is true for history as well as memory, both dependant on processes of distortion such as narrativization, condensation, and conventionalization in order to make sense.

III

However radical Borges' conflation of history and narrative may be, a story such as "The Theme of the Traitor and the Hero" assumes that history can in fact be known. Although by the end of this fiction historical truth has become far more complex than either the history books or cultural memory conventionally allows, one of its narrators can confidently assert that "This is what happened." Official histories may tell convenient and comforting lies, but in the archive the truth can be discovered by the diligent and imaginative investigator. Although the presence and behavior of the story's original narrator suggests that fictional form permeates historical narrative, his narrative creation, Ryan, succeeds in distinguishing one from the other. Even though the official lies may be perpetuated, at least someone will know the truth, will recognize the distortions that narrative form has imposed on historical facts.

In Danilo Kiš' "To Die for One's Country Is Glorious," this is not the case, the categories of hero and coward not simply confused, but ultimately unknowable. Kiš' version of Borges' tale also contains two main characters, "the young Esterházy," who has participated in a doomed revolt against the Habsburg dynasty and now awaits his death, and his mother, who in a brief visit in the days prior to the execution has promised to do all she can to secure "the Emperor's mercy" and have her son's sentence commuted: "'I shall be standing on the balcony,' she said, all but inaudibly. 'If I am in white, it means that I have succeeded.'"[16] We meet the young prisoner on the morning of his execution, and it soon becomes clear that on this final day he must direct all of his energies toward the goal of dying in a noble fashion: "All that mattered to him…was to preserve the dignity required of an Esterházy at such a moment" (126). Although the story begins with the protagonist attended by a priest, participating in his last "conversation with God," religious consolation—with its own specific narrative forms that represent divine closure—plays no part in Esterházy's preparations for death, which are governed instead by a set of established conventions that define and demonstrate heroic behavior. Sleep deserted him on the night before his execution, for example, but he forced himself to lie with his eyes shut, without stirring or uttering a sigh, so that the guard might testify to his utter fearlessness:

> And, in a strange inversion of time, he could already hear the guard telling the officers' mess, "Gentlemen, the young Esterházy slept quite soundly that

night, without so much as a sigh, as if going to his wedding rather than to his
hanging. I give you my word as an officer! Gentlemen, let us render him his
due!" After which was heard—he heard—the crystal ping of glasses. "Bottoms
up!" (127)

This vision of the future, which includes both dialogue and stage properties,
an entire narrative ready-to-hand, prepares the prisoner for the role he must
play if he is to successfully mime heroic performance. Again and again, he
constructs his actions on his final day through a series of behaviors that obey
the protocols of heroic narrative.

The repeated emphasis on "Gentlemen" in these imagined, future sce-
narios, these "strange inversion[s] of time" that accompany his memorial
dreams, suggests their rigorous class coding, the way in which aristocratic
behavior depends on a series of established conventions that provide its legitimacy and make it readable as "superiority" of rank and station. A reader
might even be tempted to provide a class reading of the story, except that
even the lower orders, Kiš suggests, possess little beyond the established and
time-worn narratives that determine their behavior and hold them prisoner
as well: "Through the intermittent drumrolls he heard the buzz of the
crowd, its threatening murmur; he saw fists raised in hate. The crowd was
cheering Imperial justice, because the mob always cheers the victor" (129).
Borges provided a type of dignity for his hero by constructing heroic narrative through Shakespearean drama; in Kiš, however, models for human
behavior seem governed by the grade B movie and comic strip. In "To Die
for One's Country is Glorious," the human actors Kiš presents seem unable
to respond to history beyond the most facile attention to cliché, observing
their stock parts as "hero" or "angry mob," or, as the crowd's frenzy begins
to affect the young Esterházy's behavior, "coward."

What transforms both the arc of the count's performance and the complexity of the story is the presence of Esterházy's formidable mother. Indeed,
even more than the force of her considerable personality, it is her clothing
that impresses itself on the story and her son, for, when he sees in the distance the promised balcony, "he glimpsed a blinding white spot...Leaning
over the railing, all in white, stood his mother": "Immediately, almost inso-
lently, he straightened up wishing to make it clear to the threatening mob
that an Esterházy could not die just like that, that he could not be hanged
like some highwayman." The count's aristocratic certainty that a world of
difference divides an Esterházy from a highwayman is perhaps undermined
when the execution proceeds without a last-minute reprieve.

Kiš' short, apparently simple, parable-like fiction asks a number of questions about the relationship between history and collective memory. Certainly
the most direct is posed by the "two possible conclusions" that the narrator
defines: "Either the young aristocrat died a brave and noble death, fully
conscious of the certainty thereof, his head held high, or the whole thing
was merely a clever bit of playacting directed by a proud mother" (130–31).
These binary oppositions direct, in fact, the dual, self-serving interpretations

offered up by the "historians," the first, heroic version proffered by "the sans-culottes and Jacobins," the second account, designed to present the rebel as a coward unworthy of emulation, "recorded by the official historians of the powerful Habsburg dynasty" (131).

Borges' tale suggests that even though the "official" version of history possesses an authority not easily challenged, the archive does preserve the evidence that allows for the recovery of historical truth, however inconvenient, complex, or even logically inconceivable it may be. Indeed, Borges' tale insists on the possibility that Kilpatrick fulfills *both* the roles of traitor and hero. In Kiš' narrative, on the other hand, it seems impossible to know whether the young Esterházy actually plays the hero or the coward. Borges composes an outlandish dramatic and intellectual conundrum in which one man can be both a traitor and a hero; Kiš presents a parallel narrative in which we cannot determine whether a man achieves heroism or surrenders to his fears.

But Kiš' story also suggests that we go beyond the simple binary presented by only "two possible conclusions," for it ends with a more complex formulation in which "History is written by the victors. Legends are woven by the people. Writers fantasize. Only death is certain" (131): history—legend—fantasy—death. I have argued that during the seventeenth and eighteenth centuries, memory was located between fame and history, defining a middle ground of contestation and struggle where writers attempted to construct places for themselves within an evolving cultural memory that might transcend mere transient fame and imitate the ostensible permanence of history. At the end of the twentieth century, however, when, as Yael Zerubavel writes, "the line separating 'history' from 'legend' is neither that clear nor necessarily consistent," when "the cultural interplay of 'history' and 'legend' reveals the transformative character of collective memory and its susceptibility to conflicting views that turn the past into a contested area,"[17] the normative power of both history and memory can only be confused and uncertain. To the question "is the young Esterházy a hero or a coward?" we may not only answer "we cannot know," but even "does it matter?" for in the face of the one certainty, death, of what significance is his sterile and banal performance? Nothing in Kiš' fiction suggests the end of the Empire—in a region that for centuries has simply seen one Empire replace another—or even a political evolution that can defeat the repeated cycles of revolt and punishment, "heroic" rebels and angry mobs; nothing in his tale suggests that either Esterházy's heroism or pusillanimity will make any difference to the historical processes that seem to hold all human actors within their brutal grip. By its conclusion, Kiš' story has little interest in whether Esterházy achieves heroism or not; its denouncement focuses primarily on how Esterházy's story becomes appropriated by different historiographical traditions, the grim predictability of that process part of what now makes history difficult to distinguish from legend or fantasy. In a story whose simple, declarative title makes it available to interpretations both straightforward and ironic, both sincere and cynical, what can heroism possibly mean, or how can history or memory assert their prominence, importance, or truth?

Kiš asks similar questions even more powerfully in the title story from his collection *The Encyclopedia of the Dead*, where the tale's subtitle "(A Whole Life)" points to the desire to fill in the gaps that apparently make the young Esterházy's life so difficult to interpret. Like both "Funes the Memorious" and "The Library of Babel," "The Encyclopedia of the Dead" is fascinated by visions of totality, by the modernist ambition to encompass All. Kiš' story locates this desire not in the individual memory, nor in a universal library, but in a single reference work that records everything. This reference work is discovered by the story's narrator, an unnamed Serbian woman visiting Sweden shortly after the death of her father. While there, her hostess takes her one night to the Royal Library and leaves her alone to enjoy its collection. As the narrator moves through the library's rooms she soon discovers that what lies before her is "the celebrated Encyclopedia of the Dead." This encyclopedia is unique, according to the narrator, not only because there exists only one copy, but "because it records everything. Everything" (42), and her progress through the entry on her father gradually teaches us just what such a claim means.

At first the narrator explains it by noting that "the reference (for example) to my father's place of birth is not only complete and accurate ('Kraljevčani, Glina township, Sisak district, Banija province') but is accompanied by both geographical and historical details" (42). As she continues reading, the proliferation of detail becomes even more overwhelming. When her father goes to Ruma, for example, to receive his secondary-school education, we find "a brief history of Ruma, a meteorological map, a description of the railway junction; the name of the printer and everything printed at the time—every newspaper, every book; the plays put on by itinerant companies and the attractions of touring circuses" (46–47). Eventually, the narrator comes to understand that "for *The Encyclopedia of the Dead*, history is the sum of human destinies, the totality of ephemeral happenings. That is why it records every action, every thought, every creative breath, every spot height in the survey, every shovelful of mud, every motion that cleared a brick from the ruins" (56). Like Borges' insistence in "Funes the Memorious" on the sacred nature of the verb *remember*, Kiš' tale recognizes the divine aspirations of the modernist memorial project, which would, in the *Encyclopedia*, affirm that "every human being is sacred" (51). The attempt to provide an exhaustive biography of the life of the narrator's father—who we ironically come to know only as Djuro M.—to completely capture his unique story and so provide consolation for a grieving daughter, represents the extravagant ambitions of a modernism that would faultlessly chronicle its own evolution and eventual apotheosis.[18]

As the narrator completes the entry on her father's life, however, copying out what the *Encyclopedia* identifies as "the basic floral pattern" (64) in the drawings that preoccupied her father in his final years, she "let out a scream. I awoke drenched in sweat. I immediately wrote down all of the dream I remembered. And this is what remains of it" (65). That dream, in short, is really a nightmare, the library in which the *Encyclopedia* rests "like a dungeon" (40), the volumes that compose it both unread "in a long time" and "fettered to one another like galley slaves" (41). The infinite accumulation of archival information and memories does not provide consolation or freedom, not the realization of a dream of total knowledge, the ability to understand "a whole life," but the experience of a frightening, uncontrollable, and cancerous growth, for the basic floral pattern that concludes the entry and narrator's notes "looked exactly like the sarcoma in my father's intestine" (65).

In "The Encyclopedia of the Dead," Kiš replaces the obscure romanticism of "To Die for One's Country," which he locates in an unlocalized eighteenth- or nineteenth-century Austro-Hungarian Empire, with a much more historically precise twentieth-century landscape; the narrator's father, a surveyor for successive Serbian governments, lives from 1910 to 1979. Indeed, in charting the evolution of Serbian nationalism from World War I through the Cold War, Kiš begins to suggest some of the harsh political processes that have impinged on and even deformed the development of collective memory during the last century. The German invasion and subsequent occupation of Serbia, as well as the Belgrade street battles of 1944 and partisan warfare that helped liberate the country from the German yoke, all find a place in the annals of this life.[19] The bloody territorial upheavals of the first two world wars is then replaced by the ominous specter of Communist political domination, when Djuro M.'s "muffled 'F—Stalin!'" introduces us to the *Encyclopedia*'s ability to create "the spirit of the time" by providing a catalog of the grim consequences of political control by a centralized state apparatus: "The fear in which my father lived and the silence I myself remember—a heavy, oppressive silence—are construed by the book as infectious" (58). Now "the State Security Building" comes briefly into prominence, as do denunciations, beatings, and the naming of names. The narrator's father successfully maneuvers his way through to retirement and a miserable pension, but in touching, however briefly, on the brutal visage of the modern totalitarian state, represented by both the fascists of Nazi Germany and the communist regimes of the Soviet Union and Eastern Europe, the story illuminates one of the primary political forces that has transformed the way in which we conceive of and respond to both individual and collective memory in the twentieth century.

From the notorious Moscow Show Trials of 1936–1938, to the absurd reports and photographs of a Mao in his early seventies swimming fifteen kilometers in the Yangtze River a month before launching the Cultural Revolution in August 1966, the centralized communist state has provided some of the most conspicuous and dramatic examples of the desire and ability not simply to fabricate history, but to confuse propaganda and fact in ways that have made it even more difficult to distinguish historical truth from political invention. Only after the fall of the Berlin Wall, dissolution of East Germany, and subsequent availability of Stasi dossiers did it become apparent how many people were directly and indirectly involved in the creation of such inventions, a staggering percentage of the East German population employed in the activities of surveillance, denunciation, and the policing of everyday lives.[20] The political revelations concerning the communist state that have marked the last two decades only prove the prescience of Orwell's *1984*, which registers with a terrible clarity the way in which the modern totalitarian state, with its prodigious technological sophistication and resources, can not simply transform fiction into history, but control and rewrite the individual memories of its citizens. In such a context, Francis Fukuyama's "end of history," which trumpeted the Western victory over communism, takes on a more ominous meaning than he intended; and the supreme arrogance of a senior adviser to president Bush who, during the summer of 2002, explained that "We're an empire now, and when we act, we create our own reality," suggests that the "winners" of the Cold War are not themselves immune from the desire to transform ideological fantasy into history.[21]

IV

While the histrionics of the totalitarian state have had a powerful influence on the way in which memory is imagined and understood at the conclusion of the twentieth century, the most profound challenge to the modernist compulsion toward memorial certainty and authority has been presented by a complex historical event whose ghastly power and unique nature is acknowledged by its reduction to a single epithet: the Holocaust, or Shoah. The attempt by Nazi Germany to exterminate the Jewish people was neither the first nor the last genocide of the twentieth century: the Turkish massacre of its Armenian minority might be said to have introduced the last century to its hideous, recurring historical nightmare, which has continued, in Rwanda and Sudan, even into the new millennium. But the systematic thoroughness and bureaucratic efficiency of the Nazis, their ferocious ideological commitment to the extermination of a single race, and the way in which they exploited the technologies of a modern state to achieve their aim have never been equaled. By 1945, two out of every three European Jews was dead.[22] While the numbers defy comprehension, six million Jews joined by an equal number of "deviant" races, sexualities, and nationalities in the death camps, so too does its occurrence in the very heart of Europe, the ostensibly "civilized" and "civilizing" center of the global order forged by colonialism over the last five hundred years.

The command "Never Forget," which became attached to the Holocaust when after the war the Jewish people began to comprehend the full extent of the Nazi agenda that threatened their existence, indissolubly links the Holocaust to the power and authority of memory. Like no event before it, the Holocaust seems to demand that the normal processes of memory, which inevitably include distortion, decay, and forgetting, be transcended. Both the Jews who almost suffered extinction and the Germans who perpetuated the crime, have recognized the ethical necessity of impressing the Holocaust so firmly in their collective memories that such an event could never happen again, and the Holocaust has thus remained a constant feature of the German, Israeli, and Jewish political landscape for the last fifty years. Even today, memorials to the Holocaust, which continue to be built, and the fate of the death camps themselves, raise contentious and haunting questions about the nature and power of memory, for "Never Forget" functions not simply as a command and moral imperative, but as a plea, a prayer, and an exhortation that recognizes the impossibility of that which it demands. As the numbers of Holocaust survivors dwindle, as the event becomes part of past history— now more than a half century old—rather than present memory, as other genocides and horrors jostle for a place in our conscience, there can be little doubt that the vulnerability and fragility of collective memory will be hard pressed to keep alive the cultural and ethical obligations that "Never Forget" demands.[23]

In the words of Dominick LaCapra, the Holocaust stands "at the intersection of history and memory,"[24] its traumatic destabilization of Western identities and moralities problematizing an already complex relationship between these two intellectual categories through which we construct and preserve our past. Moreover, the Holocaust continues to exert its traumatic presence in contemporary memorial politics: the recent international conference held in Teheran on December 11–12, 2006, "Review of the Holocaust: Global Vision," convened by Mahmoud Ahmadinejad, the president of Iran, used the Holocaust to dramatically raise issues concerning national identity and the "ownership" of history. In Germany, Holocaust denial remains a crime punishable by up to five years in prison, but Ahmadinejad's provocative flaunting of his denial at the center of the world's political stage asks the question "Whose collective memory?" in ways that are profoundly disturbing, for it reminds us that the Holocaust's status as an historical fact has been questioned, even in the West, from the very beginning. As Manouchehr Mottaki, the Iranian minister of foreign affairs, announced on the first day of the conference in a speech to the assembled participants,

> The critics of the formalistic interpretation of [the events of World War II], believing that history is written by the victors, sought to write the contemporary world history on the basis of actual evidence and documents. They criticize the writing of history on the basis of an analytical interpretative method. In this context, criticism of the holocaust as a historical event constitutes part of the critical approach to the contemporary history…those who took for granted the previous interpretations of such events as unquestionable facts are now skeptical about their reality and take this skepticism as the basis of their new inquiry.[25]

In spite of tens of thousands of survivors, public trials and confessions, buildings full of documents and libraries overflowing with books, photographic and cinematic evidence, and the camps themselves, there remain many who regard the Holocaust as an invention or exaggeration and who refuse to believe that it ever occurred. In the face of such a conviction, motivated primarily by anti-Semitism and ideological bad faith, the "actual evidence and documents" that ostensibly legitimize and privilege history are finally powerless to compel belief.[26]

These complexities of collective memory and historical truth, and the contradictions that undermine their authority, form the subject matter of four novels by W.G. Sebald that appeared between 1990 and 2001. His second novel, *The Emigrants*, presents the "biographies" of three Germans and a Lithuanian, born between 1886 and 1924, who chose or were forced to live their lives as exiles from the country of their birth. Three of the four are Jewish, and *The Emigrants* eulogizes a German Jewish culture in the process of its disappearance and loss.[27] It acknowledges the terrible contradiction that lies at the heart of "Never Forget" by struggling to imaginatively recover and document the lives of a people displaced, dispersed, and murdered, even as it recognizes the impossibility of such a task. Sebald's novel dramatizes the heroic and moving task of protecting memory from the ravages of time, of prolonging the life of a German Jewish heritage that, because of the thoroughness of the crimes perpetrated by the Nazis, now hardly exists. But even as it does so, this knowing and perceptive book confesses its inability to make permanent what has been lost. This is a terribly sad novel, whose pain stems directly from the failures of modern memory and the horrors of history at the end of the twentieth century. As the third of its biographical subjects, Ambros Adelwarth, writes at the conclusion of his pocket diary, "Memory...often strikes me as a kind of dumbness. It makes one's head heavy and giddy, as if one were not looking back down the receding perspectives of time but rather down on the earth from a great height, from one of those towers whose tops are lost to view in the clouds" (145). Memory in such a formulation provides not security or knowledge, certainty or futurity, but exists instead as a form of muteness that generates disorientation and vertigo, and evokes the historical disenfranchisement of individuals sundered from their geographical and cultural roots. This tower represents an inverted version of Babel, its incomprehensibility located not in noise but in an even more ominous and frightening silence. Adelwarth's nephew Kasimir, who left Germany for America in 1929 and returned thereafter to Europe only for brief visits, suggests a similar sense of existential dislocation when walking on a New Jersey beach and gazing out at the ocean that separates him from his supposed homeland: "I often come out here...it makes me feel that I am a long way away, though I never quite know from where" (89).

That "where" includes not simply the Germany that Kasimir left when still a young man because he could not find work in Weimer Germany, but Jerusalem as well, which comes to represent the original homeland from which the Jewish people have been exiled. In the long sweep of historical time, their forced displacement from Germany marks just one of the multiple geographical and cultural upheavals that have made it impossible for Jews to maintain a conventional relationship to a "homeland." Such a history has forced them to forge a racial memory that can replace the memorial stability that place normally helps to provide.[28]

Yet Kasimir is not Jewish, and, in one of the many ironies that pervade the novel, the one character who does visit Jerusalem, Ambros Adelwarth, is not a Jew either, although his travels to Turkey, the Middle East, Jerusalem, and

the Dead Sea during the winter of 1913 are undertaken with a Jewish travel-
ing companion, Cosmo Solomon, who is Adelwarth's employer, friend, and
probably lover. Their visit, which forms the conclusion and emotional climax
to Adelwarth's biography, presents Jerusalem as the "Holy Land," the spiritual homeland of Christians and Moslems as well as Jews. In describing the
city as he sees it on the morning after they arrive, Adelwarth marvels at the
"hordes" of Christian "pilgrims from all around the world" who fill the city.
At the same time, he sees himself surrounded by "decay, nothing but decay,
marasmus and emptiness"; he comes upon "a knacker's yard...Coagulated
blood, heaps of entrails, blackish-brown tripes, dried and scorched by the
sun"; after that, "one church after another, monasteries, religious and
philanthropic establishments of every kind and domination" (137). What
follows is a bewildering, Babel-like catalog of forty-five different religious
and charitable institutions, ranging from the German Asylum for the Deaf
and Dumb and the Armenian Orthodox Monastery of Mount Zion, to the
Russian Orthodox Church of Mary Magdalene, the Coptic Monastery, and
the School of the Frères de la Doctrine Chrétienne.

The violent juxtaposition between Jerusalem's filth and emptiness and
its teeming theological and philanthropic establishments suggests the spiritual inadequacy and even betrayal of those institutions. What might be the
spiritual center of the world fills Adelwarth with horror, for he experiences
Jerusalem as a foul and leprous city "filled with the rubbish of a thousand
years" (140). Nothing seems to remain of the once great beauty and wealth
"of the Promised Land but dry stone and a remote idea in the heads of
its people, now dispersed throughout the world" (142). For Adelwarth,
Jerusalem provides little comfort and no sense of home, but only reiterates
for many peoples the painful historical lessons of Jewish alienation and
displacement.

The novel emphasizes the significance of this failed visit to Jerusalem
through the penetrating silence that reoccurs in three of the four biographies. Adelwarth "would never answer questions" about that journey to
Jerusalem, just as Dr. Henry Selwyn, the subject of the first biography, and
Max Ferber, the subject of the fourth, find themselves unable to speak of
their experiences of World War II: "The years of the second war, and the
decades after, were a blinding, bad time for me, about which I could not say
a thing even if I wanted to" (21); "It had been a terribly bad time for him, a
time scarcely to be endured, a time he could not bear to say any more about"
(167). These silences echo throughout the novel, the inability or unwilling-
ness to recall, or articulate, or confess just one aspect of the voicelessness that
isolates these characters from their fellows, alienates them from their own
histories, and prevents them from even imagining a cultural memory that
might preserve the past or grant the promise of futurity. Instead, Adelwarth
longs "for extinction as total and irreversible as possible" (114), while Ferber
perceives time as "nothing but a disquiet of the soul. There is neither a past
nor a future. At least, not for me" (181). Given their traumatic experiences of
history, these characters long not for a second life in time, but for oblivion;

memory for such individuals can only be a prison, a recurring delirium from which they long to be released into silence and death.[29] Two of the novel's biographical subjects commit suicide, while a third (Adelwarth) becomes the willing patient of a doctor who subjects him to repeated electrotherapy shock treatments.

The overpowering presence of silence in the novel is one reason that images take on such importance in Sebald's fiction. In *The Emigrants*, each biography presents numerous photographs that ostensibly document the lives of the individuals chronicled in each section, although the novel contains no explanation about either the provenance of the photographs, or their relationship to the text. As Maya Jaggi notes during a conversation with Sebald, "Your books have a documentary feel, using captionless black-and-white photographs, but their status is unclear."[30] The often ominous silence of the individuals themselves is implicitly juxtaposed to this rich conversation of images, which appear to speak volumes about the lives they record and document. In the account of Paul Bereyter, the second of the four biographical subjects, the narrator is given access to a large photographic album and he "returned to it time and again, because, looking at the pictures in it, it truly seemed to me, and still does, as if the dead were coming back" (46). For the narrator, photographs possess an unquestioned memorial power, this invention of the nineteenth-century one of the technological advances that seems to surpass even the printing press in terms of memorial authority. In the third biography (that of Adelwarth) the narrator is even driven to his task of researching his forebear by a photograph album, "which contained pictures quite new to me of our relatives who had emigrated during the Weimar years. The longer I studied the photographs, the more urgently I sensed a growing need to learn more about the lives of the people in them" (71). Photographs speak even when their subjects are dumb, and their images not only connect us to a past that might otherwise be hidden from us, but can even generate the desire to recover that past and make it live again. As Susan Sontag writes in *On Photography*, "the most grandiose result of the photographic enterprise is to give us the sense that we can hold the whole world in our heads—as an anthology of images. To collect photographs is to collect the world... Photographs really are experience captured, and the camera is the ideal arm of consciousness in its acquisitive phase."[31]

Yet for all of their memorial power, the photographs and images in *The Emigrants* are sometimes quite inexplicable, their relationship to both the text and futurity problematic. In the section on Paul Bereyter, the narrator suggests as much when he emphasizes that while examining the pictures in the album it not only seemed that "the dead were coming back," but that "*we were on the point of joining them*" (46; emphasis added). If photographs of the past allow the dead to live on in the imaginations of the living, they also imply that one day the living will be no more than photographic images, that life will be subsumed by death and the living reduced to mere images in an album devoted to the past. According to Christian Metz, photography possesses a "deeply rooted kinship with death," and however much it may seem to bring its subjects back to life it "maintains the memory of the dead *as being dead*."[32] This seems particularly inauspicious in a novel in which the four main characters die childless, and which passes over in silence the family status of the unnamed narrator of the four biographies; he seems to possess a wife, Clara, who plays a minor role in the first biography (of Henry Selwyn), but she never reappears. The photographic albums will, of course, live on, but the rich and complicated genealogical histories that they allow the novel to reconstruct are in the process of coming to an end. There are many children in the novel, but all belong, like the photographs, to the past.

The complex and problematic relationship of photography to memory and the past that all of Sebald's novels raise becomes particularly important in Marianne Hirsch's conception of postmemory, for "photographs in their enduring 'umbilical' connection to life are precisely the medium connecting first- and second-generation remembrance, memory and postmemory. They are the leftovers, the fragmentary sources and building blocks, shot through with holes, of the work of postmemory." Sebald himself bears witness to the intimate relationship between photography and traumatic postmemory when he writes, in *On the Natural History of Destruction* (2003), that

> At the end of the war I was just one year old, so I can hardly have any impressions of that period of destruction based on personal experience. Yet to this day, when I see photographs or documentary films dating from the war I feel as if I were its child, so to speak, as if those horrors I did not experience cast a shadow over me, and one from which I shall never entirely emerge.[33]

In this account, Sebald becomes the child of a war that ended just after his birth and whose horrors he never experienced. Yet the images of that war not only mediate, but engender his relationship to a past through which he never lived but that nonetheless determines his life. Hirsch identifies the "shadow" from which Sebald can never emerge as the "ghostly revenant" of photography, which emphasizes both the traumatic power of the past and "at the same time, its immutable and irreversible pastness and irretrievability."[34]

The memorial and archival power of photographs and images is further questioned in one particularly significant moment in the final section of the novel, the biography of the painter Max Ferber. Born in 1924—the youngest of the four biographical subjects in the novel—Ferber remembers a particular photograph, and its complicated history should be quoted at length:

> I now remember (said Ferber) that Uncle Leo, who taught Latin and Greek at a grammar school in Würzburg until he was dismissed, once showed Father a newspaper clipping dating from 1933, with a photograph of the book burning on the Residenzplatz in Würzburg. That photograph, said Uncle, was a forgery. The burning of the books took place on the evening of the 10th of May, he said—he repeated it several times—the books were burnt on the evening of the 10th of May, but since it was already dark, and they couldn't take any decent photographs, they simply took a picture of some other gathering outside

the palace, Uncle claimed, and added a swathe of smoke and a dark night sky. In other words, the photographic document published in the paper was a fake. And just as that document was a fake, said Uncle, as if his discovery were the one vital proof, so too everything else has been a fake, from the very start. But Father shook his head without saying a word, either because he was appalled or because he could not assent to Uncle Leo's sweeping verdict. At first I too found the Würzburg story, which Ferber said he was only then remembering for the first time, somewhat on the improbable side; but in the meantime I have tracked down the photograph in question in a Würzburg archive, and as one can easily see there is indeed no doubt that Ferber's uncle's suspicions were justified. (183–84)

This passage provides a exemplary example of the types of narrative shifts that destabilize Sebald's prose, distancing both his characters and their stories from a reader. Here the *I* who begins the passage (the biographical subject Max Ferber) is not the *I* who ends it (the unnamed narrator of Ferber's life). And in the middle, the passage uses its reiteration of the *10th of May* to mimic a third voice, that of Uncle Leo, as he tells a story to Ferber's father that Ferber—a twelve-year-old at the time—only *now remembers*. The passage concludes with a copy of a suspicious-looking photograph that the narrator has recovered from the archives. The dislocating effect of the passage is exacerbated by its position in the middle of an extended, almost eight-page paragraph that reverses the narrative shift found in the above passage: the unnamed narrator begins the paragraph as the *I* who recounts a reunion with Ferber in which Ferber, who ends the paragraph as the narrative *I*, recalls the story of his escape from Nazi Germany in 1939 and the last time he saw his parents alive. They were deported in 1941, "their fate unknown," although the unnamed narrator later visits the Jewish cemetery in Kissingen where Uncle Leo has erected a gravestone to both Ferber's grandparents and parents. But only one body, that of Ferber's grandmother who committed suicide, "lies in that grave" (225).

Both the photograph and the gravestone call into question, in ways that mirror the dizzying narrative structure, the authority of memory and the documents and memorials through which it constitutes itself. The narrative shifts that divert readers from the unnamed narrator to Ferber to Uncle Leo certainly make it difficult for readers to firmly locate themselves in the narrative; throughout the novel, the deliberately disorienting narrative shifts, and welter of narrative voices—some of them poorly or only partially identified—place the novel at a distance from its readers and dramatically shape its emotional texture and affect, which, although moving, remains remote and fragile, abstract and tenuous in spite of its great attention to detail and historical specificity. But the "false" gravestone and questionable photograph undermine the novel's memorial project in much more profound and disturbing ways, for they question the very notion of documentary evidence and historical proof.[35]

The gravestone, which declares the presence of four bodies when only one is present, calls attention to the horrors and depredations of the

Holocaust, reminding us of the mass graves and ovens that were the fate of so many; but it also accentuates, in a new and particularly frightening fashion, the dubious memorial authority of marble and stone that writers from Virgil to Milton have always understood. The gravestone assumes deaths that cannot be proven, and implies a guilt that cannot be demonstrated, while the questionable "photographic document" destabilizes the very categories of historical evidence and verification. Uncle Leo's insistent questioning of the photograph contains a bitter irony, because as a Jew he calls into question the very evidence that might "prove" a Holocaust that others would deny. Although Uncle Leo does not dispute the reality of the book burning, which he knows took place on the evening of May 10, his insistence that the photograph itself is a "fake" and a "forgery" leads him to the type of radical questioning that those who deny the Holocaust use to cast doubt on the Final Solution: "And just as that document was a fake, said Uncle, as if his discovery were the only vital proof, so too everything else has been a fake, from the very start." Of what exactly does this single suspicious photograph provide "vital proof?" What precisely is the "everything else" that has been faked? Here Leo's justified frustrations and fears as a Jew in Nazi Germany unfortunately speak the same language as those who would deny the Holocaust that would shortly engulf Leo and his family.

Sebald himself, in an interview with Arthur Lubow, emphasizes the importance of this particular photograph:

> I thought very consciously that this is a place to make a declaration. It couldn't be more explicit. It acts as a paradigm for the whole enterprise. The process of making a photographic image, which purports to be the real thing and isn't anything like, has transformed our self-perception, our perception of each other, our notion of what is beautiful, our notion of what will last and what won't.[36]

I certainly do not mean to lend intellectual credence to those who deny the Holocaust, or to recruit Sebald to their ranks, although, as Mark M. Anderson notes, Sebald has had a much more complex reception in Germany than in America or Great Britain, for in his homeland he "has been charged with contesting the legitimacy of public historiography."[37] Sebald is passionate about the relationship of memory and literature, convinced that "the moral backbone of literature is about that whole question of memory...Without memories there wouldn't be any writing: the specific weight an image or phrase needs to get across to the reader can only come from things remembered—not from yesterday but from a long time ago."[38] Yet to the extent that this novel questions the memorial authority and power of the narratives and photographs and gravestones that are almost all that remain of a people marked out for extermination, it undermines the documentary status of the archive, destabilizes the privileged status of historical knowledge, and questions what James Clifford admits are already less than ideal "standards of textual proof":

> History feeds on what finds its way into a limited textual record. A historian needs constant skepticism and a willingness to read imaginatively "against" the sources, to divine what is not represented in the accumulated selection of the archive. Ultimately, however, even the most imaginative history is tied to standards of textual proof.[39]

Near the end of Ambros Adelwarth's life, he takes into his confidence his niece Fini, telling her stories about his past life that she finds incredible: "At times I thought the things he said he had witnessed, such as beheadings in Japan, were so improbable that I supposed he was suffering from Korsakov's syndrome: as you may know, said Aunt Fini, it is an illness which causes lost memories to be replaced by fantastic inventions" (102). Korsakov's (or Korsakoff's) syndrome describes, in fact, a genuine medical pathology, normally associated with a dementia observed during the last stages of chronic alcoholism when short-term memory may be lost and the patient confuses imagination with memory, indulging in confabulations that substitute imaginary for actual memories.[40] Adelwarth, Fini comes to recognize, does not suffer from such a dementia, but, in *The Emigrants*, Korsakov's syndrome might be said to define the modern condition in which it has become difficult to distinguish imaginary memories from real ones, fiction from history, confabulation from truth. By the end of the twentieth century, the desire to remember everything, to create memorials whose authority cannot be questioned, to ground futurity in a privileged collective memory ends here, in a world in which dreams of memorial power and authority become nightmares from which we cannot awake, and the simplest memory can be confused with the most outrageous invention. Historical truth has been relativized by the saturation of information generated by our technological ability to store and retrieve so much. The epigram to the first biography in the novel (that of Dr. Henry Selwyn) reads, "And the last remnants memory destroys."[41] In such a world, memory has become its opposite, destruction and not preservation its goal, forgetting rather than remembering what we ask of memories that have become only a personal and historical burden.

V

The fragility and vulnerability of modern memory, represented in *The Emigrants* by the faded, possibly faked photographs disinterred from the archive, and the traumatic narratives of a diminishing population of survivors and witnesses, stands in stark contrast to a postmodern memory described, at least in its technical register, by Ikka Tuomi in his exploration of "The Lives and Death of Moore's Law":

> Starting with Intel's 486 processor series, so-called cache memory began to be included on the same silicon die as the processor. Processor chips, therefore,

became a combination of processors and memory. As memory chips have a considerably higher density of transistors than micro-processor chips, this combination of memory with processors led to rapid increase in the number of transistors on such integrated processor chips. The first memory that was included on the chip was called L1 cache. For almost a decade, this cache memory was supplemented by fast external memory chips called L2 cache.[42]

Gordon E. Moore, cofounder of Intel, first articulated what later became known as his "law" in a 1965 publication entitled "Cramming More Components Onto Integrated Circuits," where he predicted—in its most popular (and erroneous) formulation—that the number of transistors on integrated circuits would double every eighteen months.[43] "Moore's Law" eventually served as an industrial benchmark that drove both the marketing and engineering of semiconductor manufacturers, the miniaturization of the computer chip an essential factor in the decreasing cost and increasing speed, power, and memory that has marked the advent and evolution of the personal computer.

The astonishing materialization of memory that lies at the heart of the computer and its transformation of the world in which we live manifests itself in a bewildering technical vocabulary describing "cache memory," "memory chips," and "fast external memory," which exist as discreet, singular units within a larger economic, scientific, and cultural system that Tuomi calls "the memory market" and "the memory business." In the computer chip *memory* has become not simply reified but literalized; at the same time, *memory* has become one of the foundational metaphoric tropes of the computer, the industry that produces and markets it, and the cyberspace it has created. *Memory*, precisely quantified and mechanically (re)produced on a silicon chip, lies at the heart of the new world order that the computer has begun to fashion. When he wrote "Funes the Memorious," Borges' fiction represented an impossible and unrealizable dream or nightmare; part of the story's intellectual charm depends on the very outlandishness of its premise. At the start of the new millennium, however, researchers at British Telecommunications are trying to produce the endearingly named "Soul Catcher," "a micromemory chip implanted in the human brain, implanted for the whole of a lifetime, meant to record the whole of that lifetime."[44] Soon, we may all be Funes, "enjoying" perfect access to a lifetime of memories recorded by, stored in, and even transmitted from a sophisticated circuitry implanted in our brain.

Considerable debate, of course, surrounds the nature of artificial intelligence, and particularly its relationship to human memory and thought. For Steven Rose, "brains do not work with information in the computer sense," and, particularly in respect to memory, he suggests the incommensurability between machine and human: "Our human memories are not embedded in a computer, they are encoded in the brain, in the ten thousand million nerve cells that comprise the human cerebrum—and the ten million million connections and pathways between those cells. Memories are living processes, which become transformed, imbued with new meanings, each time we recall them."[45] Hans Moravec, on the other hand, imagines a not-too-distant future "when virtually no essential human function, physical or mental, will lack an artificial counterpart," and he looks forward to a continued machine "evolution" in which we create "machines [that] are powerful enough to approximate the human intellect."[46] Indeed, Manfred Clynes, who originally coined the term *cyborg* with Nathan S. Kline in their 1960 essay on "Cyborgs and Space," projects a future in which "it should be possible to tap human memory in such a way that you can make people learn some things without the effort of learning."[47] Learning without effort, what Swift, with great disdain in *Tale of a Tub* dubbed "mechanical inspiration," represents a cherished intellectual fantasy that the computer may very well place within our reach.

At the end of the twentieth and beginning of the twenty-first century, the figure of the cyborg has come to fascinate popular and literary culture precisely because its hybridity, its often uncomfortable merging of the biological and the technological, poses most clearly questions about the relationship of the machine to the human; and about whether we should share or reject Swift's conservative response to mechanical inspiration. As Steve Mann, who has worn a mobile computer processor since the 1970s and considers himself to be a cyborg, suggests, "in marrying the body with the computer, we have a new approach to technology, to mechanism, and ultimately to memory and being ... Can we extend our projection and memory storage capacities without reducing what makes us, ultimately, human?"[48]

Nowadays, few seem willing to provide a definitive answer to that question. Mann, for instance, remains deeply committed to what he now defines as his cyborg nature, and is convinced that while, in regard to memory, his Visual Memory Prosthetic cannot *replace* his memory, it can nonetheless *augment* it, and in doing so perhaps lead to "a new way to remember [that] promises a new way to think, leading to new ways of 'being.' "[49] At the same time, he recognizes that the cyborg generates both fascination and horror, and that the merging of the human and the technological leads to what he calls both "cyborg envy" as well as "cyborg fear," both boundless optimism and great despair as we contemplate our technological future.

No one has more fully explored the "new ways of 'being' " that Mann imagines than the historian of science and feminist theorist Donna J. Haraway, who, in a series of essays and books written since the 1980s, has constructed the cyborg as "simultaneously a myth and a tool, a representation and an instrument, a frozen moment and a motor of social and imaginative reality."[50] Ironically, Haraway, who writes about Margaret Cavendish in her latest book *Modest_Witness@Second_Millennium*—which takes its conception of a "modest witness" from Robert Boyle's construction of modern experimental science during the mid-seventeenth century—situates the cyborg "where the boundary between human and animal is transgressed" (*Simians* 152); such a description at once recalls and reformulates Cavendish's division between animals, who possess no past, and humans, whose collective memory generates both history and identity. For Haraway, the cyborg puts an end to such comfortable and easy distinctions, forcing us to radically reimagine ourselves, our political constructions, and our futures.

Perhaps our most profound transformations will involve gender, for the cyborg allows Haraway and other feminists to imagine a world that can overturn the "sexual difference founded on compulsory heterosexuality [that] is itself the key technology for the production and perpetuation of western Man" (*Primate Visions* 352). By sundering women from the burden of reproduction, by generating a world based on mechanical replication rather than biological reproduction, the cyborg subverts the patriarchal structures that have governed the history of Man. As Adele Clarke rapturously suggests, new reproductive technologies "are transforming... conceptions of what it is to be human, male, female, reproductive, parent, child, fetus, family, race, and even population. That is, the 'new' reproductive technologies in their postmodern splendor are constitutive of what Paul Rabinow... termed the remaking of life itself."[51]

The millennial enthusiasm that marks many celebrations of the cyborg is tempered, in Haraway, by her refusal to ignore its genesis. Clynes and Kline, she notes, coined the term in order to imagine a man–machine hybrid who could survive the rigors of space travel and extraterrestrial environments (*Modest_Witness* 51–52), and she remains suspicious of a being situated at the heart of the military and scientific nexus of twentieth-century capitalism: "The main trouble with cyborgs, of course, is that they are the illegitimate offspring of militarism and patriarchal capitalism, not to mention state socialism. But illegitimate offspring are often exceedingly unfaithful to their origins" (*Simians* 151). As her last remark suggests, however, Haraway also possesses a hopefulness about the potential of the cyborg that allows her to look beyond the specific historical factors influencing its birth and imagine ways in which this figure, who, because it might help rewrite and reconfigure the politics of reproduction, possesses the power to "change what counts as women's experience in the late twentieth century" (*Simians* 149). Like Astell three centuries ago, Haraway looks for a way to seize the male pen, imagining the cyborg as precisely the figure who may allow a postmodern world to rewrite the history of masculine hegemony:

> Writing is pre-eminently the technology of cyborgs, etched surfaces of the late twentieth century. Cyborg politics is the struggle for language and the struggle against perfect communication, against the one code that translates all meaning perfectly, the central dogma of phallogocentrism. That is why cyborg politics insist on noise and advocate pollution, rejoicing in the illegitimate fusions of animal and machine. These are couplings which make Man and Woman so problematic, subverting the structure of desire, the force imagined to generate language and gender. (*Simians* 176)

If modern memory exhausts itself in the fictions of Borges and Kiš, where the search for totality, completeness, and perfection—for the library or reference work that contains "everything"—ends with the recognition that such dreams can only be nightmares, postmodern memory begins with the cyborg, whose frightening yet alluring vision of technological and biological "couplings" suggests a new way to conceive of memory, gender, language, and what it means to be human.

NOTES

INTRODUCTION: THE INVENTION OF MODERN MEMORY

1. Alkon, *Memory's Voice*, p. 255, note 1.
2. The decade beginning January 1, 1990, was declared "The Decade of the Brain" by the 101st Congress in House Joint Resolution 174, July 25, 1989, and confirmed in Presidential Proclamation 6158, signed July 17, 1990. The "Project on the Decade of the Brain," an interagency collaboration between The Library of Congress and National Institute of Mental Health, initiated a series of activities and publications designed to advance some of the goals set forth by congress and the president.
3. For a much more disapproving account of the recent academic interest in memory studies—what he calls "the memory industry"—see Klein, "On the Emergence of *Memory* in Historical Discourse," pp. 127–50. While admitting the importance of "trauma" to the new memory work, Klein thinks that the "rise of memory discourse" should more cynically be attributed to the identity politics of post-1960s America, a response to the challenges posed by poststructuralism, and the need for a therapeutic alternative to historical discourse. For an introduction to the large and growing literatures concerning first "recovered memory," and then memory and the Holocaust, see Loftus and Ketcham, ed., *The Myth of Repressed Memory*; Crews and His Critics, *The Memory Wars*; Pope and Brown, *Recovered Memories of Abuse*; Conway, ed., *False Memories and Recovered Memories*. Friedlander, *Memory, History and the Extermination of the Jews of Europe*; Young, *The Texture of Memory*; Roth, *The Ironist's Cage*; LaCapra, *History and Memory After Auschwitz*; Novick, *The Holocaust in American Life*. I will deal with the Holocaust more fully in the concluding chapter of this book.
4. For a consideration of the types of "histories" that might be written about memory, see Geary, *Phantoms of Remembrance*.
5. Horace, Ode 3.30, in *Horace: The Odes and Epodes*, p. 279.
6. Pope to Warburton, September 20, 1741, in *The Correspondence of Alexander Pope*, 4: 362. All quotations from the correspondence of Pope are from this edition.
7. For an introduction to the extensive and growing scholarship concerned with the construction of authorship during the Middle Ages, particularly in Chaucer and Langland, see Patterson, ed., *Literary Practice and Social Change in Britain*; Patterson, *Chaucer and the Subject of History*; Carlson, *English Humanist Books*; Lerer, *Chaucer and His Readers*; Carlson, "Chaucer, Humanism, and Printing," pp. 274–88; Justice, *Writing and Rebellion*; Justice and Kerby-Fulton, ed., *Written Work: Langland, Labor, and Authorship*; Krier, ed., *Refiguring Chaucer in the Renaissance*; Carlson, *Chaucer's Jobs*.

8. *The Countesse of Pembrokes Arcadia* appeared in 1590, four years after Sidney's death; *Astrophel and Stella* was first published in 1591, and the *Apologie for Poetrie* in 1595. For two slightly different accounts of Sidney's authorial example, see Wall, *The Imprint of Gender*, p. 13; and Blaine, "Milton and the Monument Topos," p. 223.

9. Newton, "Jonson and the (Re-)Invention of the Book," p. 34. In "Printing and 'The Multitudinous Presse': The Contentious Texts of Jonson's Masques," in *Ben Jonson's 1616 Folio*, pp. 168–91, Joseph Loewenstein argues that "the publication of the masques...was an important turning point in his [Jonson's] intellectual career—perhaps an important moment in the history of Western literary culture" (182).

10. Although the volume contains dedications to seven plays and the *Epigrammes*, the folio itself asks for and recognizes no single patron. For an important discussion of Jonson's 1616 *Workes*, see Murray, *Theatrical Legitimation*, pp. 64–93. For a sustained look at the volume from diverse perspectives by a number of critics, see *Ben Jonson's 1616 Folio*.

11. Jonson, *The New Inne*, in *The Complete Plays of Ben Jonson*, 4: 363–473.

12. Addison, "The Spectator No. 166," 2: 154. Anderson, *Imagined Communities*, calls the book "the first modern-style mass-produced industrial commodity...a distinct, self-contained object, exactly reproduced on a large scale" (38).

13. Grafton, in the "The Ways of Genius," 2: 38–40, even argues that the late seventeenth century marks the moment in modern science when "what matters is not simply arriving at the truth, but arriving there first. Modern scientists...establish their ownership of a fact or a principle only by publishing it before anyone else" (39). Grafton credits Robert Merton for this insight: "Priorities in Scientific Discovery," pp. 635–59. Eisenstein, *The Printing Press as an Agent of Change*, reiterates that in early-modern Europe "publication was indispensable for anyone seeking to make a scientific contribution" (694).

14. Jonson, "To the Memory of My Beloved," in *Ben Jonson*, pp. 453–55, lines 22–23; Greenblatt, *Will in the World*, p. 194.

15. Addison, "The Spectator No. 166," 2: 154.

16. Naudé, *Instructions Concerning Erecting of a Library*, p. 6.

17. The Court of Star Chamber was certainly not the only way in which the governments of James I and Charles I exercised control over the print trade. For a sophisticated account of the varied and complex mechanisms of censorship in the early seventeenth century, see Clegg, *Press Censorship in Jacobean England*. For a recent account of the relationship between print and politics in the mid-seventeenth century, see Peacey, *Politicians and Pamphleteers*.

18. The simple numbers from the first three years of Thomason's collection testify eloquently to the transformation in the political climate and publishing landscape. In 1640 Thomason purchased 22 items; in 1641 he purchased 721; in 1642, 2,133. These numbers, provided by MacLean in *Time's Witness*, p. 291, n. 66, include manuscripts as well as newspapers, and are therefore slightly higher than the numbers provided by Fortescue in his "Preface" to the two-volume *Catalogue of the Pamphlets, Books, Newspapers, and Manuscripts*.

19. Chartier, *The Order of Books*, pp. 70 and 88.

20. Sir Francis Bacon to Sir Thomas Bodley, 1605–1606, in *The Works of Francis Bacon*, 10: 253. It is worth noting that when Bacon published *The Advancement of Learning* in 1605 he included a similar passage, though without the doubts he expressed in his letter to Bodley: "libraries, which are as the shrines where all the relics of the ancient saints, full of true virtue, and without delusion or imposture, are preserved and reposed." In this "public" version, delusion and imposture characterize only the shrines of the ancient saints. See Bacon, *The Advancement of Learning and New Atlantis*, pp. 61–62.
21. For more on the growth and evolution of the Bodleian Library, and its importance in turn-of-the-century England, see chapter two.
22. Bacon, *The Advancement of Learning*, pp. 58–59.
23. Eisenstein, *The Printing Press as an Agent of Change*, and Foucault, "What Is an Author?" pp. 141–60. An introduction to criticism concerned with the genesis and evolution of the early modern author would include Helgerson, *Self-Crowned Laureates*; Woodmansee, "The Genius and the Copyright," pp. 425–48; Loewenstein, "The Script in the Marketplace," pp. 101–14, and "For a History of Literary Property," pp. 389–412; Rose, "The Author as Proprietor," pp. 51–85, and *Authors and Owners*; Saunders and Hunter, "Lessons from the 'Literatory,'" pp. 479–509; Woodmansee and Jaszi, ed., *The Construction of Authorship*; Pask, *The Emergence of the English Author*; Hammond, *Professional Imaginative Writing in England*.
24. In *The Boundaries of Fiction*, Zimmerman argues compellingly that "these novelists [do not] insist that their writings be taken *as* authentic histories. They appear rather to be demanding that the relationship of their fictions to history be considered seriously…The novel implies that it is a needed supplement to history" (1). This subject will be considered more fully in chapter four.
25. Ezell, *The Patriarch's Wife*; *Writing Women's Literary History*; *Social Authorship and the Advent of Print*. Summit, *Lost Property*. Wall, *The Imprint of Gender*; and *Staging Domesticity*. There is a large and growing literature on female authorship during the sixteenth through eighteenth centuries, as well as on the history of the reception of women authors from these centuries. Studies that I have found particularly helpful would include the following: Hobby, *Virtue of Necessity*; Krontiris, *Oppositional Voices*; Grundy and Wiseman, ed., *Women, Writing, History 1640–1740*; Gallagher, *Nobody's Story*; Greer, *Slip-Shod Sibyls*; Nicolay, *Gender Roles, Literary Authority, and Three American Woman Writers*; Traub, Kaplen, and Callaghan, ed., *Feminist Readings of Early Modern Culture*; Chedgzoy, Hansen, and Trill, ed., *Voicing Women*; Summers and Pebworth, ed., *Representing Women in Renaissance England*; McDowell, *The Women of Grub Street*; Todd, *The Critical Fortunes of Aphra Behn*; Burke, Donawerth, Dove, and Nelson, ed., *Women, Writing, and the Reproduction of Culture in Tudor and Stuart Britain*; Smith and Appelt, ed., *Write or Be Written*; McGrath, *Subjectivity and Women's Poetry*.
26. In "The Early Woman Writer and the Uses of Loss," the introduction to her book *Lost Property*, Jennifer Summit argues that in early modern England, "while the printing press brings men's works to public attention, it denies the same service to women, consigning them instead to the textual obscurity and fragility of the manuscript" (2). But she goes on to insist that

> the universal "oblivion" of women writers needs to be understood not as an accurate description of women writers' "loss" from literary history but as an active construction of it, which obscures the specific historical

processes through which women's writing was culturally defined, circulated, and assigned value, by turning women writers themselves into history's shadowy ghosts…it is my argument that producing the woman
writer as "lost" from literary history was part of the process of conceiving
what literary history was in a fundamental way. (5)
I will argue, in a similar fashion, that portraying women as cultural memory's
marginalized "other" was a fundamental part of the process of constructing
modern memory.

27. Wall, *The Imprint of Gender*, p. 12.
28. Fentress and Wickham, *Social Memory*, pp. 8 and 106.
29. Dolan, "Ashes and 'the Archive,'" p. 397.
30. Cressy, "National Memory in Early Modern England," pp. 61–62. Cressy
    describes some of the parameters of this national memory in *Bonfires and
    Bells*. He argues that the seventeenth-century English calendar "was based
    on, and gave expression to, a mythic and patriotic sense of national identity"
    (xi). For a sustained examination of the processes that governed England's
    growth into a "modern" nation, see Helgerson, *Forms of Nationhood*. His
    book studies the way in which that nation formed itself through the conflict
    between "royal prerogative, subjects' rights, and the cultural system" (2).
31. Kroll, *The Material Word*, p. 34.
32. Dryden, "To My Honored Friend, Dr. Charleton," in *The Works of John Dryden*,
    1: 43–44. All quotations from the poetry of Dryden are from this edition.
33. Rose, *The Making of Memory*, p. 326.
34. Charleton, one of the earliest fellows admitted to the Royal Society, on
    May 15, 1661, was not an inconsiderable figure, but his theories concerning
    Stonehenge were mired in controversy and supported almost entirely by spec-
    ulation. He designed his book proposing the Danish origins of the antiquity
    to counter *The Most Notable Antiquity of Great Britain*. This book, begun
    by Inigo Jones and completed by his assistant John Webb, argued that the
    ruin represented a Roman temple built to the god Coelus. After the publica-
    tion of Charleton's book, Webb replied with *A Vindication of Stone-Heng
    Restored*. Neither man, however, based their theories on careful fieldwork
    or new observations, an oversight not repeated by John Aubrey, who linked
    Stonehenge to the great earthworks and stone circle at Avebury in Wiltshire,
    prepared surveys of both sites, the former in 1666, the later in 1663, and took
    issue with both Charleton and Webb: "There have been several Books writt by
    learned men concerning Stoneheng, much differing from one another, some
    affirming one thing, some another. Now I come in the Rear of all by com-
    parative Arguments to give clear evidence that these monuments were Pagan
    Temples; which was not made out before" (quoted in Powell, *John Aubrey
    and His Friends*, p. 108). The history of attempts to identify Stonehenge
    can be surveyed in the following: Tylden-Wright, *John Aubrey*; Chippindale,
    Stonehenge Complete; and Burl and Mortimer, ed. *Stukeley's 'Stonehenge': An
    Unpublished Manuscript 1721–1724.*
35. Kroll, *The Material Word*, p. 86.
36. Popular Memory Group, "Popular Memory: Theory, Politics, Method,"
    p. 207.
37. Summit, *Lost Property*, pp. 144–46.
38. Weever, *Ancient Funerall Monuments within the Vnited Monarchie of Great
    Britaine*; "The Avthor to the Reader." All quotations are from this edition.

See Terry, *Poetry and the Making of the English Literary Past*, for a discussion of Weever, and a sense of the way in which "he was racing against time as the stones and inscriptions crumbled around him" (89).

39. Coiro, "Milton and Class Identity: The Publication of *Areopagitica* and the 1645 *Poems*," p. 266.

40. Evelyn, letter to Pepys, August 26, 1689, in *Particular Friends*, p. 191.

41. Kroll, *The Material Word*, p. 299. Kroll thinks of books, coins, and medals as "the inscribed, exemplary tokens for a new cultural economy" (183).

42. Bacon, *The Advancement of Learning*, p. 58.

43. Assmann, "Texts, Traces, Trash," p. 127. For an important consideration of fashion and the literary marketplace in eighteenth-century England, see Mackie, *Market a la Mode*.

44. Pope, "Preface" to the 1717 *Works*, , in *The Poems of Alexander Pope*, 1: 7 and 9.

45. Connell, "Death and the Author," pp. 557–85. Connell links the "commercialization of the book" to the "commodification of the literary monument" (560). For the history and significance of Westminster Abbey as a literary monument, see also Terry, *Poetry and the Making of the English Literary Past*, pp. 37–39.

46. Braudy, *The Frenzy of Renown*, pp. 236, 294, and 308–09. For a more specialized study, which focuses on how a medieval tradition took shape from Christian attempts to employ a classical vocabulary of fame, see Koonce, *Chaucer and the Tradition of Fame*.

47. Bacon, "Of Praise," in *The Essayes, or Counsels, Civill and Morall*, p. 159.

48. Terry, *Poetry and the Making of the English Literary Past*, pp. 91–92; and Sabl, "Noble Infirmity: Love of Fame in Hume," pp. 542–68. Sabl argues that "Hume's inability to reach a final position on fame...illuminates the larger tragedy, or irony, of a thinker poised between different traditions of fame" (543).

49. Donne to Sir Henry Goodyer, September 1608, in *John Donne: Selected Letters*, pp. 35–36.

50. Guibbory, *The Map of Time*, p. 90.

51. Donne, "Goodfriday, 1630. Riding Westward," in *John Donne: The Divine Poems*, pp. 30–31, lines 21, 23–24, and 33–36.

52. Pocock, in *Virtue, Commerce, and History* notes that "as English political and historical thought...passes from the seventeenth into the eighteenth century...We seem—though it is possible to overstate this point—to be passing out of a period in which it was generally supposed that contingent time and its events were the creation of God" (93). For my description of early-modern historiography I have relied on Pocock, as well as on Walsh, *An Introduction to the Philosophy of History*; Levy, *Tudor Historical Thought*; Guibbory, *The Map of Time*; Ferguson, *Clio Unbound*; Loewenstein, *Milton and the Drama of History*; Ankersmit and Kellner, ed., *A New Philosophy of History*. A collection of essays particularly attentive to the early-modern relationship between history and literature is Kelley and Sacks, ed., *The Historical Imagination in Early Modern Britain*.

53. For the importance of the concept of anachronism see particularly Levy, *Tudor Historical Thought*.

54. Bacon, *New Organon*, p. 70. J.G.A. Pocock levels similar although more fully developed and articulated charges against classical historiography in *The*

Ancient Constitution and the Feudal Law: "they [the Greeks and Romans] did not quite reach the point of postulating that there existed, in the past of their own civilization, tracts of time in which the thoughts and actions of men had been so remote in character from those of the present as to be intelligible only if the entire world in which they had occurred were resurrected, described in detail and used to interpret them" (1).

55. Jonson, "The Mind of the Frontispiece to a Book," in *Ben Jonson*, p. 346. The frontispiece that shaped Jonson's reflections on history was designed by Sir Walter Ralegh for his *History of the World*. Published in 1614, Ralegh's historiography reflects an awkward and uneasy balance between the providential and the secular. Eloquent on the way in which history "hath triumphed ouer time...hath made vs acquainted with our dead Ancestors; and, out of the depth and darkenesse of the earth, deliuered vs their memory and fame," Ralegh nonetheless insisted that history was ultimately defined by the First Cause: "God, who is the Author of all our tragedies, hath written out for vs, and appointed vs all the parts we are to play." See Patrides, ed., *The History of the World*, pp. 48 and 70.

56. Hamilton, Harris, and Reid, "Introduction," in *Refiguring the Archive*, p. 15.

57. Blouin, Jr., "History and Memory: The Problem of the Archive," p. 296.

58. Derrida, *Archive Fever*, p. 4. The arguments of Blouin and Derrida suggest why Raphael Samuel is correct to argue in *Theatres of Memory* that history as an academic discipline "fetishizes archive-based research" (3).

59. Samuel, in *Theatres of Memory*, argues that much of contemporary ethnography is based on the assumption that memory "is dialectically related to historical thought, rather than being some kind of negative other to it" (x), and a number of the scholars I have consulted certainly agree with this general formulation. Carolyn Steedman, for instance, in *Dust*, suggests that contemporary scholars need to "begin to disinter the ways in which, over the last 300 years or so, History has shaped Memory" (67), while Paul Ricoeur, in *Memory, History, Forgetting*, insists on the necessity for an "open dialectic" that avoids "history's claim to reduce memory to the level of one of its objects, and on the other hand, the claim of collective memory to subjugate history" (392–93). But Dominick LaCapra, in *History and Memory After Auschwitz*, claims that "the binary opposition between memory and history is very prevalent in recent thought" (17), a position with which Kerwin Lee Klein ("On the Emergence of *Memory*") agrees: "the declaration that history and memory are not really opposites has become one of the clichés of our new memory discourse. In preface after preface, an author declares that it would be simplistic to imagine memory and history as antitheses and then proceeds to use the words in antithetical ways in the body of the monograph" (128). My triangulation of fame, memory, and history, based on a specifically early-modern literary paradigm, certainly favors dialectic rather than opposition.

60. Halbwachs, *The Social Frameworks of Memory*, pp. 43 and 38.

61. Halbwachs, *The Collective Memory*, pp. 50–51.

62. Samuel, *Theatres of Memory*, pp. ix–x.

63. Fentress and Wickham, *Social Memory*, pp. ix–x.

64. Misztal, *Theories of Social Remembering*, pp. 50–74.

65. Assmann, "Collective Memory and Cultural Identity," pp. 129 and 131.

66. For the canon's assumption of its definitive, modern shape, and the concomitant "invention" of English literary history, see Kramnick, *Making the English Canon* and Terry, *Poetry and the Making of the English Literary Past*.

67. Assmann, "Collective Memory and Cultural Identity," p. 132. For a historian's articulation of how cultural formation occurs see Pocock, *Politics, Language and Time*: "But the variety of the ways in which societies have conceived the transmission of their traditions is very great indeed...Social activities and structures vary widely, and it cannot be predicted with certainty what elements of them will become institutionalised to the point of having stable and continuous images" (234).
68. Ray, "Forward" to Misztal's *Theories of Social Remembering*, p. x.
69. Marvell, *The Rehearsal Transpos'd*, pp. 4–5.
70. Rose, *The Making of Memory*, p. 60.
71. Backscheider, *Spectacular Politics*. For an historical supplement to Backscheider's primarily literary account, see Harris, *London Crowds in the Reign of Charles II*.
72. For two examinations of the evolution of memory theory during the seventeenth and eighteenth centuries, see Sutton, *Philosophy and Memory Traces*, and Wolff, "When I Imagine a Child," pp. 377–401.
73. Hobbes, "The Answer of Mr Hobbes to Sr Will. Davenant's Preface Before Gondibert," p. 78.
74. Locke, *An Essay Concerning Human Understanding*, pp. 151–52.
75. Misztal, in *Theories of Social Remembering*, speaks for many researchers in other disciplines when she declares that "artists, who have always been fascinated by memory, seem to be better equipped not only to grasp the depth of memory but also to popularize their penetrating insights into its workings. We owe a deeper and more insightful understanding of the workings of memory to creative writing" (3).
76. Cavendish, *CCXI Sociable Letters*, p. 178. All quotations from this text are from this edition.
77. Ricoeur, *Memory, History, Forgetting*, p. 21.

1 "Building Castles in the Air": Margaret Cavendish and the Anxieties of Monumentality

1. Cavendish, *Poems, and Fancies*, p. A7v. All quotations are from this edition. The pagination of *Poems, and Fancies* goes seriously awry after page 160, when poem titles rather than pages will have to suffice as references. When referring to material that appears after page 160 I'll attempt to locate quotations by describing their position in the volume.
2. Milton, *Areopagitica*, in the Yale edition of *The Complete Prose Works of John Milton*, 2: 558. All quotations from Milton's prose are from this edition. All quotations from Milton's poetry are from *John Milton: Complete Poems and Major Prose*.
3. Shapin, *A Social History of Truth*, p. 369.
4. Astell, *Reflections upon Marriage*, p. 115.
5. Behn, "Preface" to *The Luckey Chance*, in *The Works of Aphra Behn*, 7: 217.
6. Whitaker, *Mad Madge*, p. 1; Hobby, *Virtue of Necessity*, p. 6. More generous figures are provided by Crawford, "Women's Published Writings, 1660–1700," pp. 211–82. Stevenson, *Milton to Pope*, reminds us that, given the importance of manuscript circulation during this period, "publication and literary productivity, even literary recognition, are not to be equated" (30).

7. Ferguson, "Renaissance Conceptions of the 'Woman Writer,'" in *Wilcox, Women and Literature in Britain, 1500-1700*, p. 145; Lamb, *Gender and Authorship in the Sidney Circle*, p. 4.
8. McGrath, *Subjectivity and Women's Poetry in Early Modern England*, p. 2.
9. McDowell, *The Women of Grub Street*, pp. 30 and 125. McDowell ironizes the phrase "peripheral book trade activity," which she quotes from Harris, "Periodicals and the Book Trade," p. 89.
10. Scholars specializing in Cavendish have tried to qualify their excitement with various caveats, but nonetheless the following claims for the originary status of *Poems, and Fancies* cannot stand: "In 1653 the *Poems, and Fancies* was the first book of English poetry to be deliberately published by a woman under her own name" (Whitaker, *Mad Madge*, p. 1); "This volume…was also a new departure in being, and consciously being, very nearly the first collection of poems in English by a woman ever to be published" (Sokol, "Margaret Cavendish's *Poems and Fancies* and Thomas Harriot's Treatise on Infinity," p. 156). These claims would seem to be contradicted by both the 1611 publication of Lanyer's *Salve Deus Rex Iudaeorum* and the following two publications of Whitney: *The Copy of a letter* and *A Sweet nosgay*.

    Given her extensive list of publications, the case for Cavendish as the first "professional" woman writer in England is perhaps stronger: "Cavendish was arguably the first Englishwoman to fashion herself as an author" (Clucas, "Introduction," in *A Princely Brave Woman*, p. 1); "She was the first woman in England to write specifically for publication, and certainly the first to consider herself primarily as a writer" (Jones, *A Glorious Fame*, p. 1). But Renaissance scholars have made strong cases for their own favorites. Lynette McGrath, in *Subjectivity and Women's Poetry*, flatly states that "Pending further scholarly discoveries, Isabella Whitney's remains the first woman's name we are able to attach to a substantial body of published poetry in England. For her contemporary readers, as well as for subsequent aspirants to poetry, she therefore publicly modeled the newly viable possibility of woman's poetic subjectivity" (123). Susanne Woods, however, in *Lanyer: A Renaissance Woman Poet*, mentions Whitney only once and dismisses her as someone who "published secular poems filled with moral precepts and admonitions for minor gentry who find themselves in service" (vii). She insists that "Aemilia Lanyer was the first woman writing in England who clearly sought professional standing as a poet" (vii).

    I am not inclined to join such debates because I agree with Goldberg, in *Desiring Women Writing*, who implies that the desire to determine a series of feminist "firsts"—the "first" female writer to publish a romance, the first female writer to publish an original drama—is politically conservative and intellectually misleading. Ezell, in *Writing Women's Literary History*, even argues that "this adherence to a linear narrative of women's literary history has directed the type of questions we ask about early women writers" (22).
11. Wendy Wall argues that the necessity to imagine how women writers might disrupt this male literary succession does not stem from "a hazy psychological concern over [women's] exclusion from literary history, but an awareness that their task transgressed both gender boundaries and the decorum of literary presentation. If women were tropes necessary to the process of writing, with what authority could a woman publish?" See "Our Bodies/Our Texts?: Renaissance Women and the Trials of Authorship," in Singley and Sweeney, ed., *Anxious Power*, p. 52.

12. Levinson, *Written in Stone*, p. 7.

13. Bradstreet, *The Tenth Muse Lately sprung up in America*. All quotations are from this edition. For information about the printing of the volume and speculation about the extent of Bradstreet's knowledge of the project, see Hensley's "Anne Bradstreet's Wreath of Thyme," the introduction to Hensley, ed., *The Works of Anne Bradstreet.*

14. Ward, *The Simple Cobler of Aggawam in America*. The long descriptive title of this work (see the bibliography) provides at least a taste of the book's home-spun charm. For details about Bowtell's career, see Plomer, et al., *Dictionaries of the Printers and Booksellers*. For details about Ward's career, see Zell's edition of *The Simple Cobler of Aggawam in America*.

15. Cowell, "The Early Distribution of Anne Bradstreet's Poem," p. 271.

16. Griffin, "Introduction," in *The Faces of Anonymity*, p. 10.

17. Goldberg, *Writing Matter*, pp. 49–50.

18. Behn, *Oroonoko: Or, The Royal Slave. A True History*, p. 36.

19. Eberwein, " 'No Rhet'ric We Expect,' " pp. 218–25, discusses the complexities of reading tone and irony in "The Prologue." While she recognizes that structurally the poem seems to divide at stanza five, she insists that the poem is ironic about gender issues throughout.

20. For an exciting consideration of Bradstreet's lines about "A Poets Pen" in relationship to Cavendish, see Sherman, "Trembling Texts," pp. 192–93.

21. For a discussion of printing practices in the colonies, see Nicolay, *Gender Roles*, pp. 11–12.

22. Jones, *The Currency of Eros*, p. 29.

23. Collins, *Divine Songs and Meditacions*, pp. 1–2. All quotations are from this edition.

24. Gottlieb, "An Collins and the Experience of Defeat," pp. 121–35.

25. Cavendish, *CCXI Sociable Letters*, pp. 225–26.

26. "To the most Excellently accomplish'd, Mrs. *K. Philips*" was published in Vaughan's *Olor Iscanus*. Patrick Thomas designates this as the poem that "first drew public attention to [Philips's] poetry." See Thomas, ed., *The Collected Works of Katherine Philips*, p. 7. All quotations from the poetry of Philips are from this edition.

27. Ezell, " 'By a Lady,' " in *The Faces of Anonymity*, p. 66.

28. Plomer, *Dictionaries of the Printers and Booksellers*, pp. 2–3.

29. For an excellent account of women in the print trade, and particularly the relationship of wives and widows to their husbands' businesses, see McDowell, *The Women of Grub Street.*

30. Whitaker, *Mad Madge*, p. 251.

31. For discussions of the history and iconography of these portraits, see Whitaker, *Mad Madge*, pp. 178–80, and Fitzmaurice, "Front Matter and the Physical Make-Up of *Natures Pictures*," p. 354.

32. Walter Charleton, letter dated May 7, 1667, in *Letters and Poems in Honour of the Incomparable Princess, Margare*, p. 108.

33. Ibid., letter dated December 16, 1667, from "The Vicechancellor and the whole Senate of the University of Cambridge," p. 24; Thomas Tully, letter dated June 30, 1663, p. 95.

34. Huyssen, *Twilight Memories*, p. 13.

35. See Whitaker, *Mad Madge*, pp. 172–73 and 243–44, for a discussion of how Cavendish learned to supervise the printing of her books.

36. Cavendish, *The Philosophical and Physical Opinions*, p. A4. All quotations are from this edition.

37. Fulton, *Feeling as a Foreign Language*, p. 123.

38. Price, "Feminine Modes of Knowing and Scientific Enquiry," p. 133. For discussions of paratext, see Tribble, *Margins and Marginality*; Genette, *Paratexts*; and Voss, "Books for Sale," pp. 733–756. Summit, in *Lost Property*, argues that "paratextual signals about the woman writer take their place among the other markers of literary meaning…Such moments are crucial to the understanding of how the figure of the woman writer signifies to a larger literary culture" (20).

39. For details about Cavendish's life in London during the years 1651–1653 see Whitaker, *Mad Madge*, pp. 133–59. For a discussion of the collaborative processes that were a normal and integral part of the seventeenth-century book trade, see Dobranski, *Milton, Authorship, and the Book Trade*. Cavendish, I am arguing, decisively rejected what Wendy Wall, in *The Imprint of Gender*, has characterized as a Tudor and early-Stuart understanding that "writing was not an individual activity…texts were seen as porous and variable scripts for performance" (31).

40. For a discussion of "the Newcastle circle" in Paris during the 1640s and 1650s, see Kroll, *The Material Word*, pp. 156–65; and Whitaker, *Mad Madge*, pp. 89–97.

41. For two studies on the subject of early modern needlework, see Parker, *The Subversive Stitch*; and Jones and Stallybrass, *Renaissance Clothing and the Materials of Memory*. Both books convincingly argue, in the words of Parker, that while embroidery may have fashioned women, "it also enabled them to negotiate the constraints of femininity" (11). Catty, *Writing Rape*, touches on the way in which classical mythology portrayed weaving as a type of female utterance "explicitly associated with resistance" (123).

42. For Denny's letter of February 26, 1621/22 to Wroth, from which I quote, the complete text of Denny's poem, and the history of his quarrel with Wroth, see Roberts, ed., *The Poems of Lady Mary Wroth*, pp. 31–35 and 238–39. This incident is also discussed by Lamb, *Gender and Authorship in the Sidney Circle*, pp. 30 and 152–54.

43. Cavendish, *Natures Pictures Drawn by Fancies Pencil to the Life*, p. 385.

44. Cavendish, *The Life of William Cavendish Duke of Newcastle*, p. 175. All quotation from *A True Relation* are from this edition.

45. Osborne, letter of April 14, 1653, in *Letters to Sir William Temple*, p. 75.

46. Evelyn, kalendarium entries for April 18 and 27, in *The Diary of John Evelyn*, 3: 478 and 481.

47. Cavendish, *CCXI Sociable Letters*, p. b.

48. Jones and Stallybrass, *Renaissance Clothing*, pp. 5 and 277.

49. Hobby, in *Virtue of Necessity*, notes that "the most ubiquitous concern of Cavendish's writings is her attempts to ensure her acceptance and fame as an author" (195).

50. Lilley, "True State Within," p. 73.

51. Popular Memory Group, "Popular Memory: Theory, Politics, Method," p. 210.

52. Sherman, "Trembling Texts," p. 188.

53. Cavendish, *Observations upon Experimental Philosophy*, p. 121. All quotations are from this edition.

54. Cavendish, *Playes*, p. A8. All quotations are from this edition. See Summit, *Lost Property*, pp. 205–09, for an insightful exploration of the way in which Cavendish "made uniqueness into an authorial stance" (206).
55. Cavendish, *Plays, Never before Printed*, "To the Readers."
56. Donoghue, *The Fame Machine*.
57. Jonson, "Epigram to My Bookseller," in *Ben Jonson*, p. 386, lines 7–8.
58. Cavendish, *The Worlds Olio*, (1655), p. 3.
59. Pepys, *The Diary of Samuel Pepys*, entries for 11 April, 1 May, 26 April, 8: 163, 186–87, 196. All quotations from *The Diary* are from this edition.
60. See Whitaker, *Mad Madge*, who talks at length about Cavendish's sense of dress and fashion, and first drew my attention to her "hybrid male-female outfit[s]" 297.
61. Pepys, *The Diary*, entry for May 30, 1667, 8: p. 243.
62. Cavendish, *Plays, Never before Printed*, "To the Readers."
63. Cavendish, *The Philosophical and Physical Opinions*, p. 53.
64. Rose, *The Making of Memory*, p. 326.
65. Fulton, in *Feeling as a Foreign Language*, writes that Cavendish's "deepest subject is not man's relation to God, but man's relation to the natural world" (89).
66. Edelman, *Bright Air, Brilliant Fire*, pp. 204 and 207.
67. Cavendish was not alone in speculating about the immortality of memory. The Cambridge Platonist Henry More, in *A Platonick Song of the Soul*, specifies that "memorie [is] the very bond of life":

    > But if dispersed lifes collection,
    > Which is our memory, safely survive
    > (Which well it may, sith it depends not on
    > The *Mundane* spirit)...

    See *A Platonick Song of the Soul*, p. 537. For a discussion of More's complex understanding of memory, see Sutton, *Philosophy and Memory Traces*, pp. 144–48.
68. McDowell, *The Women of Grub Street*, pp. 122–23.
69. Woolf, *The Common Reader*, p. 101.
70. The most complete examination of the figure of Penelope in Cavendish's work is provided by Rees, "A Well-Spun Yarn," pp. 171–82.
71. Cavendish, *The Worlds Olio (1655)*, pp. A2–A2v. Chalmers, "Dismantling the Myth of 'Mad Madge,' " pp. 323–39, suggests the complexity of Cavendish's relationship to her husband: "Cavendish's emphasis on the centrality of the role played by her husband in the authorial process may be seen as a gesture of self-effacement akin to that frequently discernible in the writings of her female predecessors and contemporaries. However, in her case, it plays a key role in enabling the outspoken rhetoric of authorship in which she frankly and repeatedly states her ambition to win public acclaim through printing her works" (325).
72. Pepys, *The Diary*, entry for March 18, 1668, 9: p. 123.
73. Lord, ed., A Session of the Poets," in *Poems on Affairs of State*, ed. Lord, 1: 327–37, lines 85–92.
74. Pepys, *The Diary*, entries for April 11, 1667, and March 30, 1667, 8: pp. 137 and 163–64.
75. Behn, "A Pindaric Poem to the Reverend Doctor Burnet," in *The Works of Aphra Behn*, 1: 307–10, lines 98–103.
76. McDowell, *The Women of Grub Street*, p. 293.

77. "To her Excellency the Lady Marchioness of Newcastle, on her Incomparable Works," in *Letters and Poems*, p. 157.
78. Beal, *In Praise of Scribes*, pp. 165–67.
79. Fulton, *Feeling as a Foreign Language*, pp. 106 and 120.
80. Popular Memory Group, "Popular Memory: Theory, Politics, Method," pp. 207 and 211.
81. Summit, *Lost Property*, p. 5.

2   "A SPACE FOR NARRATION": MILTON AND THE POLITICS OF COLLECTIVE MEMORY

1. Lewalski, *The Life of John Milton*, provides a full discussion of the date of the volume's publication. According to Lewalski it was licensed for publication on July 2, 1670, and advertised in the *Term Catalogues* of November 22, 1670, although "the title pages of all copies are dated for the new year, as often happens with late-year publications" (p. 692, n.21). My emphasis here on the end of Milton's career suggests my position on the vexed question of the date of *Samson Agonistes'* composition. I agree with Michael Lieb's conclusion, in *Milton and the Culture of Violence*, that "despite all the debate concerning such matters, I still do not think it possible to know conclusively either when the work was written or what the immediate occasion of its composition was" (227). Unless new evidence comes to light, a definitive answer to these questions seems unlikely. Nonetheless, I find most compelling the arguments that place *Samson Agonistes* late in Milton's career, composed after *Paradise Lost*. Radzinowicz, *Towards Samson Agonistes*, and Coiro, "Fable and Old Song," pp. 123–52, are most persuasive here, particularly the latter's argument that the poem's "evocative recall" of Milton's earlier works represents a deliberate parody on his part, rather than evidence for an early date of composition (124). As this chapter will make clear, I believe that the political and cultural tensions of the poem place it near the end of Milton's career.
2. Fish, *How Milton Works*, p. 238.
3. For the challenges presented to memory by the rapid social changes wrought by modernity, see Terdiman, *Present Past*. Terdiman writes specifically about the years of revolution in Europe from 1789 to 1815, but his book can apply as well to England during the period from 1642 to 1660.
4. Marvell, "An Horatian Ode Upon Cromwel's Return from Ireland," in *The Poems and Letters of Andrew Marvell*, 1: 87–90, lines 1–6.
5. Sidney, *An Apologie for Poetrie*, sig Br-v. A less ironic demonstration of the privileging of military virtue can be seen in Samson Lennard's translation of Peter Charron's *Of Wisdome*: "For to some and the greater part this qualitie [nobilitie] is militarie, to others it is politike, literarie of those that are wise,…But the militarie hath the aduantage aboue the rest: for besides the seruice which it yeeldeth to the weale-publike as the rest do, it is painfull, laborious, dangerous; whereby it is accounted more worthy and commendable" (210).
6. According to Stevenson, *Milton to Pope*, Milton's *Paradise Lost* emphatically asserts the irrelevance of warfare to true heroism: "Explicitly at the beginning of Book IX, and implicitly in Books VI-VII, the narrator dismisses war as central to heroism" (37).
7. Radzinowicz, *Toward Samson Agonistes*, discusses the importance of "the individual act of bearing witness" (164) in Milton's prose; see particularly

pp. 145–66. Fish, in *How Milton Works*, emphasizes that in Milton "success is measured not by the battles you won or the poems you have written, but by the witness you give to what you believe" (569).

8. Schudson, "Dynamics of Distortion in Collective Memory," p. 352; Fentress and Wickham, *Social Memory*, p. 127.
9. Le Goff, *History and Memory*, p. 54.
10. Griffin, "Introduction," in *The Faces of Anonymity*, p. 2.
11. Fish, *How Milton Works*, p. 7.
12. Leonard, "'Trembling ears,'" p. 73.
13. Fish, *How Milton Works*, p. 270.
14. Hanson, "To Smite Once and Yet Once More," p. 75.
15. Fish, *How Milton Works*, pp. 256–80; Evans, *The Miltonic Moment*, p. 112.
16. Dietz, "'Thus sang the uncouth Swain,'" p. 43.
17. Weber, *Paper Bullets*, pp. 143–47. *Areopagitica*'s complex ambivalences toward censorship and the print trade have interested scholars for over two decades. For a select history of this conversation see Barker, *The Tremulous Private Body*; Blum, "The Author's Authority," pp. 74–96; Wilding, "Milton's *Areopagitica*," pp. 7–38; Mendle, "De Facto Freedom, De Facto Authority," pp. 307–332; Dobranski, *Milton, Authorship, and the Book Trade*, pp. 104–24; Fish, *How Milton Works*, pp. 187–214; Egan, "*Areopagitica* and the Tolerationist Rhetorics of the 1640s," pp. 165–90.
18. Klinge, "The Grotesque in *Areopagitica*," p. 118.
19. Proclamation No. 272, "Prohibiting Heretical Books; Requiring Printer to Identify Himself, Author of Book, and Date of Publication," in *Tudor Royal Proclamations*, 1: 374.
20. Proclamation No. 129, "Prohibiting Erroneous Books and Bible Translations," in *Tudor Royal Proclamations*, 1:, 194.
21. For an important discussion of the movement enacted in *Areopagitica* from the "overt violence of the older settlement to a more indirectly ideological control implanted in the new subjectivity," see Barker, *The Tremulous Private Body*, pp. 46–47.
22. Klinge, "The Grotesque in *Areopagitica*," p. 113.
23. Translations from the ode are those of Hughes, ed. *John Milton*, pp. 146–49, lines 24, 29–30, 34–37.
24. For a brief history of the ode—which was published only in the 1673 second edition of *Poems of Mr. John Milton*—see Bush, Shaw, and Giamatti, ed., *A Variorum Commentary on the Poems of John Milton*, pp. 324–31. For an extended critical account of the poem, see Revard, *Milton and the Tangles of Neaera's Hair*, chapter 8.
25. On the use of Latin as a "truth-language," see Anderson, *Imagined Communities*. He emphasizes the way in which Latin functioned as "the media through which the great global communities of the past were imagined" (21). Further, he insists that its use contained "an impulse largely foreign to nationalism" (22). One of the most important of those communities for Milton was that of book professionals, and in *Milton, Authorship, and the Book Trade*, Dobranski argues that in spite of a poetic self-fashioning that often juxtaposed Milton to a despicable world of commerce, that group of professional publishers, editors, booksellers, and printers "cooperates to create the individual, who exists not by separating himself from a community, but by participating in it" (101).
26. For the history of the library at Oxford I have depended on Philip, *The Bodleian Library in the Seventeenth and Eighteenth Centuries*, and Fletcher,

The Intellectual Development of John Milton. For a history of the library in England, see Stewart and Sullivan, Jr., " 'Worme-eaten, and full of canker holes,' " pp. 215–38; and Summit, "Monuments and Ruins," pp. 1–34. The latter in particular calls our attention to the reinvention of the library by Protestant reformers:

> With the Dissolution of the Monasteries came the dispersal and widescale destruction of the monastic libraries, which had housed the bulk of England's textual heritage. When, in the Reformation's wake, Protestant collectors sought to recover the books formerly owned by the monastic libraries, they did so in an effort to preserve the nation's past. In the process they reinvented the library itself from an ecclesiastical receptacle of written tradition to a state-sponsored center of national history" (2).

27. Coiro, "Milton and Class Identity," pp. 288–89.
28. Burke, "History as Social Memory," p. 97.
29. Hobsbawm, "Introduction: Inventing Tradition," in *The Invention of Tradition*, p. 14; Dolan, "Ashes and 'the Archive,' " p. 381.
30. Teski, "The Remembering Consciousness of a Polish Exile Government," p. 50.
31. Schudson, "Dynamics of Distortion in Collective Memory," p. 355.
32. Lieb, *Milton and the Culture of Violence*, p. 16. Fish, in *How Milton Works*, recognizes that when Milton raises the question of what he is "doing when he puts pen to paper"—a question he poses and considers "endlessly in his prose and poetry"—he inevitably links writing and warfare: "That activity is inscribing, the making of marks, the institution of divisions and distinctions. The instrument is not the pen, but the sword" (496). In light of both Lieb and Fish, we might consider the relevance to Milton of Paul Ricoeur's insistence in *Memory, History, Forgetting* that "there is no historical community that has not arisen out of what can be termed an original relation to war. What we celebrate under the heading of founding events are, essentially, violent acts legitimated after the fact by a precarious state of right" (82). This speaks to both Milton's reasons for writing *A Second Defence*, and the violent acts, including his self-destruction, that define Samson's heroic career in *Samson Agonistes*.
33. A number of the essays in *Milton Studies* 42 (2002)—dedicated to "*Paradise Regained* in Context: Genre, Politics, Religion"—provide intriguing readings of the two poems. Corns, " 'With Unaltered Brow,' " pp. 106–21, surveys the critical history of the "range of political interpretation" raised by the two poems. In "Republican Occasions in *Paradise Regained*," pp. 122–48, David Norbrook emphasizes that while the "diptychlike character of the 1671 volume" has led some to see the two poems "as offering opposed models of behavior" (122), a renewed attention to "Restoration oppositional discourse" suggests that "there was no clear-cut opposition between the pacific Son and the riddling, violent Samson" (132). And Coffey, "Pacifist, Quietist, or Patient Militant," pp. 149–74, insists that "Milton is not, I think, presenting his readers with an either/or proposition; the poems do not offer alternative routes to liberation. Instead, there is a striking consistency between the two poems" (169).
34. Parker, *Milton: A Biography*, suggests that during Milton's final years "half a dozen London booksellers were making the discovery that writings by John Milton had commercial value" (1: 606). *Paradise Lost* had sold between thirteen hundred and fifteen hundred copies by April 1669, and during the final

six years of his life Milton published one or more books every year (1: 603–07). See Dobranski, *Milton, Authorship, and the Book Trade*, pp. 41–61, for an extended discussion of the printing of this volume. Dobranski focuses particularly on what the "Omissa" tells us about its printing.

35. Radzinowicz's *Toward Samson Agonistes* probably represents the high-water mark of interpretations of the poem that stress the progressive growth of Samson and unequivocal celebration of his triumph. While many contemporary critics would take issue with the radical indeterminacy that Stanley Fish attributes to the poem in "Spectacle and Evidence in *Samson Agonistes*," pp. 556–86, the last two decades have nonetheless seen a powerful shift to interpretations that emphasize uncertainty, doubt, and ambiguity in the poem's resolution. *Milton Studies* 33 (1996), a special issue devoted to "The Miltonic Samson," contains a number of essays that question the extent of Samson's triumph. Rose, " 'Vigorous Most / When Most Unactive Deem'd,' " pp. 83–109, argues that in the poem "heroism is presented at best as ambivalent and compromised, at worst as bitter and scathing" (105). Michael Lieb, in " 'Our Living Dread,' " pp. 3–25, assumes an even more extreme stance when he calls the poem "a work of harsh and uncompromising violence, indeed, a work that exults in violence, while it gives expression to profound and deeply disturbing elements of vehemence and rage" (4).

36. Rumrich, "Milton's *Theanthropos*," pp. 50–67.

37. Corns, " 'With Unaltered Brow,' " discusses how "the Son recontextualizes earthly fame in a larger perspective, attributing its acquisition, for the most part, to the judgment of a degenerate multitude, and contrasting it with the achievements of those who retain a pious uprightness" (117).

38. Donne, "A Lent-Sermon Preached before the King, at White-Hall, February 16, 1620 [1620/1621]," in *The Sermons of John Donne*, 3: 218.

39. Keeble, "Wilderness Exercises," p. 97; Knoppers, "Satan and the Papacy in *Paradise Regained*," p. 69, and *Historicizing Milton*, pp. 13–41. For extended considerations of civic pageantry and public politics during Charles's reign, see Backscheider, *Spectacular Politics*, and Harris, *London Crowds in the Reign of Charles II*.

40. Guillory, "The Father's House," pp. 148–76, provides an illuminating reading of these lines in the context of how "the antinomies of election and reprobation are redefined as election and *obscurity*" (157; emphasis added).

41. For an exciting investigation of sexual roles in *Samson Agonistes*, see Guillory, "Dalila's House," in *Rewriting the Renaissance*, pp. 106–22, where his focus on the gendered division of labor links this essay to his exploration of the historical evolution of the Protestant concept of "vocation" in "The Father's House."

42. Coiro, "Fable and Old Song," p. 143. In addition to Coiro, see also Wittreich, *Shifting Contexts*, where he admits that Milton allows Dalila "some compelling discourse" (142); Mueller, "Just Measures? Versification in *Samson Agonistes*," pp. 47–82, who argues that in "the prosody [of *Samson Agonistes*], Dalila makes a bid for full gender equality" (71); and Shawcross, "Misreading Milton," pp. 181–203, who explains that Milton acknowledges Samson's failings "by assigning to Dalila a character that is not simply venal" (200).

43. Chaucer, "The Wife of Bath's Prologue," in *The Canterbury Tales*, p. 114, lines 721–23. All quotations from Chaucer are to this edition.

44. Teski and Climo, "Introduction," in *The Labyrinth of Memory*, p. 9.

45. Radzinowicz, *Toward Samson Agonistes*, p. 175.

46. For a complete survey of these traditions, see *Interpreting Samson Agonistes* and *Shifting Contexts*. In the first Wittreich argues that "Samson's last act is left ambiguous, deliberately so, with the probable implication that Milton's poem is not about Samson's regeneration but, instead, his second fall" (80). In the second he insists that "Samson as a divided image, complicated in his character and ambiguous in his heroism, is traceable to Milton's own time. Indeed, his Samson emerges not from a hermeneutics and poetics of consensus but of conflict" (71).

47. Fish, "Spectacle and Evidence in *Samson Agonistes*," p. 584; Haskin, *Milton's Burden of Interpretation*, p. 118.

48. MacCallum, "*Samson Agonistes*: The Deliverer as Judge," p. 264.

49. Ibid.

50. Cavendish, *CCXI Sociable Letters*, p. 178. In *The Philosophical and Physical Opinions*, she locates the passions in the heart, the functions of imagination and memory in the brain: "all passions are made in the heart; as Love, Hate, Fear, Anger, Grief, Jealousie, Envy, Malice, and the like; and also the Will, and opinions, which are a Kinde of passions; and that imaginations, conceptions, fancies, understanding, judgment, memory, and remembrance is made in the brain" (106).

51. I am indebted throughout my discussion of "On Shakespeare" to Cori Perdue's unpublished essay, " 'The Spirit within Shall on the Heart Engrave.' "

52. Fentress and Wickham, *Social Memory*, p. 9.

53. For an important consideration of the tension between performance and text in Milton, see Helgerson, "Milton Reads the King's Book," pp. 1–25.

54. Cressy, *Bonfires and Bells*, p. xiv.

55. Loewenstein, *Milton and the Drama of History*, p. 28.

3   "OH GRANT AN HONEST FAME, OR GRANT ME NONE!": THE ETHICS OF MEMORIALIZATION IN POPE'S ARCHIVES OF DULNESS

1. Pope, *The Temple of Fame*, in *The Poems of Alexander Pope*, 2: 2, lines 523–24. Except for quotations from *The Dunciad*, all references to the poetry of Pope are to this Twickenham edition. For reasons that will become clear later in the chapter, quotations from the successive editions of *The Dunciad* come from multiple volumes. References from the 1743 *Dunciad, in Four Books*, come from the Twickenham edition of the poem edited by James Sutherland, volume 5 in that series. Quotations from the 1728 *Dunciad* are to Vander Meulen, ed., *Pope's Dunciad of 1728*, while quotations from the 1729 *Dunciad Variorum* are from Day, ed., *Alexander Pope: Poems in Facsimile*.

2. Milton, *Areopagitica*, in *The Complete Prose Works of John Milton*, 2: 514.

3. Ingrassia, "Dissecting the Authorial Body," in *"More Solid Learning": New Perspectives on Pope's Dunciad*, p. 151. A number of other essays in this collection consider Pope's *Dunciad* in light of its performance of gender. See in particular Rousseau, " 'et in Acadio homo,' " pp. 33–61; Rosenthal, " 'Trials of Manhood,' " pp. 81–105; and Chandler, "Pope's 'Girl of the Game,' " pp. 106–28. Other important considerations of Pope's masculinity can be found in Deutsch, *Resemblance and Disgrace*; Williams, *Pope, Homer, and Manliness*; and Rumbold, *Women's Place in Pope's World*.

4. Foxon, *Pope and the Early Eighteenth-Century Book Trade*, shows how Pope exploited the Copyright Act of 1710 much more successfully than his contemporaries, for while this act was "supposed to have brought a new alliance of author and bookseller,...from the 1720s Pope was using it to strengthen his own position and lesson his dependence on the book trade" (237). Winn, "On Pope, Printers, and Publishers," pp. 93–102, argues that "Pope's success in his dealings with the 'trade' is the more remarkable for having occurred in a period when most writers were at a disadvantage...Pope effectively defeated this monopoly by understanding it perfectly and shifting his methods when necessary" (94).

5. The figure of Pope as the "reluctant modern" can be found to different degrees in Deutsch, *Resemblance and Disgrace*; Stallybrass and White, *The Politics and Poetics of Transgression*; Levine, *The Battle of the Books*; Hunter, "From Typology to Type," pp. 41–69; Griffin, *Literary Patronage in England*; Hammond, *Professional Imaginative Writing in England*.

6. In his book on the growth of writing as a profession, Brean S. Hammond argues that for all of his complaints against the corruption wrought by modern notions of progress, "in some respects, Pope embodied the direction taken by progress," a work such as *The Dunciad* ideologically "rooted in the value systems that it ostensibly opposes...its energy borrowed from the lowbrow and demotic forms that it affects to despise" (*Professional Imaginative Writing*, pp. 2 and 209).

7. Pope to Cromwell, November 1, 1708, *in The Correspondence of Alexander Pope*, 1: 52.

8. Pope to Warburton, September 20, 1741, in *The Correspondence*, 4: 362. Thorne, "Thumbing Our Nose at the Public Sphere," pp. 531–44, provides a link for the Tory satirists between gender politics and a deformed modernity that threatens the survival of cultural memory: "Modernity, in this vision, is a fall from grace, a deplorable break from a past marked by manly earnestness and into a feminized present of hypocrisy and superficial luxury" (533).

9. Hill to Pope, February 10, 1730/1, *The Correspondence*, 3: 174.

10. Connerton, *How Societies Remember*, p. 62.

11. McKitterick, "Bibliography, Bibliophily, and the Organization of Knowledge," p. 31.

12. Irwin, *The Origins of the English Library*, p. 140.

13. The 1715 edition of *The Temple of Fame* emphasizes the poet's youth by noting that it was "Written in the Year 1711." But Geoffrey Tillotson's edition of *The Rape of the Lock and Other Poems*, volume two of *The Poems of Alexander Pope*, suggests that this date doesn't quite fit with other evidence that the poem was substantially complete in 1710 (243). Mack, *Alexander Pope*, agrees that an early draft was extant "probably by the autumn of 1710" (163).

14. For two accounts of how Chaucer's depiction of Fama stems from and fits within classical and medieval contexts, see Delany, *Chaucer's House of Fame*; and Koonce, *Chaucer and the Tradition of Fame*.

15. In regard to the relationship between *The Temple of Fame* and *The Dunciad*, Tillotson (*The Poems of Alexander Pope*) has remarked that the second half of the former "may be considered as a tryout for the fourth Book of the Dunciad" (2: 239). In regard to the relationship between Pope and his poetic forebears, Stevenson, *Milton to Pope*, suggests that "one of the striking characteristics of his poetry is its homage to a host of earlier writers" (99), English as well as classical.

16. See Mack's *Alexander Pope* for a more sympathetic reading of the conclusion to *The Temple of Fame*. Mack insists that the poem ends with "an attitude toward the writer's life that will never leave him, though it will never deter him either. The poem ends, appropriately, with what I believe we must consider a heartfelt prayer" (167).

17. Rumbold, in *Women's Place in Pope's World*, reminds us that during the first half of the eighteenth century one "can write at length about the human race as if it were entirely masculine" (1).

18. See Wilmot, earl of Rochester, "Womans Honour Song," in *The Works of John Wilmot*, p. 21.

19. Rumbold, *Women's Place in Pope's World*, p. 153.

20. Connell, "Death and the Author," p. 565.

21. Although almost four decades old, Mack's *The Garden and the City* remains an indispensable guide to the literary ambitions and personal self-conceptions that Pope embodied in his Twickenham estate. More recent considerations of Pope's architectural and landscape aesthetics can be found in Brownell, *Alexander Pope and the Arts of Georgian England*; Martin, *Pursuing Innocent Pleasures*; Batey, *Alexander Pope*.

22. McLaverty, *Pope, Print, and Meaning*, p. 56.

23. Pope to Swift, January 1727/8, in *The Correspondence*, 2: 468.

24. For an extended discussion of Pope's survey of the eighteenth-century academy, see Rousseau, "Pope and the Tradition in Modern Humanistic Education," pp. 199–239. Rousseau concludes that "if the satire on education was a literary achievement, it was something else as well: a moment in the history of Western education" (227).

25. According to the *Oxford English Dictionary*, this modern definition of the term *museum* was in use as early as 1656 and 1660. The former date, in fact, saw the publication in London of *Musaeum Tradescantianum: or, A Collection of Rarities. Preserved at South Lambeth neer London*, a catalog of the collection from which the Ashmolean grew. The *OED* also notes that, within a century, there appeared a derogatory use of the term that called attention to "any large or motley collection of things, esp. outmoded or useless ones." For the history of the Ashmolean see Ovenell, *The Ashmolean Museum*. On the opening of the Ashmolean and its part in the evolution of the archive, see Taylor, "Holdings: Refiguring the Archive," p. 251.

26. In *Market a la Mode*, Erin Mackie looks at these lines in order to explicate the "fetishization of objects" (57) that accompanied both the new science and the burgeoning retail trade.

27. Johnson and Harris, *History of Libraries in the Western World*, p. 119.

28. For the history of the library in England I have depended on, in addition to the works by Irwin, Johnson and Harris, and McKitterick already cited, Savage, *Old English Libraries*; Wormald and Wright, ed., *The English Library Before 1700*; Irwin, *The English Library*; Feather and McKitterick, *The History of Books and Libraries*.

29. Drury, *The Reformed Librarie-Keeper*, p. 14.

30. Yates, *The Art of Memory*, p. 127. See Carruthers, *The Book of Memory* for a study of medieval memory, particularly for an exploration of how the glossed book provided a functional model for the relationship between authorship and textual authority during the Middle Ages.

31. Brown, *Alexander Pope*, p. 132.

32. Naudé, *Instructions Concerning Erecting of a Library*, p. 75.
33. Pope to the earl of Oxford, September 15, 1729 and October 6, 1729, in *The Correspondence* 3: 54–56.
34. Pope to the earl of Oxford, October 1, 1730, in *The Correspondence* 3:136.
35. Irwin, *The Origins of the English Library*, p. 132.
36. Mbembe, "The Power of the Archive and Its Limits," p. 20.
37. Swift to Pope and Bolingbroke, April 5, 1729, in *The Correspondence* 3: 29.
38. Swift, *A Tale of a Tub*, pp. 55 and 56.
39. Braudy, *The Frenzy of Renown*, p. 361.
40. McLaverty, *Pope, Print and Meaning*, p. 209.
41. Ibid., p. 109.
42. See Foxon, *Pope and the Early Eighteenth-Century Book Trade*, for a careful examination of both the economics and aesthetics of the printing of the *Iliad* (pages 51–86). Foxon argues that "with Pope's return to original composition with the *Dunciad* of 1728, we find a completely new relationship with the book trade, one in which the author takes charge, choosing his own printer and publisher and directing operations himself" (102).
43. Jones, "Pope and Dulness," p. 647.
44. Chambers, *Cyclopaedia: Or, An Universal Dictionary of Arts and Sciences*. All quotations are from the first volume of this edition.
45. Cave, *The Gentleman's Magazine, or Trader's Monthly Intelligencer*. All quotations are from this edition.
46. For discussions of periodical literature in eighteenth-century Britain, see Rogers, *Grub Street: Studies in a Subculture*; Reitan, "Introduction" to *The Best of the Gentleman's Magazine*, pp. 1–23; Shevelow, *Women and Print Culture*; Ballaster, Beetham, Frazer, and Hebron, *Women's Worlds*; and Sommerville, *The News Revolution in England*. Both Hunter, *Before Novels* and Hammond, *Professional Imaginative Writing in England*, also consider periodical printing.
47. Deutsch, *Resemblance and Disgrace*, p. 170.
48. Swift, *A Tale of a Tub*, p. 34.
49. Horace, Ode 3.30, in *Horace: The Odes and Epodes*, p. 279.
50. Deutsch, *Resemblance and Disgrace*, p. 182.
51. For the evolution of satire as a form, and its magical origins, see Elliott, *The Power of Satire*, particularly chapters one and two. McLaverty, *Pope, Print and Meaning*, writes insightfully about the way in which "naming becomes quasi-magical and divorced from issues of reference; to name someone is analogous to cursing" (223).
52. Nora, "Between Memory and History," p. 13.
53. Pope to Sheridan, October 12, 1728, in *The Correspondence* 2: 523. In regard to the question of "ownership," see Staves, "Pope's Refinement," pp. 145–63, which provides an exciting discussion of how Pope would have considered himself "the proprietor of his poems" and the ways in which "the Copyright Act imagines the author as an individual owner of property" (158). She argues that the appearance of the revised version of *The Dunciad* in 1743 depended on the reversion to Pope of the original copyright.
54. Hamilton, Harris, and Reid, "Introduction," in *Refiguring the Archive*, p. 15.
55. Kinsley, "The Dunciad as Mock-Book," p. 717 and pp. 866–67, n. 39.
56. Pope to Swift, June 28, 1728, in *The Correspondence* 2: 503.
57. Kotre, *White Gloves*, p. 116.

58. Fentress and Wickham, *Social Memory*, pp. xi and 59.

59. Hammond, *Professional Imaginative Writing*, p. 195. McLaverty, in *Pope, Print and Meaning*, emphasizes Pope's success, not just in *The Dunciad* but throughout his oeuvre, in "mesmerizing posterity": "What is striking over 250 years later is how successful Pope was in steering criticism of his work" (241).

60. Johnson, *Lives of the English Poets*, 3: 145 and 241–42.

61. De Quincey, "Alexander Pope," in *The Collected Writings of Thomas De Quincey*, 4: 270. The poetry of Pope presented an interesting problem for De Quincey, who, according to John E. Jordan, composed five separate papers on Pope. For a much more detailed consideration of De Quincey's attitudes toward Pope than I can provide, see his *Thomas De Quincey Literary Critic*, particularly pp. 153–74.

62. De Quincey, "Schlosser's Literary History of the Eighteenth Century," in *The Collected Waitings of Thomas De Quincey*, 11: 33–35. The work that De Quincey reviewed in *Tait's Magazine* for September and October 1847 was a translation by D. Davidson of Schlosser's six volume *Geschichte des 18ten Jahrhunderts und des 19ten bis zum Sturz des französischen Kaiserreichs*; this work had originally been published between 1836–1848, while the translation had appeared between the years 1843 and 1852.

63. For a consideration of this lecture series and its great success, as well as Thackeray's rank as a critic of the eighteenth century, see Ray, *Thackeray: The Age of Wisdom*, pp. 138–48.

64. Thackeray, *The English Humourists of the Eighteenth Century*, pp. 155–56, 182–83 and 185–86.

65. Stephen, *Alexander Pope*, pp. 133 and 124.

66. Lounsbury, *The Text of Shakespeare*, pp. 258–59, 259–60, and 271–72.

67. For an omnibus book review that affords an evaluation of current critical trends regarding Pope, see Snead, "No Exit? Recent Publications on Pope," pp. 349–55. In the "Introduction: 'More Solid Learning,'" to their collection *"More Solid Learning,"* Catherine Ingrassia and Claudia N. Thomas provide an excellent survey of *The Dunciad*'s critical reception since the mid-1960s; see pages 24–32. They note that "a re-evaluation of the professional authors he [Pope] characterized as 'hacks' is, itself, an act of literary history that challenges or revises Pope's interpretation of events." They also maintain that "work of the dominant Pope scholars of this century…largely maintained the attitudes or standards Pope established in his poem" (24).

68. Root, "Introduction," in *The Dunciad Variorum*, p. 16.

69. Abrams and Greenblatt, "Preface to the Seventh Edition," in *The Norton Anthology*, 1: xxxiii and xlii.

70. This chapter was written before *The Norton Anthology* released its newest edition in 2006. Sadly, Cavendish did not survive the passage from the seventh to the eighth edition.

71. Todd, in *Imagining Monsters*, identifies a series of similar contradictions within eighteenth-century conceptions of the imagination: "A void which is also a plenum of being, a movement toward death which is at the same time an act of life, the destruction of all creation which is simultaneously the creation of a 'new World': the 'uncreating' power of Dulness is paradoxical because Dulness represents the imagination" (197).

72. Rumbold, "Cut the Caterwauling," p. 529.

73. Kramnick, *Making the English Canon*, pp. 39–41, and Terry, *Poetry and the Making of the English Literary Past*, pp. 252–85.
74. Chandler, "Pope's 'Girl of the Game,'" p. 115. Dennis Todd, in *Imagining Monsters*, recognizes the importance of *The Dunciad* as "a succession poem": "Lineage, succession, and birth signal the extinction of identity here" (215).
75. Rogers, "Nameless Names," p. 244.
76. Stallybrass and White, *The Politics and Poetics of Transgression*, pp. 117–18.
77. McLaverty, *Pope, Print and Meaning*, p. 211.
78. Fanning, "Small Particles of Eloquence," pp. 360–92, suggests that a similar intellectual promise and betrayal was enacted by the way in which printing furthered advances in modern editing: "The advances of modern editing have only heightened our awareness of the dependence of the 'great tradition' on the physical state of texts. Printing, which originated the demand for 'perfect' texts of the ancients, has also revealed the impossibility of perfection by magnifying lacunae and drawing attention to cruces of interpretation" (369–70).

4 "GRAVEN WITH AN IRON PEN AND LEAD IN THE BOOK FOR EVER!": PAPER AND PERMANENCE IN RICHARDSON'S *CLARISSA*

1. Dryden, *Mac Flecknoe*, in *The Works of John Dryden*, 2: 2, 54–60, lines 98–103.
2. Churchyard, *A Sparke of Frendship and Warme Goodwill*, pp. Dv and D3. For the history and evolution of papermaking, as well as descriptions of the papermaking process, see Hunter, *Papermaking*; Sutermeister, *The Story of Papermaking*; and Jenkins, *Paper-Making in England*. There is a particularly succinct description of early-modern papermaking in Campbell, *The London Tradesman*, pp. 124–25.
3. Hunter, *Papermaking*, p. 11. *The London Tradesman* presents good paper, rather than metals, as the basis for permanence by patriotically contrasting European to Chinese paper:
   [The Chinese] make their Paper of that Material, which comes short of the Beauty and Firmness of our *European* Paper; and has this particular Misfortune attending it, that it is apt to breed a Worm, which destroys it. This obliges these People to transcribe their Records often, and there is not now in any of their Libraries an Original of older Date than two Thousand Years. (124–25)
4. Flynn, *Samuel Richardson*, p. 269. Flint, "In Other Words," pp. 627–72, points out that "Clarissa is not only a celebration of 'writing to the moment'; it is also an homage to what we might call 'printing to the moment'" (663). Flint's important reformulation here suggests the ways in which the material processes of the print industry were central to conceptions of authorship in the eighteenth century.
5. Berger, Jr., "The Pepys Show," pp. 557–91, possesses a particularly acute sense of the fascinating dynamic between gold and paper during the early modern. He notes that although Pepys "was a fiscal conservative in the sense that he kept most of his wealth in gold and his gold under his bed...his financial health came increasingly to depend on his ability to navigate in the precarious waters of paper instruments and promises" (557).
6. Flint, "In Other Words," p. 663.

7. McKeon, *The Origins of the English Novel*, pp. 20 and 43. Fox, "Custom, Memory and the Authority of Writing," pp. 89–116, argues that in legal, administrative, and commercials contexts, the sixteenth and seventeenth centuries mark the moment when "customary usages [were transferred] from oral memory to written record. This creation of their own transcripts of custom was a reflection, perhaps... of an increasingly legalistic and documentary culture" (106). In regard to the novel, Armstrong, in *Desire and Domestic Fiction*, notes that "Novels characteristically identify themselves as fiction and yet presume to be more faithful to life than earlier fictions" (35).

8. Derrida, *Archive Fever*, recognizes the centrality of the printer to "archival technology" and the "archival event" when he argues that "what is no longer archived in the same way is no longer lived in the same way. Archivable meaning is also and in advance codetermined by the structure that archives. It begins with the printer" (18).

9. Flint, "In Other Words," p. 662.

10. Pocock, *Virtue, Commerce, and History*, p. 99.

11. Ingrassia, in *Authorship, Commerce, and Gender in Early Eighteenth-Century England*, makes explicit the links between new forms of fiction and the development of paper credit.

12. Keymer, "Richardson's *Meditations*: Clarissa's *Clarissa*," pp. 108–09. See also Flint, "In Other Words," who carefully studies the changing printer's ornaments in successive editions of the novel to argue "that *Clarissa* was a constantly evolving text" (656). Lewis, "Clarissa's Cruelty," pp. 45–67, surveys "the massive apparatus that Richardson devised to regulate increasingly wanton interpretations of his novel. Incorporating footnotes, insertions, prefaces, and postscripts, this apparatus was meant to clarify Richardson's own 'Intentions' and 'Design' as an author" (46). But in a review essay, Richardson, "The Perils of Prolixity," pp. 314–19, suggests that "the question for scholars is whether this proliferation of text provided Richardson with the control he desired over the interpretation of his novel, or whether his grasp slipped further with each addition" (314).

13. The three volumes of *Samuel Richardson's Published Commentary on Clarissa* provide a good indication of the novel's impressive archival evolution and growth. Richardson possessed the editorial as well as economic freedom to create such an extensive archive because, as Christopher Flint points out, he fulfilled "various roles as writer, editor, printer, publisher, and even critic of his own work" (664).

14. See McKeon, *The Origins of the English Novel*, for an analysis of the ways in which "Writing 'reifies' memory. The physical presentation of knowledge produces not only documents and archives but also the conditions for the 'objective' comparison of data" (29).

15. Young, *The Texture of Memory*, pp. 2 and 6.

16. Richardson to Cheyne, January 21, 1742/3, Richardson to Hill, January 19, 1743/4, and Richardson to Hill, November 7, 1748, in *Selected Letters of Samuel Richardson*, pp. 56, 60, and 100.

17. Fielding, *Remarks on Clarissa, Addressed to the Author*, pp. 34–35.

18. Richardson to Westcomb, 1746?, in *Selected Letters*, p. 66.

19. Early in the novel, when Miss Howe's mother has first forbidden Anna and Clarissa to correspond, the latter states that she "must write on, although I were not to send it to anybody," for even without a recipient she must "gratify my passion for scribbling" (483). Later in the novel, after her rape, she uses

the term in a much darker register: "I was under a strange delirium...now weeping, now raving, now scribbling, tearing what I scribbled as fast" (1011). Lovelace, as his plans begin to go awry, tells us that "But for this scribbling vein, or I should still run mad!" (741). All quotations from the novel are from the following edition: Richardson, *Clarissa; or, The History of a Young Lady*, ed. Angus Ross (New York: Penguin Books, 1985). The significance of this identification of Clarissa, Lovelace, and even Richardson as scribblers is increased by a further seventeenth- and eighteenth-century definition of the term from the *Oxford English Dictionary* that includes "a person who scribbles wool, or who tends a scribbling-machine." The gendering of labor involved in the juxtaposition of writing to sewing, examined originally in chapter one, will be considered later in this chapter.

20. Keymer and Sabor, *Pamela in the Marketplace*, pp. 14–15.
21. For an examination of this work's relationship to Richardson's novel, see Sabor's "Introduction" to Fielding's *Remarks on Clarissa*, pp. iii–x.
22. Richardson to Dr. Young, November 19, 1747, in *The Correspondence of Samuel Richardson*, 2: 24. All further quotation from Richardson's correspondence will be from this edition.
23. Two of Richardson's biographers attest to the friendly persuasion that the novelist labored under during the fall of 1748, just prior to the publication of the final volumes of *Clarissa*. See McKillop, *Samuel Richardson*, pp. 169–71; Kinkead-Weekes, *Samuel Richardson: Dramatic Novelist*, pp. 219–20.
24. Fielding, *The Jacobite's Journal*, in *The Jacobite's Journal and Related Writings*, p. 120.
25. Keymer, *Richardson's Clarissa and the Eighteenth-Century Reader*, p. 218.
26. For two different views of the relationship between Bradshaigh and Richardson, see Barchas, "Richardson on the Margins," pp. 8–42; and Traugott, "*Clarissa*'s Richardson," pp. 157–208. Barchas likens their relationship to "an epistolary novel" (12), while Traugott laughs at "A nice little flirtation of the porcine printer and the sentimental lady. What a pair!" (160).
27. Lady Echlin's revision of *Clarissa*'s conclusion has been edited by Daphinoff as *An Alternative Ending to Richardson's Clarissa*. In her "Introduction," Daphinoff explains that Lady Echlin's alternative version "illustrates not only the intimate relationship between Richardson and his readers, but, moreover, the mutuality of the creative process that the new genre (the novel) established" (16).
28. Richardson, "Hints of Prefaces for Clarissa," pp. 3 and 5.
29. *Critical Remarks on Sir Charles Grandison, Clarissa and Pamela*, pp. 4–5.
30. Beale, *A History of the Post in England*, p.206.
31. Eagleton, *The Rape of Clarissa*, p. 80; Anderson and Ehrenpreis, "The Familiar Letter in the Eighteenth Century," p. 278. For other interesting considerations of the letter as a literary form, see Redford, *The Converse of the Pen*; Todd, "Fatal Fluency," pp. 417–34; and Gilroy and Verhoeven, ed., *Epistolary Histories*. In the "Introduction" to this last volume, Gilroy and Verhoeven write that "The most historically powerful fiction of the letter has been that which figures it as the trope of authenticity and intimacy" (1).
32. Steedman, *Dust*, suggestively notes that "the eighteenth-century reader of epistolary fiction always read something in which *the story of the letters* themselves involved their being lost, pilfered or misappropriated in some way or another" (75).
33. Stoler, "Colonial Archives and the Arts of Governance," p. 88.
34. Clanchy, *From Memory to Written Record*, pp. 63 and 68–69.

35. Anderson and Ehrenpreis, "The Familiar Letter," pp. 269–70.
36. On the manufacture and use of parchment, see Hunter, *Papermaking*, pp. 14–18; Carvalho, *Forty Centuries of Ink*; Clanchy, *From Memory to Written Record*, pp. 88–95.
37. Clanchy, *From Memory to Written Record*, p. 88.
38. Hunter, *Papermaking*, p. 35.
39. Ibid., epigraph.
40. Jones and Stallybrass, *Renaissance Clothing and the Materials of Memory*, pp. 5 and 8.
41. Hunter, *Papermaking*, p. 86.
42. Quoted in Jenkins, *Paper-Making in England*, p. 14.
43. Ibid., p. 19–20.
44. Hunter, *Papermaking*, p. 327.
45. Jenkins, *Paper-Making in England*, pp. 12–13.
46. Browne, *Getting the Message*, p. 37.
47. Favret, *Romantic Correspondence*, p. 13.
48. Fleming, *Diamonds Are Forever*, p. 140.
49. Beale, *A History of the Post*, p. 2.
50. Ibid., p. 100.
51. Peterson, "The Archives and the Political Imaginary," p. 29; Jones and Stallybrass, *Renaissance Clothing and the Materials of Memory*, pp. 156 and 261.
52. Keymer, "Richardson's *Meditations*," writes that Aaron Hill's suggestion that Richardson rename the novel "The Lady's Legacy" emphasizes the way in which the fiction moves from an opening in which Clarissa inherits, to a conclusion in which she bequeaths (89).
53. For considerations of Clarissa's posthumous power, see Marshall, "Fatal Letters," pp. 213–51; and Flynn, *Samuel Richardson*, pp. 235–62. See Zigarovich, "Courting Death," pp. 112–28, for a study of "the fetishism Clarisa displays in her posthumous will and letters which detail how she would like her corpse displayed" (123).
54. Clanchy, *From Memory to Written Record*, p. 245; Goldberg, *Writing Matter*, agrees with Clanchy: "the prototype for moveable type may more easily be seen in the seal than in the mark that served as a signature, for the seal is capable of exact duplication" (244).
55. Clanchy, *From Memory to Written Record*, p. 245.
56. Quoted in Clanchy, *From Memory to Written Record*, p. 246.
57. The story of Rowe's disappointment was sufficiently notorious to find its way into Samuel Johnson's biography of Rowe in the *Lives of the English Poets*, 2: 71–72.
58. Kroll, *The Material Word*, p. 14.
59. Kreisel, "Stealing the Pen," p. 2, in an unpublished essay.
60. Flint, "In Other Words," pp. 650–52.
61. Talon, ed. *Selections from the Journals & Papers of John Byrom*, pp. 7 and 9–10. For the history of shorthand in England prior to the eighteenth century, see Duthie, *Elizabethan Shorthand and the First Quarto of King Lear*.
62. Talon, ed. *Selections from the Journals & Papers of John Byrom*, pp. 87–88.
63. Price, "Stenographic Masculinity," p. 34. Price's essay contains a wealth of fascinating information about shorthand, although unfortunately for my study it deals primarily with the mid- and late nineteenth century.
64. Warner, *The Letters of the Republic*, p. 15. In *The Women of Grub Street*, Paula McDowell suggests that the relationship of writing to gender involved

class issues as well: "the text-based history available to a learned and leisured woman such as Astell was not available to a working woman like [Elinor] James...In late seventeenth- and early eighteenth-century London, the religio-political culture of ordinary women was still fundamentally an oral culture" (130).

65. Jones and Stallybrass, *Renaissance Clothing and the Materials of Memory*, p. 141.

66. Goldberg, *Writing Matter*, pp. 111 and 45.

67. Scribes were not always seen as mere mechanics. For a careful consideration of the power and authority of the scribe prior to the print revolution, see Beal, *In Praise of Scribes*.

68. At one point, Dorcas transcribes Lovelace's letters so that copies can be sent to Belford (731). We learn, in fact, that Clarissa is surrounded by a veritable gaggle of scribes, both Sally and Polly helping Dorcas in the transcription of Clarissa's letters (570).

69. Maaja Stewart has pointed out to me that these ink-stained fingers run counter to the ways in which most women were depicted in early modern painting, where the ideal female hand is white and child-sized, with oval-shaped finger nails and tapered fingers that are never ink-stained or needle-pricked.

70. Bloy, *A History of Printing Ink, Balls and Rollers*, p. 1.

71. Carvalho, *Forty Centuries of Ink*, p. 255.

72. Goldberg, *Writing Matter*, pp. 74–75.

73. Hunter, *Papermaking*, p. 8.

74. Eagleton, *The Rape of Clarissa*, p. 93.

75. Fielding, *Remarks on Clarissa*, p. 56. Harris, "Grotesque, Classical and Pornographic Bodies in *Clarissa*," in Rivero, *New Essays on Samuel Richardson*, asserts that for all of Clarissa's modesty and desire not to become a public figure, "Clarissa's classical and Latinate [name] means both 'clarissima' (famous) and brilliant" (102).

76. Beasley, "Richardson's Girls," pp. 43–44.

77. Nuttall, "Literature and the Archive," p. 295. On this question see as well Derrida, *Archive Fever*:

   By incorporating the knowledge deployed in reference to it, the archive augments itself, engrosses itself, it gains in *auctoritas*. But in the same stroke it loses the absolute and meta-textual authority it might claim to have. One will never be able to objectivize it with no remainder. The archivist produces more archive, and that is why the archive is never closed. It opens out of the future. (68)

78. McKeon, *The Origins of the English Novel*, p. 127.

79. Flynn, *Samuel Richardson*, p. 2.

CONCLUSION: FROM THE "GARBAGE HEAP" OF MEMORY TO THE CYBORG: THE EXHAUSTION AND REVITALIZATION OF MEMORY IN THE TWENTIETH AND TWENTY-FIRST CENTURIES

1. Richards, *The Imperial Archive*, p. 6.

2. Stewart, *On Longing*, p. 35.

3. Hirsch, "Surviving Images," p. 9.

4. Assmann, "Collective Memory and Cultural Identity," pp. 130 and 133.
5. Hirsch, "Surviving Images," p. 9.
6. Ricoeur, in *Memory, History, Forgetting*, notes that "new modes of transmitting texts in the age of the 'electronic representation'…lead to a revolution in the practice of reading, and through this, in the very practice of writing" (228). See also Rose, *The Making of Memory*, who insists that technology refashions biology, particularly in regard to memory:

    such is the powerful interaction of our technology with our biology itself that the fact of creating a technology-driven society in which metaphors for memory have become central changes the very nature of our memory itself. The act of writing…fixes the fluid, dynamic memory of oral cultures into linear form. The establishment of mass-circulation printed texts…further stabilizes and controls memory…Modern technologies…restructure consciousness and memory even more profoundly. (95)

7. In 1979, Elizabeth Eisenstein could ironically note that "however sophisticated present findings have become, we still have to call upon a fifteenth-century invention to secure them. Even at present, a given scholarly discovery…has to be registered in print—announced in a learned journal and eventually spelled out in full—before it can be acknowledged as a contribution or put to further use" (224–25). Only twenty-nine years later, I leave it to individual readers to determine just how long this will remain true.
8. Haraway, *Simians, Cyborgs, and Women*, p. 58.
9. Borges, "Funes the Memorious," in *Labyrinths*, p. 59. All quotations from the works of Borges are from this edition. Borges' emphasis on the formulation "to remember" is echoed by Paul Ricoeur, who begins his long and thoughtful meditation on modern memory, *Memory, History, Forgetting*, by focusing on the significance of this verb and what precisely it designates (56).
10. Nalbantan, *Memory in Literature*, p. 127.
11. "Borges, "The Library of Babel," p. 58. It is entirely appropriate that the first name of Letizia Álvarez de Toledo, who ends Borges' story by replacing the Library with the Volume, should have been adapted for a cyber agent "that assists a user browsing the World Wide Web." Henry Lieberman, of the Media Laboratory at MIT, has taken the name Letizia from Borges' fiction for his search agent that will assist conventional web browsers in discovering items that will interest the user: "It uses a simple set of heuristics to model what the user's browsing behavior might be." See http://lieber.www.media.mit.edu/people/lieber/Lieberary/Letizia. For a website that presents a modernistic image of Borges' Library, go to http://jubal.westnet.com/hyperdiscordia/library_of_babel.html.
12. Stewart, *On Longing*, p. 35.
13. Ricoeur, *Memory, History, Forgetting*, p. 237.
14. Kelley and Sacks, "Preface," in *The Historical Imagination in Early Modern Britain*, pp. ix–xx.
15. Bakhurst, "Social Memory in Soviet Thought," p. 212.
16. Kiš, "To Die for One's Country Is Glorious," in *The Encyclopedia of the Dead*, p. 129. All quotations from the works of Kiš are from this edition.
17. Zerubavel, "The Historic, the Legendary, and the Incredible," pp. 105 and 118.

18. In his "Postscript" to the volume, Kiš quotes at length from an account entitled "Archives," published in a Yugoslav magazine, which provides a description of the continuing project of the Genealogical Society of the Church of the Latter-Day Saints to provide accurate genealogies for "nothing less than the whole of mankind." Kiš provides the following amused but rather chilling conclusion to his story: "The person who dreamed the dream and to whom the story is dedicated awoke one day to find, not without a shudder of amazement, that her most intimate nightmares were etched in stone, like a monstrous monument" (193).

19. Belgrade, where Djuro M. lives for approximately fifty years, had been the capital of Serbia since 1404. It was chosen as the capital of the newly created "Kingdom of the Serbs, Croats, and Slovenes" in 1918, which was ruled by the Serbian royal family, the Karadjordjevics. In 1929 King Alexander I renamed the country "Kingdom of Yugoslavia"—"Land of the Southern Slavs." The city was occupied by invading German armies in 1941, and liberated in 1944 by forces of both the Soviet Red Army and the People's Liberation Army of Yugoslavia. In reading this story it is worth remembering that the assassination of the Austrian heir apparent, Archduke Franz Ferdinand, by Serbian nationalists on June 28, 1914, in Sarajevo, led directly to the outbreak of World War I.

20. By the time the Berlin Wall came down, the Stasi, or *Ministerium für Staatssicherheit*, employed over ninety thousand people and maintained an extraordinary number of citizens as informers. According to Childs, *The Fall of the GDR*, "Over the Honecker period the full-time staff of the MfS expanded from 52,700 in 1973 to 81,500 in 1981. Moreover, it employed a growing army of informers. Although no final figure can be given, it has been estimated that between one and two million citizens worked at one time or another as informers for the MfS. The MfS employed more people than Hitler's Gestapo, which is a shocking commentary on the GDR" (37). Ash, in *The File*, writes that the Stasi considered their "unofficial collaborators," *Inoffizielle Mitarbeiter* (IM for short) as one of their most important sources of information: "The numbers are extraordinary. According to internal records, in 1988—the last 'normal' year of the GDR—the Ministry for State Security had more than 170,000 'unofficial collaborators.' Of these, some 110,000 were regular informers" (84). Ash estimates that taken altogether, "about one out of every fifty adult East Germans had a direct connection with the secret police" (84).

21. Fukuyama's notorious essay "The End of History?" was published in *The National Interest*, pp. 3–18, and later turned into a book, *The End of History and the Last Man*. The quotation is provided by journalist Ron Suskind in "What Makes Bush's Presidency So Radical," p. 51.

22. In an "edited conversation" with W.G. Sebald on September 24, 2001, just a few months before his death, he told Maya Jaggi that

> You could grow up in Germany in the postwar years without ever meeting a Jewish person. There were small communities in Frankfurt or Berlin, but in a provincial town in south Germany Jewish people didn't exist. The subsequent realization was that they had been in all those places, as doctors, cinema ushers, owners of garages, but they had disappeared—or had been disappeared. (2–3)

This conversation can be found online in "The Last Word," December 21, 2001, in *Guardian Unlimited Books*, http://books.guardian.co.uk/departments/generalfiction/story/0,6000,624750,00.html.

23. As "Never Forget" itself dwindles into a cliché that becomes applied to multiple horrors, its efficacy as a command becomes even more questionable. When I initially ran a Google search to explore the history of "Never Forget," I was directed to sites concerned only with the tragedy of 9/11, which seems to have appropriated the phrase in order to assert its own historical and cultural importance.

24. LaCapra, *History and Memory after Auschwitz*, p. 2. Klein, "On the Emergence of *Memory* in Historical Discourse," suggests that the "sudden appearance of memory in academic and popular discourse" might be explained in terms of the return of the repressed: "Since memories not defined by trauma are likely to slide into nostalgia, the Holocaust, the ultimate traumatic decentering of history and subjectivity, holds a privileged philosophical place" (139).

25. The complete text of Mottaki's speech can be found at the following website: http://www.ipis.ir/English/meetings_roundtables_conferences.htm.

26. Joel Brouwer has suggested to me that, insofar as Holocaust denial may be a form of pathological denial, and not necessarily solely the result of anti-Semitism or bad faith, it can also stem from fear or anxiety. There is, of course, an extensive literature devoted to Holocaust denial. Perhaps the best introduction to this contentious and fraught issue is the trial that ushered in the new millennium, when on January 11, 2000, the British historian David Irving brought a libel suit to the High Court in London against Deborah E. Lipstadt and her publisher Penguin. In her book, *Denying the Holocaust*, Lipstadt called Irving "one of the most dangerous spokespersons for Holocaust denial." This trial can be followed in two accounts: Guttenplan, *The Holocaust on Trial*, and Lipstadt, *History on Trial*.

27. Although the topic remains beyond the scope of my brief consideration of *The Emigrants*, the novel is quite aware of the arbitrary nature of the racial and national categories that separate Jew from German in cultures that have so thoroughly interpenetrated each other. The arbitrary construction of cultural identities is most compellingly presented in the life of Paul Bereyter, the second of the novel's four biographical subjects, whose Jewish grandfather married a Christian maid. As a "Jew," Paul loses his teaching position in 1935 and watches from France the disintegration of his family under the increasing violence of the Nazi regime. Yet, "German to the marrow, profoundly attached to his native land," he returns in 1939 when, as a "three-quarter Aryan," he is conscripted into the German army, where for six years he serves "in the Greater German homeland" and several occupied countries (55–57). From such a schizophrenic history there is no reprieve: Paul himself, with a lifelong passion for railways, lies in front of a train and commits suicide on December 30, 1983. All quotations are from Sebald, *The Emigrants*.

28. Jews, of course, are not the only people whose forced migration has sundered them from a homeland. Part of the intractability of the current situation in Israel and the Occupied Territories stems from the terrible collision of two peoples, Palestinians and Jews, tragically struggling to reclaim the same "homeland." Baraka, *Black Music*, writing on behalf of an African and African American population whose enslavement over the course of centuries has robbed them of their homeland, succinctly describes how such a

profound experience of homelessness, which calls into question a people's cultural identity, can deform their experience of time: "A 'cultureless' people is a people without a memory. No history" (182).

29. Joel Brouwer has pointed out that in *Austerlitz*, Sebald's fourth novel, he takes the traumatic experience of history exemplified in the lives of Adelwarth and Ferber one awful step further: "Sebald suggests that time is not only nonlinear, but also omni-present, that 'the past' is every bit as much present as 'the present,' always. The 'disquiet of the soul' is a perpetual state, a fixed disorder."

30. Jaggi, "The Last Word," December 21, 2001, in *Guardian Unlimited Books*, p. 4. Many scholars who write about Sebald have, of course, focused on the importance of photography in his fictions. Two that I have found particularly helpful are Duttlinger, "Traumatic Photographs," pp. 155–71; Long, "History, Narrative, and Photography," pp. 117–39. Chandler, "About Loss," pp. 235–62, doesn't focus on photography, but his interest in the "image and impression" means that he often discusses related issues.

31. Sontag, *On Photography*, pp. 3–4.

32. Metz, "Photography and Fetish," pp. 157–58.

33. Sebald, *On the Natural History of Destruction*, p. 71.

34. Hirsch, *Family Frames*, pp. 23 and 20.

35. Bernard-Donals, "Beyond the Question of Authenticity," pp. 1302–15, insists that this same lack of evidentiary status attaches itself even to the testimony of those who survived the Holocaust:

> We cannot view testimony as a window on the past; at its most extreme—in memories of trauma—testimony marks the absence of events, since they did not register on, let alone become integrated into, the victim's consciousness. A testimony may be effective, and it may allow a reader to glimpse a trauma...But it alone does not provide evidence of that event. (1302–03)

36. Lubow, interview with Sebald, "Preoccupied With Death," p. 2.

37. Anderson, "The Edge of Darkness," p. 110. Anderson also responds to this quotation from the Lubow interview and has much of great interest to say about "the contradictory logic" (109) of Sebald's use of photographs.

38. Jaggi, "The Last Word," p. 3.

39. Clifford, *The Predicament of Culture*, p. 340.

40. According to Stedman, *Stedman's Medical Dictionary*, Korsakoff's psychosis is "characterized by confusion and severe impairment of memory, especially for recent events, for which the patient compensates by confabulation; typically encountered in chronic alcoholics." The *Dictionary of Biological Psychology*, explains that "the psychological disturbance in Korsakoff's syndrome is characterized by both antero-grade amnesia and retrograde amnesia, chronotaraxis, and confabulation." For a portrait of someone suffering from this dementia, see Sacks, "The Lost Mariner," in *The Man Who Mistook His Wife for a Hat*, pp. 22–41.

41. Anderson, "The Edge of Darkness," writes about the complex and even contradictory nature of the German lines being translated here: "Zerstöret das Letzte / die Erinnerung nicht": "The phrase can be translated in several contradictory ways: either as exhortation (Destroy every last thing / [but] not memory), or as a statement of fact formulated as a negative question (Doesn't memory / destroy the last remnants?)" (105). According to

Anderson, the Italian translation chose the first version, the French translation the second. The English translation, by Michael Hulse, was "carefully vetted by Sebald."

42. Tuomi, "The Lives and Death of Moore's Law," in *First Monday*. This online journal can be found at http://firstmonday.org/issues.

43. Moore, "Cramming More Components onto Integrated Circuits," in *Electronics*. Moore's prediction was later dubbed "Moore's Law" by Caltech professor Carver Mead, and it has a far more complex history and application than its simple, popular status as a cliché might suggest. For a discussion of its history, and how it has been both misunderstood and misinterpreted, see Tuomi and Stokes, "Understanding Moore's Law," in *arstechnica*. This online journal can be found at http://arstechnica.org.

44. Kotler, "The Genius Who Sticks Around Forever," p. SM102.

45. Rose, *The Making of Memory*, p. 2. Edelman, in *The Remembered Present*, would certainly agree with Rose. In this book he argues that human memory is *recategorical*, "a process involving facilitated pathways, not a fixed replica or code. It is metastable and subject to change": "Although memory so defined is associative and inexact (as a computer's replicative store is not), it is at the same time capable of remarkable degrees of generalization" (111).

46. Moravec, *Mind Children*, pp. 2 and 52.

47. Gray, "An Interview with Manfred Clynes," p. 51.

48. Mann with Niedzviecki, *Cyborg: Digital Destiny and Human Possibility*, p. 28.

49. Ibid., p. 41.

50. Haraway, *Primate Visions*, p. 139. Haraway also discusses the cyborg in *Simians, Cyborgs, and Women* and *Modest_Witness@Second_Millennium*. All quotations from Haraway are from these editions.

51. Clarke, "Modernity, Postmodernity and Reproductive Processes," p. 149.

BIBLIOGRAPHY

Abrams, M.H. and Stephen Greenblatt. "Preface to the Seventh Edition." In *The Norton Anthology of English Literature*. Ed. M.H. Abrams, Stephen Greenblatt, et al. Seventh ed. 2 vols. New York: Norton, 2000, 1: xxxiii–xlii.

Addison, Joseph. *The Spectator*. Ed. Donald F. Bond. 5 vols. Oxford: Clarendon Press, 1965.

Alkon, Daniel L. *Memory's Voice: Deciphering the Brain–Mind Code*. New York: HarperCollins, 1992.

Anderson, Benedict. *Imagined Communities: Reflections on the Origin and Spread of Nationalism*. London: Verso, 1983.

Anderson, Howard and Irvin Ehrenpreis. "The Familiar Letter in the Eighteenth Century: Some Generalizations." In *The Familiar Letter in the Eighteenth Century*. Ed. Howard Anderson, Philip B. Daghlian, and Irvin Ehrenpreis. Lawrence: University of Kansas Press, 1966, 269–82.

Anderson, Mark M. "The Edge of Darkness: On W.G. Sebald." *October* 106 (2003): 102–21.

Armstrong, Nancy. *Desire and Domestic Fiction: A Political History of the Novel*. Oxford: Oxford University Press, 1987.

Ash, Timothy Garton. *The File: A Personal History*. New York: Random House, 1997.

Assmann, Aleida. "Texts, Traces, Trash: The Changing Media of Cultural Memory." *Representations* 56 (1996): 123–34.

Assmann, Jan. "Collective Memory and Cultural Identity." *New German Critique* 65 (1995): 125–33.

Astell, Mary. *Reflections upon Marriage*. In *The First English Feminist: Reflections Upon Marriage and Other Writings by Mary Astell*. Ed. Bridget Hill. Aldershot: Gower Publishing, 1986, 67–132.

Backscheider, Paula R. *Spectacular Politics: Theatrical Power and Mass Culture in Early Modern England*. Baltimore: Johns Hopkins University Press, 1993.

Bacon, Sir Francis. *New Organon*. In *New Organon and Related Writings*. Ed. Fulton H. Anderson. Indianapolis: Bobbs-Merrill, 1960, 31–268.

———. *The Works of Francis Bacon, Baron of Verulam, Viscount St. Alban, and Lord High Chancellor of England*. Ed. James Spedding, Robert Leslie Ellis, and Douglas Denon Heath. 14 vols. 1857–1874. Rpt. New York: Garrett Press, 1968.

———. *The Advancement of Learning and New Atlantis*. Ed. Arthur Johnston. Oxford: Clarendon Press, 1974.

———. *The Essayes or Counsels, Civill and Morall*. Ed. Michael Kiernan. The Oxford Francis Bacon 15. Oxford: Clarendon Press, 1985.

Bakhurst, David. "Social Memory in Soviet Thought." In *Collective Remembering*. Ed. David Middleton and Derek Edwards. Inquiries in Social Construction. London: SAGE Publications, 1990, 203–26.

Ballaster, Ros, Margaret Beetham, Elizabeth Frazer, and Sandra Hebron. *Women's Worlds: Ideology, Femininity, and the Woman's Magazine*. London: Macmillan, 1991.

Baraka, Imamu Amiri. *Black Music*. New York: William Morrow, 1967.

Barchas, Janine. "Richardson on the Margins: An Introduction to the Bradshaigh *Clarissa*." In *The Annotations in Lady Bradshaigh's Copy of Clarissa*. Ed. Janine Barchas and Gordon D. Fulton. ELS Monograph Series No. 76. Victoria: University of Victoria, 1998, 8–42.

Barker, Francis. *The Tremulous Private Body: Essays on Subjection*. London: Methuen, 1984.

Batey, Mavis. *Alexander Pope: The Poet and the Landscape*. London: Barn Elms, 1999.

Beal, Peter. *In Praise of Scribes: Manuscripts and Their Makers in Seventeenth-Century England*. Oxford: Clarendon Press, 1998.

Beale, Philip. *A History of the Post in England from the Romans to the Stuarts*. Aldershot:Ashgate, 1998.

Beasley, Jerry C. "Richardson's Girls: The Daughters of Patriarchy in *Pamela, Clarissa*, and *Sir Charles Grandison*." In Rivero, *New Essays on Samuel Richardson*, 35–52.

Behn, Aphra. *The Works of Aphra Behn*. Ed. Janet Todd. 7 vols. Columbus: Ohio State University Press, 1992–1996.

———. *Oroonoko: Or, The Royal Slave. A True History*. Ed. Joanna Lipking. Norton Critical Editions. New York: W.W. Norton & Company, 1997.

Ben Jonson's 1616 Folio. Ed. Jennifer Brady and W. H. Herendeen. Newark: University of Delaware Press, 1991.

Berger, Jr., Harry. "The Pepys Show: Ghost-Writing and Documentary Desire in *The Diary*." *ELH* 65 (1998): 557–91.

Bernard-Donals, Michael. "Beyond the Question of Authenticity: Witness and Testimony in the *Fragments* Controversy." *PMLA* 116 (2001): 1302–15.

Blaine, Marlin E. "Milton and the Monument Topos: 'On Shakespeare,' 'Ad Joannem Rousium,' and *Poems* (1645)." *Journal of English and Germanic Philology* 99 (2000): 215–34.

Blouin, Jr., Francis X. "History and Memory: The Problem of the Archive." *PMLA* 119 (2004): 296–98.

Bloy, C.H. *A History of Printing Ink, Balls and Rollers, 1440–1850*. London: The Wynkyn de Worde Society, 1967.

Blum, Abbe. "The Author's Authority: *Areopagitica* and the Labour of Licensing." In Nyquist and Ferguson, *Re-membering Milton*, 74–96.

Borges, Jorge Luis. *Labyrinths: Selected Stories and Other Writings*. Ed. Donald A. Yates and James E. Irby. New York: New Directions Publishing Corp., 1964.

Bradstreet, Anne. *The Tenth Muse Lately sprung up in America. Or Severall Poems, compiled with great variety of Wit and Learning, full of delight. Wherein especially is contained a compleat discourse and description of The Four Elements, Constitutions, Ages of Man, Seasons of the Year. Together with an Exact Epitomie of the Four Monarchies, viz. The Assyrian, Persian, Grecian, Roman. Also a Dialogue between Old England and New, concerning the late troubles. With divers other pleasant and serious Poems*. London, 1650.

Braudy, Leo. *The Frenzy of Renown: Fame and Its History*. Oxford: Oxford University Press, 1986.

Brown, Laura. *Alexander Pope*. Oxford: Blackwell, 1985.

Browne, Christopher. *Getting the Message: The Story of the British Post Office*. Dover, New Hampshire: Alan Sutton, 1993.

Brownell, Morris R. *Alexander Pope and the Arts of Georgian England.* Oxford: Clarendon Press, 1978.

Burke, Peter. "History as Social Memory." In *Memory: History, Culture and the Mind.* Ed. Thomas Butler. Wolfson College Lectures. Oxford: Basil Blackwell, 1989, 97–113.

Campbell, R. *The London Tradesman. Being an Historical Account of All the Trades, Professions, Arts, both Liberal and Mechanic, now practiced in the Cities of London and Westminster. Calculated for the Instruction of Youth in their Choice of Business.* Third ed. London, 1765.

Carlson, David R. *English Humanist Books: Writers and Patrons, Manuscript and Print, 1475–1525.* Toronto: University of Toronto Press, 1993.

———. "Chaucer, Humanism, and Printing." *University of Toronto Quarterly* 64 (1995): 274–88.

———. *Chaucer's Jobs. The New Middle Ages.* London: Palgrave Macmillan, 2004.

Carruthers, Mary. *The Book of Memory: A Study of Memory in Medieval Culture.* Cambridge: Cambridge University Press, 1990.

Carvalho, David N. *Forty Centuries of Ink: or, A Chronological Narrative Concerning Ink and Its Backgrounds.* New York: The Banks Law Publishing Co., 1904.

Catty, Jocelyn. *Writing Rape, Writing Women in Early Modern England: Unbridled Speech.* London: Macmillan Press, 1999.

Cave, Edward. *The Gentleman's Magazine, or Trader's Monthly Intelligencer.* London: January, 1731.

Cavendish, Margaret, duchess of Newcastle. *CCXI Sociable Letters.* London, 1664.

———. *The Life of William Cavendish Duke of Newcastle To Which is Added The True Relation of My Birth Breeding and Life.* Ed. C.H. Firth. Second ed. London: George Routledge & Sons, 1906.

———. *Poems, and Fancies.* London, 1653.

———. *The Philosophical and Physical Opinions.* London, 1655.

———. *The Worlds Olio.* London, 1655.

———. *Natures Pictures Drawn by Fancies Pencil to the Life.* London, 1656.

———. *Playes.* London, 1662.

———. *CCXI Sociable Letters,* 1664.

———. *Observations upon Experimental Philosophy. To which is added, The Description of a New Blazing World.* London, 1666.

———. *Plays, Never before Printed.* London, 1668.

———. *The Worlds Olio.* The Second Edition. London, 1671.

———. *The Life of William Cavendish . . .,* 1906.

Chalmers, Hero. "Dismantling the Myth of 'Mad Madge': The Cultural Context of Margaret Cavendish's Authorial Self-Presentation." *Women's Writing* 4 (1997): 323–39.

Chambers, Ephraim. *Cyclopaedia: Or, An Universal Dictionary of Arts and Sciences; Containing the Definitions of the Terms, And Accounts of the Things Signify'd Thereby, In the Several Arts, Both Liberal and Mechanical, and the Several Sciences, Human and Divine: The Figures, Kinds, Properties, Productions, Preparations, and Uses, of Things Natural and Artificial; The Rise, Progress and State of Things Ecclesiatical, Civil, Military, and Commercial: With the Several Systems, Sects, Opinions, &c. Among Philosophers, Divines, Mathematicians, Physicians, Antiquaries, Criticks, &c. The Whole Intended as a Course of Antient and Modern LEARNING, Compiled from the Best Authors, Dictionaries, Journals, Memoirs, Transactions, Ephemerides, &c, in Several Languages.* 2 vols. London, 1728.

Chandler, Eric V. "Pope's 'Girl of the Game': The Prostitution of the Author and the Business of Culture." In Ingrassia and Thomas, *"More Solid Learning": New Perspectives on Pope's Dunciad*, 106–28.

Chandler, James. "About Loss: W.G. Sebald's Romantic Art of Memory." *South Atlantic Quarterly* 102 (2003): 235–62.

Charleton, Walter. *Chorea Gigantum; or, the most Famous antiquity of Great-Britain, vulgarly called Stone-Heng, standing on Salisbury plain, restored to the Danes.* London, 1663.

Charron, Peter. *Of Wisdome: Three Bookes.* Trans. Samson Lennard. n.d. Rpt. Amsterdam: Da Capo Press, 1971.

Chartier, Roger. *The Order of Books: Readers, Authors, and Libraries in Europe between the Fourteenth and Eighteenth Centuries.* Trans. Lydia G. Cochrane. Stanford: Stanford University Press, 1994.

Chaucer, Geoffrey. *The Canterbury Tales.* In *The Riverside Chaucer.* Ed. Larry D. Benson. Third ed. Boston: Houghton Mifflin, 1978.

Childs, David. *The Fall of the GDR: Germany's Road to Unity.* Themes in Modern German History Series. London: Longman, 2001.

Chippindale, Christopher. *Stonehenge Complete.* Third ed. New York: Thames & Hudson, 2004.

Churchyard, Thomas. *A Sparke of Frendship and Warme Goodwill, That Shewes the Effect of Trve Affection and Vnfoldes the finenesse of this world. Whereunto is ioined, the commoditie of sundrie Sciences, the benefit that paper bringeth, with many rare matters rehearsed in the same: with a description & commendation of a Paper Mill, now and of late set vp (neere the Towne of Darthford) by an high Germayn called M. Spilman, Ieweller to the Qu. most excellent Maiestie.* London, 1588.

Clanchy, M.T. *From Memory to Written Record: England, 1066–1307.* Cambridge: Harvard University Press, 1979.

Clarke, Adele. "Modernity, Postmodernity and Reproductive Processes ca. 1890–1990, or 'Mommy, Where Do Cyborgs Come From Anyway?'" In Gray, Figueroa-Sarriera, and Mentor, *The Cyborg Handbook*, 139–55.

Clegg, Cyndia Susan. *Press Censorship in Jacobean England.* Cambridge: Cambridge University Press, 2001.

Clifford, James. *The Predicament of Culture: Twentieth-Century Ethnography, Literature, and Art.* Cambridge: Harvard University Press, 1988.

Clucas, Stephen. "Introduction." In *A Princely Brave Woman: Essays on Margaret Cavendish, Duchess of Newcastle.* Ed. Stephen Clucas. Aldershot: Ashgate, 2003, 1–15.

Coffey, John. "Pacifist, Quietist, or Patient Militant? John Milton and the Restoration." *Milton Studies* 42 (2002): 149–74.

Coiro, Ann Baynes. "Milton and Class Identity: The Publication of *Areopagitica* and the 1645 *Poems.*" *Journal of Medieval and Renaissance Studies* 22 (1992): 261–89.

———. "Fable and Old Song: *Samson Agonistes* and the Idea of a Poetic Career." *Milton Studies* 36 (1998): 123–52.

Collins, An. *Divine Songs and Meditacions.* Ed. Sidney Gottlieb. Tempe: Medieval and Renaissance Texts and Studies, 1996.

Connell, Philip. "Death and the Author: Westminster Abbey and the Meanings of the Literary Monument." *Eighteenth-Century Studies* 38 (2005): 557–85.

Connerton, Paul. *How Societies Remember.* Cambridge: Cambridge University Press, 1989.

Corns, Thomas N. "'With Unaltered Brow': Milton and the Son of God." *Milton Studies* 42 (2002): 106–21.

Cowell, Pattie. "The Early Distribution of Anne Bradstreet's Poem." In *Critical Essays on Anne Bradstreet*. Ed. Pattie Cowell and Ann Stanford. Boston: G.K. Hall, 1983, 270–79.

Crawford, Patricia. "Women's Published Writings, 1660–1700." In *Women in English Society, 1500–1800*. Ed. Mary Prior. London: Methuen, 1985, 211–82.

Cressy, David. *Bonfires and Bells: National Memory and the Protestant Calendar in Elizabethan and Stuart England*. London: Weidenfeld and Nicolson, 1989.

———. "National Memory in Early Modern England." In Gillis, *Commemorations: The Politics of National Identity*, 61–73.

Crews, Frederick and His Critics. *The Memory Wars: Freud's Legacy in Dispute!* New York: New York Review of Books, 1995.

Critical Remarks on Sir Charles Grandison, Clarissa and Pamela. Enquiring, Whether they have a Tendency to corrupt or improve the Public Taste and Morals. In a Letter to the Author. By a Lover of Virtue. London, 1754.

Daphinoff, Dimiter. *An Alternative Ending to Richardson's Clarissa*. Swiss Studies in English, Vol. 107. Bern: Francke Verlag, 1982.

Delany, Sheila. *Chaucer's House of Fame: The Poetics of Skeptical Fideism*. Chicago: University of Chicago Press, 1972.

De Quincey, Thomas. *The Collected Writings of Thomas De Quincey: New and Enlarged Edition*. Ed. David Masson. 14 vols. Edinburgh: Adam and Charles Black, 1890.

Derrida, Jacques. *Archive Fever: A Freudian Impression*. Trans. Eric Prenowitz. Chicago: University of Chicago Press, 1996.

Deutsch, Helen. *Resemblance and Disgrace: Alexander Pope and the Deformation of Culture*. Cambridge: Harvard University Press, 1996.

Dictionaries of the Printers and Booksellers Who Were at Work in England, Scotland and Ireland 1557–1775. Ed. H.R. Plomer, et al. Yorkshire: The Bibliographical Society, 1977.

Dictionary of Biological Psychology. Ed. Philip Winn. London: Routledge, 2001.

Dietz, Michael. "'Thus sang the uncouth Swain': Pastoral, Prophecy, and Historicism in *Lycidas*." *Milton Studies* 35 (1997): 42–72.

Dobranski, Stephen B. *Milton, Authorship, and the Book Trade*. Cambridge: Cambridge University Press, 1999.

Dolan, Frances E. "Ashes and 'the Archive': The London Fire of 1666, Partisanship, and Proof." *The Journal of Medieval and Early Modern Studies* 31(2001): 379–408.

Donne, John. *John Donne: The Divine Poems*. Ed. Helen Gardner. Oxford: Clarendon Press, 1952.

———. *The Sermons of John Donne*. Ed. George R. Potter and Evelyn M. Simpson. 10 vols. Berkeley: University of California Press, 1953–1962.

———. *John Donne: Selected Letters*. Ed. P.M. Oliver. Manchester: Carcanet Press, 2002.

Donoghue, Frank. *The Fame Machine: Book Reviewing and Eighteenth-Century Literary Careers*. Stanford: Stanford University Press, 1996.

Drury, John. *The Reformed Librarie-Keeper with a Supplement to the Reformed-School, as Subordinate to Colleges in Universities*. London, 1650.

Dryden, John. *The Works of John Dryden*. Ed. Edward N. Hooker, H.T. Swedenburg, Jr., et al. 20 vols. Berkeley: University of California Press, 1956–2005.

Duthie, George. *Elizabethan Shorthand and the First Quarto of King Lear.* Oxford: Basil Blackwell, 1949.

Duttlinger, Carolin. "Traumatic Photographs: Remembrance and the Technical Media in W.G. Sebald's *Austerlitz.*" In *W.G. Sebald—A Critical Companion.* Ed. J.J. Long and Anne Whitehead. Literary Conjugations Series. Seattle: University of Washington Press, 2004, 155–71.

Eagleton, Terry. *The Rape of Clarissa: Writing, Sexuality, and Class Struggle in Samuel Richardson.* Oxford: Basil Blackwell, 1982.

Eberwein, Jane Donahue. " 'No Rhet'ric We Expect': Argumentation in Bradstreet's 'The Prologue.' " In Cowell and Stanford, *Critical Essays on Anne Bradstreet,* 218–25.

Edelman, Gerald M. *The Remembered Present: A Biological Theory of Consciousness.* New York: Basic Books, 1989.

———. *Bright Air, Brilliant Fire.* New York: Basic Books, 1992.

Egan, James. "*Areopagitica* and the Tolerationist Rhetorics of the 1640s." *Milton Studies* 46 (2007): 165–90.

Eisenstein, Elizabeth L. *The Printing Press as an Agent of Change: Communications and Cultural Transformations in Early-Modern Europe.* Cambridge: Cambridge University Press, 1980.

Elliott, Robert C. *The Power of Satire: Magic, Ritual, Art.* Princeton: Princeton University Press, 1960.

Epistolary Histories: Letters, Fiction, Culture. Ed. Amanda Gilroy and W.M. Verhoeven. Charlottesville: University Press of Virginia, 2000.

Evans, J. Martin. *The Miltonic Moment.* Lexington: The University Press of Kentucky, 1998.

Evelyn, John. *The Diary of John Evelyn.* Ed. E.S. De Beer. 6 vols. Oxford: Clarendon Press, 1955.

Ezell, Margaret J.M. " 'By a Lady': The Mask of the Feminine in Restoration, Early Eighteenth-Century Print Culture." In Griffin, *The Faces of Anonymity,* 63–79.

———. *The Patriarch's Wife: Literary Evidence and the History of the Family.* Chapel Hill: University of North Carolina Press, 1987.

———. *Writing Women's Literary History.* Baltimore: Johns Hopkins University Press, 1993.

———. *Social Authorship and the Advent of Print.* Baltimore: Johns Hopkins University Press, 1999.

False Memories and Recovered Memories. Ed. M.A. Conway. Oxford: Oxford University Press, 1997.

Fanning, Christopher. "Small Particles of Eloquence: Sterne and the Scriblerian Text." *Modern Philology* 100 (2003): 360–92.

Favret, Mary A. *Romantic Correspondence: Women, Politics, and the Fiction of Letters.* Cambridge: Cambridge University Press, 1993.

Feather, John P. and David McKitterick. *The History of Books and Libraries: Two Views.* Washington, D.C.: Library of Congress, 1986.

Feminist Readings of Early Modern Culture: Emerging Subjects. Ed. Valerie Traub, M. Lindsay Kaplen, and Dympna Callaghan. Cambridge: Cambridge University Press, 1996.

Fentress, James and Chris Wickham. *Social Memory.* Oxford: Basil Blackwell, 1992.

Ferguson, Arthur B. *Clio Unbound: Perception of the Social and Cultural Past in Renaissance England*. Duke Monographs in Medieval and Renaissance Studies 2. Durham: Duke University Press, 1979.

Ferguson, Margaret. "Renaissance Conceptions of the 'Woman Writer.'" In Wilcox, *Women and Literature in Britain, 1500–1700*, 143–68.

Fielding, Henry. *The Jacobite's Journal and Related Writings*. Ed. W.B. Coley. Oxford: Oxford University Press, 1975.

Fielding, Sarah. *Remarks on Clarissa, Addressed to the Author. Occasioned by some critical Conversations on the Characters and Conduct of that Work. With Some Reflections on the Character and Behaviour of Prior's EMMA*. London, 1749. Rpt. Los Angeles: William Andrews Clark Memorial Library, 1985.

Fish, Stanley. "Spectacle and Evidence in *Samson Agonistes*." *Critical Inquiry* 15 (1989): 556-86.

———. *How Milton Works*. Cambridge: Harvard University Press, 2001.

Fitzmaurice, James. "Front Matter and the Physical Make-Up of *Natures Pictures*." *Women's Writing* 4 (1997): 353–67.

Fleming, Ian. *Diamonds Are Forever*. New York: Berkley Books, 1982.

Fletcher, Harris Francis. *The Intellectual Development of John Milton*. 2 vols. Urbana: University of Illinois Press, 1961.

Flint, Christopher. "In Other Words: Eighteenth-Century Authorship and the Ornaments of Print." *Eighteenth-Century Fiction* 14 (2002): 627–72.

Flynn, Carol Houlihan. *Samuel Richardson: A Man of Letters*. Princeton: Princeton University Press, 1982.

Flynn, Carol Houlihan and Edward Copeland, eds. *Clarissa and Her Readers: New Essays for the Clarissa Project*. New York: AMS Press, Inc., 1999.

Fortescue, George K., ed. *Catalogue of the Pamphlets, Books, Newspapers, and Manuscripts Relating to the Civil War, the Commonwealth, and Restoration, Collected by George Thomason, 1640–1661*. 2 vols. London: British Museum, 1908.

Foucault, Michel. "What Is an Author?" In *Textual Strategies: Perspectives in Post-Structuralist Criticism*. Ed. Josue V. Harari. Ithaca: Cornell University Press, 1979, 141–60.

Fox, Adam. "Custom, Memory and the Authority of Writing." In *The Experience of Authority in Early Modern England*. Ed. Paul Griffiths, Adam Fox, and Steve Hindle. New York: St. Martin's Press, 1996, 89–116.

Foxon, David. *Pope and the Early Eighteenth-Century Book Trade*. Ed. James McLaverty. Lyell Lectures, Oxford 1975–1976. Oxford: Clarendon Press, 1991.

Friedlander, Saul. *Memory, History and the Extermination of the Jews of Europe*. Bloomington: University of Indiana Press, 1993.

Fukuyama, Francis. "The End of History?" *The National Interest* 16 (1989): 3–18.

———. *The End of History and the Last Man*. New York: Macmillan, 1992.

Fulton, Alice. *Feeling as a Foreign Language: The Good Strangeness of Poetry*. Saint Paul, Minn: Graywolf Press, 1999.

Gallagher, Catherine. *Nobody's Story: The Vanishing Acts of Women Writers in the Marketplace, 1670–1820*. Berkeley: University of California Press, 1994.

Geary, Patrick J. *Phantoms of Remembrance: Memory and Oblivion at the End of the First Millennium*. Princeton: Princeton University Press, 1994.

Genette, Gerard. *Paratexts: Thresholds of Interpretation*. Trans. Jane E. Lewin. Cambridge: Cambridge University Press, 1997.

Gillis, John R., ed. *Commemorations: The Politics of National Identity.* Princeton: Princeton University Press, 1994.

Goldberg, Jonathan. *Writing Matter: From the Hands of the English Renaissance.* Stanford: Stanford University Press, 1990.

———. *Desiring Women Writing: English Renaissance Examples.* Stanford: Stanford University Press, 1997.

Gottlieb, Sidney. "An Collins and the Experience of Defeat." In *Representing Women in Renaissance England.* Ed. Claude J. Summers and Ted-Larry Pebworth. Columbia: University of Missouri Press, 1997, 121–35.

Grafton, Anthony. "The Ways of Genius." *The New York Review of Books* 51.19 (December 2, 2004): 38–40.

Gray, Chris Hables. "An Interview with Manfred Clynes." In Gray, Figueroa-Sarriera, and Mentor, *The Cyborg Handbook,* 43–53.

Gray, Chris Hables, Heidi J. Figueroa-Sarriera, and Steven Mentor, eds. *The Cyborg Handbook.* London: Routledge, 1995.

Greenblatt, Stephen. *Will in the World: How Shakespeare Became Shakespeare.* New York: W.W. Norton, 2004.

Greer, Germaine. *Slip-Shod Sibyls: Recognition, Rejection and the Woman Poet.* London: Viking, 1995.

Griffin, Dustin. *Literary Patronage in England, 1650–1800.* Cambridge: Cambridge University Press, 1996.

Griffin, Robert J. "Introduction." In *The Faces of Anonymity: Anonymous and Pseudonymous Publication from the Sixteenth to the Twentieth Century.* Ed. Robert J. Griffin. New York: Palgrave Macmillan, 2003, 1–17.

Guibbory, Achsah. *The Map of Time: Seventeenth-Century English Literature and Ideas of Pattern in History.* Urbana: University of Illinois Press, 1986.

Guillory, John. "Dalila's House: *Samson Agonistes* and the Sexual Division of Labor." In *Rewriting the Renaissance: The Discourses of Sexual Difference in Early Modern Europe.* Ed. Margaret W. Ferguson, Maureen Quilligan, and Nancy J. Vickers. Chicago: University of Chicago Press, 1986, 106–22.

———. "The Father's House: *Samson Agonistes* in Its Historical Moment." In Nyquist, and Ferguson, *Re-membering Milton,* 148–76.

Guttenplan, D.D. *The Holocaust on Trial.* New York: Norton, 2001.

Halbwachs, Maurice. *The Collective Memory.* Trans. Francis J. Ditter, Jr. and Vida Yazdi Ditter. New York: Harper & Row, 1980.

———. *The Social Frameworks of Memory.* In *On Collective Memory.* Ed. and trans. Lewis A. Coser. The Heritage of Sociology. Chicago: University of Chicago Press, 1992, 37–189.

Hamilton, Carolyn, Verne Harris, and Graeme Reid. "Introduction." In *Refiguring the Archive.* Ed. Carolyn Hamilton, Verne Harris, Jane Taylor, Michèle Pickover, Graeme Reid, and Razia Saleh. Dordrecht, Netherlands: Kluwer Academic Publishers, 2002, 7–17.

Hammond, Brean S. *Professional Imaginative Writing in England 1670–1740: "Hackney for Bread."* Oxford: Clarendon Press, 1997.

Hanson, Elizabeth. "To Smite Once and Yet Once More: The Transactions of Milton's *Lycidas.*" *Milton Studies* 25 (1989): 69–88.

Haraway, Donna J. *Primate Visions: Gender, Race, and Nature in the World of Modern Science.* London: Routledge, 1989.

———. *Simians, Cyborgs, and Women: The Reinvention of Nature.* New York: Routledge, 1991.

————. *Modest_Witness@Second_Millennium. FemaleMan©_Meets_ OncoMouse*™: *Feminism and Technoscience*. London: Routledge, 1997.

Harris, Jocelyn. "Grotesque, Classical and Pornographic Bodies in *Clarissa*." In Rivero, *New Essays on Samuel Richardson*, 101–16.

Harris, Michael. "Periodicals and the Book Trade." In *Development of the English Book Trade, 1700–1899*. Ed. Robin Myers and Michael Harris. Publishing Pathways Series. Oxford: Oxford Polytechnic Press, 1981, 66–94.

Harris, Tim. *London Crowds in the Reign of Charles II: Propaganda and Politics from the Restoration until the Exclusion Crisis*. Cambridge: Cambridge University Press, 1987.

Haskin, Dayton. *Milton's Burden of Interpretation*. Philadelphia: University of Pennsylvania Press, 1994.

Helgerson, Richard. *Self-Crowned Laureates: Spenser, Jonson, Milton and the Literary System*. Berkeley: University of California Press, 1983.

————. "Milton Reads the King's Book: Print, Performance, and the Making of a Bourgeois Idol." *Criticism* 29 (1987): 1–25.

————. *Forms of Nationhood: The Elizabethan Writing of England*. Chicago: University of Chicago Press, 1992.

Hensley, Jeannine. "Anne Bradstreet's Wreath of Thyme." In *The Works of Anne Bradstreet*. Ed. Jeannine Hensley. Cambridge: Belknap Press, 1967, xxiii–xxxvi.

Hirsch, Marianne. *Family Frames: Photography, Narrative, and Postmemory*. Cambridge: Harvard University Press, 1997.

————. "Surviving Images: Holocaust Photographs and the Work of Postmemory." *The Yale Journal of Criticism* 14 (2001): 5–37.

Hobbes, Thomas. "The Answer of Mr Hobbes to Sr Will. Davenant's Preface Before Gondibert." In *Gondibert: An Heroicke Poem, Written by Sr William Davenant*. London, 1651.

Hobby, Elaine. *Virtue of Necessity: English Women's Writing 1649–88*. Ann Arbor: University of Michigan Press, 1988.

Hobsbawm, Eric. "Introduction: Inventing Tradition." In *The Invention of Tradition*. Ed. Eric Hobsbawm and Terence Ranger. Past and Present Publications. Cambridge: Cambridge University Press, 1983, 1–14.

Horace. *Horace: The Odes and Epodes*. Trans. C.E. Bennett. The Loeb Classical Library. Cambridge: Harvard University Press, 1968.

Hunter, Dard. *Papermaking: The History and Technique of an Ancient Craft*. New York: Alfred A. Knopf, 1943.

Hunter, J. Paul. *Before Novels: The Cultural Contexts of Eighteenth-Century English Fiction*. New York: Norton, 1990.

————. "From Typology to Type: Agents of Change in Eighteenth-Century English Texts." In *Cultural Artifacts and the Production of Meaning: The Page, the Image, and the Body*. Ed. Margaret J.M. Ezell and Katherine O'Brien O'Keefe. Ann Arbor: University of Michigan Press, 1994, 41–69.

Huyssen, Andreas. *Twilight Memories: Marking Time in a Culture of Amnesia*. London: Routledge, 1995.

Ingrassia, Catherine. *Authorship, Commerce, and Gender in Early Eighteenth-Century England: A Culture of Paper Credit*. Cambridge: Cambridge University Press, 1998.

————. "Dissecting the Authorial Body: Pope, Curll, and the Portrait of a 'Hack Writer.'" In Ingrassia and Thomas, *More Solid Learning: New Perspectives on Pope's Dunciad*, 147–65.

Ingrassia, Catherine and Claudia N. Thomas. "Introduction: 'More Solid Learning.'" In *More Solid Learning: New Perspectives on Pope's Dunciad*. Ed. Catherine Ingrassia and Claudia N. Thomas. Lewisburg: Bucknell University Press, 2000, 13–32.

Irwin, Raymond. *The Origins of the English Library*. London: George Allen & Unwin Ltd, 1958.

———. *The English Library: Sources and History*. London: Allen & Unwin, 1966.

Jaggi, Maya. "Edited conversation [with W.G. Sebald] on 24 September 2001." In "The Last Word," December 21, 2001. *Guardian Unlimited Books*, http://books.guardian.co.uk/departments/generalfiction/story/0,6000,624750,00.html

Jenkins, Rhys. *Paper-Making in England 1495–1788*. A.A.L. Reprints No. 5. London: Association of Assistant Librarians, 1958.

Johnson, Elmer D. and Michael H. Harris. *History of Libraries in the Western World*. Third ed. Metuchen, N.J.: The Scarecrow Press, 1976.

Johnson, Samuel. *Lives of the English Poets*. Ed. George Birkbeck Hill. 3 vols. 1905. Rpt. New York: Octagon Books, 1967.

Jones, Ann Rosalind. *The Currency of Eros: Women's Love Lyric in Europe, 1540–1620*. Bloomington: Indiana University Press, 1990.

Jones, Ann Rosalind and Peter Stallybrass. *Renaissance Clothing and the Materials of Memory*. Cambridge: Cambridge University Press, 2000.

Jones, Emrys. "Pope and Dulness." In Mack and Winn, *Pope: Recent Essays by Several Hands*, 612–51.

Jones, Inigo and John Webb. *The Most Notable Antiquity of Great Britain, Vulgarly Called Stone-heng, on Salisbury Plain, Restored*. London, 1655.

Jones, Kathleen. *A Glorious Fame: The Life of Margaret Cavendish, Duchess of Newcastle, 1623–1673*. London: Bloomsbury, 1988.

Jonson, Ben. *The New Inne*. In *The Complete Plays of Ben Jonson*. Ed. G.A. Wilkes. 4 vols. Oxford: Clarendon Press, 1981–1982. 4: 363–473.

———. *Ben Jonson*. Ed. Ian Donaldson. The Oxford Authors. Oxford: Oxford University Press, 1985.

Jordan, John E. *Thomas De Quincey Literary Critic: His Method and Achievement*. Berkeley: University of California Press, 1952.

Justice, Steven. *Writing and Rebellion: England in 1381*. Berkeley: University of California Press, 1996.

Keeble, N.H. "Wilderness Exercises: Adversity, Temptation, and Trial in *Paradise Regained*." *Milton Studies* 42 (2002): 86–105.

Kelley, Donald R. and David Harris Sacks. "Preface" to *The Historical Imagination in Early Modern Britain: History, Rhetoric, and Fiction, 1500–1800*. Ed. Kelley and Sacks. Woodrow Wilson Center Series. Cambridge: Cambridge University Press, 1997, ix–xii.

Keymer, Thomas "Richardson's *Meditations*: Clarissa's *Clarissa*." In *Samuel Richardson: Tercentenary Essays*. Ed. Margaret Anne Doody and Peter Sabor. Cambridge: Cambridge University Press, 1989, 89–109.

———. *Richardson's Clarissa and the Eighteenth-Century Reader*. Cambridge Studies in Eighteenth-Century English Literature and Thought 13. Cambridge: Cambridge University Press, 1992.

Keymer, Thomas and Peter Sabor. *Pamela in the Marketplace: Literary Controversy and Print Culture in Eighteenth-Century Britain and Ireland*. Cambridge: Cambridge University Press, 2005.

Kinkead-Weekes, Mark. *Samuel Richardson: Dramatic Novelist*. Ithaca: Cornell University Press, 1973.

Kinsley, William. "The Dunciad as Mock-Book." In Mack and Winn, *Pope: Recent Essays by Several Hands,* 707–28.

Kiš, Danilo. *The Encyclopedia of the Dead.* Trans. Michael Henry Heim. Evanston: Northwestern University Press, 1997.

Klein, Kerwin Lee. "On the Emergence of *Memory* in Historical Discourse." *Representations* 69 (2000): 127–50.

Klinge, Markus. "The Grotesque in *Areopagitica.*" *Milton Studies* 45 (2006): 82–128.

Knoppers, Laura Lunger. *Historicizing Milton: Spectacle, Power, and Poetry in Restoration England.* Athens: University of Georgia Press, 1994.

———. "Satan and the Papacy in *Paradise Regained.*" *Milton Studies* 42 (2002): 68–85.

Koonce, B.G. *Chaucer and the Tradition of Fame: Symbolism in the House of Fame.* Princeton: Princeton University Press, 1966.

Kotler, Steven. "The Genius Who Sticks Around Forever." *The New York Times,* June 11, 2000, p. SM102.

Kotre, John. *White Gloves: How We Create Ourselves Through Memory.* New York: Free Press, 1995.

Kramnick, Jonathan Brody. *Making the English Canon: Print-Capitalism and the Cultural Past, 1700–1770.* Cambridge: Cambridge University Press, 1998.

Kreisel, Deanna. "Stealing the Pen: Spectacles of Abdication in Richardson's *Clarissa.*" An unpublished essay.

Kroll, Richard W.F. *The Material Word: Literate Culture in the Restoration and Early Eighteenth Century.* Baltimore: The Johns Hopkins University Press, 1991.

Krontiris, Tina. *Oppositional Voices: Women as Writers and Translators of Literature in the English Renaissance.* London: Routledge, 1992.

LaCapra, Dominick. *History and Memory after Auschwitz.* Ithaca: Cornell University Press, 1998.

Lamb, Mary Ellen. *Gender and Authorship in the Sidney Circle.* Madison: University of Wisconsin Press, 1990.

Lanyer, Aemilia. *The Poems of Aemila Lanyer: Salve Deus Rex Judaeorum.* Ed. Susanne Woods. Oxford: Oxford University Press, 1993.

Le Goff, Jacques. *History and Memory.* Trans. Steven Randall and Elizabeth Claman. New York: Columbia University Press, 1992.

Leonard, John. " 'Trembling Ears': The Historical Moment of *Lycidas.*" *The Journal of Medieval and Renaissance Studies* 21 (1991): 59–81.

Lerer, Seth. *Chaucer and His Readers: Imagining the Author in Late-Medieval England.* Princeton: Princeton University Press, 1993.

Letters and Poems in Honour of the Incomparable Princess, Margaret, Duchess of Newcastle. London: 1676.

Levine, Joseph M. *The Battle of the Books: History and Literature in the Augustine Age.* Ithaca: Cornell University Press, 1991.

Levinson, Sanford. *Written in Stone: Public Monuments in Changing Societies.* Durham: Duke University Press, 1998.

Levy, F.J. *Tudor Historical Thought.* 1967. Rpt. Toronto: University of Toronto Press, 2004.

Lewalski, Barbara K. *The Life of John Milton: A Critical Biography.* Oxford: Blackwell Publishers, 2000.

Lewis, Jayne Elizabeth. "Clarissa's Cruelty: Modern Fables of Moral Authority in *The History of a Young Lady.*" In Flynn and Copeland, *Clarissa and Her Readers: New Essays for the Clarissa Project,* 45–67.

Lieb, Michael. *Milton and the Culture of Violence*. Ithaca: Cornell University Press, 1994.

———. "'Our Living Dread': The God of *Samson Agonistes*." *Milton Studies* 33 (1996): 3–25.

Lilley, Kate. "True State Within: Women's Elegy 1640–1700." In *Women, Writing, History: 1640–1740*. Ed. Isobel Grundy and Susan Wiseman. London: B.T. Batsford, 1992, 72–92.

Lipstadt, Deborah E. *Denying the Holocaust: The Growing Assault on Truth and Memory*. New York: Penguin, 1993.

———. *History on Trial: My Day in Court with Daniel Irving*. New York: Ecco, 2005.

Locke, John. *An Essay Concerning Human Understanding*. Ed. Peter H. Nidditch. The Clarendon Edition of the Works of John Locke. Oxford: Clarendon Press, 1975.

Loewenstein, David. *Milton and the Drama of History: Historical Vision, Iconoclasm, and the Literary Imagination*. Cambridge: Cambridge University Press, 1990.

Loewenstein, Joseph. "The Script in the Marketplace." *Representations* 12 (1985): 101–14.

———. "For a History of Literary Property: John Wolfe's Reformation." *English Literary Renaissance* 18 (1988): 389–412.

———. "Printing and the 'Multitudinous Presse': The Contentious Texts of Jonson's Masques." In *Ben Jonson's 1616 Folio*, 168–91. Ed. Jennifer Brady and W.H. Herendeen. Newark: University of Delaware Press, 1991, 168–91.

Long, J.J. "History, Narrative, and Photography in W.G. Sebald's *Die Ausgewanderten*." *Modern Language Review* 98 (2003): 117–39.

Lounsbury, Thomas R. *The Text of Shakespeare. Its History from the Publication of the Quartos and Folios Down to and Including the Publication of the Editions of Pope and Theobald*. New York: Scribner's Sons, 1906.

Lubow, Arthur. Interview with G.W. Sebald. "Preoccupied With Death, but Still Funny." *New York Times*, December 11, 2001, section E, 1–2.

MacCallum, Hugh. "*Samson Agonistes*: The Deliverer as Judge." *Milton Studies* 23 (1987): 259-90.

Mack, Maynard. *The Garden and the City: Retreat and Politics in the Later Poetry of Pope 1731–1743*. Toronto: University of Toronto Press, 1969.

———. *Alexander Pope: A Life*. New York: Norton, 1985.

Mack, Maynard and James A. Winn, eds. *Pope: Recent Essays by Several Hands*. Hamden, Conn.: Archon, 1980.

Mackie, Erin. *Market a la Mode: Fashion, Commodity, and Gender in The Tatler and The Spectator*. Baltimore: The Johns Hopkins University Press, 1997.

MacLean, Gerald M. *Time's Witness: Historical Representation in English Poetry, 1603–1660*. Madison: University of Wisconsin Press, 1990.

Mann, Steve with Hal Niedzviecki. *Cyborg: Digital Destiny and Human Possibility in the Age of the Wearable Computer*. Canada: Doubleday, 2001.

Marshall, David. "Fatal Letters: Clarissa and the Death of Juilie." In Flynn and Copeland, *Clarissa and Her Readers*, 213–51.

Martin, Peter. *Pursuing Innocent Pleasures: The Gardening World of Alexander Pope*. Hamden, Conn.: Archon Books, 1984.

Marvell, Andrew. *The Poems and Letters of Andrew Marvell*. Ed. H.M. Margoliouth. 2 vols. Oxford: Clarendon Press, 1927.

———. *The Rehearsal Transpos'd and The Rehearsal Transpos'd, The Second Part*. Ed. D.I.B. Smith. Oxford: Clarendon Press, 1971.

Mbembe, Achille. "The Power of the Archive and Its Limits." In Hamilton et al., *Refiguring the Archive*, 19–26.

McDowell, Paula. *The Women of Grub Street: Press, Politics, and Gender in the London Literary Marketplace 1678–1730*. Oxford: Clarendon Press, 1998.

McGrath, Lynette. *Subjectivity and Women's Poetry in Early Modern England: "Why on the ridge should she desire to go?"* Aldershot: Ashgate, 2002.

McKeon, Michael. *The Origins of the English Novel, 1600–1740*. Baltimore: The Johns Hopkins University Press, 1987.

McKillop, Alan Dugald. *Samuel Richardson: Printer and Novelist*. 1936. Rpt. n.p.: Shoe String Press, 1960.

McKitterick, David. "Bibliography, Bibliophily, and the Organization of Knowledge." In *The Foundations of Scholarship: Libraries & Collecting, 1650–1750*. Papers Presented at a Clark Library Seminar, March 9, 1985, by David Vaisey and David McKitterick. Los Angeles: Clark Library, 1992, 29–61.

McLaverty, James. *Pope, Print, and Meaning*. Oxford: Oxford University Press, 2001.

Mendle, Michael. "De Facto Freedom, De Facto Authority: Press and Parliament, 1640–1643." *The Historical Journal* 38 (1995): 307–32.

Merton, Robert. "Priorities in Scientific Discovery: A Chapter in the Sociology of Science." *American Sociological Review* 22 (1957): 635–59.

Metz, Christian. "Photography and Fetish." In *The Critical Image: Essays on Contemporary Photography*. Ed. Carol Squiers. Seattle: Bay Press, 1990, 155–64.

Milton, John. *The Complete Prose Works of John Milton*. Ed. D.M. Wolfe et al. 8 vols. New Haven: Yale University Press, 1953–82.

———. *John Milton: Complete Poems and Major Prose*. Ed. Merritt Y. Hughes. The Odyssey Press. New York: The Bobbs-Merrill Company, 1957.

Misztal, Barbara A. *Theories of Social Remembering*. *Theorizing Society*. Maidenhead, Berks.: Open University Press, 2003.

Moore, Gordon E. "Cramming More Components onto Integrated Circuits." *Electronics* 38.8, April 19, 1965.

Moravec, Hans. *Mind Children: The Future of Robot and Human Intelligence*. Cambridge: Harvard University Press, 1988.

More, Henry. *A Platonick Song of the Soul*. Ed. Alexander Jacob. London: Associated University Presses, 1998.

Mottaki, Manouchehr. Opening Speech to "Review of the Holocaust: Global Vision." Online at the following website: http://www.ipis.ir/English/meetings_roundtables_conferences.htm

Mueller, Janel. "Just Measures? Versification in *Samson Agonistes*." *Milton Studies* 33 (1996): 47–82.

Murray, Timothy. *Theatrical Legitimation: Allegories of Genius in Seventeenth-Century England and France*. Oxford: Oxford University Press, 1987.

Musaeum Tradescantianum: or, A Collection of Rarities. Preserved at South Lambeth neer London. London, 1656.

The Myth of Repressed Memory: False Memories and Allegations of Sexual Abuse. Ed. Elizabeth F. Loftus and Katherine Ketcham. New York: St. Martin's Press, 1994.

Nalbantan, Suzanne. *Memory in Literature: From Rousseau to Neuroscience*. London: Palgrave Macmillan, 2003.

Naudé, Gabriel. *Instructions Concerning Erecting of a Library: Presented to My Lord The President De Mesme*. Trans. John Evelyn. London, 1661.

A New Philosophy of History. Ed. Frank Ankersmit and Hans Kellner. Chicago: University of Chicago Press, 1995.

Newton, Richard C. "Jonson and the (Re-)Invention of the Book." In *Classic and Cavalier: Essays on Jonson and the Sons of Ben*. Ed. Claude J. Summers and Ted-Larry Pebworth. Pittsburgh: University of Pittsburgh Press, 1982, 31–55.

Nicolay, Theresa Freda. *Gender Roles, Literary Authority, and Three American Woman Writers: Anne Dudley Bradstreet, Mercy Otis Warren, Margaret Fuller Ossoli*. New York: Peter Lang, 1995.

Nora, Pierre. "Between Memory and History: Les Lieux de Mémoire." *Representations* 26 (1989): 7–25.

Norbrook, David. "Republican Occasions in *Paradise Regained* and *Samson Agonistes*." *Milton Studies* 42 (2002): 122–48.

Novick, Peter. *The Holocaust in American Life*. Boston: Houghton Mifflin, 1999.

Nuttall, Sarah. "Literature and the Archive: The Biography of Texts." In Hamilton et al., *Refiguring the Archive*, 283–99.

Nyquist, Mary and Margaret W. Ferguson, eds. *Re-membering Milton: Essays on the Texts and Traditions*. New York: Methuen, 1987.

Osborne, Dorothy. *Letters to Sir William Temple*. Ed. Kenneth Parker. London: Penguin Books, 1987.

Ovenell, R.F. *The Ashmolean Museum 1683–1894*. Oxford: Clarendon Press, 1986.

Parker, Rozsika. *The Subversive Stitch: Embroidery and the Making of the Feminine*. London: The Woman's Press, 1984.

Parker, William Riley. *Milton: A Biography*. 2 vols. Oxford: Clarendon Press, 1968.

Particular Friends: The Correspondence of Samuel Pepys and John Evelyn. Ed. Guy de la Bédoyère. Woodbridge, Suffolk: The Boydell Press, 1997.

Pask, Kevin. *The Emergence of the English Author: Scripting the Life of the Poet in Early Modern England*. Cambridge: Cambridge University Press, 1996.

Patterson, Lee, ed: *Literary Practice and Social Change in Britain 1380–1530*. Berkeley: University of California Press, 1990.

———. *Chaucer and the Subject of History*. Madison: University of Wisconsin Press, 1991.

Peacey, Jason. *Politicians and Pamphleteers: Propaganda during the English Civil Wars and Interregnum*. Aldershot: Ashgate, 2004.

Pepys, Samuel. *The Diary of Samuel Pepys*. Ed. Robert Latham and William Matthews. 11 vols. Berkeley: University of California Press, 1970–1983.

Perdue, Cori. " 'The Spirit within Shall on the Heart Engrave': Milton's 'Live-long Monument.' " An unpublished essay.

Peterson, Bhekizizwe. "The Archives and the Political Imaginary." In Hamilton et al., *Refiguring the Archive*, 29–35.

Philip, Ian. *The Bodleian Library in the Seventeenth and Eighteenth Centuries*. Lyell Lectures, Oxford 1980–1981. Oxford: Clarendon Press, 1983.

Philips, Katherine. *The Collected Works of Katherine Philips: The Matchless Orinda. Volume I. The Poems*. Ed. Patrick Thomas. Essex: Stump Cross Books, 1990.

Pocock, J.G.A. *Politics, Language and Time: Essays on Political Thought and History*. New York: Atheneum, 1971.

———. *Virtue, Commerce, and History: Essays on Political Thought and History, Chiefly in the Eighteenth Century*. Cambridge: Cambridge University Press, 1985.

———. *The Ancient Constitution and the Feudal Law: A Study of English Historical Thought in the Seventeenth Century, A Reissue with a Retrospect*. Cambridge: Cambridge University Press, 1987.

Pope, Alexander. *The Poems of Alexander Pope*. Ed. John Butt et al. 11 vols. London: Methuen, 1939–69.

———. *The Correspondence of Alexander Pope*. Ed. George Sherburn. 5 vols. Oxford: Clarendon Press, 1956.

———. *Alexander Pope: Poems in Facsimile*. Ed. Geoffrey Day. Aldershot: Scolar, 1988.

———. *Pope's Dunciad of 1728: A History and Facsimile*. Ed. David L. Vander Meulen. Bibliographical Society of the University of Virginia. Charlottesville: University Press of Virginia, 1991.

Pope, Kenneth S. and Laura S. Brown. *Recovered Memories of Abuse: Assessment, Therapy, Forensics*. Psychotherapy Practitioner Resource Books. New York: American Psychological Association, 1996.

Popular Memory Group. "Popular Memory: Theory, Politics, Method." In *Making Histories: Studies in History-Writing and Politics*. Ed. Richard Johnson, Gregor McLennan, Bill Schwarz, and David Sutton. Centre for Contemporary Cultural Studies. London: Hutchinson, 1982, 205–52.

Powell, Anthony. *John Aubrey and His Friends*. New York: Charles Scribner's Sons, 1948.

Price, Bronwen. "Feminine Modes of Knowing and Scientific Enquiry: Margaret Cavendish's Poetry as Case Study." In Wilcox, *Women and Literature in Britain, 1500–1700*, 117–39.

Price, Leah. "Stenographic Masculinity." In *Literary Secretaries/ Secretarial Culture*. Ed. Leah Price and Pamela Thurschwell. Aldershot: Ashgate, 2005, 32–47.

Radzinowicz, Mary Ann. *Towards Samson Agonistes: The Growth of Milton's Mind*. Princeton: Princeton University Press, 1978.

Ralegh, Sir Walter. *The History of the World*. Ed. C.A. Patrides. Philadelphia: Temple University Press, 1971.

Ray, Gordon N. *Thackeray: The Age of Wisdom 1847–1863*. 1958. Rpt. New York: Octagon Books, 1972.

Ray, Larry. "Forward" to Misztal, *Theories of Social Remembering*, ix–xi.

Redford, Bruce. *The Converse of the Pen: Acts of Intimacy in the Eighteenth-Century Familiar Letter*. Chicago: The University of Chicago Press, 1986.

Rees, Emma L.E. "A Well-Spun Yarn: Margaret Cavendish, and Homer's Penelope." In Clucas, *A Princely Brave Woman*, 171–82.

Refiguring Chaucer in the Renaissance. Ed. Theresa M. Krier. Gainesville: University Press of Florida, 1998.

Reitan, E.A. "Introduction." *The Best of the Gentleman's Magazine 1731–1754*. Ed. E.A. Reitan. Studies in British History 4. Lewiston, N.Y.: Edwin Mellen, 1987, 1–23.

Representing Women in Renaissance England. Ed. Claude J. Summers and Ted-Larry Pebworth. Columbia: University of Missouri Press, 1997.

Revard, Stella P. *Milton and the Tangles of Neaera's Hair: The Making of the 1645 Poems*. Columbia: University of Missouri Press, 1997.

Richards, Thomas. *The Imperial Archive: Knowledge and the Fantasy of Empire*. London: Verso, 1993.

Richardson, Leslie. "The Perils of Prolixity: New Work on Reading and Writing *Clarissa*." *Eighteenth-Century Studies* 37 (2004): 314–19.

Richardson, Samuel. *Selected Letters of Samuel Richardson*. Ed. John Carroll. Oxford: Clarendon Press, 1964.

———. "Hints of Prefaces for Clarissa." In *Samuel Richardson, Clarissa: Preface, Hints of Prefaces, and Postscript*. Ed. R.F. Brissenden. The Augustan Reprint Society, Number 103. Los Angeles: William Andrews Clark Memorial Library, 1964.

————. *The Correspondence of Samuel Richardson*. Ed. Anna Laetitia Barbauld. 6 vols. 1804. Rpt. New York: AMS Press, 1966.

————. *Clarissa; or, The History of a Young Lady*. Ed. Angus Ross. New York: Penguin Books, 1985.

Samuel Richardson's Published Commentary on Clarissa, 1747–1765. Ed. Florian Stuber and Margaret Anne Doody. 3 vols. London: Pickering & Chatto, 1998.

Ricoeur, Paul. *Memory, History, Forgetting*. Chicago: University Press of Chicago, 2004.

Rivero, Albert J., ed. *New Essays on Samuel Richardson*. New York: St. Martin's Press, 1996.

Rogers, Pat. *Grub Street: Studies in a Subculture*. London: Methuen, 1972.

————. "Nameless Names: Pope, Curll, and the Uses of Anonymity." *New Literary History* 33 (2002): 233–45.

Root, Robert Kilburn. "Introduction." In *The Dunciad Variorum With the Prolegomena of Scriblerus by Alexander Pope. Reproduced in Facsimile from the First Issue of the Original Edition of 1729*. Princeton: Princeton University Press, 1929, 1–42.

Rose, Mark. "The Author as Proprietor: *Donaldson v. Beckett* and the Genealogy of Modern Authorship." *Representations* 23 (1988): 51–85.

————. *Authors and Owners: The Invention of Copyright*. Cambridge: Harvard University Press, 1993.

Rose, Mary Beth. "'Vigorous Most / When Most Unactive Deem'd': Gender and the Heroes of Endurance in Milton's *Samson Agonistes*, Aphra Behn's *Oroonoko*, and Mary Astell's *Some Reflections Upon Marriage*." *Milton Studies* 33 (1996): 83–109.

Rose, Steven. *The Making of Memory: From Molecules to Mind*. New York: Doubleday, 1992.

Rosenthal, Laura J. "'Trials of Manhood': Cibber, *The Dunciad*, and the Masculine Self." In Ingrassia and Thomas, *"More Solid Learning": New Perspectives on Pope's Dunciad*, 81–105.

Roth, Michael S. *The Ironist's Cage: Memory, Trauma, and the Construction of History*. New York: Columbia University Press, 1995.

Rousseau, G.S. "'et in Acadio homo': Opera, Gender, and Sexual Politics in *The Dunciad*." In Ingrassia and Thomas, *"More Solid Learning": New Perspectives on Pope's Dunciad*, 3–61.

————. "Pope and the Tradition in Modern Humanistic Education: '...in the pale of Words till death.'" In *The Enduring Legacy: Alexander Pope Tercentenary Essays*. Ed. G.S. Rousseau and Pat Rogers. Cambridge: Cambridge University Press, 1988, 199–239.

Rumbold, Valerie. *Women's Place in Pope's World*. Cambridge: Cambridge University Press, 1989.

————. "Cut the Caterwauling: Women Writers (Not) in Pope's *Dunciad*." *The Review of English Studies* 52 (2001): 524–39.

Rumrich, John. "Milton's *Theanthropos*: The Body of Christ in *Paradise Regained*." *Milton Studies* 42 (2002): 50–67.

Sabl, Andrew. "Noble Infirmity: Love of Fame in Hume." *Political Theory* 34 (2006): 542–68.

Sabor, Peter. "Introduction." In Fielding, *Remarks on Clarissa, Addressed to the Author*, pp. iii–x.

Sacks, Oliver. "The Lost Mariner." In *The Man Who Mistook His Wife for a Hat and Other Clinical Tales*. New York: Simon and Schuster, 1985, 22–41.

Samuel, Raphael. *Theatres of Memory. Volume I: Past and Present in Contemporary Culture.* London: Verso, 1994.

Saunders, David and Ian Hunter. "Lessons from the 'Literatory': How to Historicize Authorship." *Critical Inquiry* 17 (1991): 479–509.

Savage, Ernest A. *Old English Libraries: The Making, Collection, and Use of Books During the Middle Ages.* London: Methuen, 1912.

Schudson, Michael. "Dynamics of Distortion in Collective Memory." In *Memory Distortion: How Minds, Brains, and Societies Reconstruct the Past.* Ed. Daniel L. Schacter. Cambridge: Harvard University Press, 1995, 346–64.

Sebald, W.G. *The Emigrants.* Trans. Michael Hulse. London: The Harvil Press, 1996.

———. *On the Natural History of Destruction.* Trans. Anthea Bell. New York: Random House, 2003.

"A Session of the Poets." In *Poems on Affairs of State: Augustan Satirical Verse, 1660–1714.* Ed. George deForest Lord. 7 vols. New Haven: Yale University Press, 1963–1975, 1: 327–37.

Shapin, Steven. *A Social History of Truth: Civility and Science in Seventeenth-Century England.* Chicago: University of Chicago Press, 1994.

Shawcross, John T. "Misreading Milton." *Milton Studies* 33 (1996): 181–203.

Sherman, Sandra. "Trembling Texts: Margaret Cavendish and the Dialectic of Authorship." *English Literary Renaissance* 24 (1994): 184–210.

Shevelow, Kathryn. *Women and Print Culture: The Construction of Femininity in the Early Periodical.* London: Routledge, 1989.

Sidney, Sir Philip. *An Apologie for Poetrie.* 1595. Rpt. Amsterdam: Da Capo Press, 1971.

Snead, Jennifer. "No Exit? Recent Publications on Pope." *Eighteenth-Century Studies* 38 (2005): 349–55.

Sokol, B.J. "Margaret Cavendish's *Poems and Fancies* and Thomas Harriot's Treatise on Infinity." In Clucas, *A Princely Brave Woman,* 156–70.

Sommerville, C. John. *The News Revolution in England: Cultural Dynamics of Daily Information.* Oxford: Oxford University Press, 1996.

Sontag, Susan. *On Photography.* New York: Farrar, Straus and Giroux, 1973.

Stallybrass, Peter and Allon White. *The Politics and Poetics of Transgression.* London: Methuen, 1985.

Staves, Susan. "Pope's Refinement." *The Eighteenth Century: Theory and Interpretation* 29 (1988): 145–63.

Stedman, Thomas Lathrop. *Stedman's Medical Dictionary.* Twenty-fourth ed. Baltimore: Williams and Wilkins, 1982.

Steedman, Carolyn. *Dust.* Manchester: Manchester University Press, 2001.

Stephen, Leslie. *Alexander Pope.* New York: Harper & Brothers, 1880.

Stevenson, Kay Gilliland. *Milton to Pope, 1650–1720.* London: Palgrave, 2001.

Stewart, Alan and Garrett A. Sullivan Jr. "'Worme-eaten, and full of canker holes': Materializing Memory in *The Faerie Queene* and *Lingua.*" *Spenser Studies* 17 (2003): 215–38.

Stewart, Susan. *On Longing: Narratives of the Miniature, the Gigantic, the Souvenir, the Collection.* Baltimore: The Johns Hopkins University Press, 1984.

Stokes, Jon Hannibal. "Understanding Moore's Law." *arstechnica,* Thursday, February 20,2003, http://arstechnica.org.

Stoler, Ann Laura. "Colonial Archives and the Arts of Governance: On the Content in the Form." In Hamilton et al., *Refiguring the Archive,* 83–101.

Stukeley's "Stonehenge": An Unpublished Manuscript 1721–1724. Ed. Aubrey Burl and Neil Mortimer. New Haven: Yale University Press, 2005.

Summit, Jennifer. *Lost Property: The Woman Writer and English Literary History, 1380–1589.* Chicago: University of Chicago Press, 2000.

———. "Monuments and Ruins: Spenser and the Problem of the English Library." *ELH* 70 (2003): 1–34.

Suskind, Ron. "What Makes Bush's Presidency So Radical—Even to Some Republicans—Is His Preternatural, Faith-Infused Certainty in Uncertain Times. Without a Doubt." *The New York Times Magazine* (154) October 17, 2004: 44–106.

Sutermeister, Edwin. *The Story of Papermaking.* New York: R.R. Bowker Company, 1954.

Sutton, John. *Philosophy and Memory Traces: Descartes to Connectionism.* Cambridge: Cambridge University Press, 1998.

Swift, Jonathan. *A Tale of a Tub.* Ed. A.C. Guthkelch and D. Nichol Smith. Second ed. Oxford: Clarendon, 1958.

Talon, Henri ed. *Selections from the Journals & Papers of John Byrom: Poet-Diarist-Shorthand Writer 1691–1763.* London: Rockliff, 1950.

Taylor, Jane. "Holdings: Refiguring the Archive." In Hamilton et al., *Refiguring the Archive*, 243–81.

Terdiman, Richard. *Present Past: Modernity and the Memory Crisis.* Ithaca: Cornell University Press, 1993.

Terry, Richard. *Poetry and the Making of the English Literary Past 1660–1781.* Oxford: Oxford University Press, 2001.

Teski, Marea C. "The Remembering Consciousness of a Polish Exile Government." In *The Labyrinth of Memory: Ethnographic Journeys.* Ed. Marea C. Teski and Jacob J. Climo. Westport, CT.: Bergin & Garvey, 1995, 49–58.

Teski, Marea C. and Jacob J. Climo. "Introduction." In Teski and Climo, *The Labyrinths of Memory*, 1–10.

Thackeray, W.M. *The English Humourists of the Eighteenth Century. A Series of Lectures.* New York: Harper & Brothers, 1853.

Thorne, Christian. "Thumbing Our Nose at the Public Sphere: Satire, the Market, and the Invention of Literature." *PMLA* 116 (2001): 531–44.

Todd, Dennis. *Imagining Monsters: Miscreations of the Self in Eighteenth-Century England.* Chicago: University of Chicago Press, 1995.

Todd, Janet. *The Critical Fortunes of Aphra Behn.* Columbia, S.C.: Camden House, 1998.

———. "Fatal Fluency: Behn's Fiction and the Restoration Letter." *Eighteenth-Century Fiction* 12 (2000): 417–34.

"To her Excellency the Lady Marchioness of Newcastle, on her Incomparable Works." In *Letters and Poems in Honour of the Incomparable Princess, Margaret, Duchess of Newcastle*, 155–58.

Traugott, John. "*Clarissa's* Richardson: An Essay to Find the Reader." In *English Literature in the Age of Disguise.* Ed. Maximillian E. Novak. Berkeley: University of California Press, 1977, 157–208.

Tribble, Evelyn B. *Margins and Marginality: The Printed Page in Early Modern England.* Charlottesville: University Press of Virginia, 1993.

Tudor Royal Proclamations. Ed. Paul L. Hughes and James F. Larkin. 3 vols. New Haven: Yale University Press, 1964–1969.

Tuomi, Ikka. "The Lives and Death of Moore's Law." *First Monday*, 7.11 (November 2002), http://firstmonday.org/issues.

Tylden-Wright, David. *John Aubrey: A Life*. New York: HarperCollins, 1991.

A Variorum Commentary on the Poems of John Milton. Volume One. Ed. Douglas Bush, J.E. Shaw, and A. Bartlett Giamatti. New York: Columbia University Press, 1970.

Vaughan, Henry. "To the most Excellently accomplish'd, Mrs. *K. Philips*." In *Olor Iscanus. A Collection of Some Select Poems, and Translations, Formerly written by Mr. Henry Vaughan Silurist*. London, 1651. In *The Complete Poetry of Henry Vaughan*. Ed. French Fogle. New York: W.W. Norton, 1969, 86–87.

Voicing Women: Gender and Sexuality in Early Modern Writing. Ed. Kate Chedgzoy, Melanie Hansen, and Suzanne Trill. Edinburgh: Edinburgh University Press, 1996.

Voss, Paul J. "Books for Sale: Advertising and Patronage in Late Elizabethan England." *Sixteenth Century Journal* 29 (1998): 733–56.

Wall, Wendy. *The Imprint of Gender: Authorship and Publication in the English Renaissance*. Ithaca: Cornell University Press, 1993.

———. "Our Bodies/Our Texts?: Renaissance Women and the Trials of Authorship." In *Anxious Power: Reading, Writing, and Ambivalence in Narrative by Women*. Ed. Carol J. Singley and Susan Elizabeth Sweeney. Albany: State University of New York Press, 1993, 51–71.

———. *Staging Domesticity: Household Work and English Identity in Early Modern Drama*. Cambridge Studies in Renaissance Literature and Culture. Cambridge: Cambridge University Press, 2002.

Walsh, W.H. *An Introduction to the Philosophy of History*. 1951. Rpt. Sussex: Harvester Press, 1976.

Ward, Nathaniel. *The Simple Cobler of Aggawam in America. Willing To help 'mend his Native Country, lamentably tattered, both in the upper-Leather and sole, with all the honest stitches he can take. And as willing never to bee paid for his work, by Old English wonted pay. It is his Trade to patch all the year long, gratis. Therefore I pray Gentlemen keep your purses*. London, 1647.

Warner, Michael. *The Letters of the Republic: Publication and the Public Sphere in Eighteenth-Century America*. Cambridge: Cambridge University Press, 1990.

Webb, John. *A Vindication of Stone-Heng Restored: In which the Orders and Rules of Architecture Observed by the Ancient Romans, are Discussed*. London, 1665.

Weber, Harold. *Paper Bullets: Print and Kingship under Charles II*. Lexington: The University Press of Kentucky, 1996.

Weever, John. *Ancient Funerall Monuments within the Vnited Monarchie of Great Britaine, Ireland, and the Islands Adiacent with the Dissolued Monasteries Therein Contained: Their Founders, and What Eminent Persons Haue Beene in the Same Interred. As Also the Death and Buriall of Certaine of the Bloud Royale, the Nobilitie and Gentrie of These Kingdomes Entombed in Forraine Nations. A Worke Reuiuing the Dear Memory of the Royall Progenie, the Nobilitie, Gentrie, and Communaltie, of These His Maiesties Dominions. Intermixed and Illustrated with Variety of Historicall Obseruations, Annotations, and Brief Notes, Extracted Out of Approued Authors. Whereunto is Prefixed a Discourse of Funerall Monuments*. London, 1631.

Whitaker, Katie. *Mad Madge: Margaret Cavendish, Duchess of Newcastle, Royalist, Writer, and Romantic*. London: Chatto and Windus, 2003.

Whitney, Isabella. *The Copy of a letter; lately written in meeter, by a yonge Gentilwoman: To her unconstant Lover. With an Admonition to al yong Gentilwomen, and to all other Mayds in general to beware of mennes Flattery*. London, 1567.

———. *A Sweet nosgay, or pleasant posye: containing a hundred and ten phylosophicall Flowers*. London, 1573.

Wilcox, Helen, ed. *Women and Literature in Britain, 1500–1700*. Cambridge: Cambridge University Press, 1996.

Wilding, Michael. "Milton's *Areopagitica*: Liberty for the Sects." In *The Literature of Controversy: Polemical Strategies from Milton to Junius*. Ed. Thomas N. Corns. London: Frank Cass, 1987, 7–38.

Williams, Carolyn D. *Pope, Homer, and Manliness*. Routledge: London, 1993.

Wilmot, John, earl of Rochester. *The Works of John Wilmot, Earl of Rochester*. Ed. Harold Love. Oxford: Oxford University Press, 1999.

Winn, James A. "On Pope, Printers, and Publishers." *Eighteenth-Century Life* 6 (1980–81): 93-102.

Wittreich, Joseph. *Interpreting Samson Agonistes*. Princeton: Princeton University Press, 1986.

———. *Shifting Contexts: Reinterpreting Samson Agonistes*. Pittsburgh: Duquesne University Press, 2002.

Wolff, Larry. "When I Imagine a Child: The Idea of Childhood and the Philosophy of Memory in the Enlightenment." *Eighteenth-Century Studies* 31 (1998): 377–401.

Women, Writing, and the Reproduction of Culture in Tudor and Stuart Britain. Ed. Mary E. Burke, Jane Donawerth, Linda L. Dove, and Karen Nelson. Syracuse: Syracuse University Press, 2000.

Women, Writing, History 1640–1740. Ed. Isobel Grundy and Susan Wiseman. London: B.T. Batsford, 1992.

Woodmansee, Martha. "The Genius and the Copyright: Economic and Legal Conditions of the Emergence of the 'Author.'" *Eighteenth-Century Studies* 17 (1984): 425–48.

Woodmansee, Martha, and Peter Jaszi, eds. *The Construction of Authorship: Textual Appropriation in Law and Literature*. Durham: Duke University Press, 1994.

Woods, Susanne. *Lanyer: A Renaissance Woman Poet*. Oxford: Oxford University Press, 1999.

Woolf, Virginia. *The Common Reader*. New York: Harcourt, Brace and Company, 1925.

Wormald, Francis and C.E. Wright, eds. *The English Library Before 1700*. London: Athlone, 1958.

Write or Be Written: Early Modern Women Poets and Cultural Constraints. Ed. Barbara Smith and Ursula Appelt. Aldershot: Ashgate, 2001.

Written Work: Langland, Labor, and Authorship. Ed. Steven Justice and Kathryn Kerby-Fulton. Philadelphia: University of Pennsylvania Press, 1997.

Wroth, Lady Mary. *The Poems of Lady Mary Wroth*. Ed. Josephine A. Roberts. Baton Rouge: Louisiana State University Press, 1983.

Yates, Frances A. *The Art of Memory*. Chicago: University of Chicago Press, 1966.

Young, James E., *The Texture of Memory: Holocaust Memorials and Meaning*. New Haven: Yale University Press, 1994.

Zell, P.M., ed. *The Simple Cobler of Aggawam in America. By Nathaniel Ward*. Lincoln: University of Nebraska Press, 1969.

Zerubavel, Yael. "The Historic, the Legendary, and the Incredible: Invented Tradition and Collective Memory in Israel." In Gillis, *Commemorations: The Politics of National Identity*, 105–123.

Zigarovich, Jolene. "Courting Death: Necrophilia in Samuel Richardson's *Clarissa*." *Studies in the Novel* 32 (2000): 112-28.

Zimmerman, Everett. *Boundaries of Fiction: History and the Eighteenth-Century British Novel*. Ithaca: Cornell University Press, 1996.

INDEX

9/11, 230n23

Abrams, M. H., 130
Addison, Joseph, 5–7, 15, 129
Ahmadinejad, Mahmoud, 190
Alexander the Great, 90, 104
Alexander I (King of Yugoslavia), 229n19
Alkon, Daniel L., 1–2
Allestrye, James, 37–8, 40
Anderson, Benedict, 215n25
Anderson, Howard, 148, 150
Anderson, Mark M., 196, 231n37, 231n41
archives
    and the illusion of objectivity, 20, 38, 80–1, 156–7, 175–6, 182–4, 186
    relationship to cultural memory, 6–8, 10, 14, 20, 38, 80–1, 106–7, 123–7, 130–1, 141–3, 156–7, 182–4, 186
    see also libraries and museums
Aristotle, 11–12
Armstrong, Nancy, 223n7
Ash, Timothy Garton, 229n20
Ashmolean Museum, see museums
Assmann, Aleida, 16
Assmann, Jan, 22, 177
Astell, Mary, 28, 33, 43, 61, 163, 165, 200, 217n35, 226n64
    Reflections Upon Marriage, 28
Athens: as a representation of the West's classical heritage in Milton, 72, 91
Aubry, John, 206n34
Augustine, Saint, 24
Austro-Hungarian Empire, 188

Babel
    "The Library of Babel," 180–2, 187, 228n11
    Tower of, 46, 86–7, 108, 122, 191–2

Backscheider, Paula R., 209n71, 217n39
Bacon, Sir Francis, 8, 13, 15–16, 18–19, 75, 205n20
    Advancement of Learning, The, 8, 16, 205n20
    "Of Praise," 18
    New Organon, 19
Bakhurst, David, 184
Ballaster, Ros, 221n46
Baraka, Imamu Amiri, 230n28
Barchas, Janine, 225n26
Barker, Francis, 215n17, 215n21
Bastwick, John, 71
Batey, Mavis, 220n21
Bathurst, Allen, first Earl Bathurst, 119, 139
Beal, Peter, 62, 227n67
Beale, Philip, 148, 155
Beasley, Jerry C., 172
Beetham, Margaret, 221n46
Behn, Aphra, 28–9, 31–2, 36, 60–1
    Luckey Chance, The, 28–9
    Oroonoko, 32, 217n35
    "Pindaric Poem to the Reverend Doctor Burnet," 60–1
"Belfour," see Bradshaigh, Lady Dorothy
Belgrade, 188, 229n19
Bentley, Richard, 128, 130, 134
Berger, Harry Jr., 223n5
Berlin Wall, 188, 229n20
Bernard-Donals, Michael, 231n35
Blaine, Marlin E., 204n8
Blouin, Francis X., Jr., 20, 208n58
Blount, Martha, 109
Bloy, C.H., 169
Blum, Abbe, 215n17
Bodley, Sir Thomas, 8, 79–80, 205n20
Boileau-Despréaux, Nicholas, 124
Bolingbroke, first Viscount (Henry St. John), 118
Bond, James, 155

books
  as literary monuments, 3–9, 13–19,
      24–5, 27–8, 29–30, 74–8, 81–2,
      85, 96–101, 110–11, 124–7,
      133–6, 137–141, 147, 176
  as spiritual objects, 5–8, 15–17, 24–5,
      53–4, 97–101, 176,
      181–2
  in Borges, 180–3
  in Cavendish, 27–8, 35–49, 63–4, 65,
      112
  in Kiš, 186–8
  in Milton, 74–86, 96–101
  in Pope, 16, 105–7, 111–27, 133–6,
      137–8
  in Richardson, 139–43, 171–4
Borges, Jorge Luis, 176–7, 179–87, 198,
      201
  "Funes the Memorius," 179–80, 187,
      198
  "Library of Babel, The," 180–2, 187,
      228n11
  "Theme of the Traitor and the Hero,"
      182–6
Bowtell, Stephen, 31, 211n14
Boyle, Robert, 13, 199
Bradstreet, Anne, 31–5, 35, 39–41, 50–1
  Tenth Muse Lately sprung up in
      America, The, 31–4, 40–1, 50–1
Bradshaigh, Lady Dorothy ("Belfour")
      145–6, 225n26
Braudy, Leo, 17–18, 118
British Museum Act, 106
British Telecommunications, 198
Brouwer, Joel, 230n26, 231n29
Brown, Laura, 115
Brown, Laura S., 203n3
Browne, Christopher, 154
Brownell, Morris R., 220n21
Budgell, Eustace, 130
Bunyan, John, Grace Abounding, 162
Burke, Peter, 80–1
Burl, Aubrey, 206n34
Burlington, third earl of (Richard Boyle),
      119
Burnet, Gilbert, bishop of Salisbury, 60
Burton, Henry, 71
Burton, Robert, 113
Bush, Douglas, 215n24
Bush, George H.W. (President), 2
Bush, George W. (President), 189
Byrom, John, 162–4

Cade, Jack, 153
Caesar, Julius, 90, 104, 163–4, 182
Camden, William, 28
Campbell, R., The London Tradesman,
      223n2, 223n3
Carlson, David R., 203n7
Carruthers, Mary, 220n30
Carteret, Lady Elizabeth, 167
Carteret, Sir Philip, 167
Cartwright, William, 36
Carvalho, David N., 170, 226n36
Caryll, John, second baron Caryll, 110
Catty, Jocelyn, 212n41
Cave, Edward, Gentleman's Magazine, or
      Trader's Monthly Intelligencer, The,
      121–3, 130
Cavendish, Sir Charles, 42
Cavendish, Margaret, duchess of
      Newcastle, 4, 7, 12, 19, 24, 27–64,
      70, 75, 80, 86, 97, 100, 108, 109,
      112, 122, 149, 160, 163, 165, 167,
      176, 180, 199–200
  Blazing World, The, 39, 131
  CCXI Sociable Letters, 24, 34, 45,
      63–4, 97–8, 218n50
  "Elysium, The," 53, 56
  "Epistle to Mistris Toppe, An," 30,
      47–8
  Life of the thrice Noble, High and
      Puissant Prince William
      Cavendishe, The, 36
  Life of William Cavendish Duke of
      Newcastle To Which is Added The
      True Relation of My Birth Breeding
      and Life, The, 44, 50, 51, 131
  Natures Pictures Drawn by Francies
      Pencil to the Life, 43
  Observations Upon Experimental
      Philosophy. To which is added, The
      Description of a New Blazing
      World, 49
  Philosophical and Physical Opinions,
      The, 38, 44, 52, 218n50
  Philosophicall Fancies, 40
  Playes, 37, 41, 58
  Plays, Never before Printed, 6, 49
  Poems, and Fancies, 2, 9–10, 27–8,
      29–30, 32–3, 35–58, 62, 65,
      68–9, 77, 86, 131, 165,
      210n10
  Worlds Olio, The, 38, 41, 51, 54, 57–8,
      65, 67

Cavendish, William, first duke of
    Newcastle, 36–8, 41–2, 49, 57–62,
    167
    Humourous Lovers, The, 59–60
    Letters and Poems in Honour of the
        Incomparable Princess, Duchess of
        Newcastle, 38, 61–2
Caxton, William, 116, 120, 153
censorship, 7, 32–4, 71, 74–8
Cervantes, Miguel de, *Don Quixote*, 160
Chalmers, Hero, 213n71
Chambers, Ephraim, *Cyclopaedia* 121–3,
    130, 136, 181
Chandler, Eric V., 134, 218n3
Charles I (King of England), 11, 36, 71,
    79, 155, 204n17
Charles II (King of England), 11, 14, 36,
    85, 90, 217n39
Charleton, Walter, 11, 13–14, 16–17,
    37–8, 206n34
Chorea Gigantum, 13–14, 206n34
Charron, Peter, *Of Wisdome*, 214n5
Chartier, Roger, 7–8
Chaucer, Geoffrey, 3, 17–18, 92–3, 104,
    107–9, 203n7
    Canterbury Tales, The, 92–3
    House of Fame, 107–9, 207n46, 219n14
Cheyne, George, 224n16
Childs, David, 229n20
Chippindale, Christopher, 206n34
Church of the Latter-Day Saints, 229n18
Churchyard, Thomas, *Sparke of Frendship*
    and Warme Goodwill, A, 138
Cibber, Colley, 105, 112, 113, 115–16,
    128–9, 134
Cibber, Theophilus, 130
Clanchy, M.T., 149–51, 159, 226n36
Clarke, Adele, 200
Clarke, Samuel, 128
Clegg, Cyndia Susan, 204n17
Cleland, William, 124
Clifford, James, 197
Climo, Jacob J., 93
clothing
    as a vehicle of memory, 44–6,
        152–3
    in Cavendish, 30, 43–6, 51–2, 56
    in *Clarissa*, 152–3, 157
    in Kiš, 185
    see also sewing
Clucas, Stephen, 210n10
Clynes, Manfred, 199–200

Cobham, Thomas, 79
Coffey, John, 216n33
Coiro, Ann Baynes, 15, 80, 92, 214n1
Collins, An, 33–5, 39–40, 47–8
    Divine Songs and Meditacions, 33–5
Columbus, 12–13
commercial print industry
    in early modern Britain, 2–10, 16–18,
        22–5, 28–39, 74–8, 100–1,
        105–7, 111, 117–27, 133–6,
        138–47, 151–4, 161–2, 171
    see also censorship *and* paper
computers
    compared to human brain, 198–9
    relationship to collective memory, 23,
        178–9, 197–202
Connell, Philip, 17, 111, 207n45
Connerton, Paul, 106
Copyright Act of 1710, 9, 121, 219n4,
    221n53
Corns, Thomas N., 216n33, 217n37
Cotton, Sir Robert, 15, 80, 113
Cowell, Pattie, 32
Cowper, Judith, 110
Crawford, Patricia, 209n6
Cressy, David, 11, 101, 206n30
Crews, Frederick, 203n3
Critical Remarks on Sir Charles
    Grandison, Clarissa and Pamela (by
    a Lover of Virtue), 147
Cromwell, Henry, 105
Cromwell, Oliver, 66, 84–5
Cowley, Abraham, 38
Curll, Edmund, 117, 126, 132, 134, 138
Cyborg, 12, 178–9, 199–201

Daphinoff, Dimiter, 225n27
"Decade of the Brain," 2, 203n2
Defoe, Daniel, 130
Delany, Sheila, 219n14
Delany, Reverend Patrick, 145
Dennis, John, 129–30
Denny, Sir Edward, 43, 165,
    212n42
De Quincey, Thomas, 128, 222n61,
    222n62
Derrida, Jacques, 20, 208n58, 224n8,
    227n77
Descartes, René, 23
Deutsch, Helen, 123, 125, 218n3, 219n5
Diepenbecke, Abraham van, 37
Dietz, Michael, 74

Dobranski, Stephen B., 212n39, 215n17, 215n25, 216n34
Dolan, Frances E., 10–11, 81
Donne, John, 18–19, 89, 113
  "Goodfriday, 1613. Riding Westward," 19
Donoghue, Frank, 50
Drew, Sarah, 110
Drury, John, *The Reformed Librarie-Keeper*, 114–15
Dryden, John, 11–17, 19, 37, 111, 120, 137–8
  Mac Flecknoe, 137–8
  "To My Honored Friend, Dr. Charleton," 11–17
Du Bartas, Guillaume de Salluste, 33
Duthie, George, 226n61
Duttlinger, Carolin, 231n30

Eagleton, Terry, 148, 172
Eberwein, Jane Donahue, 211n19
Echlin, Lady Elizabeth, 146, 225n27
Edelman, Gerald M., 54, 232n45
Egan, James, 215n17
Ehrenpreis, Irvin, 148, 150
Eisenstein, Elizabeth L., 9, 204n13, 228n7
Elizabeth I (Queen of England), 33
Elliott, Robert C., 221n51
English Civil War, 67, 74, 104
Ent, Sir George, 13
Evans, J. Martin, 73
Evelyn, John, 6, 15–16, 23, 44
Ezell, Margaret J. M., 9, 29, 36, 205n25, 210n10

Fairfax, Thomas, third Lord Fairfax, 79, 84
fame
  and its traditions, 9–10, 12–14, 16–20, 46–9, 69–70, 72–3, 88–91, 107–9, 132–3
  distrusted by Milton and Pope, 46, 51, 68–74, 83–93, 103–110, 116, 123–7, 132–4
  embraced by Cavendish, 29–30, 34, 42–55, 61–4
  relationship to memory, 9–10, 12–21, 29–30, 147, 184–7
Fanning, Christopher, 223n78
Favret, Mary A., 154–5
Feather, John P., 220n28

Fentress, James, 10, 21, 68, 100, 127
Ferdinand, Archduke Franz (of Austria), 229n19
Ferguson, Arthur B., 207n52
Ferguson, Margaret, 29
Fielding, Henry, 144–5, 163
  Jacobite's Journal, The, 145
  Joseph Andrews, 144, 163
  Shamela, 144
Fielding, Sarah, *Remarks on Clarissa*, 142, 144, 172
Figueroa-Sarriera, Heidi J., 232n47
Finch, Anne, countess of Winchilsea, 110
Fish, Stanley, 66, 69, 71, 73, 95, 214n7, 215n17, 216n32, 217n35
Fitzmaurice, James, 211n31
Fleming, Ian, 155
Fletcher, Harris Francis, 215n26
Flint, Christopher, 140, 162, 223n4, 224n12, 224n13
Flynn, Carol Houlihan, 139, 173, 226n53
Fortescue, George K., 204n18
Foucault, Michel, 9, 205n23
Fox, Adam, 223n7
Foxon, David, 219n4, 221n42
Frazer, Elizabeth, 221n46
Friedlander, Saul, 203n3
Fukuyama, Francis, 189, 229n21
Fulton, Alice, 39, 62, 213n65

Gallagher, Catherine, 205n25
Gay, John, 128
Geary, Patrick J., 203n4
gender
  and the early modern print industry, 28–39, 40–1, 43, 47–8, 60–1, 105–6, 132–5, 164–8
  in Cavendish, 9–10, 28–49, 56–64, 109
  in Milton, 72–3, 76–8, 92–6, 110
  in Pope, 104–6, 109–10, 131–5
  in Richardson, 156–8, 159–74
  in the electronic age, 178–9, 200–1
  relationship to memory, 3, 8–10, 28–30, 47–8, 92–3, 133–4, 166–8, 172
Genette, Gerard, 212n38
Gentleman's Magazine, or Trader's Monthly Intelligencer, The, see Edward Cave
Giamatti, A. Bartlett, 215n24

Gilbert, William, 13, 17
Gillis, John R., 206n30
Gilliver, Lawton. 119
Gilroy, Amanda, 225n31
Goldberg, Jonathan, 32, 168, 170,
    210n10, 226n54
Gottlieb, Sidney, 35
Grafton, Anthony, 204n13
Gray, Chris Hables, 232n47
Gray, Thomas, 129
Greenblatt, Stephen, 5, 130
Greer, Germaine, 205n25
Gregg, John Robert, 163
Griffin, Dustin, 219n5
Griffin, Robert J., 32, 69
Grubstreet, 123–35, 138, 144
Guibbory, Achsah, 18–19, 207n52
Guillory, John, 217n40, 217n41
Gutenberg, Johannes, 159, 169
Guttenplan, D.D., 230n26

Halbwachs, Maurice, 20–2
Hamilton, Carolyn, 20, 126
Hammond, Brean S., 127, 205n23,
    219n5, 219n6, 221n46
handwriting, 143, 160–2
Hanson, Elizabeth, 73
Haraway, Donna J., 178–9, 199–201,
    232n50
Harris, Jocelyn, 227n75
Harris, Michael, 210n9
Harris, Michael H., 112–13
Harris, Tim, 209n71, 217n39
Harris, Verne, 20, 126
Harvey, William, 13, 17
Haskin, Dayton, 95
Haywood, Eliza, 133
Hebron, Sandra, 221n46
Helgerson, Richard, 205n23, 206n30,
    218n53
Henry II (King of England), 150, 159
Henry VIII (King of England), 11,
    74–6
Hensley, Jeannine, 211n13
Hewet, John, 110
Heywood, Peter, 153
Hill, Aaron, 106, 128, 142, 224n16
Hirsch, Marianne, 177–8, 194
history
    evolution as a field, 11, 13–14, 17–21
    relationship to memory, 11–12, 14–21,
        62–4, 66–8, 80–7, 91–101,

        140–3, 164–8, 171–4, 176–9,
        182–97
Hobbes, Thomas, 23
Hobby, Elaine, 29, 205n25, 212n49
Hobsbawm, Eric, 81
Holocaust, The, 2, 177–8, 189–97,
    203n3
Homer, *Iliad*, 104, 119, 121, 221n42
Hooke, Robert, 23
Horace, "Ode 3.30," 2, 100, 124–5
Hulse, Michael, 230n27, 231n41
Hume, David, 18, 207n48
Hunter, Dard, 138, 151–3, 153, 171,
    223n2, 226n36
Hunter, Ian, 205n23
Hunter, J. Paul, 219n5, 221n46
Huyssen, Andreas, 38

Ingrassia, Catherine, 104, 222n67,
    224n11
Intel, 197–8
Irving, David, 230n26
Irwin, Raymond, 106, 117–18, 220n28

Jaggi, Maya, 193, 229n22, 231n30,
    231n38
Jenkins, Rhys, 223n2, 226n42, 226n43,
    226n45
Jerusalem, 191–2
Johnson, Elmer D., 112–13
Johnson, Richard, 206n36
Johnson, Samuel, 127–9,
    226n57
    Lives of the English Poets, 127–8,
        226n57
Jones, Ann Rosalind, 33, 45, 152, 156,
    165, 212n41
Jones, Emrys, 120
Jones, Inigo, 206n34
Jones, Kathleen, 210n10
Jonson, Ben, 3–5, 19–20, 27–8, 50, 80,
    98, 144
    "Epigram to My Bookseller," 50
    "Mind of the Frontispiece to a Book,
        The," 19, 208n55
    New Inne, The, 3–4
    "To the Memory of My Beloved,
        The Author, Mr. William
        Shakespeare," 5
    Workes, 4, 27–8, 204n10
Jordan, John E., 222n61
Justice, Steven, 203n7

Keeble, N.H., 90
Kelley, Donald R., 183
Kerby-Fulton, Kathryn, 203n7
Ketcham, Katherine, 203n3
Keymer, Thomas, 141, 144–5, 226n52
King, Edward, 69, 74
Kinkead-Weekes, Mark, 225n23
Kinsley, William, 126
Kiš, Danilo, 176, 184–8, 201
    "Encyclopedia of the Dead, The," 187–8
    "To Die for One's Country Is
        Glorious," 184–6, 188
Klein, Kerwin Lee, 203n3, 208n59,
    230n24
Kline, Nathan S., 199–200
Klinge, Markus, 75, 77
Knoppers, Laura Lunger, 90
Koonce, B.G., 207n46, 219n14
Korsakov's Syndrome (also Korsakoff's),
    197, 231n40
Kotler, Steven, 198
Kotre, John, 127
Kramnick, Jonathan Brody, 133, 208n66
Kreisel, Deanna, 161–2
Kroll, Richard W.F., 11, 13, 16–17, 161,
    212n40
Krontiris, Tina, 205n25

LaCapra, Dominick, 190, 203n3, 208n59
Lamb, Mary Ellen, 29, 212n42
Langland, William, 3
Lanyer, Aemilia, 34, 210n10
Lawes, Henry, 42
Le Goff, Jacques, 68
Leonard, John, 71
Lerer, Seth, 203n7
letters
    history in the West, 148–50, 154–60
    use by Richardson, 147–50, 154–64,
        171–4
    see also postal system
    Letters and Poems in Honour of the
        Incomparable Princess, Margaret,
        Duchess of Newcastle, 38, 61–2
Levine, Joseph M., 219n5
Levinson, Sanford, 30
Levy, F.J., 207n52, 207n53
Lewalski, Barbara K., 214n1
Lewis, Jayne Elizabeth, 224n12
libraries
    Bodleian, 8, 79–80
    British, 80, 117–18

evolution and development of, 6–8,
    106–7, 112–14, 136
    in Borges, 180–2
    in Cavendish, 30, 38, 55, 56, 112
    in Kiš, 187–9
    in Milton, 78–81
    in Pope, 106–7, 112–19, 124–6,
        136
    relationship to cultural memory, 6–8,
        10, 15–17, 106–7, 112–19, 121–2,
        124–6, 136, 175–6, 190
Lieb, Michael, 84, 214n1, 217n35
Lieberman, Henry, 228n11
Lilley, Kate, 49
Lintot, Bernard, 119, 138
Lipstadt, Deborah E., 230n26
Locke, John, 23–4
Loewenstein, David, 101, 207n52
Loewenstein, Joseph, 204n9, 205n23
Loftus, Elizabeth F., 203n3
Long, J.J., 231n30
Lounsbury, Thomas R., 129–30
Lowell, Robert, 39
Lubow, Arthur, 196

MacCallum, Hugh, 96
Mack, Maynard, 219n13, 220n16,
    220n21
Mackie, Erin, 207n43, 220n26
MacLean, Gerald M., 204n18
Macocke, John, 87
Mann, Steve, 199
Marshall, David, 226n53
Martin, John, 37–8, 40
Martin, Peter, 220n21
Marvell, Andrew, 22; "An Horatian
    Ode," 67–8, 78, 82–3, 90–1, 94
Maxwell, Anne, 37, 39
Mbembe, Achille, 118
McDowell, Paula, 29, 55, 61, 205n25,
    210n9, 211n29, 226n64
McGrath, Lynette, 29, 205n25, 210n10
McKeon, Michael, 140, 173, 224n14
McKillop, Alan Dugald, 225n23
McKitterick, David, 106, 220n28
McLaverty, James, 111, 118–19, 135,
    221n51, 222n59
McLennan, Gregor, 206n36
Mead, Carver, 232n43
memory
    collective memory, 10–11, 17–25,
        67–8, 177–9

neuroscience and, 1–2, 12, 54, 198–9
postmemory, 177–8, 194
relationship to fame, 9–10, 12–14,
  17–21, 42–3, 46–56, 63–4,
  69–74, 83–102, 103–11, 116–19,
  123–7, 184–6
relationship to history, 11–21, 60–4,
  66–8, 80–1, 83–102, 140–3,
  156–60, 164–74, 175–9, 182–97
Mendle, Michael, 215n17
Mentor, Steven, 232n47
Merton, Robert, 204n13
Metz, Christian, 193–4
Milton, John, 2, 4, 7, 9–10, 17, 19, 24,
  27, 35–6, 46, 50–2, 62, 65–104,
  108, 122, 147, 176, 180, 183, 196
  Areopagitica, 27, 66, 74–9, 80, 83, 98,
    100
  History of Britain, 96
  Lycidas, 32, 66, 68–74, 76, 83, 6,
    88–9, 95, 110
  Mask Presented at Ludlow Castle, 69,
    101
  "On Shakespeare," 97–100
  Paradise Lost, 51, 68, 73, 86, 87, 97,
    108, 147
  Paradise Regained, 2, 51, 66, 72,
    87–91, 92, 96–7, 98
  Poems of Mr. John Milton, 39, 74, 78–9,
    81
  Readie and Easie Way, The, 85–7, 160
  Samson Agonistes, 2, 9, 62, 66, 68, 73,
    87–9, 91–6, 101, 134, 171, 183
  Second Defence of the English People, A,
    66, 74, 81–6, 91–2, 95
  "To John Rouse," 66, 74, 78–81, 83,
    95, 117
Ministerium für Staatssicherheit, 188–9,
  229n20
Misztal, Barbara A., 21–2, 209n75
Montagu, Lady Mary Wortley, 110, 131
monuments
  relationship to collective memory, 2,
    13–17, 19, 22, 27, 45–9, 51, 62–4,
    72, 78, 86–7, 92–101, 110–11,
    117–19, 124–7, 133–6, 138,
    167–8, 189–90, 195–7
  see also Babel *and* books
Moore, Gordon E., 197–8, 232n43
Moore's Law, 197–8, 232n43
Moravec, Hans, 199
More, Henry, 23, 213n67

Morley, John, 129
Mortimer, Neil, 206n34
Moscow Show Trials, 188
Moseley, Humphrey, 38
Mottaki, Manouchehr, 190, 230n25
Mueller, Janel, 217n42
Murray, Timothy, 204n10
museums
  Ashmolean, 112
  evolution and development of, 111–12,
    115
  relationship to cultural memory, 106–7,
    111–12, 126

Nalbantan, Suzanne, 180
Naudé, Gabriel, *Advis pour dresser une
  bibliothèque*, 6–7, 15, 114–15
New England Historical Society, 117
Newton, Richard C., 3
Nicolay, Theresa Freda, 205n25, 211n21
Niedzviecki, Hal, 232n48
Nora, Pierre, 126
Norbrook, David, 216n33
*Norton Anthology of English Literature,
  The*, 130–1, 222n70
novels
  relationship to history, 9, 140–3,
    171–4, 191, 196–7
Novick, Peter, 203n3
Nuttall, Sarah, 173

Orwell, George, *1984*, 189
Osborne, Dorothy, 44
Ovenell, R.F., 220n25
Overton, Robert, 84
Oxford, first earl of (Robert Harley),
  117–19, 160

paper
  as a vehicle of memory, 137–40, 150–4,
    156, 181–2
  history of papermaking, 138, 150–4
  in *Clarissa*, 139–40, 150–4, 156, 168,
    169–71
  in Pope, 125, 137–40
Parker, Rozsika, 212n41
Parker, William Riley, 216n34
Pask, Kevin, 205n23
Patterson, Lee, 203n7
Peacey, Jason, 204n17
People's Liberation Army of Yugoslavia,
  229n19

Pepys, Samuel, 15–16, 23, 51–2, 59–60,
 113, 223n5
Perdue, Cori, 218n51
Peterson, Bhekizizwe, 156
Petrarch, 18
Philip, Ian, 215n26
Philips, Ambrose, 130
Philips, Katherine, 31, 35–6, 42, 211n26
Pickover, Michèle, 208n56
photography
 as a vehicle of memory, 193–7
Pitman, Sir Isaac, 163
Plomer, H.R., 37, 211n14
Pocock, J.G.A., 141, 207n52, 207n54,
 209n67
"Poets' Corner," see Westminster Abbey
Pompey, 90
Pope, Alexander, 2, 4, 7, 9, 19, 24, 51, 62,
 103–36, 137–40, 141–2, 176, 180–1
 and his composition of epitaphs,
 110–11
 Dunciad, The, 2, 9, 106–21, 123–36,
 137–8, 141–2, 158, 181
 Epistle to Dr. Arbuthnot, An,
 108
 Essay on Criticism, An, 103,
 116
 Moral Essays, 131, 138–9
 Pastorals, The, 105
 Rape of the Lock, The, 104, 111, 120,
 135
 Temple of Fame, The, 103–4, 107–11,
 132, 134
 "To a Lady with the Temple of Fame,"
 109
 Windsor-Forest, 104
 Works (1717), 16, 111
 Works (1735), 111
Pope, Kenneth S., 203n3
Popular Memory Group, 14, 23, 49, 63
postal system, 150, 154–6, 159
postmemory, see memory
Powell, Anthony, 206n34
Price, Bronwen, 41
Price, Leah, 163
Prior, Matthew, 128
Proust, Marcel, 24
Prynne, William, 71
Pugliano, John Pietro, 67

Radzinowicz, Mary Ann, 95, 214n1,
 214n7, 217n35

Rabinow, Paul, 200
Ralegh, Sir Walter, 208n55
Ray, Gordon N., 222n63
Ray, Larry, 22
readers
 distinguished from theatrical spectator,
 3–5, 144
 in Cavendish, 4, 47, 49–50, 52–3,
 65–6
 in Collins, 34
 in Jonson, 3–5, 50, 144
 in Milton, 4, 50, 52, 69, 78–81, 95–6,
 97–8
 in Pope, 4, 129
 in Richardson, 3, 143–7
Redford, Bruce, 225n31
Rees, Emma L.E., 213n70
Regii sanguinis clamor ad coelum adversus
 parricidas Anglicanos, 81
Reid, Graeme, 20, 126
Reitan, E.A., 221n46
Revard, Stella P., 215n24
Richards, Thomas, 175
Richardson, Leslie, 224n12
Richardson, Samuel, 2, 4, 9, 18–19, 24,
 62, 137–74, 176, 182–3
 Clarissa, 1, 9, 32, 137–74, 183
 Collection of Moral and Instructive
 Sentiments, Maxims, Cautions
 and Reflections Contained in the
 Histories of Pamela, Clarissa and
 Sir Charles Grandison, A, 141
 Hints of Prefaces for Clarissa, 141,
 146–7
 Letters and Passages Restored from the
 Original Manuscripts of the History
 of Clarissa, 141
 Meditations Collected from the Sacred
 Books, 141
 Pamela, 139, 142, 144
 Sir Charles Grandison, 139
Ricoeur, Paul, 25, 183, 208n59, 216n32,
 228n6, 228n9
Rivero, Albert J., 227n75
Rogers, Pat, 135, 221n46
Rolleston, John, 41
Root, Robert Kilburn, 130
Rose, Mark, 205n23
Rose, Mary Beth, 217n35
Rose, Steven, 12, 23, 54, 198–9, 228n6
Rosenthal, Laura J., 218n3
Roth, Michael S., 203n3

Rousseau, G. S., 218n3, 220n24
Rowe, Nicholas, 110–11, 160, 226n57
Royal Society, 13, 51–2, 106, 163
    Transactions Philosophical, 163
Roycroft, Thomas, 37
Rumbold, Valerie, 110, 133, 218n3,
    220n17
Rumrich, John, 88

Sabl, Andrew, 18, 207n48
Sabor, Peter, 144, 225n21
Sacks, David Harris, 183
Sacks, Oliver, 231n40
Saleh, Razia, 208n56
Samuel, Raphael, 21, 208n58, 208n59
Saunders, David, 205n23
Savage, Ernest A., 220n28
Saye and Sele, first Baron (James Fiennes),
    153
Schlosser, Friedrich Christoph, 128,
    222n62
Schudson, Michael, 68, 84
Schwarz, Bill, 206n36
Scipio Africanus, 84, 90
Sebald, W.G., 176–8,
    191–7
    Austerlitz, 231n29, 231n30
    Emigrants, The, 191–7
    On the Natural History of Destruction,
    194
"Session of the Poets," 59
sewing
    and its relationship to writing, 32, 42,
    76–7, 165–8
    in Cavendish, 32, 42–6, 56, 76–7, 165
    in *Clarissa*, 165–8
Shakespeare, William, 5, 17, 69, 97–100,
    130, 153, 158, 182, 185
    Hamlet, 158
    2 Henry IV, 153
    Macbeth, 182
Shapin, Steven, 28
Shaw, J.E., 215n24
Shawcross, John T., 217n42
Sheridan, Thomas, 126
Sherman, Sandra, 49, 211n20
Shevelow, Kathryn, 221n46
shorthand, 162–4
Shorthand Society, 163
Sidney, Sir Philip, 3, 18, 33, 67, 204n8
    Apologie for Poetrie, An, 67
Sloane, Sir Hans, 117–18

Smith, D. Nicol, 130
Smollett, Tobias, *Humphry Clinker*, 163
Smythe, James Moore, 128
Snead, Jennifer, 222n67
Sokol, B.J., 210n10
Sommerville, C. John, 221n46
Sontag, Susan, 193
"Soul Catcher," 198
South Sea Bubble, 141
Spilman, John, 138, 152
Stallybrass, Peter, 45, 135, 152, 156, 165,
    212n41, 219n5
Star Chamber, 7, 71, 74, 204n17
Starkey, John, 87
Stasi, *see* Ministerium für Staatssicherheit
Stationers' Company, 37, 71, 74, 77, 152
Staves, Susan, 221n53
Stedman, Thomas Lathrop, 231n40
Steedman, Carolyn, 208n59, 225n32
Stephen, Leslie, 129
Stevenson, Kay Gilliland, 209n6, 214n6,
    219n15
Stewart, Alan, 215n26
Stewart, Maaja, 227n69
Stewart, Susan, 176, 182
Stokes, Jon Hannibal, 232n43
Stoler, Ann Laura, 149
Stonehenge, 14, 16–17, 206n34
Sullivan, Garrett A., Jr., 215n26
Summit, Jennifer, 9–10, 14, 63,
    205n25, 205n26, 212n38,
    213n54, 215n26
Suskind, Ron, 229n21
Sutherland, James, 119
Sutermeister, Edwin, 223n2
Sutton, Donald, 206n36
Sutton, John, 209n72, 213n67
Swift, Jonathan, 111, 117–18, 122, 124,
    126, 180–1, 199
    Gulliver's Travels, 180
    Tale of a Tub, A, 118, 124, 199

Talon, Henri, 162–3
Taylor, Jane, 208n56, 220n25
Temple, Sir William, 44
Terdiman, Richard, 214n3
Terry, Richard, 18, 133, 206n38, 207n45,
    208n66
Teski, Marea C., 82, 93
Thackeray, William Makepeace, *English
    Humourists of the Eighteenth
    Century, The*, 128–9

Theobald, Lewis, 112–13, 115–16, 128–30
Thomas, Claudia N., 218n3, 222n67
Thomas, Elizabeth, 133
Thomas, Patrick, 211n26
Thomason, George, 7, 204n18
Thorne, Christian, 219n8
Todd, Dennis, 222n71, 222n74
Todd, Janet, 205n25, 225n31
Transactions Philosophical, see Royal Society
Traugott, John, 225n26
Tribble, Evelyn B., 212n38
Tuomi, Ikka, 197–8, 232n43
Tylden-Wright, David, 206n34

Vaughan, Henry, "To the most Excellently accomplish'd Mrs. *K. Philips*," 36, 211n26
Verhoeven, W.M., 225n31
Virgil, 71, 196
Visual Memory Prosthetic, *see* Mann, Steve
Voss, Paul J., 212n38

Wall, Wendy, 9–10, 204n8, 205n25, 210n11, 212n39
Walpole, Robert, first earl of Orford, 132
Walsh, W.H., 207n52
Warburton, William, bishop of Gloucester, 105–6
Ward, Nathanial, *Simple Cobler Of Aggawam in America, The,* 31, 211n14
Warner, Michael, 165
Webb, John, 206n34
Weber, Harold, 2, 74
Weever, John
     Ancient Funerall Monuments within the Vnited Monarchie of Great Britaine, 15, 24, 78, 206n38

Westcomb, Sophia, 224n18
Westminster Abbey, 17, 62, 167, 207n45
     "Poets' Corner," 17
Westminster School, 28
Whitaker, Katie, 29, 37, 210n10, 211n31, 211n35, 212n39, 212n40, 213n60
White, Allon, 135, 219n5
Whitney, Isabella, 210n10
Wickham, Chris, 10, 21, 68, 100, 127
Wilcox, Helen, 210n7
Wilding, Michael, 215n17
Williams, Carolyn D., 218n3
Wilmot, John, earl of Rochester, "Womans Honour," 109–110
Wilson, William, 37–9
Winn, James A., 219n4
Wittreich, Joseph, 95, 217n42, 218n46
Wolff, Larry, 209n72
Woodbridge, John, 31
Woodmansee, Martha, 205n23
Woods, Susanne, 210n10
Woolf, Virginia, *Common Reader, The,* 56, 62
World War I, 175, 188, 229n19
World War II, 175–6, 188, 190, 192, 229n19, 230n27
Wormald, Francis, 220n28
Wright, C.E., 220n28
Wright, John, 119
Wroth, Lady Mary, *Countess of Montgomery's Urania, The,* 43, 212n42
Wycherley, William, 117

Yates, Frances A., 115
Young, Edward, 291–2, 296–7
Young, James E., 142

Zell, P.M., 211n14
Zerubavel, Yael, 186
Zigarovich, Jolene, 226n53
Zimmerman, Everett, 205n24

Breinigsville, PA USA
03 February 2010
231868BV00002B/36/P